ISAIAH

THE IGNATIUS CATHOLIC STUDY BIBLE

REVISED STANDARD VERSION
SECOND CATHOLIC EDITION

ISAIAH

With Introduction, Commentary, and Notes

by

Scott Hahn and Curtis Mitch

with Mark Giszczak

and

with Study Questions by

Dennis Walters

IGNATIUS PRESS   SAN FRANCISCO

Published with ecclesiastical approval
Original Bible text: Revised Standard Version, Catholic Edition
Nihil Obstat: Thomas Hanlon, S.T.L., L.S.S., Ph.L.
Imprimatur: +Peter W. Bartholome, D.D.
Bishop of Saint Cloud, Minnesota
May 11, 1966

Introduction, commentaries, and notes:
Nihil Obstat: Ruth Ohm Sutherland, Ph.D., Censor Deputatus
Imprimatur: +The Most Reverend Salvatore Cordileone
Archbishop of San Francisco
December 10, 2018

The *nihil obstat* and *imprimatur* are official declarations that a book or pamphlet is free of doctrinal or moral error. No implication is contained therein that those who have granted the *nihil obstat* and *imprimatur* agree with the contents, opinions, or statements expressed.

Second Catholic Edition approved by the
National Council of the Churches of Christ in the USA

Cover art:
The Prophet Isaiah (Detail of Interior Mosaic in St. Mark's Basilica, Venice)
12th century. Artist: Byzantine Master
HIP/Art Resource, New York

Cover design by Riz Boncan Marsella

Published by Ignatius Press in 2019

CONTENTS

INTRODUCTION TO
THE IGNATIUS STUDY BIBLE

by Scott Hahn, Ph.D.

You are approaching the "word of God". This is the title Christians most commonly give to the Bible, and the expression is rich in meaning. It is also the title given to the Second Person of the Blessed Trinity, God the Son. For Jesus Christ became flesh for our salvation, and "the name by which he is called is The Word of God" (Rev 19:13; cf. Jn 1:14).

The word of God is Scripture. The Word of God is Jesus. This close association between God's *written* word and his *eternal* Word is intentional and has been the custom of the Church since the first generation. "All Sacred Scripture is but one book, and this one book is Christ, 'because all divine Scripture speaks of Christ, and all divine Scripture is fulfilled in Christ'[1]" (CCC 134). This does not mean that the Scriptures are divine in the same way that Jesus is divine. They are, rather, divinely inspired and, as such, are unique in world literature, just as the Incarnation of the eternal Word is unique in human history.

Yet we can say that the inspired word resembles the incarnate Word in several important ways. Jesus Christ is the Word of God incarnate. In his humanity, he is like us in all things, except for sin. As a work of man, the Bible is like any other book, except without error. Both Christ and Scripture, says the Second Vatican Council, are given "for the sake of our salvation" (*Dei Verbum* 11), and both give us God's definitive revelation of himself. We cannot, therefore, conceive of one without the other: the Bible without Jesus, or Jesus without the Bible. Each is the interpretive key to the other. And because Christ is the subject of all the Scriptures, St. Jerome insists, "Ignorance of the Scriptures is ignorance of Christ"[2] (CCC 133).

When we approach the Bible, then, we approach Jesus, the Word of God; and in order to encounter Jesus, we must approach him in a prayerful study of the inspired word of God, the Sacred Scriptures.

Inspiration and Inerrancy The Catholic Church makes mighty claims for the Bible, and our acceptance of those claims is essential if we are to read the Scriptures and apply them to our lives as the Church intends. So it is not enough merely to nod at words like "inspired", "unique", or "inerrant". We have to understand what the Church means by these terms, and we have to make that understanding our own. After all, what we believe about the Bible will inevitably influence the way we read the Bible. The way we read the Bible, in turn, will determine what we "get out" of its sacred pages.

These principles hold true no matter what we read: a news report, a search warrant, an advertisement, a paycheck, a doctor's prescription, an eviction notice. How (or whether) we read these things depends largely upon our preconceived notions about the reliability and authority of their sources—and the potential they have for affecting our lives. In some cases, to misunderstand a document's authority can lead to dire consequences. In others, it can keep us from enjoying rewards that are rightfully ours. In the case of the Bible, both the rewards and the consequences involved take on an ultimate value.

What does the Church mean, then, when she affirms the words of St. Paul: "All Scripture is inspired by God" (2 Tim 3:16)? Since the term "inspired" in this passage could be translated "God-breathed", it follows that God breathed forth his word in the Scriptures as you and I breathe forth air when we speak. This means that God is the primary author of the Bible. He certainly employed human authors in this task as well, but he did not merely assist them while they wrote or subsequently approve what they had written. God the Holy Spirit is the *principal* author of Scripture, while the human writers are *instrumental* authors. These human authors freely wrote everything, and only those things, that God wanted: the word of God in the very words of God. This miracle of dual authorship extends to the whole of Scripture, and to every one of its parts, so that whatever the human authors affirm, God likewise affirms through their words.

The principle of biblical inerrancy follows logically from this principle of divine authorship. After all, God cannot lie, and he cannot make mistakes. Since the Bible is divinely inspired, it must be without error in everything that its divine and human authors affirm to be true. This means that biblical inerrancy is a mystery even broader in scope than infallibility, which guarantees for us that the Church will always teach the truth concerning faith and morals. Of course the mantle of inerrancy likewise covers faith and morals, but it extends even farther to ensure that all the facts and events of

---

[1] Hugh of St. Victor, *De arca Noe* 2, 8: PL 176, 642: cf. ibid. 2, 9: PL 176, 642–43.
[2] *DV* 25; cf. Phil 3:8 and St. Jerome, *Commentariorum in Isaiam libri xviii*, prol.: PL 24, 17b.

salvation history are accurately presented for us in the Scriptures. Inerrancy is our guarantee that the words and deeds of God found in the Bible are unified and true, declaring with one voice the wonders of his saving love.

The guarantee of inerrancy does not mean, however, that the Bible is an all-purpose encyclopedia of information covering every field of study. The Bible is not, for example, a textbook in the empirical sciences, and it should not be treated as one. When biblical authors relate facts of the natural order, we can be sure they are speaking in a purely descriptive and "phenomenological" way, according to the way things appeared to their senses.

Biblical Authority Implicit in these doctrines is God's desire to make himself known to the world and to enter a loving relationship with every man, woman, and child he has created. God gave us the Scriptures not just to inform or motivate us; more than anything he wants to save us. This higher purpose underlies every page of the Bible, indeed every word of it.

In order to reveal himself, God used what theologians call "accommodation". Sometimes the Lord stoops down to communicate by "condescension"—that is, he speaks as humans speak, as if he had the same passions and weakness that we do (for example, God says he was "sorry" that he made man in Genesis 6:6). Other times he communicates by "elevation"—that is, by endowing human words with divine power (for example, through the Prophets). The numerous examples of divine accommodation in the Bible are an expression of God's wise and fatherly ways. For a sensitive father can speak with his children either by condescension, as in baby talk, or by elevation, by bringing a child's understanding up to a more mature level.

God's word is thus saving, fatherly, and personal. Because it speaks directly to us, we must never be indifferent to its content; after all, the word of God is at once the object, cause, and support of our faith. It is, in fact, a test of our faith, since we see in the Scriptures only what faith disposes us to see. If we believe what the Church believes, we will see in Scripture the saving, inerrant, and divinely authored revelation of the Father. If we believe otherwise, we see another book altogether.

This test applies not only to rank-and-file believers but also to the Church's theologians and hierarchy, and even the Magisterium. Vatican II has stressed in recent times that Scripture must be "the very soul of sacred theology" (*Dei Verbum* 24). As Joseph Cardinal Ratzinger, Pope Benedict XVI echoed this powerful teaching with his own, insisting that "the *normative theologians* are the authors of Holy Scripture" (emphasis added). He reminded us that Scripture and the Church's dogmatic teaching are tied tightly together, to the point of being inseparable: "Dogma is by definition nothing other than an interpretation of Scripture." The defined dogmas of our faith, then, encapsulate the Church's infallible interpretation of Scripture, and theology is a further reflection upon that work.

The Senses of Scripture Because the Bible has both divine and human authors, we are required to master a different sort of reading than we are used to. First, we must read Scripture according to its *literal* sense, as we read any other human literature. At this initial stage, we strive to discover the meaning of the words and expressions used by the biblical writers as they were understood in their original setting and by their original recipients. This means, among other things, that we do not interpret everything we read "literalistically", as though Scripture never speaks in a figurative or symbolic way (it often does!). Rather, we read it according to the rules that govern its different literary forms of writing, depending on whether we are reading a narrative, a poem, a letter, a parable, or an apocalyptic vision. The Church calls us to read the divine books in this way to ensure that we understand what the human authors were laboring to explain to God's people.

The literal sense, however, is not the only sense of Scripture, since we interpret its sacred pages according to the *spiritual* senses as well. In this way, we search out what the Holy Spirit is trying to tell us, beyond even what the human authors have consciously asserted. Whereas the literal sense of Scripture describes a historical reality—a fact, precept, or event—the spiritual senses disclose deeper mysteries revealed through the historical realities. What the soul is to the body, the spiritual senses are to the literal. You can distinguish them; but if you try to separate them, death immediately follows. St. Paul was the first to insist upon this and warn of its consequences: "God ... has qualified us to be ministers of a new covenant, not in a written code but in the Spirit; for the written code kills, but the Spirit gives life" (2 Cor 3:5–6).

Catholic tradition recognizes three spiritual senses that stand upon the foundation of the literal sense of Scripture (see CCC 115). **(1)** The first is the *allegorical* sense, which unveils the spiritual and prophetic meaning of biblical history. Allegorical interpretations thus reveal how persons, events, and institutions of Scripture can point beyond themselves toward greater mysteries yet to come (OT) or display the fruits of mysteries already revealed (NT). Christians have often read the Old Testament in this way to discover how the mystery of Christ in the New Covenant was once hidden in the Old and how the full significance of the Old Covenant was finally made manifest in the New. Allegorical significance is likewise latent in the New Testament, especially in the life and deeds of Jesus recorded in the Gospels. Because Christ is the Head of the Church and the source of her spiritual life, what was accomplished in Christ the Head during his earthly life prefigures what he continually produces in his members through grace. The allegorical sense builds up the virtue of faith. **(2)** The second is the *tropological* or *moral* sense, which reveals how the actions of God's people in the Old Testament and the life of Jesus in the New Testament prompt us to form virtuous habits in our own lives. It therefore draws from Scripture warnings against sin and vice as well as inspirations to pursue holiness and purity. The moral sense is intended to build up the virtue of charity. **(3)** The third is the *anagogical* sense, which points upward to heavenly glory. It shows us how countless events in the Bible prefigure our final union with God in eternity and how things that are "seen" on earth are figures of things "unseen" in heaven. Because the anagogical sense leads us to contemplate our destiny, it is meant to build up the virtue of hope. Together with the literal sense, then, these spiritual senses draw out the fullness of what God wants to give us through his Word and as such comprise what ancient tradition has called the "full sense" of Sacred Scripture.

All of this means that the deeds and events of the Bible are charged with meaning beyond what is immediately apparent to the reader. In essence, that meaning is Jesus Christ and the salvation he died to give us. This is especially true of the books of the New Testament, which proclaim Jesus explicitly, but it is also true of the Old Testament, which speaks of Jesus in more hidden and symbolic ways. The human authors of the Old Testament told us as much as they were able, but they could not clearly discern the shape of all future events standing at such a distance. It is the Bible's divine Author, the Holy Spirit, who could and did foretell the saving work of Christ, from the first page of the Book of Genesis onward.

The New Testament did not, therefore, abolish the Old. Rather, the New fulfilled the Old, and in doing so, it lifted the veil that kept hidden the face of the Lord's bride. Once the veil is removed, we suddenly see the world of the Old Covenant charged with grandeur. Water, fire, clouds, gardens, trees, hills, doves, lambs—all of these things are memorable details in the history and poetry of Israel. But now, seen in the light of Jesus Christ, they are much more. For the Christian with eyes to see, water symbolizes the saving power of Baptism; fire, the Holy Spirit; the spotless lamb, Christ crucified; Jerusalem, the city of heavenly glory.

The spiritual reading of Scripture is nothing new. Indeed, the very first Christians read the Bible this way. St. Paul describes Adam as a "type" that prefigured Jesus Christ (Rom 5:14). A "type" is a real person, place, thing, or event in the Old Testament that foreshadows something greater in the New. From this term we get the word "typology", referring to the study of how the Old Testament

prefigures Christ (CCC 128–30). Elsewhere St. Paul draws deeper meanings out of the story of Abraham's sons, declaring, "This is an allegory" (Gal 4:24). He is not suggesting that these events of the distant past never really happened; he is saying that the events both happened *and* signified something more glorious yet to come.

The New Testament later describes the Tabernacle of ancient Israel as "a copy and shadow of the heavenly sanctuary" (Heb 8:5) and the Mosaic Law as a "shadow of the good things to come" (Heb 10:1). St. Peter, in turn, notes that Noah and his family were "saved through water" in a way that "corresponds" to sacramental Baptism, which "now saves you" (1 Pet 3:20–21). It is interesting to note that the expression translated as "corresponds" in this verse is a Greek term that denotes the fulfillment or counterpart of an ancient "type".

We need not look to the apostles, however, to justify a spiritual reading of the Bible. After all, Jesus himself read the Old Testament this way. He referred to Jonah (Mt 12:39), Solomon (Mt 12:42), the Temple (Jn 2:19), and the brazen serpent (Jn 3:14) as "signs" that pointed forward to him. We see in Luke's Gospel, as Christ comforted the disciples on the road to Emmaus, that "beginning with Moses and all the prophets, he interpreted to them in all the Scriptures the things concerning himself" (Lk 24:27) It was precisely this extensive spiritual interpretation of the Old Testament that made such an impact on these once-discouraged travelers, causing their hearts to "burn" within them (Lk 24:32).

Criteria for Biblical Interpretation We, too, must learn to discern the "full sense" of Scripture as it includes both the literal and spiritual senses together. Still, this does not mean we should "read into" the Bible meanings that are not really there. Spiritual exegesis is not an unrestrained flight of the imagination. Rather, it is a sacred science that proceeds according to certain principles and stands accountable to sacred tradition, the Magisterium, and the wider community of biblical interpreters (both living and deceased).

In searching out the full sense of a text, we should always avoid the extreme tendency to "over-spiritualize" in a way that minimizes or denies the Bible's literal truth. St. Thomas Aquinas was well aware of this danger and asserted that "all other senses of Sacred Scripture are based on the literal" (*STh* I, 1, 10, *ad* 1, quoted in CCC 116). On the other hand, we should never confine the meaning of a text to the literal, intended sense of its human author, as if the divine Author did not intend the passage to be read in the light of Christ's coming.

Fortunately the Church has given us guidelines in our study of Scripture. The unique character and divine authorship of the Bible call us to read it "in the Spirit" (*Dei Verbum* 12). Vatican II outlines this teaching in a practical way by directing us to read the Scriptures according to three specific criteria:

1. We must "[b]e especially attentive 'to the content and unity of the whole Scripture'" (CCC 112).

2. We must "[r]ead the Scripture within 'the living Tradition of the whole Church'" (CCC 113).

3. We must "[b]e attentive to the analogy of faith" (CCC 114; cf. Rom 12:6).

These criteria protect us from many of the dangers that ensnare readers of the Bible, from the newest inquirer to the most prestigious scholar. Reading Scripture out of context is one such pitfall, and probably the one most difficult to avoid. A memorable cartoon from the 1950s shows a young man poring over the pages of the Bible. He says to his sister: "Don't bother me now; I'm trying to find a Scripture verse to back up one of my preconceived notions." No doubt a biblical text pried from its context can be twisted to say something very different from what its author actually intended.

The Church's criteria guide us here by defining what constitutes the authentic "context" of a given biblical passage. The first criterion directs us to the literary context of every verse, including not only the words and paragraphs that surround it, but also the entire corpus of the biblical author's writings and, indeed, the span of the entire Bible. The *complete* literary context of any Scripture verse includes every text from Genesis to Revelation—because the Bible is a unified book, not just a library of different books. When the Church canonized the Book of Revelation, for example, she recognized it to be incomprehensible apart from the wider context of the entire Bible.

The second criterion places the Bible firmly within the context of a community that treasures a "living tradition". That community is the People of God down through the ages. Christians lived out their faith for well over a millennium before the printing press was invented. For centuries, few believers owned copies of the Gospels, and few people could read anyway. Yet they absorbed the gospel—through the sermons of their bishops and clergy, through prayer and meditation, through Christian art, through liturgical celebrations, and through oral tradition. These were expressions of the one "living tradition", a culture of living faith that stretches from ancient Israel to the contemporary Church. For the early Christians, the gospel could not be understood apart from that tradition. So it is with us. Reverence for the Church's tradition is what protects us from any sort of chronological or cultural provincialism, such as scholarly fads that arise and carry away a generation of interpreters before being dismissed by the next generation.

The third criterion places scriptural texts within the framework of faith. If we believe that the Scriptures are divinely inspired, we must also believe them to be internally coherent and consistent with all the doctrines that Christians believe.

Remember, the Church's dogmas (such as the Real Presence, the papacy, the Immaculate Conception) are not something *added* to Scripture; rather, they are the Church's infallible interpretation *of* Scripture.

Using This Study Guide This volume is designed to lead the reader through Scripture according to the Church's guidelines—faithful to the canon, to the tradition, and to the creeds. The Church's interpretive principles have thus shaped the component parts of this book, and they are designed to make the reader's study as effective and rewarding as possible.

Introductions: We have introduced the biblical book with an essay covering issues such as authorship, date of composition, purpose, and leading themes. This background information will assist readers to approach and understand the text on its own terms.

Annotations: The basic notes at the bottom of every page help the user to read the Scriptures with understanding. They by no means exhaust the meaning of the sacred text but provide background material to help the reader make sense of what he reads. Often these notes make explicit what the sacred writers assumed or held to be implicit. They also provide a great deal of historical, cultural, geographical, and theological information pertinent to the inspired narratives—information that can help the reader bridge the distance between the biblical world and his own.

Cross-References: Between the biblical text at the top of each page and the annotations at the bottom, numerous references are listed to point readers to other scriptural passages related to the one being studied. This follow-up is an essential part of any serious study. It is also an excellent way to discover how the content of Scripture "hangs together" in a providential unity. Along with biblical cross-references, the annotations refer to select paragraphs from the *Catechism of the Catholic Church*. These are not doctrinal "proof texts" but are designed to help the reader interpret the Bible in accordance with the mind of the Church. The *Catechism* references listed either handle the biblical text directly or treat a broader doctrinal theme that sheds significant light on that text.

Topical Essays, Word Studies, Charts: These features bring readers to a deeper understanding of select details. The *topical essays* take up major themes and explain them more thoroughly and theologically than the annotations, often relating them to the doctrines of the Church. Occasionally the annotations are supplemented by *word studies* that put readers in touch with the ancient languages of Scripture. These should help readers to understand better and appreciate the inspired terminology that runs throughout the sacred books. Also included are various *charts* that summarize biblical information "at a glance".

Icon Annotations: Three distinctive icons are interspersed throughout the annotations, each one corresponding to one of the Church's three criteria for biblical interpretation. Bullets indicate the passage or passages to which these icons apply.

Notes marked by the book icon relate to the "content and unity" of Scripture, showing how particular passages of the Old Testament illuminate the mysteries of the New. Much of the information in these notes explains the original context of the citations and indicates how and why this has a direct bearing on Christ or the Church. Through these notes, the reader can develop a sensitivity to the beauty and unity of God's saving plan as it stretches across both Testaments.

Notes marked by the dove icon examine particular passages in light of the Church's "living tradition". Because the Holy Spirit both guides the Magisterium and inspires the spiritual senses of Scripture, these annotations supply information along both of these lines. On the one hand, they refer to the Church's doctrinal teaching as presented by various popes, creeds, and ecumenical councils; on the other, they draw from (and paraphrase) the spiritual interpretations of various Fathers, Doctors, and saints.

Notes marked by the keys icon pertain to the "analogy of faith". Here we spell out how the mysteries of our faith "unlock" and explain one another. This type of comparison between Christian beliefs displays the coherence and unity of defined dogmas, which are the Church's infallible interpretations of Scripture.

Putting It All in Perspective Perhaps the most important context of all we have saved for last: the interior life of the individual reader. What we get out of the Bible will largely depend on how we approach the Bible. Unless we are living a sustained and disciplined life of prayer, we will never have the reverence, the profound humility, or the grace we need to see the Scriptures for what they really are.

You are approaching the "word of God". But for thousands of years, since before he knit you in your mother's womb, the Word of God has been approaching you.

One Final Note. The volume you hold in your hands is only a small part of a much larger work still in production. Study helps similar to those printed in this booklet are being prepared for *all* the books of the Bible and will appear gradually as they are finished. Our ultimate goal is to publish a single, one-volume Study Bible that will include the entire text of Scripture, along with all the annotations, charts, cross-references, maps, and other features found in the following pages. Individual booklets will be published in the meantime, with the hope that God's people can begin to benefit from this labor before its full completion.

We have included a long list of Study Questions in the back to make this format as useful as possible, not only for individual study, but for group settings and discussions as well. The questions are designed to help readers both "understand" the Bible and "apply" it to their lives. We pray that God will make use of our efforts and yours to help renew the face of the earth! «

INTRODUCTION TO ISAIAH

Author and Date The Book of Isaiah is an anthology of prophecies that were written down at different times and combined into a single work. Jewish and Christian tradition attributes the collection to Isaiah of Jerusalem, a prophet who spoke the word of God in Judah from 740 until at least 701 B.C. The earliest witness to this tradition is Sirach 48:24–25, written about 175 B.C., which admires the prophet Isaiah as one who "comforted those who mourned in Zion" (alluding to Is 40:1–2; 61:2–3) and revealed "hidden things before they came to pass" (alluding to Is 46:10; 48:6). From the first century A.D., we have the testimony of Jesus and the authors of the NT, who shared the early Jewish belief that all parts of the Book of Isaiah come from the prophet Isaiah (Mt 3:3; 8:17; 12:17–21; Mk 7:6–7; Lk 3:4–6; Jn 12:38–41; Acts 28:25–27; Rom 9:27–29; 15:12, etc.). The Jewish historian Josephus, also writing in the first century A.D., contends that Isaiah predicted the rise of Cyrus II of Persia more than a century before his time (*Antiquities* 11.5–6, referring to Is 44:28; 45:1). A few centuries later, rabbinic scholars add the detail that Isaiah's prophecies were compiled into a single work in the days of King Hezekiah of Judah, who was a contemporary of Isaiah (Babylonian Talmud, *Baba Bathra* 15a). Together these ancient voices testify to a tradition that Isaiah of Jerusalem stands behind the entire book that bears his name. They further imply that, while others may have played a role in preserving Isaiah's oracles and assembling them into a single work, the substance of the book may be dated near the end of the prophet Isaiah's lifetime, that is, before the middle of the seventh century B.C.

Today the traditional view is a minority position among scholars, although academic defenses of the Isaianic authorship and date of the book continue to be made. Arguments made in support of the tradition include the following. **(1)** The opening verse attributes the work to "Isaiah the son of Amoz" (1:1). This passage appears to be a heading, not merely for the book's opening chapter or section, but for the entire canonical work, as indicated by the reference to Isaiah's prophetic gift of "seeing" extending over the reigns of several kings of Judah. **(2)** There are no oracles in the book attributed to a prophet other than Isaiah, nor has history preserved any alternative tradition to suggest that oracles uttered by other prophets have been added to the collection of prophecies preserved in Isaiah's name. **(3)** The book presents Isaiah, not only as a prophet who spoke to his own generation in the eighth century B.C., but also as one who foretold events of the sixth century B.C., such as the Babylonian Exile of Judah (39:6) and the fall of Babylon itself (13:1–22). Assuming the possibility of predictive prophecy, these internal claims of the book are consistent with its contents, parts of which deal with the eighth century (chaps. 1–39), and parts of which deal with the sixth and fifth centuries (chaps. 40–66). **(4)** It is increasingly recognized among scholars that the Book of Isaiah is a unified literary work. A clear indication of this is the recurrence of images and expressions that stretch across the entire book from beginning to end. For instance, (a) the Lord is called "the Holy One of Israel" throughout the book, in early chapters as well as later ones (1:4; 10:20; 17:7; 41:14; 43:3; 54:5; 60:9); (b) the eschatological visions of the book consistently focus on Zion, the Lord's holy mountain, as the place where Israel and all nations will assemble for worship (2:2–3; 11:9; 25:6–9; 56:7–8; 65:25; 66:20); (c) the way of salvation for God's people reappears throughout the book as a highway that runs through the wilderness (11:16; 19:23; 35:8; 40:3; 62:10); and (d) the Lord's holy "arm", signifying his saving power, is an image distributed across all parts of the book (30:32; 33:2; 40:10; 48:14; 59:16; 63:12). Such consistency of language and imagery is readily explained—and even to be expected—if a single prophet stands behind the entire work. And since ancient sources are unanimous in crediting the book to a single prophet, Isaiah of Jerusalem, modern-day proponents insist that the tradition of Isaianic authorship remains a defensible position on internal grounds.

That said, a majority of modern scholars have come to different conclusions regarding the origins of Isaiah. Many accept that the prophet Isaiah authored select parts of the book that bears his name; however, the view that became dominant by the early twentieth century holds that the Book of Isaiah also incorporates the work of anonymous authors and editors from later centuries. Advocates segment the book into three parts: First Isaiah (chaps. 1–39, also called Proto-Isaiah), Second Isaiah (chaps. 40–55, also called Deutero-Isaiah), and Third Isaiah (chaps. 56–66, also called Trito-Isaiah). First Isaiah is thought to have its background in *preexilic* Jerusalem in the latter decades of the eight century B.C. Isaiah's oracles form the bulk of this collection, although several chapters are alleged to come from later contributors to the book. Second Isaiah is said to reflect an *exilic* setting in Babylon around the midpoint of the sixth century B.C. Its author is unknown beyond the fact that he was deeply influenced by Isaiah's theology.

It is widely held that the anonymous prophet responsible for Second Isaiah also made editorial insertions into First Isaiah. Third Isaiah is said to address *postexilic* Jerusalem, where the Jewish community that had returned from Babylon was struggling to rebuild the nation after the trauma of the Exile, most likely in the fifth century B.C. Its author is likewise unnamed and unknown, although it is held that he was intimately familiar with First and Second Isaiah, whose work he edited in turn. On this modern hypothesis, the Book of Isaiah was written and compiled by several authors and editors between the eighth and fifth centuries B.C. A number of scholars further maintain that the Isaiah Apocalypse (chaps. 24–27) is an independent segment that was added to the book as late as the fourth or third century B.C.

Many reasons are given for this modern account of Isaiah's origins, among which are the following. **(1)** The name "Isaiah" appears more than fifteen times in chapters 1–39 but disappears entirely from chapter 40 onward. This could suggest that chapters 40–66 were not part of the original collection of Isaiah's oracles. **(2)** The literary style and mood of chapters 1–39 are markedly different from those of chapters 40–66. The former is dominated by a serious tone and a heavy concentration of oracles threatening doom; the latter features a profusion of oracles promising deliverance and is expressed in some of the most lyrical poetry found in the Bible. Again, a shift is noticeable in chapter 40 that is readily explained if the sayings of one or more other prophets have been added to Isaiah's prophecies. **(3)** The oracles of the book address different historical audiences: Isaiah's contemporaries in Judah in the eighth century (chaps. 1–39), the exiles of Judah living in Babylon in the middle of the sixth century (chaps. 40–55), and the community of former exiles living in Judah in the fifth century (chaps. 56–66). On the premise that prophets usually address their contemporaries rather than future generations, even when speaking about future events, the internal evidence of three different audiences suggests to many scholars that the oracles of the book stem from three different prophets. **(4)** Two passages, 44:28 and 45:1, announce God's plan to raise up a figure named "Cyrus" to accomplish his purposes for Israel. Explicit reference to this figure, which all agree is Cyrus II of Persia, the conqueror of Babylon in 539 B.C., suggests to many commentators that the prophet who delivered these oracles must have lived in the sixth century B.C. rather than the eighth century B.C., since predictions made by the prophets almost never identify persons to come in the future by name. Together these observations combine into a plausible case that more than one prophet, writing in more than one century, had a hand in producing the book we know today.

In the end, the origin of the Book of Isaiah is patient of more than one explanation. Proponents of various views appeal to internal elements in the text to construct hypotheses for how the book came to be written. But these elements are subject to diverse interpretations by Catholic as well as non-Catholic scholars. Depending on one's evaluation of the evidence, the book can be viewed as a *compositional unity*, the masterwork of Isaiah of Jerusalem, or as an *editorial unity*, a composite work that started out as a collection of Isaiah's prophecies and grew over time as later prophets who internalized Isaiah's preaching added their own contributions. Regardless of the position one adopts, the Catholic Church contends that all sixty-six chapters of the Book of Isaiah are divinely inspired and canonical, whether they were written by a single prophet or by a succession of prophets whom God commissioned to speak his word over the span of three or more centuries.

Title The opening verse entitles the book: "The vision of Isaiah the son of Amoz" (1:1). Later this would be simplified to *Yesha 'yahu* (or the abbreviated *Yesha 'yah*), the Hebrew name for Isaiah meaning "the LORD saves". In the Greek Septuagint, the title is simply the name of the prophet, transliterated as *Ēsaias*. Manuscripts of the Latin Vulgate supply a fuller heading, either *Isaias Propheta* ("Isaiah the Prophet") or *Liber Isaiae* ("The Book of Isaiah").

Place in the Canon In the Jewish Bible, or Tanakh, which is divided into three parts, Isaiah is located among the *Nevi 'im*, or Prophets, where it stands as the first of the "Latter Prophets", followed by the books of Jeremiah and Ezekiel. The Greek Septuagint, followed by the Latin Vulgate, places Isaiah among the "Major Prophets" (with Jeremiah, Ezekiel, and Daniel), which are either followed or preceded in ancient codices of the LXX by the twelve "Minor Prophets" (Hosea–Malachi). Isaiah's canonical status as an inspired book of Scripture has never been seriously questioned in either Judaism or Christianity.

Structure The Book of Isaiah divides into two major movements, the first dominated by oracles of confrontation (chaps. 1–39) and the second by oracles of consolation (chaps. 40–66). The second movement is further divided into prophecies spoken to Jewish exiles living in Babylon (chaps. 40–55) and prophecies spoken to the Jewish community who returned from Babylon (chaps. 56–66). Isaiah thus has three major sections. In the first, the Southern Kingdom of Judah is brought to trial and judgment for its sins against the covenant. For the most part, this takes place in the historical context of Assyria's interventions in Palestine. In the second, the exiles of Judah are comforted with a message that God is coming to save them from captivity in Babylon. In the third, the Jewish returnees from Babylon are rebuked for falling back into sinful ways but are also encouraged with visions of God glorifying his people, gathering all nations to Zion, and creating a new heaven and a new earth. For a more detailed breakdown, see outline.

The Prophet and His Times Isaiah of Jerusalem was an extraordinary prophet and man of God. As a theologian and poet of the highest caliber, he has been called the Fifth Evangelist and the Shakespeare of ancient Israel. Nevertheless, little is known about the prophet's life except what filters through the book that bears his name. Isaiah lived in Israel's capital city, and, judging from his close association with the royal court, he was probably a member of the Jerusalem nobility. He was the husband of a prophetess (8:3), the father of two sons (7:3; 8:3), and the leader of a group of disciples (8:16). Isaiah was called to prophetic ministry about 740 B.C., the year that King Uzziah of Judah died (6:1–13), and he continued to serve as the Lord's messenger under Uzziah's successors: Jotham, Ahaz, and Hezekiah (1:1). Jewish tradition holds that Isaiah died as a martyr under the wicked King Manasseh of Judah (696–642 B.C.), who had him sawn in two (*Martyrdom and Ascension of Isaiah* 5, 1–16; *Lives of the Prophets* 1, 1; cf. Heb 11:37).

Isaiah's ministry began when the kingdoms of Israel (northern) and Judah (southern) enjoyed economic prosperity and military strength. For the most part, it was a time of peace and optimism. But all of that was about to change. Threats to Israel's social stability were lurking within, and threats to Israel's national security were gathering like storm clouds on the horizon without. **(1)** Internally, material wealth bred various forms of social injustice and religious corruption. Oppression of the poor, bribery in the courts, hedonism among the rich and ruling classes, brazen acts of idolatry, and empty liturgical worship are just a few of the evils singled out for condemnation. **(2)** Externally, Israel and Judah had reason to fear the rise of Assyria. Beginning around 745 B.C., the Assyrian king Tiglath-Pileser III, followed by a series of like-minded successors, used ruthless military force to fulfill their imperialist ambitions on a colossal scale. By the end of Isaiah's ministry, much of the Near East from Palestine to the Persian Gulf had been forced under the yoke of Assyrian rule. Key events forming the background to Isaiah's ministry include the death of King Uzziah of Judah (740 B.C.), the Syro-Ephraimite conflict (735 B.C.), the conquest of Samaria and the demise of the Northern Kingdom of Israel (722 B.C.), the death of the Assyrian king Sargon II (705 B.C.), and the siege of Jerusalem by the Assyrian king Sennacherib (701 B.C.).

The Message of the Prophet The Book of Isaiah stands in a class by itself. It is not only the longest prophetic book of the Old Testament; it is also the most luminous. It takes readers into the drama of Israel's history at various points along a timeline that covers more than two centuries. And yet the prophet's insights into God's ways are not restricted to the major events that impacted his people in OT times. Numerous passages in the book take readers beyond these particular historical moments and present a vision of God's ultimate plan of salvation for Israel and the world. Little wonder the Book of Isaiah has been one of the most treasured writings of Scripture in Jewish and Christian communities alike.

But if Isaiah's vision is breathtaking and grand, it is marked by a certain simplicity. The book expounds only a modest number of themes for its length, and yet these core motifs reappear again and again as one reads through the book. Its most obvious pattern may be outlined in three steps: first, Isaiah addresses a historical and spiritual crisis in the life of Israel, a crisis occasioned in part by the sinfulness of the nation; second, the prophet calls for repentance and a renewed trust in the Lord— otherwise the covenant people will face God's judgment; and third, he promises that even if God's warnings go unheeded and judgment must come, hope for the future remains because the Lord's mercy is never exhausted for those who desire it. A fuller account of this pattern will encompass much of Isaiah's message.

(1) *Condemnation of Sin.* Many of Isaiah's oracles begin with stern denunciations of evil. Time and again the prophet charges Judah and Jerusalem with rebellion against God and his covenant. Foremost among their sins is idolatry. In some cases, this involves a wholesale abandonment of the Lord to serve the gods of other nations; in others, it takes the form of syncretism, i.e., adopting pagan cult practices alongside the observances of Israel's religion (2:8; 65:2–5). Either way, the chosen people stand guilty of turning their backs on the unique and exclusive relationship between God and Israel. Other sins decried by the prophet pertain to social injustice and immorality. Having rejected the Torah (5:24), Judah and Jerusalem are charged with exploiting the poor, oppressing widows and orphans, corrupting justice by the acceptance of bribes, reveling in drunkenness, and instigating violence (1:17, 21, 23; 3:14–15; 5:7, 11, 22–23; etc.). Isaiah describes this as a time when God's people have lost their way to such an extent that good is mistaken for evil and evil for good (5:20). Another problem the prophet confronts is the corruption of worship. Many who participate in the liturgy of the Temple and perform acts of piety such as fasting are accused of perpetrating evil against fellow members of the community (1:12–17; 58:1–7). Some he faults for mechanically "going through the motions" without seeking God in their hearts, as if performing liturgical rituals could substitute for a living relationship with the Lord (29:13). Finally, Judah and Jerusalem are imperiled by a crisis of godly leadership. Royal and religious authorities seek security in politics instead of the Lord's guidance for Israel. This plays out as government leaders forge alliances with regional states such as Assyria, Egypt, and Babylonia, despite Isaiah's pleas to rely on the wisdom and power of God rather than the wisdom and power of the world (7:3–9; 30:1–18; 31:1–9; 39:1–7).

(2) *Call for Repentance.* Isaiah responds to these alarming developments by urging Judah and Jerusalem to cease from their rebellion and return to the Lord. God's people must renounce their wickedness and seek justice for the entire covenant community, especially its most vulnerable members (58:6–7). Israel must also repudiate the idols of the nations for what they really are—lifeless creations that can never benefit their devotees or influence the course of history (41:21–24; 44:9–20). Not even worshiping the one true God is acceptable unless liturgy and life form a unity, so that serving God in the Temple flows out into a life of serving others as well (1:16–17). And if the kingdom of Judah is to return to God's favor, the people must learn to trust the Lord in difficult times (7:9; 28:16) with a serene confidence that his plans will be fulfilled (30:15). Fear of the Lord must take precedence over human fears (7:4–8; 8:12–13; 10:24–27). And Isaiah issues this call to national repentance not only by promising restored blessings but also by warning of dreadful judgments. Unless God's people reform their lives and renew their commitment to the covenant, they will bring upon themselves the humiliation that their rebellion deserves. The Lord will allow his vineyard to be ravaged by enemies (5:1–7). He will rouse mighty armies as instruments of his will (9:11; 10:5–6) to devastate the land and drive the survivors of his people into exile (6:11–12). Even Gentile nations beyond Israel will be held accountable to the Lord for their proud and wicked ways (chaps. 13–23).

(3) *Comfort after Judgment.* Besides oracles of warning and woe, Isaiah also speaks words of encouragement and hope. More than once in his lifetime, and many more times in the history of Israel, the chosen people reaped the bitter consequences of breaking the covenant. And yet, according to the prophet, judgment on sin is never the end of the story. Isaiah is adamant that God will never cast off or abandon his beloved people, even if he must humble them for a time (41:8–10; 45:17). On the contrary, the Lord desires to bless them in unprecedented ways in the days to come. The northern tribes of Israel, scattered among the nations by Assyrian conquerors in the eighth century B.C., will be restored (27:12–13; 49:6). The southern tribes of Judah, exiled by Babylonian conquerors in the sixth century B.C., will be freed and led home to rebuild their lives in the Promised Land (48:20; 52:9–12). Beyond that, all nations will hear the tidings of salvation (49:6; 66:18–21), the call to join themselves to the God of Israel and to become members of the covenant people alongside Israel (2:2–4; 18:7;

19:19–25; 56:6–8). The focal point of these prophecies is Mount Zion. In Isaiah's day, Jerusalem was in revolt against the Lord (1:21–23); and even after the exiles returned home from Babylon, the holy city lapsed back into its wicked ways (57:1–13). The Lord, however, announces a plan for the purification (1:25–27), exaltation (2:2–3), and glorification of Zion (4:5–6; 60:1–22). In the "latter days" of eschatological fulfillment (2:1), the Lord will draw all peoples to Zion for a banquet of choice foods (25:6–8). There they will bring their riches (60:4–14), and there they will come to receive instruction (2:1–4). At that time, Jerusalem will become the Lord's bridal city once again (54:5; 62:1–5). The NT will interpret Isaiah's vision of the ideal Zion, not as referring to the historical city as such, but as the transcendent reality symbolized by the earthly capital—the heavenly elevation where the Lord draws the faithful of all nations into everlasting peace and worship (see Heb 12:22–24; Rev 21:2).

Alongside these expectations of Zion's transformation, Isaiah announces many "new things" that await God's people (42:9; 48:6). He foretells a *new exodus* in which the Lord will show himself a mighty Savior once again, just as he did when he rescued Israel from bondage in Egypt. Memories linked with this event such as crossing the sea on dry land and providing water in the wilderness are called to mind as signs of a new and greater act of deliverance (11:15–16; 43:16–21). Initially the prophet has in mind the liberation of the Jewish captives from Babylon in the sixth century B.C. (45:1, 13; 48:20–21); ultimately, however, he foresees a spiritual restoration, a salvation from sin, that God accomplishes through a messianic figure identified only as the Servant of the Lord (49:6; 53:10–12). Isaiah likewise speaks of a *new covenant* in which the Lord will unite himself to his people in a new way. It is a covenant that will grant forgiveness (27:9) and peace to God's people (54:10) and impart new life through an outpouring of the Spirit (59:21; cf. 32:15; 44:3). Closely related to this, the prophet unveils the divine plan for a *new kingdom* that extends beyond Israel to embrace all nations. This kingdom is viewed as the fulfillment of God's covenant of kingship with David (55:3–5). Its agent is the Davidic Messiah, a figure who will rule from the throne of David (9:6–7), who will be richly endowed with the Spirit (11:1–5), who will be sought by the nations (11:10), and who will govern the world with perfect justice (16:5; 32:1). Finally, Isaiah foresees a *new creation*, the coming of a "new heavens" and a "new earth" where peace and righteousness prevail (65:17–25). In this new creation, which will remain forever, all people and nations will worship the Lord God of Israel (66:22–23) as the only true God (43:10–11; 45:5–6).

Christian Perspective Isaiah is the OT book most frequently quoted in the NT after the Psalms. This is not surprising, since the entire scope of the

Christian message is present in Isaiah in prophetic outline. John the Baptist is the voice crying in the wilderness, making the Lord's people ready for his coming (40:3; Mt 3:3; Jn 1:23). Jesus is the Immanuel child who is born of a virgin Mother (7:14; Mt 1:23) and is destined to rule upon David's throne over an everlasting kingdom (9:6–7; Lk 1:32–33). Jesus' Baptism reveals him to be the royal branch of Jesse and the Servant who is pleasing to the Lord (11:1–2; 42:1; Mt 3:16–17), while his residence in Galilee fulfills the expectation of a great light shining upon Galilee (9:1–2; Mt 4:12–16) and bringing good news to the poor (61:1–3; Lk 4:16–21). Jesus is also the precious stone laid on Zion, so that those who believe in him find salvation, while those who do not stumble over him (28:16; Rom 9:33; 1 Pet 2:6–8). Ultimately, Jesus fulfills the mission of Isaiah's Suffering Servant, who was reckoned among transgressors (53:12; Lk 22:37), even though no deceit was found in his mouth (53:9; 1 Pet 2:22) and he sacrificed his life

for the sins of others (53:10–12; Mk 10:45; 14:22–24; Acts 8:26–35). In the wake of his rejection and death, he is revealed as the divine Lord, before whom all creatures will bend the knee (45:23; Phil 2:9–11). And beyond being the Redeemer of Israel, Jesus is the hope of the nations as well (11:10; Rom 15:12), with the Church sharing in his mission to be a light to all nations (49:6; Acts 13:47). Lastly, God's redemption will have its full effect when death is destroyed and the bodies of the dead are raised (25:8; 26:19; 1 Cor 15:51–54). Then every tear will be wiped away (25:8; Rev 7:17; 21:4), and the present world will give way to a new heaven and a new earth (65:17; 2 Pet 3:13; Rev 21:1). Beyond the pages of the NT, the Book of Isaiah is frequently expounded in the writings of the Fathers and Doctors of the Church. Its ongoing relevance for the Church today is reflected in the Roman lectionary, which draws more Mass readings from Isaiah than from any other prophetic book of the OT.

OUTLINE OF ISAIAH

1. The Message and Ministry of Isaiah (chaps. 1–12)
  A. Judah and Jerusalem under Judgment (1:1—5:30)
  B. The Call of Isaiah (6:1–13)
  C. The Book of Immanuel (7:1—12:6)

2. Oracles concerning the Nations (chaps. 13–27)
  A. Babylon, Assyria, Philistia, Moab (13:1—16:14)
  B. Syria, Israel, Ethiopia, Egypt (17:1—20:6)
  C. Babylon, Edom, Arabia, Jerusalem, Tyre (21:1—23:18)
  D. The Isaiah Apocalypse (24:1—27:13)

3. Jerusalem, Egypt, and Redemption (chaps. 28–35)
  A. Woes on Judah, ally of Egypt (28:1—33:24)
  B. The Coming Judgment and Salvation (34:1—35:10)

4. Historical Section on Isaiah and Hezekiah (chaps. 36–39)
  A. Hezekiah and Sennacherib's Invasion (36:1—37:38)
  B. Hezekiah's Sickness and Recovery (38:1–22)
  C. Hezekiah and Babylon's Envoys (39:1–8)

5. The Consolation of Zion (chaps. 40–55)
  A. The Return from Exile (40:1—41:29)
  B. The Servant of the Lord (42:1—53:12)
  C. The Blessing of Zion (54:1—55:13)

6. The Glorification of Zion (chaps. 56–66)
  A. The Scope of the Coming Salvation (56:1—59:21)
  B. Zion Shines with God's Glory (60:1–22)
  C. Glad Tidings for Zion (61:1—62:12)
  D. God's Recompense for the Faithful and the Unfaithful (63:1—64:12)
  E. The New Heavens and the New Earth (65:1—66:24)

THE BOOK OF THE PROPHET

ISAIAH

The Sinfulness of Judah

1 The vision of Isai′ah the son of A′moz, which he saw concerning Judah and Jerusalem in the days of Uzzi′ah, Jo′tham, A′haz, and Hezeki′ah, kings of Judah.
²Hear, O heavens, and give ear, O earth;
 for the LORD has spoken:

"Sons have I reared and brought up,
 but they have rebelled against me.
³The ox knows its owner,
 and the donkey its master's crib;
but Israel does not know,
 my people does not understand."

1:1 The vision of Isaiah: A title for the book, which records the divine revelation given to the prophet Isaiah. NOTE TO THE READER: Since the only name attached to the contents of the book is Isaiah's, the annotations herein refer to "Isaiah" or "the prophet" without presuming a particular solution to the modern debates concerning authorship. For different views on the origin of the book, see introduction: *Author and Date*. **which he saw:** Suggests that God imparts his message to the prophets in ways that are visual as well as verbal (2:1; 6:1; Ezek 7:26). **Amoz:** Otherwise unknown, although an ancient Jewish tradition identifies him as the brother of King Amaziah of Judah (796–767 B.C.). **Judah and Jerusalem:** Isaiah ministered in the Southern Kingdom of Judah and its capital. **kings of Judah:** The length of Isaiah's career is measured by a succession of Davidic kings. He was called to be a prophet in the final year of Uzziah (740 B.C.), and he continued to speak the word of God during the reigns of Jotham (750–731 B.C.), Ahaz (735–715 B.C.), and Hezekiah (729–686 B.C.). For the overlap in royal tenures, see chart: *Kings of the Divided Monarchy* at 1 Kings 13.

1:2–20 Isaiah's opening tirade takes the rhetorical form of a covenant lawsuit. The prophet assumes the stance of a prosecutor who represents the Lord, bringing the people of Israel to trial for mass defection from the covenant, while heaven and earth are summoned as witnesses. • Isaiah charges Israel with violating the covenant of Deuteronomy,

which was ratified by oath before "heaven and earth" (Deut 4:23–26; 30:19; 31:28–29). He also evokes key images and ideas found in the Song of Moses in Deut 32, a poem in which Moses foresees Israel's future disobedience. Among the parallels: both begin by summoning the heavens and the earth to hear a divine proclamation (1:2; Deut 32:1); both characterize the Israelites as the faithless children of the Lord, their Father (1:2, 4; Deut 32:6, 19–20); both blame Israel for a lack of understanding (1:3; Deut 32:28); both accuse Israel of acting corruptly (1:4; Deut 32:5); both compare Israel to Sodom and Gomorrah (1:9–10; Deut 32:32); and both threaten judgment with the image of a devouring sword (1:20; Deut 32:41–42). See essay: *Covenant Lawsuit* at Mic 6:1.

1:2 heavens ... earth: In the theology of Isaiah, the existing creation will give way to a new creation in the future. The heavens and the earth of the present time are witnesses to the iniquity of the covenant people. The time will come, however, when the Lord will redeem Israel and all the nations, establishing a "new heavens" and a "new earth" that are filled with righteousness (65:17; 66:22). **Sons:** Kinship with the Lord as adopted sons and daughters is one of the great blessings of the Mosaic covenant (Deut 14:1; Rom 9:4). Rebellious children, however, are liable to the death penalty in the Mosaic Law (Deut 21:18–21).

1:3 ox ... donkey: Even brute animals have more sense than stubborn Israel (Jer 8:7). • When the shepherds and the wise men came to Jesus, the ox recognized its owner and the donkey its master's crib. From the Jews came the horned ox, and from the Gentiles came the donkey. Now the Owner of the ox and the Master of the donkey lies in a manger, providing food for both (St. Augustine, *Sermons* 204, 2).

The Books of Prophecy

In ancient times there were prophets of many different religions, men who claimed to speak in the name of their gods; and not infrequently they existed in large groups. Thus Elijah had to confront no less than 450 prophets of Baal on the occasion of the contest on Mount Carmel (1 Kings 18). There were similar groups of prophets who spoke in the name of Yahweh. These prophets experienced ecstasies and trances often induced by the playing of music (1 Sam 10:5), and seem to have been organized into communities (2 Kings 2:3–18).

The prophets, however, whom we know by name and whose actions are recorded in the Bible, were very different from these and their influence on Israel was much more profound. So far from their seeking prophecy as a profession, it was imposed on them by God and they could not refuse (Jer 1:9; Amos 3:8). So far from their trying by fair words to please their hearers, they often had to announce approaching disaster as punishment for sin. Not only their words, their whole life was given up to the ministry, and they had to lead a life of great penance and sacrifice often ending in violent death. The prophet received an inner, wordless message, which he was then compelled to communicate, sometimes in lyric poetry, sometimes in prose, often making use of parables, allegories, and symbolic actions. When disaster had fallen on the nation, then the role of the prophet changed from one of threat to one of consolation (Is 40ff.). It was in such times as these that many Messianic prophecies were uttered, foretelling the coming of God's kingdom in "the last days" heralded by God's anointed or "messiah." The character and mission of Christ are vividly portrayed in Isaiah and even his sufferings are there described, though it does not follow that those who first heard the prophecies understood all that was being said. Many prophecies were fully understood only when they came to pass.

The Book of Isaiah

Isaiah, the greatest of all the prophets, lived at a critical time in Israel's history. The very existence of the people was threatened by the king of Assyria in the latter part of the eighth century B.C. The well-known and beautiful Immanuel prophecies (chapters 6–12) were uttered on occasions of great national danger when Judah was ruled by an unworthy king—Ahaz. Under his successor, Hezekiah, a good and prudent king, Isaiah, who was himself of noble birth, occupied a position of influence in promoting religious reform, and many of his prophecies are to be ascribed to this period. He was by now a national figure with a large following. He appears last of all in the great crisis of 701 B.C. when, as he had promised, Jerusalem was saved from destruction by the Assyrians.

His prophecies are distinguished both for their poetical quality and for the elevation of their thought. The monotheism of Isaiah is declared in eloquent terms. Likewise, his Messianic predictions attain a clarity that has induced some to give him the title of "evangelist." The second part of the book (chapters 40–55), quite different from the first and perhaps even more sublime, is generally held now not to be by Isaiah himself but by a later prophet writing at the time of the Exile, doubtless a member of the Isaian school and following in his tradition. These chapters are remarkable for the words of comfort and encouragement they contain and perhaps even more for the remarkable "Servant Songs," prophecies about the Messiah to come, foretelling his sufferings. The remaining chapters (56–66) contain a varied selection of prophecies of different dates.

⁴Ah, sinful nation,
    a people laden with iniquity,
offspring of evildoers,
    sons who deal corruptly!
They have forsaken the LORD,
    they have despised the Holy One of Israel,
    they are utterly estranged.

⁵Why will you still be struck down,
    that you continue to rebel?
The whole head is sick,
    and the whole heart faint.
⁶From the sole of the foot even to the head,
    there is no soundness in it,
but bruises and sores
    and bleeding wounds;
they are not pressed out, or bound up,
    or softened with oil.

⁷Your country lies desolate,
    your cities are burned with fire;
in your very presence
    strangers devour your land;
    it is desolate, as overthrown by strangers.
⁸And the daughter of Zion is left
    like a booth in a vineyard,
like a lodge in a cucumber field,
    like a besieged city.

⁹If the LORD of hosts
    had not left us a few survivors,

we should have been like Sodom,
    and become like Gomor'rah.

¹⁰Hear the word of the LORD,
    you rulers of Sodom!
Give ear to the teaching of our God,
    you people of Gomor'rah!
¹¹"What to me is the multitude of your sacrifices?
    says the LORD;
I have had enough of burnt offerings of rams
    and the fat of fed beasts;
I do not delight in the blood of bulls,
    or of lambs, or of he-goats.

¹²"When you come to appear before me,
    who requires of you
    this trampling of my courts?
¹³Bring no more vain offerings;
    incense is an abomination to me.
New moon and sabbath and the calling of
        assemblies—
    I cannot endure iniquity and solemn assembly.
¹⁴Your new moons and your appointed feasts
    my soul hates;
they have become a burden to me,
    I am weary of bearing them.
¹⁵When you spread forth your hands,
    I will hide my eyes from you;
even though you make many prayers,
    I will not listen;
    your hands are full of blood.

1:9: Rom 9:29.

1:4 the Holy One of Israel: Isaiah's signature epithet for the Lord, appearing 25 times in the book (also attributed to Isaiah in 2 Kings 19:22). It encapsulates the revelation given to the prophet that God is holy in the superlative degree (6:3). It also underscores the gaping divide between the Lord, who is infinite in holiness, and his unholy people, who have strayed far from him by their transgressions.

1:5-6 Isaiah puzzles over the foolishness of Israel. Failing to learn from past mistakes, the people continue to revel in sin and provoke the Lord's discipline, despite being ill and badly injured already.

1:7-9 A picture of Jerusalem under siege and surrounded by devastation. The historical situation in view is the Assyrian campaign of Sennacherib against Hezekiah of Judah in 701 B.C. The extant *Annals of Sennacherib* describe how the Assyrian army ravaged the Judean countryside, captured 46 towns and fortifications, deported more than 200,000 exiles, and cooped up Hezekiah within his capital "like a bird in a cage". Amidst the duress of these circumstances, Isaiah counseled Hezekiah to trust in the Lord for deliverance and to make a courageous stand against the boastful invaders; as a result of his trust, Jerusalem was spared by a miracle of God (36:1—37:38; 2 Kings 18:13—19:36).

1:8 the daughter of Zion: Jerusalem, personified as a young woman under the watchful protection of her father (37:22).

1:9 the LORD of hosts: A title for the Lord as the commander of the heavenly armies of angels (Josh 5:14) as well as the military forces of Israel (1 Sam 17:45). **a few survivors:** Elsewhere called "the surviving remnant of the house

of Judah" (37:31). Thanks to an act of divine protection, Jerusalem narrowly escaped Assyrian conquest. Had the Lord not shown this mercy, Jerusalem would have suffered the fate of **Sodom** and **Gomorrah**, two cities annihilated by the fiery judgments of God (Gen 19:1–23). • Paul cites this verse in Rom 9:29 to show that God always preserves a remnant of Israel with whom he fulfills his promises, even in times of national catastrophe. Here the remnant is a small segment of the Southern Kingdom of Judah in Jerusalem (1:1).

1:10-17 The prophet denounces ritual presumption, the mistaken belief that correct cultic observance substitutes for a lack of moral obedience (1 Sam 15:22; Ps 40:6-8; Mic 6:6-8). Liturgy and life form a unity in biblical teaching, so that the service of God is inseparable from service to neighbor (Amos 5:21-24). Isaiah's polemic is not against the rites of Mosaic worship themselves, which had been divinely instituted at Sinai, but against the hypocrisy of Israel's leaders, who make a show of religious piety while ignoring the needs of the poor and powerless (1:17).

1:10 Sodom: A subversive description of sinful Jerusalem (3:9; Jer 23:14; Rev 11:8). It calls to mind the moral depravity of the ancient city whose sins were "very grave" (Gen 18:20).

1:12 appear before me: I.e., attend festal worship at the sanctuary in Jerusalem. This was required for Israelite men three times a year (Ex 23:17; Deut 16:16).

1:15 spread forth your hands: A traditional posture for prayer (1 Kings 8:22; Ezra 9:5; Ps 63:4). **I will not listen:** That iniquity can render prayer ineffective; see Ps 66:18 and 1 Pet 3:7. **full of blood:** I.e., guilty of oppression (1:17) and murder (1:21).

¹⁶Wash yourselves; make yourselves clean;
  remove the evil of your doings
    from before my eyes;
  cease to do evil,
¹⁷ learn to do good;
  seek justice,
    correct oppression;
  defend the fatherless,
    plead for the widow.

¹⁸"Come now, let us reason together,
    says the LORD:
  though your sins are like scarlet,
    they shall be as white as snow;
  though they are red like crimson,
    they shall become like wool.
¹⁹If you are willing and obedient,
    you shall eat the good of the land;
²⁰but if you refuse and rebel,
    you shall be devoured by the sword;
  for the mouth of the LORD has spoken."
²¹How the faithful city
    has become a harlot,
    she that was full of justice!
  Righteousness lodged in her,
    but now murderers.
²²Your silver has become dross,
    your wine mixed with water.
²³Your princes are rebels
    and companions of thieves.
  Every one loves a bribe
    and runs after gifts.
  They do not defend the fatherless,
    and the widow's cause does not come to them.

²⁴Therefore the Lord says,
    the LORD of hosts,
    the Mighty One of Israel:
  "Ah, I will vent my wrath on my enemies,
    and avenge myself on my foes.
²⁵I will turn my hand against you
    and will smelt away your dross as with lye
    and remove all your alloy.
²⁶And I will restore your judges as at the first,
    and your counselors as at the beginning.
  Afterward you shall be called the city of
    righteousness,
    the faithful city."

²⁷Zion shall be redeemed by justice,
    and those in her who repent, by righteousness.
²⁸But rebels and sinners shall be destroyed
    together,
  and those who forsake the LORD shall be
    consumed.
²⁹For you shall be ashamed of the oaks
    in which you delighted;
  and you shall blush for the gardens
    which you have chosen.
³⁰For you shall be like an oak
    whose leaf withers,
    and like a garden without water.
³¹And the strong shall become tow,
    and his work a spark,
  and both of them shall burn together,
    with none to quench them.

The Lord's Universal Reign

2 The word which Isai′ah the son of A′moz saw concerning Judah and Jerusalem.

1:16–17 An appeal for national repentance. Israel must depart from the sinful ways of the past (**evil**) and set out on a new path committed to righteous and responsible living (**good**).

1:17 the fatherless ... the widow: Those most vulnerable in the ancient world. Concern for the welfare of widows and orphans is exemplified by the Lord (Ps 68:5) and is laid upon his people as one of the social demands of the covenant (Ex 22:22; Deut 14:29; Ps 82:3; Jas 1:27; CCC 2208).

1:18 let us reason: Or "let us set matters right". **scarlet:** Evokes the image of blood (1:15).

1:19–20 The "two ways" of the covenant are set before Jerusalem, which must choose either obedience leading to blessings or rebellion leading to curses (Deut 30:15–20). Although not apparent in translation, the same Hebrew verb (′akal) appears in both verses, indicating that Israel can choose to "eat" from the land and live (1:19) or else "be devoured" by the sword of judgment and die (1:20).

1:21–31 Isaiah laments the infidelity of Jerusalem (1:21–23), at the same time announcing its future restoration (1:24–31). Because the city refuses to purge itself of iniquity, the Lord will impose purification so that "Zion shall be redeemed by justice" (1:27).

1:21 harlot: Jerusalem, the bride of the Lord by covenant (Jer 2:1), is guilty of spiritual prostitution, i.e., abandoning her Husband for the worship of other gods (Ex 34:14–16). • Harlotry is a common metaphor in prophetic descriptions of sin. The same charge against Jerusalem is made by Jeremiah (Jer 3:1–2) and Ezekiel (Ezek 16:1–34) and likewise informs

the vision of the great harlot city in the Book of Revelation (Rev 17:1–18).

1:25 smelt away your dross: Divine testing and judgment is likened to the refinement of precious metals by fire (Job 23:10; Sir 2:4–5; 1 Pet 1:6–7). The prophet envisions Jerusalem undergoing this process, which will burn away the rebels (1:28) but will redeem those who repent (1:27). **lye:** A cleansing agent (Job 9:30; Jer 2:22).

1:26 restore your judges: A promise to restore the Davidic institutions of justice formerly established for the tribes of Israel (Ps 122:3–5). This is one aspect of the larger, messianic restoration of Davidic kingship that appears in the book (9:6–7; 11:1–16; 55:3–5). The point is not that God wishes to reinstate the charismatic model of leadership seen in the Book of Judges. **the faithful city:** The Greek LXX reads "the faithful mother city".

1:27 Zion shall be redeemed: One of the great themes running through Isaiah and rising to a crescendo in chaps. 40–66.

1:29 oaks ... gardens: Sacred groves that served as shrines in ancient Canaanite religion. The prophets denounced these cultic sites as places of idolatry and sexual impurity (57:5; 65:3; Hos 4:13–14). It was not until the reign of King Hezekiah, late in the career of Isaiah, that a systematic effort was made to destroy the pagan "high places" that dotted the landscape of ancient Israel (2 Kings 18:4).

2:1 The word: A section heading for chaps. 2–4 (or possibly for chaps. 2–12). It resembles the book's title in 1:1.

²It shall come to pass in the latter days
    that the mountain of the house of the Lᴏʀᴅ
shall be established as the highest of the
    mountains,
    and shall be raised above the hills;
and all the nations shall flow to it,
³   and many peoples shall come, and say:
"Come, let us go up to the mountain of the Lᴏʀᴅ,
    to the house of the God of Jacob;
that he may teach us his ways
    and that we may walk in his paths."
For out of Zion shall go forth the law,
    and the word of the Lᴏʀᴅ from Jerusalem.
⁴He shall judge between the nations,
    and shall decide for many peoples;

and they shall beat their swords into plowshares,
    and their spears into pruning hooks;
nation shall not lift up sword against nation,
    neither shall they learn war any more.*

⁵O house of Jacob,
    come, let us walk
    in the light of the Lᴏʀᴅ.

⁶For you have rejected your people,
    the house of Jacob,
because they are full of diviners[a] from the
    east
    and of soothsayers like the Philis'tines,
    and they strike hands with foreigners.

2:2–4: Mic 4:1–3.

2:2–4 A vision of Jerusalem's future glory. Its focal point is the Temple Mount (= Mount Moriah, 2 Chron 3:1), which will tower above all other heights and become a magnet drawing the world back to God. This will coincide with an era of peace, when disputes are resolved by the Lord, making war a thing of the past. The same vision appears in Mic 4:1–3 among the sayings of the prophet Micah, a contemporary of Isaiah. In the biblical world, mountains were viewed as places of contact between heaven and earth, the divine and human realms, making them ideal locations for sanctuaries of worship.

2:2 highest: The exaltation of the Temple Mount, which sits lower than its neighboring elevations, Mount Scopus and the Mount of Olives. The language of the prophet is figurative, not a literal prediction of future changes in the landscape around Jerusalem. **all the nations:** Isaiah sees all nations converging as pilgrims on Jerusalem, an expectation further elucidated in later chapters, especially in 60:1–7 and 66:18–20. • The extension of divine blessing to "all the nations" will signal the fulfillment of the Abrahamic covenant (Gen 22:16–18).

2:3 Zion: Another name for the elevated city of Jerusalem, which encompasses the Temple Mount. Originally, however, the word "Zion" had a more restricted meaning, referring to the southeastern ridge of the city where King David built his royal residence (2 Sam 5:6–12) and stationed the Ark of the Covenant (1 Chron 15:1). • According

to the NT, the summit of Zion, crowned with the city of Jerusalem, is a historical sign of a heavenly reality: the celestial Mount Zion, also called the Jerusalem above, where angels and saints worship the Lord without ceasing (Gal 4:26; Heb 12:22–24; Rev 21:2, 10). **the law:** The Hebrew is *torah*, meaning "instruction" as well as "law". • Jesus seems to have this passage in mind when he commissions the apostles to preach the gospel "to all nations, beginning from Jerusalem" (Lk 24:47). • How should one identify the law going forth from Zion, which differs from the law of Sinai, except as the word of the gospel, which goes forth from Zion to all nations? Jerusalem is where our Savior taught and where the law of the New Covenant began and spread out to all people (Eusebius of Caesarea, *Demonstration of the Gospel* 1, 4).

2:4 He shall judge: The Lord will administer divine justice, leading to a time of divine peace. The prophet later specifies that God will accomplish this work through the Davidic Messiah (see 11:1–9). **plowshares ... pruning hooks:** The weapons of the warrior will be refashioned into the tools of the farmer. For the opposite use of this imagery, see Joel 3:10.

2:5 O house of Jacob: An appeal to the twelve tribes of Israel, which descend from the twelve sons of the patriarch Jacob (Gen 49:1–28).

2:6 rejected your people: Israel is handed over to judgment for the sin of trusting in idols and superstitions (2:6, 8) as well as material wealth and military strength (2:7). Though one can speak of times of divine discipline for the nation, Scripture insists that God will never abandon Israel in a definitive way (1 Sam 12:22; Ps 94:14; Rom 11:1–2).

---

[a] Cn: Heb lacks *of diviners*.
* 2:2–4: Note the universalism of this prophecy.

WORD STUDY

The Latter Days (2:2)

'aḥarit hayyamim (Heb.): A phrase that appears 14 times in the Hebrew Bible meaning "the days that come after" or simply "the future". Occasionally, the expression foresees a time of judgment for Israel (Deut 4:30; 31:29) or a time of restoration for Gentile nations following judgment (Jer 48:47; 49:39). In another instance, Jacob peers ahead to the latter days and predicts the fortunes of the twelve tribes descended from him (Gen 49:1). The phrase is thus linked to the eschatological hopes of Israel. The latter days mark a time when the covenant people anticipate the rising of a star as ruler (Num 24:14), the restoration of Israel from exile (Ezek 38:16), the exaltation of Zion and the ingathering of the nations (Is 2:2; Mic 4:1), the reign of a Davidic king (Hos 3:5), and the worldwide expansion of God's kingdom (Dan 2:28). The latter days, then, are not the same as the last days of history, sometimes called the "end times". The expression points instead to a time of fulfillment within the flow of history when God's purposes for Israel and the world are realized more fully than ever before. The latter days of OT prophecy thus correspond to "messianic times"—an era of history having its own stages of fulfillment leading up to the Second Coming.

7Their land is filled with silver and gold,
  and there is no end to their treasures;
their land is filled with horses,
  and there is no end to their chariots.
8Their land is filled with idols;
  they bow down to the work of their hands,
  to what their own fingers have made.
9So man is humbled,
  and men are brought low—
  forgive them not!
10Enter into the rock,
  and hide in the dust
from before the terror of the LORD,
  and from the glory of his majesty.
11The haughty looks of man shall be brought low,
  and the pride of men shall be humbled;
and the LORD alone will be exalted in that day.

12For the LORD of hosts has a day
  against all that is proud and lofty,
  against all that is lifted up and high;[b]
13against all the cedars of Lebanon,
  lofty and lifted up;
  and against all the oaks of Bashan;
14against all the high mountains,
  and against all the lofty hills;
15against every high tower,
  and against every fortified wall;
16against all the ships of Tar'shish,
  and against all the beautiful craft.
17And the haughtiness of man shall be humbled,
  and the pride of men shall be brought low;
and the LORD alone will be exalted in that
  day.
18And the idols shall utterly pass away.
19And men shall enter the caves of the rocks
  and the holes of the ground,

from before the terror of the LORD,
  and from the glory of his majesty,
  when he rises to terrify the earth.

20In that day men will cast forth
  their idols of silver and their idols of gold,
which they made for themselves to worship,
  to the moles and to the bats,
21to enter the caverns of the rocks and the clefts of
  the cliffs,
from before the terror of the LORD,
  and from the glory of his majesty,
  when he rises to terrify the earth.
22Turn away from man
  in whose nostrils is breath,
  for of what account is he?

The Lord's Judgment

3 For behold, the Lord, the LORD of hosts,
  is taking away from Jerusalem and from
    Judah
stay and staff,
  the whole stay of bread,
  and the whole stay of water;
2the mighty man and the soldier,
  the judge and the prophet,
  the diviner and the elder,
3the captain of fifty
  and the man of rank,
the counselor and the skilful magician
  and the expert in charms.
4And I will make boys their princes,
  and infants shall rule over them.
5And the people will oppress one another,
  every man his fellow
  and every man his neighbor;
the youth will be insolent to the elder,
  and the base fellow to the honorable.

2:8 the work of their hands: A standard critique of idols, highlighting how these "gods" are nothing more than products of human ingenuity and craftsmanship (40:18–20; Deut 4:28; Ps 115:4; 135:15; Jer 10:1–10).
2:10 Enter ... hide: I.e., seek shelter from the coming storm of divine wrath (cf. Rev 6:12–17).
2:11 the pride of men: Placing trust in things other than God is one of the besetting sins of Isaiah's generation. Humiliation by judgment is thus a means of regaining perspective on the Lord's preeminence over all aspects of life.
2:12 the LORD ... has a day: The "day of the Lord" is announced by the prophets as a day of terrifying judgment, when God manifests his power and justice over the nations and their evildoing (13:6–9; Joel 1:15; Zeph 1:14 18). Sometimes it is a day of reckoning for Gentile peoples (Ezek 30:1–5; Jer 50:25–27; Obad 15 16); other times it is a day when God settles accounts with sinful Israel (Ex 32:34; Amos 5:18–20). Theologically, every "day of the Lord" throughout history offers a glimpse of the final and universal Day of Judgment to

come at the end of history (Mt 25:31–46; Rev 20:11–15). See essay: *The Day of the Lord* at Joel 1:15.
2:13 cedars of Lebanon: Renowned in the biblical world for being rigid, straight, and tall. **oaks of Bashan:** Woodlands east of the Sea of Galilee.
2:16 ships of Tarshish: Merchant vessels built for long-distance travel and trade.
2:22 breath: The "breath of life" infused into man at creation (Gen 2:7). Isaiah invokes this tradition as a reminder that human life is fragile (Ps 146:4) and that human destiny rests in the hands of God (Job 34:14–15; Ps 104:29).
3:1—4:6 Isaiah warns that God will judge the Southern Kingdom of Judah and Jerusalem, its capital. He will exercise impartial justice by punishing the wicked (3:1–4:1) and protecting the righteous (4:2–6).
3:1 stay and staff: Means "support" and "supply". All that sinful Jerusalem relies on in the way of natural and human resources will be swept away in the coming distress (food and water, military personnel, public officials, occult advisors). It was the deportation policy of the Assyrians and Babylonians to take captives from the skilled, educated, and ruling classes, leaving behind a remnant of peasantry.
3:5 oppress one another: The disappearance of civil authorities leads to lawlessness.

[b] Cn Compare Gk: Heb *low.*

⁶When a man takes hold of his brother
    in the house of his father, saying:
  "You have a mantle;
    you shall be our leader,
  and this heap of ruins
    shall be under your rule";
⁷in that day he will speak out, saying:
  "I will not be a healer;
    in my house there is neither bread nor
      mantle;
  you shall not make me
    leader of the people."
⁸For Jerusalem has stumbled,
    and Judah has fallen;
  because their speech and their deeds are against
      the LORD,
    defying his glorious presence.

⁹Their partiality witnesses against them;
    they proclaim their sin like Sodom,
    they do not hide it.
  Woe to them!
    For they have brought evil upon themselves.
¹⁰Tell the righteous that it shall be well with
    them,
    for they shall eat the fruit of their deeds.
¹¹Woe to the wicked! It shall be ill with him,
    for what his hands have done shall be done to
      him.
¹²My people—children are their oppressors,
    and women rule over them.
  O my people, your leaders mislead you,
    and confuse the course of your paths.

¹³The LORD has taken his place to contend,
    he stands to judge his people.ᵈ
¹⁴The LORD enters into judgment
    with the elders and princes of his people:

"It is you who have devoured the vineyard,
    the spoil of the poor is in your houses.
¹⁵What do you mean by crushing my people,
    by grinding the face of the poor?" says the
      Lord GOD of hosts.

¹⁶The LORD said:
Because the daughters of Zion are haughty
    and walk with outstretched necks,
    glancing wantonly with their eyes,
  mincing along as they go,
    tinkling with their feet;
¹⁷the Lord will strike with a scab
    the heads of the daughters of Zion,
    and the LORD will lay bare their secret parts.

18 In that day the Lord will take away the finery of the anklets, the headbands, and the crescents; ¹⁹the pendants, the bracelets, and the scarfs; ²⁰the headdresses, the armlets, the sashes, the perfume boxes, and the amulets; ²¹the signet rings and nose rings; ²²the festal robes, the mantles, the cloaks, and the handbags; ²³the garments of gauze, the linen garments, the turbans, and the veils.
²⁴Instead of perfume there will be rottenness;
    and instead of a belt, a rope;
  and instead of well-set hair, baldness;
    and instead of a rich robe, a putting on of
      sackcloth;
  instead of beauty, shame.ᵉ
²⁵Your men shall fall by the sword
    and your mighty men in battle.
²⁶And her gates shall lament and mourn;
    ravaged, she shall sit upon the ground.
4 And seven women shall take hold of one man in that day, saying, "We will eat our own bread and wear our own clothes, only let us be called by your name; take away our reproach."

3:6 heap of ruins: Jerusalem in the aftermath of divine judgment (1 Kings 9:8).

3:7 in that day: The "day of the Lord". See note on 2:12. **I will not be a healer:** Equivalent to saying "I am not the solution to this crisis." **neither bread nor mantle:** Circumstances in which no one is available to serve as a leader.

3:8 his glorious presence: The sins of Judah are especially grave since the Lord dwells in the Jerusalem sanctuary (1 Kings 8:11).

3:9 partiality: Favoritism and discrimination in the courts. **like Sodom:** An indication of how brazen Jerusalem has become in its evildoing (1:10; Rev 11:8).

3:10–11 The Lord treats his people as their actions deserve. Judgment according to works is a doctrine taught throughout the Bible, in the OT (Ps 62:12; Prov 24:12; Sir 16:14) as well as the NT (Mt 16:27; Rom 2:6–10; 2 Cor 5:10; 1 Pet 1:17).

3:10 the righteous: Those in Zion "who repent" (1:27).

3:12 children ... women: Judah's leaders are chided for their weakness of will. Instead of doing what is right, they indulge their childish desires and cater to the whims of the affluent ladies who surround them (3:16–17).

3:13–17 The leading men are guilty of oppression and abuse of power (3:13–15), while the leading women are charged with arrogance and vanity (3:16–17). When God's judgment comes, many men will be slain (3:25) and the city's noblewomen will be reduced to disgraced and desperate widows (4:1).

3:15 grinding ... the poor: Instead of protecting the needy, rulers in Jerusalem plundered them of their minimal resources (3:14; 10:1–3). They had forgotten that the Lord defends the cause of the poor and takes action against those who mistreat them (25:4).

3:18–23 The extravagant wardrobe and jewelry worn by women of high society. Vanities such as these will pass away when the Lord comes in judgment.

3:18 In that day: The "day of the Lord". See note on 2:12.

4:1 in that day: The "day of the Lord." See note on 2:12. **seven women ... one man:** Death and exile will drastically reduce Judah's male population.

ᵈGk Syr: Heb *judge peoples.*
ᵉOne ancient Ms: Heb lacks *shame.*

2 In that day the branch of the Lord shall be beautiful and glorious, and the fruit of the land shall be the pride and glory of the survivors of Israel. ³And he who is left in Zion and remains in Jerusalem will be called holy, every one who has been recorded for life in Jerusalem, ⁴when the Lord shall have washed away the filth of the daughters of Zion and cleansed the bloodstains of Jerusalem from its midst by a spirit of judgment and by a spirit of burning. ⁵Then the Lord will create over the whole site of Mount Zion and over her assemblies a cloud by day, and smoke and the shining of a flaming fire by night; for over all the glory there will be a canopy and a pavilion. ⁶It will be for a shade by day from the heat, and for a refuge and a shelter from the storm and rain.

The Parable of the Vineyard

5 *Let me sing for my beloved
  a love song concerning his vineyard:
My beloved had a vineyard
  on a very fertile hill.

²He dug it and cleared it of stones,
  and planted it with choice vines;
he built a watchtower in the midst of it,
  and hewed out a wine vat in it;
and he looked for it to yield grapes,
  but it yielded wild grapes.

³And now, O inhabitants of Jerusalem
  and men of Judah,
judge, I beg you, between me
  and my vineyard.
⁴What more was there to do for my vineyard,
  that I have not done in it?
When I looked for it to yield grapes,
  why did it yield wild grapes?

⁵And now I will tell you
  what I will do to my vineyard.
I will remove its hedge,
  and it shall be devoured;

4:2: Jer 23:5; 33:15; Zech 3:8; 6:12.   **5:1–7:** Mt 21:33–46; Mk 12:1–12; Lk 20:9–19.

4:2–6 Another vision of glorified Zion, following 1:27 and 2:2 4. Once the city of Jerusalem is purged of its wrongdoing, God will enfold the remnant of his people in glory, protecting them from harm. Memories of Israel's wandering in the wilderness in 4:5 suggest that Zion is the final encampment of the Lord's pilgrim people, the destiny to which he is leading them. See note on 2:3.

4:2 branch of the Lord: A title used by the prophets for the coming Davidic Messiah, who is both a royal and priestly figure (Jer 23:5; 33:15; Zech 3:8; 6:12). Isaiah also describes this anointed descendant of David as a "shoot" or "branch" (11:1). The meaning of the image in this passage is disputed, whether it refers to the Messiah and the abundant blessings he will bring or to the remnant of Israel and the fruit it bears for the Lord. Perhaps both are in view: the Messiah is the one who brings God's purposes into bloom, while the remnant is the beneficiary of messianic fulfillment. **fruit of the land:** Abundant vegetation is a sign that life continues in the aftermath of judgment. It also represents a blessing of the covenant for those who remain faithful to the covenant (Deut 11:13–17; 28:2–4).

4:3 will be called holy: The remnant that escapes the purging judgment of Zion (4:4) will embody the covenant ideal of being the Lord's "holy nation" (Ex 19:6). **recorded for life:** I.e., in the Book of Life, portrayed elsewhere as a registry kept in heaven and inscribed with the names of the righteous elect (Ex 32:32; Ps 69:28; 87:5–6; Lk 10:20; Phil 4:3).

4:4 daughters of Zion: The women condemned in 3:16–17. **bloodstains:** The Hebrew *damim* means "bleeding", which refers to murder (1:21; 5:7) or possibly to the vanities of the sinful women, which are implicitly compared to the ritual uncleanness of menstruation (cf. 64:6; Lev 15:19–31). **by a spirit of burning:** For purification and refinement by fire, see Num 31:21–23 and Zech 13:8 9. • The remnant of Jerusalem will be saved by the Baptism of the Savior, in which sins will be forgiven and sinners will be cleansed by his blood. The Lord will cleanse the filth of the daughters of Jerusalem by a spirit of judgment and the blood of Jerusalem by a spirit of burning. John the Baptist spoke about these in the Gospel, saying: "I baptize you with water, but the one coming after me will

baptize you with the Holy Spirit and with fire" (St. Jerome, *Commentary on Isaiah* 2, 4).

4:5 cloud by day . . . fire by night: As during the Exodus, when God guided and protected the Israelites with a pillar of cloud and fire during their journey through the wilderness (Ex 13:21–22; Neh 9:12). **the glory:** The visible manifestation of God's presence among his people, often appearing as a thick cloud, sometimes dark and sometimes luminous (Ex 40:34–35; 1 Kings 8:10–11). In rabbinic theology, the glorious cloud of divine Presence is called the "Shekinah". **canopy:** Formed by the Lord's glory settling on Mount Zion, just as it once enveloped Mount Sinai (Ex 19:16–18) and descended upon the wilderness Tabernacle (Num 9:15–23). It gave shelter to the pilgrims of Israel when they escaped Egypt (Ps 105:39). The Hebrew term for canopy, *huppah*, refers to a bridal pavilion or bedchamber in which newlyweds consummate their marriage (see Ps 19:5; Joel 2:16).

5:1–7 The Song of the Vineyard, a juridical parable that indicts Israel for resisting the Lord's will. Similar to Nathan's parable in 2 Sam 12:1–7, Isaiah's song elicits an incriminating judgment on Judah and Jerusalem (5:3). The sad story of unreciprocated love announces that the Lord (**my beloved**) has just cause to abandon his people (**my vineyard**) to judgment for yielding a bitter harvest (**wild grapes**). The parable stresses that God went to great lengths to bring a profitable yield from his people, yet his attentions were spurned or ignored. Some scholars suggest that Isaiah's parable inspired the botanical imagery in the Song of Solomon. For the grapevine as a representation of Israel, see Ps 80:8–16; Jer 2:21; Hos 10:1. • Jesus draws from Isaiah's Song of the Vineyard when he utters the parable of the Wicked Tenants against the obstinate leaders of Israel in his own day (Mt 21:33–46; Mk 12:1–12).

5:1 on a very fertile hill: The Hebrew is literally "on a horn, a son of oil". It refers either to the land of Canaan or more specifically to the city of Jerusalem (Ex 15:17).

5:2 watchtower: Sometimes identified as the Temple in Jewish tradition (e.g., *1 Enoch* 89, 73; *Targum on Isaiah* 5, 2). **wine vat:** A stone-cut trough used to collect juice from pressed grapes. **grapes:** God looked for "justice" and "righteousness" (5:7), but all he found were the **wild grapes** of "bloodshed" and the "cry" of the oppressed (5:7). Wild grapes are sour and ill-suited for winemaking.

5:5 hedge . . . wall: Natural barriers and fences were placed around vineyards to keep out animals and thieves.

---

*5:1–7: This moving allegory may be compared with similar passages in the New Testament, e.g., Mt 21:33–41; Jn 15:1–2.

I will break down its wall,
and it shall be trampled down.
⁶I will make it a waste;
it shall not be pruned or hoed,
and briers and thorns shall grow up;
I will also command the clouds
that they rain no rain upon it.

⁷For the vineyard of the Lord of hosts
is the house of Israel,
and the men of Judah
are his pleasant planting;
and he looked for justice,
but behold, bloodshed;
for righteousness,
but behold, a cry!

⁸Woe to those who join house to house,
who add field to field,
until there is no more room,
and you are made to dwell alone
in the midst of the land.
⁹The Lord of hosts has sworn in my hearing:
"Surely many houses shall be desolate,
large and beautiful houses, without inhabitant.
¹⁰For ten acres of vineyard shall yield but one
bath,
and a homer of seed shall yield but an ephah."

¹¹Woe to those who rise early in the morning,
that they may run after strong drink,
who linger late into the evening
till wine inflames them!
¹²They have lyre and harp,
timbrel and flute and wine at their feasts;
but they do not regard the deeds of the Lord,
or see the work of his hands.

¹³Therefore my people go into exile for want of
knowledge;
their honored men are dying of hunger,
and their multitude is parched with thirst.
¹⁴Therefore Sheol has enlarged its appetite
and opened its mouth beyond measure,
and the nobility of Jerusalem *ᶠ* and her multitude
go down,
her throng and he who exults in her.
¹⁵Man is bowed down, and men are brought low,
and the eyes of the haughty are humbled.
¹⁶But the Lord of hosts is exalted in justice,
and the Holy God shows himself holy in
righteousness.
¹⁷Then shall the lambs graze as in their pasture,
fatlings and kids *ᵍ* shall feed among the ruins.

¹⁸Woe to those who draw iniquity with cords of
falsehood,
who draw sin as with cart ropes,
¹⁹who say: "Let him make haste,
let him speed his work
that we may see it;
let the purpose of the Holy One of Israel draw
near,
and let it come, that we may know it!"
²⁰Woe to those who call evil good and good evil,
who put darkness for light
and light for darkness,
who put bitter for sweet
and sweet for bitter!
²¹Woe to those who are wise in their own eyes,
and shrewd in their own sight!
²²Woe to those who are heroes at drinking wine,
and valiant men in mixing strong drink,
²³who acquit the guilty for a bribe,
and deprive the innocent of his right!

Here they represent the Lord's blessings of protection. Once removed, Israel will be left vulnerable to enemy hordes, such as the Assyrians.

5:6 briers and thorns: Signs of abandonment (7:23) as well as burnable fuel (9:18; 10:17; 27:4). **no rain upon it:** One of the curses of the covenant (Deut 28:23–24).

5:7 Israel . . . Judah: Both the Northern and Southern Kingdom stand under God's judgment.

5:8–24 Isaiah decries the evil flourishing in his time. Prefacing his words with six "woes" (5:8, 11, 18, 20, 21, 22), he denounces unrestrained greed (5:8), overindulgence in alcohol (5:11, 22), moral confusion (5:20), intellectual conceit (5:21), and rank injustice in the courts (5:23). The painful consequences wrought by these sins are spelled out in 5:9 and in the three passages that begin with "Therefore" (5:13, 14, 24).

5:8 Woe: A cry of lamentation. See word study: *Woe* at 28:1. **house to house . . . field to field:** A hoarding of property, probably by unjust means.

5:10 bath: A liquid measure roughly equal to six gallons. **homer:** A dry measure roughly equal to six bushels. **ephah:** One-tenth of a homer.

5:11 strong drink: Beer or ale rather than distilled liquor.

5:13 go into exile: God's initial judgments on Israel took the form of Assyrian deportations from Galilee (2 Kings 15:29) and the Transjordan (1 Chron 5:26). **want of knowledge:** Not complete ignorance of the law but a foolish disregard for its precepts (Hos 4:1–2).

5:14 Sheol: Hebrew name for the netherworld or realm of the dead. It is here imagined as a ravenous creature devouring its victims. See word study: *Sheol* at Num 16:30.

5:17 among the ruins: A picture of once-thriving Judah left desolate (cf. 17:1; Jer 2:15).

5:19 Let him make haste: The words of irreverent scoffers who challenge God to speed up his plans, perhaps even daring him to bring swift judgment.

5:20 evil good and good evil: The moral disorientation that follows habitual immersion in sin. The more a society descends into godlessness, the more its ability to distinguish right from wrong is diminished. Over time, wanton iniquity causes the mind to become "darkened" to the truth of God's moral order (Rom 1:21; Eph 4:18).

5:21 wise in their own eyes: A form of pride that Scripture warns is foolishness (Prov 3:7; 26:5; Rom 11:25).

ᶠ Heb *her nobility.*
ᵍ Cn Compare Gk: Heb *aliens.*

²⁴Therefore, as the tongue of fire devours the
     stubble,
  and as dry grass sinks down in the flame,
so their root will be as rottenness,
  and their blossom go up like dust;
for they have rejected the law of the Lord of
     hosts,
  and have despised the word of the Holy One of
     Israel.
²⁵Therefore the anger of the Lord was kindled
     against his people,
  and he stretched out his hand against them
     and struck them,
  and the mountains quaked;
and their corpses were as refuse
  in the midst of the streets.
For all this his anger is not turned away
  and his hand is stretched out still.

²⁶He will raise a signal for a nation afar off,
  and whistle for it from the ends of the earth;
and behold, swiftly, speedily it comes!
²⁷None is weary, none stumbles,
  none slumbers or sleeps,
not a waistcloth is loose,
  not a sandal-thong broken;

²⁸their arrows are sharp,
  all their bows bent,
their horses' hoofs seem like flint,
  and their wheels like the whirlwind.
²⁹Their roaring is like a lion,
  like young lions they roar;
they growl and seize their prey,
  they carry it off, and none can rescue.
³⁰They will growl over it on that day,
  like the roaring of the sea.
And if one look to the land,
  behold, darkness and distress;
and the light is darkened by its clouds.

A Vision of the Lord in the Temple

6 *In the year that King Uzzi′ah died I saw the
Lord sitting upon a throne, high and lifted up;
and his train filled the temple. ²Above him stood the
seraphim; each had six wings: with two he covered
his face, and with two he covered his feet, and with
two he flew. ³And one called to another and said:
  "Holy, holy, holy is the Lord of hosts;
  the whole earth is full of his glory."
⁴And the foundations of the thresholds shook at
the voice of him who called, and the house was filled
with smoke. ⁵And I said: "Woe is me! For I am lost;
for I am a man of unclean lips, and I dwell in the

6:3· Rev 4:8.   6:4: Rev 15:8.

5:25 the anger of the Lord: The passage shows strong thematic links with chaps. 9–10, leading some scholars to hypoth-
esize that 6:1–9:6 was inserted as a block into the midst of a
longer, continuous oracle that is now split apart. **his hand is
stretched out still:** A refrain that appears in 9:12, 17, 21; 10:4.
It means that God is not finished unleashing his judgments on
Israel, i.e., he remains ready to strike another blow.

5:26 a nation afar off: The Assyrians, whom God will use
as the "rod" of his anger to chastise wayward Israel (10:5).
The underlying premise is that the Lord can summon even
godless nations to accomplish his purposes (Deut 28:49–51;
Jer 5:15–17).

6:1–13 The call of Isaiah. The account reads like an autobi-
ographical memoir expressed in the first person (= I, me, my).
The occasion is a vision of God, Israel's divine King, enthroned
in heavenly majesty. This is generally viewed as the inaugural
event that launched Isaiah's long career as a prophet.

6:1 the year that King Uzziah died: About 740 B.C. **I saw
the Lord sitting:** A throne vision also granted to the prophets
Micaiah (1 Kings 22:19) and Ezekiel (Ezek 1:4–28). **a throne:**
Represented in the sanctuaries of Israel by the wings of the
cherubim outstretched over the Ark of the Covenant (37:16;
1 Sam 4:4). **high and lifted up:** The language of exaltation,
also used of the Lord in 57:15 and of the Lord's Servant in
52:13. **the temple:** The sanctuary built by King Solomon
in Jerusalem, which is an earthly image of the celestial sanctuary of God in heaven (Ps 11:4; Wis 9:8; Heb 8:2–5; Rev
11:19). See essay: *Theology of the Temple* at 2 Chron 5.

6:2 seraphim: Literally "burning ones". These are angels
surrounding the Lord's throne while shielding themselves
from the overpowering intensity of his glory. They are depicted
symbolically as hybrid creatures that have animal features

(wings) as well as rational intelligence (the ability to worship
and speak). • Catholic tradition identifies the seraphim as the
highest of the nine choirs of angels, those who are first in
rank among created spirits (e.g., St. Thomas Aquinas, *Summa
Theologiae* 1, 108, 6). **he covered ... he flew:** Describes the
posture and movement of each individual seraph.

6:3 Holy, holy, holy: Repeated three times for emphasis
(Jer 22:29; Ezek 21:27). The expression is probably
equivalent to the superlative degree ("holiest of all"). It means
that the Lord is the Perfect One who towers above the created
order, set apart from sin and free from every defect. Isaiah
was deeply impacted by this encounter with divine holiness, as
shown by his repeated references to the Lord as "the Holy One
of Israel" throughout the book (1:4; 5:19, 24; 10:20; 12:6,
etc.). • The "Holy, holy, holy" was sung in Christian liturgies
from ancient times (Rev 4:8) and came to be called the *Sanc-
tus* (Latin for "holy"). The threefold acclamation is traditionally
said to address each of the three Persons of the Trinity. • The
cry "Holy, holy, holy" is both from us and from the seraphim,
for Christ has removed the barrier and made peace between
things in heaven and on earth. Initially the hymn was sung
only in heaven; but when the Lord came to earth, he brought
this music to us. When the great high priest stands at his holy
table, offering spiritual worship and performing the unbloody
sacrifice, he urges all to sing this majestic chant and to lift our
thoughts from earth to heaven (St. John Chrysostom, *Homilies
on Isaiah* 6). **the whole earth:** The world is represented by the
architectural design and furnishings of the Temple. See essay:
Theology of the Temple at 2 Chron 5.

6:4 smoke: A visible manifestation of divine glory (Ex
19:18), reproduced in the Temple as billowing clouds of
incense (Lev 16:13).

6:5 Woe is me!: A cry of fear and dread, reflecting the
belief that seeing God could be fatal for mortals (Ex 33:20;
Judg 13:22). **I am lost:** Or "I am silenced". Isaiah is overwhelmed by an awareness of his sin and confesses himself

---

*6:1–13: This vision stresses the solemnity of the prophet's calling. The
"Holy, holy, holy" is fittingly included in the Mass. The vision also serves
to introduce the Immanuel prophecies.

midst of a people of unclean lips; for my eyes have seen the King, the Lord of hosts!"

6 Then flew one of the seraphim to me, having in his hand a burning coal which he had taken with tongs from the altar. ⁷And he touched my mouth, and said: "Behold, this has touched your lips; your guilt is taken away, and your sin forgiven." ⁸And I heard the voice of the Lord saying, "Whom shall I send, and who will go for us?" Then I said, "Here am I! Send me." ⁹And he said, "Go, and say to this people:

'Hear and hear, but do not understand;
see and see, but do not perceive.'
¹⁰Make the heart of this people fat,
    and their ears heavy,
    and shut their eyes;
lest they see with their eyes,
    and hear with their ears,
and understand with their hearts,
    and turn and be healed."

¹¹Then I said, "How long, O Lord?"
And he said:
"Until cities lie waste
    without inhabitant,
and houses without men,
    and the land is utterly desolate,
¹²and the Lord removes men far away,
    and the forsaken places are many in the midst
    of the land.
¹³And though a tenth remain in it,
    it will be burned again,
like a terebinth or an oak,
    whose stump remains standing
    when it is felled."
The holy seed is its stump.

Isaiah Reassures King Ahaz

7 In the days of A'haz the son of Jo'tham, son of Uzzi'ah, king of Judah, Re'zin the king of Syria and Pe'kah the son of Remali'ah the king of Israel

---

6:9–10: Mt 13:14–15; Mk 4:12; Lk 8:10; Jn 12:39–41; Acts 28:26–27.

---

unfit to stand in the presence of the Holy One (cf. Lk 5:8). **a man of unclean lips:** Recalls how Moses initially objected to his prophetic call, claiming to be "a man of uncircumcised lips" (Ex 6:12). The responses of both reflect a proper attitude of humility when a prophet is given a divine mission.

6:6 a burning coal: Taken from the fires of the altar hearth. • One of the seraphim is sent with a burning coal from the altar. This signifies Christ, who offered himself to the Father as an unblemished spiritual sacrifice and is now received from the altar. He is compared to a coal because Scripture compares the divine nature to fire, as when God appeared to the people of Israel at Mount Sinai (St. Cyril of Alexandria, *Commentary on Isaiah* 6, 6). Let us approach the Eucharist with burning desire and receive the body of the crucified One. Let us receive the burning coal, so that its fire might increase our desire, consume our sins, and enlighten our hearts, and so that by communion with divine fire we might be set aflame and deified (St. John of Damascus, *On the Orthodox Faith* 4, 13).

6:7 touched my mouth: A communication of grace, also noted in Jeremiah's call to prophetic ministry (Jer 1:9). **your guilt is taken away:** Isaiah is purged from sin in preparation for his mission to speak in the name of the Lord. Granting forgiveness through an ember of the altar symbolizes how the ministries of the Temple are God's provision for dealing with Israel's sin.

6:8 who will go for us?: For the divine use of "us" in the OT, see note on Gen 1:26. **Here am I!:** The reply of one who is ready and eager to fulfill the Lord's will (Gen 22:1; Ex 3:4; 1 Sam 3:4).

6:9–13 The commissioning of Isaiah. He is tasked with preparing the covenant people for chastisement (6:11–12) while promising the survival of a remnant (6:13).

6:9–10 Isaiah's preaching will put the Lord's punitive sentence into effect: it will induce a spiritual hardening that leaves many in Israel unresponsive to his call for repentance. It is not that divine hardening causes people to sin in the first place; rather, hardening is the Lord's disciplinary response to those who repeatedly reject his blessings. Isaiah is only an instrument in the divine plan. God is the One who hardens the heart of the disobedient as an act of judgment (29:9–10; 44:18; 63:17). For more on this theme, see notes on 63:17 and Ex 4:21. • The Lord's words to Isaiah are quoted several times in the NT to explain Jewish unbelief in the gospel. It is cited in this connection by Jesus (Mt 13:14–15), by the

evangelist John (Jn 12:40), and by the Apostle Paul (Acts 28:26–27).

6:11–12 An announcement of coming devastation and deportation. Marking the beginning of Isaiah's ministry in 740 B.C., the oracle forecasts the Assyrian conquest of Samaria in 722 B.C., which saw the invasion of Israel and thousands forced into exile, as well as the Assyrian siege of Jerusalem in 701 B.C., when Judah was laid waste and thousands more were taken into exile. See note on 1:7–9.

6:13 a tenth: The Southern Kingdom of Judah, which survived the fall of the Northern Kingdom of Israel (722 B.C.), but not without facing a judgment of its own two decades later (701 B.C.). **stump:** An image of hope in the midst of ruin. Despite drastic reduction, the nation is not fully uprooted. The Lord preserves a stump of survivors so that the covenant people can sprout and flourish once again. See note on 11:1. **holy seed:** The sanctified remnant of Israel that will emerge from the purging fires of judgment (4:3). Isaiah often uses the term "seed" (Heb., *zera*', also translated "offspring" or "descendants") to speak of God's favored ones (41:8; 43:5; 45:25; 65:9; 66:22).

7:1—12:6 Often called the Book of Immanuel, a collection of oracles named after the child in 7:14 and 8:8. The royal son of David who appears in 9:6–7 and 11:1-5 is probably to be identified with this same individual.

7:1–9:7 Isaiah addresses a crisis of faith in the kingdom of Judah. *Historically*, events take place against the background of the Syro-Ephraimite conflict around 735 B.C. (2 Kings 16:1–20; 2 Chron 28:1–27). Rezin, the king of Aram (= Syria), in alliance with Pekah, king of Israel (= Ephraim), marched against Jerusalem with the aim of unseating Ahaz, the Davidic king of Judah, and replacing him with a puppet ruler: "the son of Tabeel" (7:7). It appears that Ahaz refused to join a coalition of regional states in opposing Assyria's expansion westward. Isaiah reassures Ahaz that God will protect the ruling house of David from this plot, but Ahaz falters in faith by calling on Assyria for help instead of trusting the Lord. *Theologically*, the survival of the Davidic monarchy, and thus the continuance of the Davidic covenant, seemed to be in jeopardy before the Syro-Ephraimite threat. Ahaz is urged to believe (7:9) that God will stand by his commitment to establish Davidic kingship for all time (2 Sam 7:12–16; Ps 89:3–4, 28–37; 132:11–12). See essay: *The Davidic Covenant* at 2 Sam 7.

7:1 Ahaz: The eleventh king of Judah (ca. 735 to 715 B.C.). Memory of his reign is marred by crimes of idolatry (2 Kings

came up to Jerusalem to wage war against it, but they could not conquer it. [2]When the house of David was told, "Syria is in league with E'phraim," his heart and the heart of his people shook as the trees of the forest shake before the wind.

3 And the Lord said to Isai'ah, "Go forth to meet A'haz, you and She'arjash'ub[h] your son, at the end of the conduit of the upper pool on the highway to the Fuller's Field, [4]and say to him, 'Take heed, be quiet, do not fear, and do not let your heart be faint because of these two smoldering stumps of firebrands, at the fierce anger of Re'zin and Syria and the son of Remali'ah. [5]Because Syria, with E'phraim and the son of Remali'ah, has devised evil against you, saying, [6]"Let us go up against Judah and terrify it, and let us conquer it for ourselves, and set up the son of Ta'be-el as king in the midst of it," [7]thus says the Lord God:

It shall not stand,
    and it shall not come to pass.
[8]For the head of Syria is Damascus,
    and the head of Damascus is Re'zin.
(Within sixty-five years E'phraim will be broken to pieces so that it will no longer be a people.)
[9]And the head of E'phraim is Samar'ia,
    and the head of Samaria is the son of Remali'ah.
If you will not believe,
    surely you shall not be established.'"

The Sign of Immanuel

10 Again the Lord spoke to A'haz, [11]"Ask a sign of the Lord your God; let it be deep as Sheol or high as heaven." [12]But A'haz said, "I will not ask, and I will not put the Lord to the test." [13]And he said, "Hear then, O house of David! Is it too little for you to weary men, that you weary my God also? [14]Therefore the Lord himself will give you a sign.

7:14: Mt 1:23.

16:2–4) and cultic innovation (2 Kings 16:10–18; 2 Chron 28:22–25). **Rezin:** King of the Aramean state of Syria, north of Israel. **Pekah:** An army officer who seized the throne of Israel (ca. 740 to 732 B.C.).

7:3 Shearjashub: The older of Isaiah's two sons. His name means "a remnant will return" or "a remnant will repent". The younger son is Maher-shalal-hash-baz (8:3). **the conduit of the upper pool:** The king is inspecting Jerusalem's water supply while (or before) the city is under siege (2 Kings 16:5). Three decades later, the Assyrians will demand the surrender of Jerusalem at this very spot (2 Kings 18:17).

7:4 do not fear: A word of encouragement for the king. It assures him that God will thwart the plans of the Syria-Israel coalition to seize control of Jerusalem and dethrone Ahaz. The prophet declares that this scheme "shall not come to pass" (7:7). **two smoldering stumps:** The threats from Syria and Israel will soon be extinguished.

7:5 Ephraim: The Northern Kingdom of Israel, here named after its leading tribe.

7:6 the son of Tabeel: A prince of uncertain nationality. Significantly, this figure is not from the dynastic line of David and is thus ineligible for the throne of Judah.

7:8 Damascus: The capital of the kingdom of Syria, which will fall to the Assyrians in 732 B.C. **sixty-five years:** The Northern Kingdom of Israel (**Ephraim**) will undergo a process of transformation from a sovereign state to a region of mixed ethnicity and culture. Assyrian conquests and deportations will begin around 732 B.C., the fall of Samaria will take place in 722, and a succession of Assyrian kings from Sargon II to Esarhaddon will repopulate central Israel with vanquished peoples from other lands. Following generations of intermarriage, the Ephraimites and other northern Israelites ceased to be recognizable as a **people** distinct from Gentiles (see 2 Kings 17:24–41; Ezra 4:2).

7:9 Samaria: The capital of the kingdom of Israel, nearly 40 miles north of Jerusalem in central Canaan. **If you will not believe:** A test of faith is set before Ahaz—a test he will fail. He is urged to believe in Isaiah's word and to trust in the Lord for protection. But instead he invests his faith in a political solution: Ahaz negotiates to make Judah a vassal state of the Assyrian Empire in exchange for military intervention and protection against Syrian-Israelite aggression (2 Kings 16:7). His actions are a betrayal of the Lord. **you shall not be established:** An allusion to the Lord's oath in 2 Sam

7:16 to "establish" Davidic kingship forever. Included in this royal covenant is a proviso that individual successors of David will be chastened if they forsake their God (2 Sam 7:14; Ps 89:30–33).

7:11 a sign: A tangible indication that the prophet's word is reliable. A sign from the Lord is often an unusual or miraculous event (38:7–8; Ex 4:1–9; Num 17:1–10; Judg 6:36–40). **Sheol:** Hebrew name for the netherworld of the dead (5:14).

7:12 I will not ... test: Ahaz pretends to be concerned about strict observance of the Torah (Deut 6:17). Isaiah sees through the king's false piety and expresses exasperation at his lack of faith (7:13).

7:14–25 Isaiah's first Immanuel prophecy, which promises a **sign** of God's intervention on behalf of the royal house of David. It is difficult to interpret because the mother is left unnamed, and little is revealed about the child beyond the fact that Ahaz's enemies (Syria and Israel) are expected to face judgment before the child reaches maturity (7:16). Different interpretations have been proposed. **(1)** Some read 7:14 as announcing the birth of Hezekiah, the son and successor of Ahaz as king of Judah. If so, the sign is related to the crisis of dynastic succession facing Ahaz, and the child's mother can be identified with one of the royal wives of Ahaz (e.g., Abijah, 2 Chron 29:1). It also suggests the Immanuel child is the royal "child" from David's line described in 9:6–7. The identification of Immanuel with Hezekiah is attested in Jewish tradition (*Exodus Rabbah* 18, 5; cf. St. Justin Martyr, *Dialogue with Trypho* 43, 8). **(2)** Others read 7:14 as announcing the birth of Isaiah's son "Maher-shalal-hash-baz" to his wife "the prophetess" (8:3). This would explain why both 7:16 (Immanuel) and 8:4 (Maher-shalal-hash-baz) stress the child's young age at the time judgment comes to Damascus and Samaria and why the discussion of Immanuel continues in 8:5–8 after the birth of Isaiah's son is related in 8:3. **(3)** Still others view the mother of 7:14 as a prophetic image of Zion, elsewhere portrayed as the mother of the Lord's children (62:1–5; 66:7–8). The judgment of Syria-Israel thus represents God's protection of a faithful remnant from their enemies. • According to Mt 1:23, the prophecy is fulfilled ultimately in the conception and birth of Jesus to the Virgin Mary. This is not to deny a preliminary fulfillment in Isaiah's time, e.g., the birth of King Hezekiah. The births of Immanuel and the Messiah are intrinsically related, since both involve acts of divine intervention that uphold the Lord's covenant of kingship with David in a time of uncertainty. One can thus speak of a fulfillment in stages, so that the word of God is relevant to the time when it was spoken by the prophet, and yet it promises

---

[h] That is *A remnant shall return.*

Behold, a virgin ⁱ* shall conceive and bear ʲ a son, and shall call his name Imman′u-el.ᵏ ¹⁵He shall eat curds and honey when he knows how to refuse the evil and choose the good. ¹⁶For before the child knows how to refuse the evil and choose the good, the land before whose two kings you are in dread will be deserted. ¹⁷The Lᴏʀᴅ will bring upon you and upon your people and upon your father's house such days as have not come since the day that E′phraim departed from Judah—the king of Assyria."

18 In that day the Lᴏʀᴅ will whistle for the fly which is at the sources of the streams of Egypt, and for the bee which is in the land of Assyria. ¹⁹And they will all come and settle in the steep ravines, and in the clefts of the rocks, and on all the thornbushes, and on all the pastures.

20 In that day the Lord will shave with a razor which is hired beyond the River—with the king of Assyria—the head and the hair of the feet, and it will sweep away the beard also.

21 In that day a man will keep alive a young cow and two sheep; ²²and because of the abundance of milk which they give, he will eat curds; for every one that is left in the land will eat curds and honey.

---

something more that awaits a future fulfillment. Moreover, the name Immanuel (meaning "God is with us"), while bearing a message of hope to the house of David in the eighth century B.C., is most fully realized in the Son of God, who took flesh as David's royal heir in the first century A.D. The messianic interpretation of Isaiah's prophecy has long been featured in the Church's theological and liturgical traditions (e.g., Vatican II, *Lumen Gentium* 55; CCC 497). • The prophet Isaiah said he would be born of a virgin. God foretold that things beyond human ability would take place, so that when they occurred, people would believe because it was promised. The words "Behold, the virgin will conceive" indicate that the virgin would conceive without having sexual relations. The power of God came upon the Virgin, overshadowed her, and enabled her to conceive as a virgin (St. Justin Martyr, *First Apology* 33).

✠ **7:14 Immanuel:** Hebrew for "God is with us". • The name of the Savior, whom the prophet calls "God with us", signifies both of his natures in one person. He who was begotten of the Father before time became Immanuel in his mother's womb, having taken on the weakness of our nature.

In marvelous fashion, he began to be what we are without ceasing to be what he had been (St. Bede, *Homilies on the Gospels* 1, 5).

7:15 curds and honey: The child will grow up in the time following judgment, as suggested by 7:20–22. **knows ... evil ... good:** Often taken to mean early childhood before the age of reason, but the Hebrew idiom "knowing good and evil" probably refers to a more advanced age of maturity. In Deut 1:39, the phrase describes persons up to the age of 20 who were not counted in the first census (Num 1:3) and thus eligible for entrance into Canaan (Num 14:29). Immanuel will come of age by the time he has learned to live responsibly as a young adult. The idiom may also imply that Immanuel will possess the wisdom to judge his people as a king (as in 2 Sam 14:17 and 1 Kings 3:9).

7:17 the day that Ephraim departed: Refers to the division of Solomon's kingdom in 930 B.C., when the northern tribes of Israel (= Ephraim) broke away from the southern tribes of Judah and established a rival monarchy (1 Kings 12:1–20). **king of Assyria:** Ahaz's decision to rely on Assyria will backfire several years later. The Lord's "sign" heralds short-term relief (deliverance from Syria and Israel, 7:15) as well as long-term regret (devastation by the Assyrians, 7:18–25).

7:18 In that day: A day of distress and judgment (7:20, 21, 23). See note on 2:12.

7:20 shave: Signifies the humiliation that will come with divine judgment (cf. 2 Sam 10:4–5). **the River:** The Euphrates. **hair of the feet:** Probably a euphemism for pubic hair.

7:22 every one that is left: The fortunate few who survive the Assyrian invasion and escape deportation from the land.

ⁱ Or *young woman*.

ʲ Or *is with child and shall bear*.

ᵏ That is *God is with us*.

*7:14, *virgin* or *young woman*: The Hebrew word *'almah* is not explicit. The Greek translates this as *parthenos*, "virgin," and may be regarded as a witness to later Jewish tradition as to the meaning of the prophecy. The virginal conception is, of course, unequivocally stated in the Gospel where this prophecy is quoted (Mt 1:23; cf. also Lk 1:35).

WORD STUDY

Virgin (7:14)

'almah (Heb.): A noun used nine times in the OT for a "young woman" or "maiden" who has reached the age for marriage and motherhood. Girls at this stage of life experienced their first awakening of romantic attraction (Prov 30:19; Song 1:3). Strictly speaking, *'almah* is not the technical term in Hebrew for a virgin (*betulah*) who has never had sexual relations with a man. However, "virgin" is defensible as an interpretive translation, since virginity was always expected of unmarried girls in Israel. Given that cultural assumptions often attach to words, the Hebrew nouns "young woman" (*'almah*) and "virgin" (*betulah*) may be said to overlap in meaning. The Book of Genesis can thus describe Isaac's prospective bride, Rebekah, as a "virgin" (Gen 24:16) and as a "young woman" (24:43) without any apparent distinction. Virginity is explicit in the first term but still implicit in the second. The RSV2CE, in rendering the word "virgin" in Is 7:14, stands in a long tradition of translations stretching back to St. Jerome's Vulgate (Lat., *virgo*) and even farther to the pre-Christian Septuagint (Gk., *parthenos*). It is significant that Matthew cites the LXX version of this verse in Mt 1:23, which speaks of "the virgin", because it shows that the virginity of Immanuel's mother was already part of the ancient Jewish understanding of the prophecy and was not a Christian innovation. In the end, while it may be true that Isaiah's contemporaries understood the girl of Is 7:14 to be a virgin only before she conceived a child in the normal way, the NT points to something miraculous in Jesus, who was conceived and born of a Virgin Mother apart from any involvement of a human father (Lk 1:26–35).

23 In that day every place where there used to be a thousand vines, worth a thousand shekels of silver, will become briers and thorns. ²⁴With bow and arrows men will come there, for all the land will be briers and thorns; ²⁵and as for all the hills which used to be hoed with a hoe, you will not come there for fear of briers and thorns; but they will become a place where cattle are let loose and where sheep tread.

Isaiah's Son a Sign of Assyrian Invasion

8 Then the Lord said to me, "Take a large tablet and write upon it in common characters, 'Belonging to Ma′her-shal′al-hash″-baz.'"[1] ²And I got reliable witnesses, Uri′ah the priest and Zechari′ah the son of Jeberechi′ah, to attest for me. ³And I went to the prophetess, and she conceived and bore a son. Then the Lord said to me, "Call his name Ma′her-shal′al-hash″-baz; ⁴for before the child knows how to cry 'My father' or 'My mother,' the wealth of Damascus and the spoil of Samar′ia will be carried away before the king of Assyria."

5 The Lord spoke to me again: ⁶"Because this people have refused the waters of Shilo′ah that flow gently, and melt in fear before^m Re′zin and the son of Remali′ah; ⁷therefore, behold, the Lord is bringing up against them the waters of the River, mighty and many, the king of Assyria and all his glory; and it will rise over all its channels and go over all its banks; ⁸and it will sweep on into Judah, it will overflow and pass on, reaching even to the neck; and its outspread wings will fill the breadth of your land, O Imman′u-el."

⁹Be broken, you peoples, and be dismayed;
    give ear, all you far countries;
gird yourselves and be dismayed;
    gird yourselves and be dismayed.
¹⁰Take counsel together, but it will come to nought;
    speak a word, but it will not stand,
    for God is with us.^x

11 For the Lord spoke thus to me with his strong hand upon me, and warned me not to walk in the way of this people, saying: ¹²"Do not call conspiracy all that this people call conspiracy, and do not fear what they fear, nor be in dread. ¹³But the Lord of hosts, him you shall regard as holy; let him be your fear, and let him be your dread. ¹⁴And he will become a sanctuary, and a stone of offense, and a rock of stumbling to both houses of Israel, a trap and a snare to the inhabitants of Jerusalem. ¹⁵And many shall stumble thereon; they shall fall and be broken; they shall be snared and taken."

8:12–13: 1 Pet 3:14–15. **8:14:** Rom 9:32–33; 1 Pet 2:8.

7:23 briers and thorns: Once cultivated lands will be deserted and overgrown. This will mark the fulfillment of another judgment oracle, the Song of the Vineyard (5:6).

8:1–22 Chapter 8 reiterates the promises and warnings of chapter 7. Again, the downfall of the Syria-Israel coalition is assured, and again Judah is challenged to put faith in God rather than in a political alignment with Assyria. The two chapters differ in literary point of view, e.g., in the use of third-person ("the Lord said to Isaiah", 7:3) and first-person narration ("the Lord said to me", 8:1).

8:1 large tablet: A placard for the public display of Isaiah's message. **Maher-shalal-hash-baz:** The younger of Isaiah's two sons (8:3). His name means "the spoil speeds, the plunder hastes" and signals the coming conquest of Damascus and Samaria, the capitals of Syria and northern Israel (8:4). These events, in turn, warn of a similar fate for the Southern Kingdom of Judah. See note on 10:6.

8:2 witnesses: Individuals who could verify that Isaiah received a prophetic message from the Lord in advance of its historical fulfillment. **Uriah the priest:** Served during the reign of Ahaz (2 Kings 16:10). **Zechariah:** Possibly Ahaz's father-in-law (2 Kings 18:2).

8:3 the prophetess: Isaiah's wife, otherwise unnamed.

8:4 Damascus: The capital of Syria (7:8). **Samaria:** The capital of the Northern Kingdom of Israel (7:9). **the king of Assyria:** Tiglath-Pileser III, who launched military campaigns against Syria and northern Israel between 734 and 732 B.C., thus confirming the prophecy of judgment in 7:16.

8:6 this people: The faithless people of Judah, who walk in step with King Ahaz, trusting in political solutions instead of the Lord. **the waters of Shiloah:** A water conduit serving ancient Jerusalem. Isaiah views it as a symbol of the Lord's steady provisions for his people. Hezekiah will later upgrade the city's water supply system with a pool (2 Kings 20:20) fed by the Gihon spring through an underground tunnel (2 Chron 32:30). See note on 2 Kings 20:20. **Rezin:** King of the Aramean state of Syria, north of Israel.

8:7 the River: The Euphrates, which causes mass destruction when it floods. Isaiah sees it as a symbol of the Lord's overwhelming judgment on Judah, which will take the form of an Assyrian military assault coming from Mesopotamia.

8:8 your land: Foresees Sennacherib's invasion of Judah in 701 B.C. Since capital cities are represented as "heads" of countries in 7:8–9, the halting of the waters at the **neck** indicates that Jerusalem, the head of the land of Judah, will be surrounded but not submerged (i.e., besieged but not destroyed). See note on 1:7–9. **Immanuel:** The child promised in 7:14, his name meaning "God is with us". See note on 7:14–25.

8:9–10 A poetic exposition of the expression **God is with us**. It means that nations plot the ruin of the covenant people in vain, for the Lord's sovereign designs cannot be thwarted, especially regarding the Davidic king he established on Zion (see Ps 2:1–6).

8:11 with his strong hand: I.e., with the power of his grace. See word study: *Hand* at Neh 2:8. **the way of this people:** The way of faithless disregard for God and his word.

8:12 what they fear: Earthly kingdoms and armies (see 7:1–2).

8:13 the Lord of hosts: See note on 1:9. **holy:** See note on 1:4. **your fear:** Fear of the Lord, expressed as a holy reverence for God and a commitment to turn away from sin, is the first step toward wisdom (Job 28:28; Ps 111:10; Prov 1:7; Sir 1:27).

8:14–15 Contrasting images of God in relation to Israel. To the faithful, the Lord is a **sanctuary** of divine protection (Ezek 11:16); but to the faithless, he is a **rock of stumbling** that brings tragedies of conquest and exile (Jer 6:21). Isaiah, speaking about 735 B.C., applies this to **both houses of Israel**, anticipating how the Northern and Southern Kingdoms will draw the judgment of God upon themselves within his

---

[1] That is *The spoil speeds, the prey hastes.*
^mCn: Heb *rejoices in.*
^xHeb *immanu el.*

Disciples of Isaiah

16 Bind up the testimony, seal the teaching among my disciples. ¹⁷I will wait for the Lᴏʀᴅ, who is hiding his face from the house of Jacob, and I will hope in him. ¹⁸Behold, I and the children whom the Lᴏʀᴅ has given me are signs and portents in Israel from the Lᴏʀᴅ of hosts, who dwells on Mount Zion. ¹⁹And when they say to you, "Consult the mediums and the wizards who chirp and mutter," should not a people consult their God? Should they consult the dead on behalf of the living? ²⁰To the teaching and to the testimony! Surely for this word which they speak there is no dawn. ²¹They will pass through the land,[n] greatly distressed and hungry; and when they are hungry, they will be enraged and will curse[o] their king and their God, and turn their faces upward; ²²and they will look to the earth, but behold, distress and darkness, the gloom of anguish; and they will be thrust into thick darkness.

The Righteous Reign

9 [p]But there will be no gloom for her that was in anguish. In the former time he brought into contempt the land of Zeb'ulun and the land of Naph'tali, but in the latter time he will make glorious the way of the sea, the land beyond the Jordan, Galilee of the nations.

²[q]The people who walked in darkness
   have seen a great light;
 those who dwelt in a land of deep darkness,
   on them has light shined.
³You have multiplied the nation,
   you have increased its joy;
 they rejoice before you
   as with joy at the harvest,
   as men rejoice when they divide the spoil.
⁴For the yoke of his burden,
   and the staff for his shoulder,
   the rod of his oppressor,
   you have broken as on the day of Mid'ian.
⁵For every boot of the tramping warrior in battle tumult
   and every garment rolled in blood
   will be burned as fuel for the fire.
⁶For to us a child is born,
   to us a son is given;

8:17–18: Heb 2:13. **9:1–2:** Mt 4:15–16; Lk 1:79.

---

lifetime. Historically, this will come about with Assyria's conquest of northern Israel in 722 ʙ.ᴄ. and Assyria's invasion of Judah in 701 ʙ.ᴄ. • The depiction of the Lord as a stumbling stone is applied to Jesus in the NT. Peter and Paul both invoke Is 8:14 to caution readers that Christ is the divine, messianic stone who occasions the downfall of those who refuse faith in him (Rom 9:33; 1 Pet 2:8).

8:16–22 Isaiah calls for the preservation of his oracles (8:16), declares his patient trust in the Lord (8:17), and counsels his disciples to avoid occult practitioners who claim to know the future (8:19). The prophet and his followers are among the remnant in Israel that clings to the word of God.

8:16 Bind … seal: Refers to wrapping or tying up a scroll and stamping it with a wax seal. The message is sealed so that Isaiah's predictions can be consulted and verified when they come to pass in the future.

8:18 signs: Embodiments of a divine message. Isaiah's prophetic actions fall into this category (20:1–6), as do his two sons and their names (7:3; 8:1).

8:19 chirp and mutter: Isaiah pokes fun at spiritists who claim to communicate with the dead. The Law condemns necromancy, fortune-telling, and other superstitious practices of this kind (Lev 19:31; Deut 18:9–14).

9:1 former time: Isaiah projects himself forward in time and writes of coming judgments as if they have already happened. This is one way the prophets expressed certainty about events that God had decreed for the future. **Zebulun … Naphtali:** Tribal lands west and northwest of the Sea of Galilee (Josh 19:10–16, 32–39). These and adjacent territories were conquered by King Tiglath-Pileser III during the Assyrian campaigns waged against northern Israel between 734 and 732 ʙ.ᴄ. The conquered regions became three Assyrian provinces: Duru, the coastal strip south of Mount Carmel (**the way of the sea**); Galada, the highlands of Gilead, east of the Jordan River (**the**

land beyond the Jordan); and Magidu, the north-central territory of Israel (**Galilee**). According to Assyrian records, nearly 15,000 Israelites were taken into exile at this time. **Galilee of the nations:** Galilee was an ethnically diverse region in the eighth century ʙ.ᴄ. Reasons for this include the failure of Zebulun, Naphtali, and Asher to drive the Canaanites out of their tribal territories (Judg 1:30–33) as well as Solomon's act of giving 20 cities in Galilee to the king of Tyre (1 Kings 9:11).

9:2 a great light: A sign of coming salvation, the dawning of a new day that heals Israel of the painful judgments of its past. • Matthew sees this prophecy fulfilled in the Galilean ministry of Jesus. He is the "great light" that restores northern Israel by preaching the gospel and healing the sick. Matthew may have viewed the "great light" of Is 9 as a personal Messiah by correlating the image with later passages in Isaiah, where the Lord's messianic servant is described as a "light to the nations" (42:6) whose mission is both to restore Israel and to bring salvation to the Gentiles (49:6). • The lands of Zebulun and Naphtali in Galilee were the first to hear the Lord's proclamation, so that where Israel suffered its first captivity by the Assyrians, there the Redeemer should begin preaching (St. Jerome, *Commentary on Matthew* 1, 4, 15).

9:4 the day of Midian: The day that Gideon and his men routed the Midianite oppressors of Israel with the help of God (Judg 7:1–8:28).

9:6–7 Isaiah's second Immanuel prophecy, further identifying the "son" promised in 7:14. The **child** is here revealed as a royal descendant of **David** who will take his **throne** and rule over his **kingdom** forever. According to some scholars, these verses come from a coronation hymn that was sung each time a new Davidic heir became the king of Judah. The four titles given to the child in 9:6 would thus function as "throne names" conferred on the new ruler, a practice attested in other Near Eastern kingdoms (e.g., in Egypt). Theologically, the prophecy reaffirms the covenant of kingship that God made with David in 2 Sam 7:12–16. • The angel Gabriel alludes to this passage when he informs Mary that her son will be given "the throne of his father David" and will rule over a "kingdom" that has "no end" (Lk 1:32–33). One can probably speak of a partial fulfillment of the oracle in

---

[n] Heb *it.*
[o] Or *curse by.*
[p] Ch 8:23 in Heb.
[q] Ch 9:1 in Heb.

and the government will be upon his shoulder,
  and his name will be called
"Wonderful Counselor, Mighty God,
  Everlasting Father, Prince of Peace."*
[7]Of the increase of his government and of peace
  there will be no end,
upon the throne of David, and over his kingdom,
  to establish it, and to uphold it
with justice and with righteousness
  from this time forth and for evermore.
The zeal of the Lord of hosts will do this.

[8]The Lord has sent a word against Jacob,
  and it will light upon Israel;
[9]and all the people will know,
  E'phraim and the inhabitants of Samar'ia,
  who say in pride and in arrogance of heart:
[10]"The bricks have fallen,
  but we will build with dressed stones;
the sycamores have been cut down,
  but we will put cedars in their place."
[11]So the Lord raises adversaries[r] against them,
  and stirs up their enemies.
[12]The Syrians on the east and the Philis'tines on
  the west
  devour Israel with open mouth.
For all this his anger is not turned away
  and his hand is stretched out still.

[13]The people did not turn to him who struck
  them,
  nor seek the Lord of hosts.
[14]So the Lord cut off from Israel head and tail,
  palm branch and reed in one day—
[15]the elder and honored man is the head,
  and the prophet who teaches lies is the tail;
[16]for those who lead this people lead them
  astray,
  and those who are led by them are swallowed
  up.
[17]Therefore the Lord does not rejoice over their
  young men,
and has no compassion on their fatherless and
  widows;
for every one is godless and an evildoer,
  and every mouth speaks folly.
For all this his anger is not turned away
  and his hand is stretched out still.

[18]For wickedness burns like a fire,
  it consumes briers and thorns;
it kindles the thickets of the forest,
  and they roll upward in a column of smoke.
[19]Through the wrath of the Lord of hosts
  the land is burned,
and the people are like fuel for the fire;
  no man spares his brother.

Hezekiah, even if its ultimate fulfillment is messianic. Only in the birth and heavenly enthronement of Jesus is the exalted language of the prophecy fully met (Acts 2:29–36). So too, only with the Incarnation of the divine Son do the "throne names" of 9:6 take on their full significance as divine titles. • Scripture would not have said these things about Christ if he were no more than a man. But they testify to him in a twofold way: unlike anyone else, he was begotten of the Most High Father, and he was also born of the Virgin. He was a man of unsightly appearance, liable to suffering, despised among the people, humbling himself to the point of death, and yet he is the holy Lord, the "Wonderful Counselor" and "Mighty God" (St. Irenaeus, *Against Heresies* 3, 19, 2).

9:6 upon his shoulder: Alludes to a ceremonial act of placing a symbol of authority on the shoulder of one assuming a public office (22:22). Christian tradition relates this passage to Jesus shouldering the burden of the Cross (St. Justin Martyr, *First Apology* 35; St Ambrose, *On the Patriarchs* 6, 31). **Wonderful Counselor:** The king will be a wise teacher and guide for his people, representing the Lord, who is "wonderful in counsel" (28:29). **Mighty God:** Or "Divine Warrior". The king will be a valiant protector of his people, representing the Lord, who is "the mighty God" (10:21). Kings in the ancient Near East were often considered divine or semi-divine, but not in Israel. Yet here a king from David's line is given a divine appellation. Christian tradition understands this royal name as a witness to the divinity of Jesus. See note on 9:6–7. **Everlasting Father:** The king will be a faithful provider and protector of his people, representing the Lord, the "Father" of Israel (63:16) who inhabits "eternity" (57:15). **Prince of Peace:** The king will fulfill the mission of the Davidic Messiah to end warfare between peoples (see 11:6–9). He is thus prefigured by King Solomon, a "man of peace" (1 Chron 22:9) who ruled over Israel and neighboring nations in a time of peace (1 Kings 4:24–25).

9:7 the increase of his government: Envisions a future kingdom that is everlasting and ever-expanding (as in Dan 2:35, 44). In the OT period, the Davidic kingdom had fluctuating borders for much of its history until it collapsed entirely in 586 b.c. **The zeal of the Lord:** Means that God is eager to bring his plans to fulfillment. The expression appears again in 37:32.

9:8–10:4 Judgments against the Northern Kingdom of Israel, which serve as warnings for the Southern Kingdom of Judah. Isaiah's words are severe, since divine chastisements on Galilee (2 Kings 15:29) and the Transjordan (1 Chron 5:26) have induced, not repentance, but further rebellion (9:13). Israel thus remained under God's wrath, as shown by the refrain: "For all this his anger is not turned away" (9:12, 17, 21; 10:4).

9:9 Ephraim: The Northern Kingdom of Israel, here named after its leading tribe. **Samaria:** The capital city of the Northern Kingdom, located in central Canaan.

9:10 we will build ... we will put: As if the Lord's discipline, experienced in the devastation of war, was simply an opportunity to rebuild with finer materials.

9:12 Syrians: Controlled the territory north and northeast of Israel. **Philistines:** Controlled the coastal plain southwest of Israel. **his hand is stretched out still:** The Lord remains ready to strike another punishing blow.

9:13 did not turn: I.e., refused to repent.

9:17 every one is godless: Sin prevails among leaders and commoners alike (9:15–16).

9:18–20 The declining years of the Northern Kingdom of Israel were marked by intrigue and internal strife at the highest levels of government (2 Kings 15:10, 14–16, 25).

---

[r] Cn: Heb *the adversaries of Rezin.*
*9:6: Passage selected for the Introit of the Mass of Christmas Day, showing that the Church regards these words as being fulfilled in Jesus Christ.

²⁰They snatch on the right, but are still hungry,
  and they devour on the left, but are not
    satisfied;
  each devours his neighbor's ˢ flesh,
²¹Manas'seh E'phraim, and Ephraim Manasseh,
  and together they are against Judah.
For all this his anger is not turned away
  and his hand is stretched out still.

Judgment on the Oppressors

10 Woe to those who decree iniquitous decrees,
  and the writers who keep writing oppression,
²to turn aside the needy from justice
  and to rob the poor of my people of their right,
that widows may be their spoil,
  and that they may make the fatherless their
    prey!
³What will you do on the day of punishment,
  in the storm which will come from afar?
To whom will you flee for help,
  and where will you leave your wealth?
⁴Nothing remains but to crouch among the
    prisoners
  or fall among the slain.
For all this his anger is not turned away
  and his hand is stretched out still.

⁵Ah, Assyria, the rod of my anger,
  the staff of my fury!ᵗ
⁶Against a godless nation I send him,
  and against the people of my wrath I command
    him,
to take spoil and seize plunder,
  and to tread them down like the mire of the
    streets.
⁷But he does not so intend,
  and his mind does not so think;
but it is in his mind to destroy,
  and to cut off nations not a few;
⁸for he says:
  "Are not my commanders all kings?
⁹Is not Calno like Car'chemish?
  Is not Ha'math like Arpad?
  Is not Samar'ia like Damascus?
¹⁰As my hand has reached to the kingdoms of the
    idols
  whose graven images were greater than those
    of Jerusalem and Samar'ia,
¹¹shall I not do to Jerusalem and her idols
  as I have done to Samar'ia and her images?"

12 When the Lord has finished all his work on Mount Zion and on Jerusalem heᵘ will punish the arrogant boasting of the king of Assyria and his haughty pride. ¹³For he says:
  "By the strength of my hand I have done it,
    and by my wisdom, for I have understanding;
  I have removed the boundaries of peoples,
    and have plundered their treasures;
  like a bull I have brought down those who sat
    on thrones.
¹⁴My hand has found like a nest
  the wealth of the peoples;

10:5–34: Nahum; Zeph 2:13–15.

9:20 each devours ... flesh: An image of society destroying itself.

9:21 Manasseh ... Ephraim: The two largest tribes of the Northern Kingdom of Israel. Both are overrun by the Assyrians in 722 B.C. **against Judah:** Longstanding animosity between the Northern and Southern Kingdoms lives on, the latest instance being the Syro-Ephraimite assault on Jerusalem in 735 B.C. (7:1).

10:1 Woe: A cry of distress that signals approaching doom. Isaiah pronounces it in view of the crimes of Judah's leaders against the poor and powerless. The Southern Kingdom is repeating the mistakes that brought judgment on the Northern Kingdom.

10:5–34 The role of Assyria in the purposes of God is explained. On the one hand, the Lord will use this mighty people as an instrument of judgment to punish Judah for its defections from the covenant (10:5–6). On the other, Assyria is itself an evil nation, and so once it has served its purpose of administering the Lord's wrath, it too will face divine judgment (10:12–19, 25–34). Isaiah insists upon this second point, lest people draw the mistaken conclusion that the God of Israel is not powerful enough to protect his people from Assyrian conquest. Note that allusions are made in this chapter to the names of Isaiah's two sons, Maher-shalal-hash-baz (8:3) and Shearjashub (7:3), which convey the prophet's twofold message of (1) judgment on Israel (10:6) and (2) the salvation of a remnant (10:20–21).

10:5 Ah: Or "Woe" as in 10:1 (also 5:8, 11, 18, 20). See note on 10:1.

10:6 godless nation: Judah. **spoil ... plunder:** *Shalal* and *baz* in Hebrew, two nouns that are featured in the name of Isaiah's younger son, Maher-shalal-hash-baz (8:3). The disobedient people will be despoiled by Assyrian invaders in 701 B.C.

10:7 he does not so intend: Blinded by pride, Assyria is unaware that its victories in battle serve the designs of God's Providence.

10:9 Calno ... Damascus: Six cities, all north of Judah (mainly in Syria), that fell one by one to Assyrian invaders in the eighth century B.C.

10:11 as I have done to Samaria: Samaria was overrun in 722 B.C., leaving Jerusalem as the next major target. **her idols:** The speaker is an Assyrian who insinuates that the Lord is no different from a pagan image—a miscalculation amounting to blasphemy.

10:12 king of Assyria: Sennacherib, who threatened to conquer Jerusalem in 701 B.C. but was turned away by a miracle of God (36:1–37:38). The event shows that God exercises sovereign control over entire nations in the fulfillment of his plan.

10:13 I ... I ... I .... I: Underscores the arrogant egotism of several Assyrian monarchs in the late eighth century B.C.

10:14 like a nest: The ease with which Assyria expanded its empire is compared to stealing eggs from an unprotected bird nest.

ˢ Tg Compare Gk: Heb *the flesh of his arm.*
ᵗ Heb *a staff it is in their hand my fury.*
ᵘ Heb *I.*

and as men gather eggs that have been forsaken
    so I have gathered all the earth;
and there was none that moved a wing,
    or opened the mouth, or chirped."
¹⁵Shall the axe vaunt itself over him who hews
    with it,
    or the saw magnify itself against him who
      wields it?
As if a rod should wield him who lifts it,
    or as if a staff should lift him who is not wood!
¹⁶Therefore the Lord, the LORD of hosts,
    will send wasting sickness among his stout
      warriors,
and under his glory a burning will be kindled,
    like the burning of fire.
¹⁷The light of Israel will become a fire,
    and his Holy One a flame;
and it will burn and devour
    his thorns and briers in one day.
¹⁸The glory of his forest and of his fruitful land
    the LORD will destroy, both soul and body,
and it will be as when a sick man wastes away.
¹⁹The remnant of the trees of his forest will be so
    few
    that a child can write them down.

The Repentant Remnant of Israel

20 In that day the remnant of Israel and the survivors of the house of Jacob will no more lean upon him that struck them, but will lean upon the LORD, the Holy One of Israel, in truth. ²¹A remnant will return, the remnant of Jacob, to the mighty God. ²²For though your people Israel be as the sand of the sea, only a remnant of them will return. Destruction is decreed, overflowing with righteousness. ²³For the Lord, the LORD of hosts, will make a full end, as decreed, in the midst of all the earth.

24 Therefore thus says the Lord, the LORD of hosts: "O my people, who dwell in Zion, be not afraid of the Assyrians when they strike with the rod and lift up their staff against you as the Egyptians did. ²⁵For in a very little while my indignation will come to an end, and my anger will be directed to their destruction. ²⁶And the LORD of hosts will wield against them a scourge, as when he struck Mid'ian at the rock of Or'eb; and his rod will be over the sea, and he will lift it as he did in Egypt. ²⁷And in that day his burden will depart from your shoulder, and his yoke will be destroyed from your neck."

He has gone up from Rimmon,^v
²⁸   he has come to Ai'ath;
    he has passed through Migron,
      at Mich'mash he stores his baggage;
²⁹they have crossed over the pass,
    at Ge'ba they lodge for the night;
Ra'mah trembles,
    Gib'eah of Saul has fled.
³⁰Cry aloud, O daughter of Gallim!
    Listen, O La'ishah!
    Answer her, O An'athoth!

10:22–23: Rom 9:27–28.

10:15 axe ... saw ... rod: Reinforces the point that Assyria is merely a tool in the hand of God, not the invincible master of its fate.

10:16 wasting sickness: Perhaps the angelic scourge that decimated Sennacherib's army and forced his withdrawal from Jerusalem in 701 B.C. (37:36–37; 2 Kings 19:35–36).

10:17 light of Israel: The Lord, who is "a devouring fire" (Deut 4:24; 9:3).

10:20 the remnant of Israel: The small number of Israelites, mainly resident in Jerusalem, who escape death and deportation in connection with the Assyrian campaign against Judah in 701 B.C. Following the demise of the Northern Kingdom in 722 B.C., Jerusalem was flooded with refugees from the northern tribes, making it a city of survivors from the whole family of **Jacob**. These are the "holy seed" envisioned in 6:13. See note on 1:7–9. **no more lean upon:** When judgment finally comes, the remnant will cease relying on Assyria and turn once more to trust in the Lord. This will mark a reversal of the course followed by King Ahaz, who declined faith in God (7:9–13) and sought protection from Assyria (2 Kings 16:5–9).

10:21 A remnant will return: The expression in Hebrew is *shear yashub*, which is the name of Isaiah's older son (7:3). **the mighty God:** Or "the Divine Warrior", to whom the penitent of Israel will return in their hearts. This is also one of the throne names borne by the Davidic king promised in 9:6.

10:22–23 Sennacherib's invasion of Judah in 701 B.C. will reduce Israel to a fraction of its former size, yet the survival of a **remnant** will be a sign of God's mercy and faithfulness to his covenant. In effect, a limit is set to the scope of judgment, lest Israel perish entirely and the Lord's **righteousness** toward his people prove to be false. • Paul cites these verses in Rom 9:27–28 to show that a pattern of judgment and salvation recurs throughout Israel's history stretching into the messianic age. In times of calamity and national apostasy, the Lord always saves a remnant in his mercy.

10:23 full end: The disaster of 701 B.C. will complete the series of judgments administered by God through the hand of Assyria. **all the earth:** Or, better, "all the land", referring to the whole territory of Israel, north and south.

10:24 be not afraid: An invitation to trust in the Lord for deliverance, as in 7:4–9. **as the Egyptians:** Refers to Israel's former enslavement in Egypt prior to the Exodus (Ex 1:8–14).

10:26 Midian ... Oreb: Refers to Gideon's success in routing the Midianites and slaying their princes in the Book of Judges (Judg 7:1–25).

10:27–32 Envisions enemy forces approaching Jerusalem from the north, passing through Benjaminite territory, and reaching Mount Scopus (the location of **Nob**, 10:32) within sight of the city. The historical circumstances behind this invasion route are debated by scholars. Some think the prophet describes the movement of the Syro-Ephraimite coalition against Jerusalem in 735 B.C. Others relate it to an Assyrian show of force against Jerusalem before putting down a revolt in Gaza in 720 B.C. Still others, in view of the preceding context, think it is a poetical rather than a literal depiction of Sennacherib's march against Jerusalem in 701 B.C., since other texts indicate that Assyria advanced from Lachish, southwest of Jerusalem (36:2; 2 Kings 18:17).

---

^vCn: Heb *and his yoke from your neck, and a yoke will be destroyed because of fatness.*

³¹Madme′nah is in flight,
the inhabitants of Gebim flee for safety.
³²This very day he will halt at Nob,
he will shake his fist
at the mount of the daughter of Zion,
the hill of Jerusalem.

³³Behold, the Lord, the Lᴏʀᴅ of hosts
will lop the boughs with terrifying power;
the great in height will be hewn down,
and the lofty will be brought low.
³⁴He will cut down the thickets of the forest with
an axe,
and Lebanon with its majestic trees^w will fall.

The Shoot from the Stump of Jesse and the Peaceful Kingdom

11 *There shall come forth a shoot from the
stump of Jesse,
and a branch shall grow out of his roots.
²And the Spirit of the Lᴏʀᴅ shall rest upon him,
the spirit of wisdom and understanding,
the spirit of counsel and might,
the spirit of knowledge and the fear of the Lᴏʀᴅ.†
³And his delight shall be in the fear of the Lᴏʀᴅ.

He shall not judge by what his eyes see,
or decide by what his ears hear;
⁴but with righteousness he shall judge the
poor,
and decide with equity for the meek of the
earth;
and he shall strike the earth with the rod of his
mouth,
and with the breath of his lips he shall slay the
wicked.
⁵Righteousness shall be the belt of his waist,
and faithfulness the belt of his loins.

⁶The wolf shall dwell with the lamb,
and the leopard shall lie down with the kid,
and the calf and the lion and the fatling together,
and a little child shall lead them.
⁷The cow and the bear shall feed;
their young shall lie down together;
and the lion shall eat straw like the ox.
⁸The sucking child shall play over the hole of the
asp,
and the weaned child shall put his hand on the
adder's den.

11:1: Is 11:10; Rom 15:12.   **11:2:** 1 Pet 4:14.   **11:5:** Eph 6:14.   **11:6–9:** Is 65:25; Hab 2:14.

10:33–34 Resumes the imagery of 10:18–19, where Assyria is a mighty forest that is axed down and destroyed by the Lord. Historically, this comes about when the Assyrian army is decimated before the walls of Jerusalem (37:36) and Sennacherib flees to Nineveh, only to be assassinated (37:37–38).

10:34 Lebanon: Famous in biblical times for its massive cedar trees.

11:1–16 One of the clearest messianic visions in Isaiah. The prophet describes the coming of an ideal Davidic king (11:1), who is endowed with the Spirit (11:2), who brings justice and peace to the world (11:3–9), who draws the nations to himself (11:10), and who restores the scattered exiles of Israel (11:11–16). The vision resembles the Immanuel oracles in 7:14–17 and 9:6–7, which foresee the birth of an ideal king, but this one looks ahead to the blessings of his reign.

11:1 stump: Recalls the image in 6:13, where the remnant of Israel that survives the Assyrian assault of 701 B.C. appears as a charred tree stump, although one that is still able to sprout again. This oracle speaks of the Davidic dynasty, which remained intact despite the calamities that overwhelmed most of Israel. The preservation of David's royal lineage was an act of God, in honor of his pledge to grant the house of David everlasting kingship (2 Sam 7:12–16). **Jesse:** The father of King David (1 Sam 16:10–13). **a branch:** A shoot rising from the stump is a sign of life (Job 14:7–9). The image implies that **(1)** the tree of the Davidic monarchy will be felled for a time but that **(2)** it will not be dead but will grow again. The prophets describe the royal Messiah from David's line as a branch, i.e., as a sign that Davidic kingship will revive after its disappearance in 586 B.C. (4:2; Jer 23:5; 33:15; Zech 3:8; 6:12). • Matthew alludes to this passage when he notes that the prophets expect the Messiah to be a "Nazarene" (Mt 2:23). The interpretation involves a word play on *nēṣer*, the Hebrew term for "branch" that appears in this verse (see St. Jerome, *Commentary on Matthew* 1, 2, 23).

11:2–3a The full measure of the Spirit will rest on the Davidic Messiah, equipping him for the tasks of sacred kingship, among other things (61:1–3; CCC 436). This recalls how the Spirit came mightily upon David at the time of his anointing as king (1 Sam 16:10–13). • On the basis of this verse, Catholic tradition speaks of seven gifts of the Holy Spirit, which inspire baptized believers to follow God's will in thought and action. Only six are mentioned in the Hebrew text translated by the RSV2CE, but the Greek LXX adds "piety" (Gk., *eusebeia*) in place of "fear of the Lᴏʀᴅ" at the end of 11:2, bringing the total number of gifts to seven. The Latin Vulgate follows the LXX (CCC 1287, 1831). • The way to heaven is opened by the sevenfold grace of the Spirit. Isaiah speaks from the viewpoint of heaven, numbering the steps in descending order: wisdom and understanding, counsel and might, knowledge and piety, and fear of the Lord. Since it is written "the fear of the Lord is the beginning of wisdom", it is clear that the way ascends from fear to wisdom instead of going down from wisdom to fear. The prophet thus reasons from heavenly things to humbler things (St. Gregory the Great, *Homilies on Ezekiel* 2, 7, 7).

11:2 might: The Latin Vulgate takes this to mean "fortitude", i.e., the strength to overcome fear in order to do what is right.

11:3b–4 The Messiah will excel all others in accurate discernment and concern for the poor and helpless. He is prefigured by King Solomon, who administered justice with a more-than-human wisdom bestowed from above (1 Kings 3:16–28).

11:4 breath of his lips: By his mighty word, the Messiah will bring judgment on God's enemies. • Paul alludes to this verse when he describes Jesus defeating the Antichrist at his Second Coming. On this future day, he will slay the "lawless one" with "the breath of his mouth" (2 Thess 2:8).

11:5 Righteousness: The chief attribute of the Davidic "branch" also in Jer 23:5–6; 33:15–16. **belt:** Strapped around the midsection to secure loose clothing in preparation for action, such as charging into battle (cf. 5:27). See note on Eph 6:10–17.

11:6–9 A poetic description of messianic times. Natural enemies becoming friends in the animal world symbolizes tranquil relations among people and nations who prey upon one another

---

^wCn Compare Gk Vg: Heb *with a majestic one.*
*11:1–3: cf. 61:1–2 and Lk 4:18–19.
†11:2: The enumeration of the "gifts of the Holy Spirit" is taken from this passage.

⁹They shall not hurt or destroy
　　in all my holy mountain;
　for the earth shall be full of the knowledge of the
　　　Lord
　　as the waters cover the sea.

10　In that day the root of Jesse shall stand as an ensign to the peoples; him shall the nations seek, and his dwellings shall be glorious.

11　In that day the Lord will extend his hand yet a second time to recover the remnant which is left of his people, from Assyria, from Egypt, from Path'ros, from Ethiopia, from E'lam, from Shi'nar, from Ha'math, and from the islands of the sea.
¹²He will raise an ensign for the nations,
　　and will assemble the outcasts of Israel,
　and gather the dispersed of Judah
　　from the four corners of the earth.
¹³The jealousy of E'phraim shall depart,
　　and those who harass Judah shall be cut
　　　off;
　Ephraim shall not be jealous of Judah,
　　and Judah shall not harass Ephraim.
¹⁴But they shall swoop down upon the shoulder of
　　the Philis'tines in the west,
　and together they shall plunder the people of
　　the east.

They shall put forth their hand against E'dom
　　and Moab,
　and the Am'monites shall obey them.
¹⁵And the Lord will utterly destroy
　　the tongue of the sea of Egypt;
　and will wave his hand over the River
　　with his scorching wind,
　and strike it into seven channels
　　that men may cross dryshod.
¹⁶And there will be a highway from Assyria
　　for the remnant which is left of his people,
　as there was for Israel
　　when they came up from the land of Egypt.

Thanksgiving and Praise

12 You will say in that day:
　"I will give thanks to you, O Lord,
　　for though you were angry with me,
　your anger turned away,
　　and you did comfort me.

²"Behold, God is my salvation;
　　I will trust, and will not be afraid;
　for the Lord God is my strength and my song,
　　and he has become my salvation."

3　With joy you will draw water from the wells of salvation. ⁴And you will say in that day:

11:10: Is 11:1; Rom 15:12.

---

like beasts (5:29; 9:12). At the same time, scenes of peaceful coexistence among the earth's creatures signal a return to the conditions of Eden and thus indicate a reversal of sin's disruptive effects on the natural order (Rom 8:18–25; Rev 21:1–4).

　11:9 my holy mountain: The glorified Mount Zion (4:2–6; 65:25). See note on 2:3. **full of the knowledge:** The result of God's word radiating out from Zion to instruct the nations in his ways, as prophesied in 2:3.

　11:10 root of Jesse: Paul cites the Greek LXX version of this passage in Rom 15:12. It is one of several OT verses the apostle links together that envision Gentiles coming under the rule of the Messiah and worshiping alongside Israel as God's people. **an ensign:** A signal or banner raised on a hilltop (13:2). It could publicize a proclamation (Jer 50:2), mobilize troops for battle (Jer 4:21), or summon a gathering of people (49:22). Isaiah envisions distant **nations** coming in search of Israel's Messiah. • Jesus relates the ensign to his Cross when he prophesies: "I, when I am lifted up from the earth, will draw all men to myself" (Jn 12:32).

　11:11–16 Messianic salvation includes a **remnant** of Israel and Judah being restored from exile and reunited in peace. The Lord's mercy will reach them in such places as Mesopotamia (**Assyria, Shinar** = Babylonia), Africa (**Egypt, Pathros, Ethiopia**), Media (**Elam**), Syria (**Hamath**), and around the Mediterranean Sea (**islands**). Evidence is lacking to indicate that Israel's diaspora was this extensive in Isaiah's day. Thus, a future situation is envisioned, one that looks beyond even the Babylonian dispersions of the sixth century B.C.

　11:13 Ephraim … Judah: The leading tribes of the Northern and Southern Kingdoms of Israel respectively. The tension between them goes back to the revolt that tore Solomon's kingdom into two rival states (1 Kings 12:1–20). The Messiah will unify Israel and Judah under his rule much as David had done (2 Sam 5:4–5).

　11:15–16 Israel's future salvation, described as a new exodus. Just as the Lord divided the **sea** with a mighty **wind**, enabling his people to cross **dryshod** and escape the

bondage of **Egypt** (Ex 14:16, 21–29), so he will again deliver a **remnant** of Israel from exile in **Assyria**, bringing his people across **the River** Euphrates (cf. 27:12–13). The Exodus event is likewise invoked in later chapters to announce Israel's return from exile in Babylon (43:16–21; 50:2–3). See essay: *The New Exodus in Isaiah* at Is 43.

　11:15 the tongue: Possibly the Gulf of Suez, an inlet of the Red Sea reaching up between Egypt and the Sinai Peninsula. **wave his hand:** Perhaps an allusion to Moses stretching out his hand over the sea in Ex 14:21.

　11:16 a highway: Not a beaten path but a newly prepared road, as in 40:3–4 and 62:10.

　12:1–6 The climax of the Book of Immanuel (chaps. 7–12). It features two psalms of thanksgiving (12:1–2 and 12:4–6) sung by the "remnant" of Israel (11:16) in gratitude for the gift of "salvation" (12:2–3). God's people will sing these psalms once the Lord has fulfilled his promises. • Isaiah 12 relates to Isaiah 11 much as Exodus 15 (the Song of the Sea) relates to Exodus 14 (Israel's crossing of the sea). The promise of a new exodus in 11:10–16 calls for a new song that praises God for this new act of deliverance. References to the Lord as "my strength … my song … my salvation" in 12:2 are taken from Ex 15:2, just as the invitation to "Sing … to the Lord" for acting "gloriously" in 12:5 recalls Ex 15:21. These praises are revisited in Ps 118:14, 105:1, and 148:13.

　12:1 in that day: The day of salvation envisioned in 4:2; 10:20; 11:10. **comfort:** Anticipates the announcements in 40:1–2 and 66:13.

　12:2 trust … not be afraid: The very thing that King Ahaz and Judah refused to do in 7:1–9, suggesting the remnant of 11:16 has undergone a conversion of heart (CCC 227). **the Lord … salvation:** Possibly an allusion to Isaiah's name, which means "the Lord saves".

　12:3 the wells of salvation: The endless supply of God's grace and mercy that satisfies the spiritual thirst of his people and gives them life (55:1; Jn 4:10–14; CCC 2560–61).

"Give thanks to the LORD,
 call upon his name;
make known his deeds among the nations,
 proclaim that his name is exalted.

5"Sing praises to the LORD, for he has done
  gloriously;
 let this be known* in all the earth.
6Shout, and sing for joy, O inhabitant of Zion,
 for great in your midst is the Holy One of
  Israel."

An Oracle concerning Babylon

13 The oracle concerning Babylon which Isai′ah
the son of A′moz saw.
2On a bare hill raise a signal,
 cry aloud to them;
wave the hand for them to enter
the gates of the nobles.
3I myself have commanded my consecrated ones,
 have summoned my mighty men to execute
  my anger,
 my proudly exulting ones.

4Listen, a tumult on the mountains
 as of a great multitude!
Listen, an uproar of kingdoms,
 of nations gathering together!

The LORD of hosts is mustering
 a host for battle.
5They come from a distant land,
 from the end of the heavens,
the LORD and the weapons of his indignation,
 to destroy the whole earth.

6Wail, for the day of the LORD is near;
 as destruction from the Almighty it will
  come!
7Therefore all hands will be feeble,
 and every man's heart will melt,
8 and they will be dismayed.
Pangs and agony will seize them;
 they will be in anguish like a woman with
  labor pains.
They will look aghast at one another;
 their faces will be aflame.

9Behold, the day of the LORD comes,
 cruel, with wrath and fierce anger,
to make the earth a desolation
 and to destroy its sinners from it.
10For the stars of the heavens and their constellations
 will not give their light;
the sun will be dark at its rising
 and the moon will not shed its light.

13:1—14:23: Is 47; Jer 50–51; Hab 1—2. **13:10:** Mt 24:29; Mk 13:24; Rev 6:12; 8:12.

12:6 in your midst: An assurance that God dwells on Zion (8:18; Zeph 3:14-15), just as he dwelt among his people in the Tabernacle (Ex 25:8) and will live forever with the saints in glory (Rev 21:3). **Holy One of Israel:** See note on 1:4.

13:1—23:18 Oracles concerning the nations (Jer 46-51; Ezek 25-32; Amos 1:1-2:3). Some announce judgment on Gentile kingdoms for their pompous abuse of power; others reveal that Gentile nations are integral to the purposes of God in history, with some turning from idols to worship the Lord (19:19-25). Isaiah's point is that Israel's God is the sovereign Lord of all nations, the one to whom all peoples stand accountable. Consequently, God's people need not fear these nations, nor should they seek political alliances with them, as though their national welfare depended on it. The nations of the world rise and fall only insofar as God's plan decrees it. The prophet addresses several nations of his day: Babylon (13:1—14:23; 21:1-10), Assyria (14:24-27), Philistia (14:28-32), Moab (15:1—16:14), Syria (17:1-14), Ethiopia (18:1-7), Egypt (19:1—20:6), Edom (21:11-12), Arabia (21:13-17), and Tyre (23:1-8).

13:1—14:23 An oracle of judgment against Babylon (13:1-22), followed by a victory taunt against Babylon (14:3-23), with a promise of Israel's restoration in between (14:1-2). The Babylonians, like the Assyrians before them, will serve as an *instrument* of God's wrath against Israel (39:6-7), only to become an *object* of God's wrath in turn (13:19). Just as the mighty forest of Assyria will be felled by the Lord (10:33-34), so Babylon will lie "fallen" as well (21:9). Isaiah singles out pride as the main reason for Babylon's humiliation (13:11; 14:13-15). Also, he shows that the succession of powers in the ancient Near East—from the Assyrian Empire to the Babylonian Empire to the Medo-Persian Empire—is determined by the sovereign designs of the Lord, whose plan embraces Israel and the world. For a similar prophetic perspective, see essay: *The Four Kingdoms in Daniel* at Dan 2.

13:1 oracle: A message given to a prophet, in this case to Isaiah (15:1; 17:1; 19:1; 21:1, 11, 13; 22:1). **Babylon:** The capital of the Babylonian Empire, straddling the Euphrates River in lower Mesopotamia. In Isaiah's day, Babylonia had not yet emerged as the leading imperial power in the Near East, since it was still under Assyrian domination. Its rise to prominence would come in the late seventh century B.C. Isaiah, who prophesied in the eighth century B.C., speaks with inspired foresight of the Babylonian conquest of Judah in 586 B.C. (39:6-7) as well as the fall of Babylon in 539 B.C. (13:17-22; 21:9).

13:2 the gates of the nobles: The lavishly decorated entryways into the city of Babylon.

13:3 my consecrated ones: The armies of the Medes (and Persians), who are set apart for the task of executing God's plan to overthrow Babylon (13:17). Some think the Babylonians are meant, in which case Isaiah is looking at how God used the Babylonians to bring judgment on others, just as he had done with the Assyrians (10:5).

13:4 The LORD of hosts: The divine Commander-in-chief. See note on 1:9.

13:6 the day of the LORD: The day of coming judgment for Babylon, which foreshadows on a local scale God's future judgment of the whole world. See note on 2:12. **Almighty:** Perhaps means "the God of the mountain". See note on Job 5:17.

13:10 stars ... sun ... moon: Scenes of apocalyptic darkness, caused by portents in the day and night sky, often appear in prophetic depictions of divine judgment (34:4; Ezek 32:7-8; Joel 2:30-31; Amos 5:18-20; 8:9). The background for this motif may be the ninth plague on Egypt, when God shrouded the land of bondage with three days of dreadful darkness (Ex 10:21-23). • Jesus speaks about a cosmic blackout when he prophesies the fall of Jerusalem and the end of the world (Mt 24:29; Mk 13:24), as does the Book of Revelation (6:12; 8:12).

---

*Or *this is made known.*

¹¹I will punish the world for its evil,
    and the wicked for their iniquity;
I will put an end to the pride of the arrogant,
    and lay low the haughtiness of the ruthless.
¹²I will make men more rare than fine gold,
    and mankind than the gold of O'phir.
¹³Therefore I will make the heavens tremble,
    and the earth will be shaken out of its place,
at the wrath of the Lord of hosts
    in the day of his fierce anger.
¹⁴And like a hunted gazelle,
    or like sheep with none to gather them,
every man will turn to his own people,
    and every man will flee to his own land.
¹⁵Whoever is found will be thrust through,
    and whoever is caught will fall by the sword.
¹⁶Their infants will be dashed in pieces
    before their eyes;
their houses will be plundered
    and their wives ravished.

¹⁷Behold, I am stirring up the Medes against them,
    who have no regard for silver
    and do not delight in gold.
¹⁸Their bows will slaughter the young men;
    they will have no mercy on the fruit of the
        womb;
    their eyes will not pity children.
¹⁹And Babylon, the glory of kingdoms,
    the splendor and pride of the Chalde'ans,
will be like Sodom and Gomor'rah
    when God overthrew them.
²⁰It will never be inhabited
    or dwelt in for all generations;
no Arab will pitch his tent there,
    no shepherds will make their flocks lie down
        there.

²¹But wild beasts will lie down there,
    and its houses will be full of howling
        creatures;
there ostriches will dwell,
    and there satyrs will dance.
²²Hyenas will cry in its towers,
    and jackals in the pleasant palaces;
its time is close at hand
    and its days will not be prolonged.

Restoration of Israel

14 The Lord will have compassion on Jacob and will again choose Israel, and will set them in their own land, and strangers will join them and will cling to the house of Jacob. ²And the peoples will take them and bring them to their place, and the house of Israel will possess them in the Lord's land as male and female slaves; they will take captive those who were their captors, and rule over those who oppressed them.

3 When the Lord has given you rest from your pain and turmoil and the hard service with which you were made to serve, ⁴you will take up this taunt against the king of Babylon:
"How the oppressor has ceased,
    the insolent furyʸ ceased!
⁵The Lord has broken the staff of the wicked,
    the scepter of rulers,
⁶that struck the peoples in wrath
    with unceasing blows,
that ruled the nations in anger
    with unrelenting persecution.
⁷The whole earth is at rest and quiet;
    they break forth into singing.
⁸The cypresses rejoice at you,
    the cedars of Lebanon, saying,
'Since you were laid low,
    no hewer comes up against us.'

13:21: Rev 18:2.

13:12 Ophir: Located in southwest Arabia (or possibly along the eastern coast of Africa). It was renowned in biblical times for its premium-quality gold (1 Chron 29:4; Job 28:16; Ps 45:9).

13:17 I am stirring up: Anticipates 41:25. **the Medes:** A people of ancient Iran, southwest of the Caspian Sea. The Medes were incorporated into the growing Persian Empire by ca. 550 B.C. Babylon surrendered to Medo-Persian forces in 539 B.C. (Jer 51:11; Dan 5:30–31).

13:19 Chaldeans: Babylonians. **Sodom and Gomorrah:** Cities annihilated by the judgments of God in the patriarchal period (Gen 19:1–23). They are a prime example of the desolation that follows violent destruction (Jer 50:39–40).

13:21 satyrs: Thought to be demons who appeared as wild goats (34:14; Lev 17:7).

13:22 its time is close at hand: A word of reassurance for Isaiah's future readers who will be living in Babylonian captivity in the sixth century B.C.

14:1–2 By God's mercy, Israel will be released from captivity, restored to its homeland, and its relationship with Gentile conquerors reversed. The placement of this promise between two oracles against Babylon suggests Israel's return from Babylonian Exile in the late sixth century B.C. is in view.

14:1 Jacob: The tribal family of Israel descended from Abraham's grandson Jacob (Gen 49:1–28). **strangers:** Gentile sojourners who dwell among the people of Israel (Deut 10:19).

14:2 slaves: Or "servants". The passage predicts a reversal of roles between captives and captors, but to what extent Isaiah intended this literally is unclear. Historical data is lacking to show that a subjugated population of Babylonians lived in Israel after Jewish captives returned home from exile.

14:3–23 A taunt against the king of Babylon. The song is a parody of a funeral dirge, humiliating rather than honoring the deceased ruler and celebrating his downfall with satirical delight. It seems likely that the king in question is not any specific monarch but a personification of Babylon's arrogance (14:13–14). • Jesus alludes to Isaiah's taunt when he denounces the city of Capernaum for refusing his message despite the mighty works he performed there (Mt 11:23; Lk 10:15).

14:8 cedars of Lebanon: Premium lumber sought for large construction projects.

ʸ One ancient Ms Compare Gk Syr Vg: The meaning of the Hebrew word is uncertain.

⁹Sheol beneath is stirred up
    to meet you when you come,
it rouses the shades to greet you,
    all who were leaders of the earth;
it raises from their thrones
    all who were kings of the nations.
¹⁰All of them will speak
    and say to you:
'You too have become as weak as we!
    You have become like us!'
¹¹Your pomp is brought down to Sheol,
    the sound of your harps;
maggots are the bed beneath you,
    and worms are your covering.

¹²"How you are fallen from heaven,
    O Day Star, son of Dawn!
How you are cut down to the ground,
    you who laid the nations low!
¹³You said in your heart,
    'I will ascend to heaven;
above the stars of God
    I will set my throne on high;
I will sit on the mount of assembly
    in the far north;
¹⁴I will ascend above the heights of the
    clouds,
I will make myself like the Most High.'
¹⁵But you are brought down to Sheol,
    to the depths of the Pit.
¹⁶Those who see you will stare at you,
    and ponder over you:
'Is this the man who made the earth
    tremble,
    who shook kingdoms,

¹⁷who made the world like a desert
    and overthrew its cities,
who did not let his prisoners go home?'
¹⁸All the kings of the nations lie in glory,
    each in his own tomb;
¹⁹but you are cast out, away from your sepulchre,
    like a loathed untimely birth,ᶻ
clothed with the slain, those pierced by the sword,
    who go down to the stones of the Pit,
    like a dead body trodden under foot.
²⁰You will not be joined with them in burial,
    because you have destroyed your land,
    you have slain your people.

"May the descendants of evildoers
    nevermore be named!
²¹Prepare slaughter for his sons
    because of the guilt of their fathers,
lest they rise and possess the earth,
    and fill the face of the world with cities."

22 "I will rise up against them," says the LORD of hosts, "and will cut off from Babylon name and remnant, offspring and posterity, says the LORD. ²³And I will make it a possession of the hedgehog, and pools of water, and I will sweep it with the broom of destruction, says the LORD of hosts."

²⁴The LORD of hosts has sworn:
"As I have planned,
    so shall it be,
and as I have purposed,
    so shall it stand,
²⁵that I will break the Assyrian in my land,
    and upon my mountains trample him under foot;

14:9 Sheol: Hebrew term for the gloomy realm of the dead (5:14). **the shades:** The spirits of the dead pictured as denizens of the netherworld.

✝ **14:12 O Day Star:** A reference to the planet Venus, visible in the morning twilight but quickly eclipsed by the brightness of the rising sun. Isaiah predicts that Babylon will enjoy only a brief moment of glory. Soon after rearing up against God, it will be thrust down from the heights of arrogance to the depths of disgrace (14:15). The Latin Vulgate translates the epithet "Day Star" as *Lucifer*, meaning "light bearer". Catholic tradition reads this passage in connection with God's judgment on Satan, whose pride led to his fall **from heaven** (cf. Lk 10:18; Rev 12:9) (CCC 391–95). • The one who was Lucifer has fallen from heaven. If he was a being of darkness, why is it said that he was once a bearer of light? Furthermore, the Savior teaches us about the devil: "I saw Satan fall like lightning from heaven." The Lord shows that he was once in heaven and shared in the light of the holy ones (Origen of Alexandria, *On First Principles* 1, 5, 5). The devil is the head of the wicked, who may be said to form his body, just as Christ is the head of the Church, which is his body. One must distinguish between what applies to the head and what applies to the members, for Scripture sometimes speaks of what concerns the devil's body rather than the devil himself. The words of Isaiah, "How you are fallen from heaven, Lucifer, son of the dawn", are understood of the devil under the guise of the king

of Babylon. However, the following words, "How you are cut down to the ground" do not refer entirely to the devil himself but to his body (St. Augustine, *On Christian Doctrine* 3, 37).

14:13 I will ascend to heaven: The boast of one who aspires to become a god (Ezek 28:2; Dan 11:36; 2 Thess 2:3–4). **the mount of assembly:** The sacred elevation where gods and goddesses were believed to hold council together. It is the Canaanite equivalent to Mount Olympus in Greek mythology. See note on 2:2–4. **in the far north:** Or "on the heights of Zaphon", which is the name of a mountain said to be located in northern Syria.

14:15 the Pit: Another name for Sheol or the netherworld of the dead (14:9).

14:19 cast out: The king is denied not only a state funeral but even the honor of a proper burial. In the biblical world, lack of burial for the dead, along with the maltreatment of human corpses, was a severe indignity—almost a fate worse than death itself. It is frequently a sign of stern judgment (34:3; 66:24; Jer 14:16; 36:30).

14:24–27 An oracle against Assyria. By swearing a divine oath, the Lord assures Israel that his purposes for history cannot be thwarted or confounded by any earthly state, no matter how mighty. Just as the boasting of Babylon will come to nothing, as indicated in 14:3–23, so will the arrogance of Assyria, as indicated previously in 10:5–34.

14:25 the Assyrian in my land: Isaiah foretells the miraculous end to Sennacherib's siege of Jerusalem in 701 B.C., an event narrated in chaps. 36–37.

ᶻ Cn Compare Tg Symmachus: Heb *a loathed branch.*

and his yoke shall depart from them,
    and his burden from their shoulder."
26This is the purpose that is purposed
    concerning the whole earth;
and this is the hand that is stretched out
    over all the nations.
27For the Lord of hosts has purposed,
    and who will annul it?
His hand is stretched out,
    and who will turn it back?

28In the year that King A'haz died came this oracle:
29"Rejoice not, O Philis'tia, all of you,
    that the rod which struck you is broken,
for from the serpent's root will come forth an
    adder,
    and its fruit will be a flying serpent.
30And the first-born of the poor will feed,
    and the needy lie down in safety;
but I will kill your root with famine,
    and your remnant I[a] will slay.
31Wail, O gate; cry, O city;
    melt in fear, O Philis'tia, all of you!
For smoke comes out of the north,
    and there is no straggler in his ranks."
32What will one answer the messengers of the
    nation?
"The Lord has founded Zion,
    and in her the afflicted of his people find
    refuge."

An Oracle concerning Moab

15 An oracle concerning Moab.
Because Ar is laid waste in a night
Moab is undone;

because Kir is laid waste in a night
    Moab is undone.
2The daughter of Di'bon[b] has gone up
    to the high places to weep;
over Nebo and over Med'eba
    Moab wails.
On every head is baldness,
    every beard is shorn;
3in the streets they put on sackcloth;
    on the housetops and in the squares
    every one wails and melts in tears.
4Heshbon and E"lea'leh cry out,
    their voice is heard as far as Ja'haz;
therefore the armed men of Moab cry aloud;
    his soul trembles.
5My heart cries out for Moab;
    his fugitives flee to Zoar,
    to Eg'lath-shelish'iyah.
For at the ascent of Lu'hith
    they go up weeping;
on the road to Horona'im
    they raise a cry of destruction;
6the waters of Nimrim
    are a desolation;
the grass is withered, the new growth fails,
    the verdure is no more.
7Therefore the abundance they have gained
    and what they have laid up
they carry away
    over the Brook of the Willows.
8For a cry has gone
    round the land of Moab;
the wailing reaches to Egla'im,
    the wailing reaches to Be'er-e'lim.

14:29–31: Jer 47; Ezek 25:15–17; Joel 3:4–8; Amos 1:6–8; Zeph 2:4–7; Zech 9:5–7.
15–16: Is 25:10–12; Jer 48; Ezek 25:8–11; Amos 2:1–3; Zeph 2:8–11.

14:26 the hand ... stretched out: The Lord is ready to smite the nations with judgment, just as he had done to Israel. See note on 5:25.

14:28–32 An oracle against Philistia, whose cities (especially Ashdod) joined a conspiracy with Egypt and Ethiopia to break free from Assyrian rule while the latter was experiencing a brief period of decline. Isaiah warned Judah against joining this revolt, since it was doomed to fail (see 20:1).

14:28 King Ahaz died: About 715 B.C.

14:29 the rod: The Assyrians, whom the Lord was using to execute his wrath against Israel and its neighbors in the eighth century B.C. (10:5). **flying serpent:** Perhaps a winged cobra such as those that appear in Egyptian artwork (30:6).

14:30 the poor ... the needy: The afflicted of Judah (14:32).

14:31 smoke: Signals the approach of the Assyrian army.

14:32 messengers: Envoys who pressed Judah to join the anti-Assyrian coalition. **The Lord:** The Protector of Jerusalem and its people when they keep the covenant and heed the words of his prophets.

15:1—16:14 An oracle concerning Moab, located directly east of the Dead Sea. It has four main parts: **(1)** a lament

over the invasion of Moab by unnamed conquerors (15:1–9), **(2)** an appeal to Judah to shelter refugees fleeing from Moab (16:1–5), **(3)** Judah's reaction to the Moabite appeal (16:6–12), and **(4)** a prophecy that Moab will suffer these humiliations in three years (16:13–14). Parts of this oracle will be cited and expanded by the prophet Jeremiah (compare 15:2–3 and 16:6–12 with Jer 48:29–38).

15:1–9 Moab bewails the destruction that fills its land. Isaiah is so certain this catastrophe is coming that he speaks as if it had already happened. Multiple towns and villages are named in the oracle, showing the extent of the devastation, but not all of them have been located by historians and archaeologists with certainty.

15:1 Ar ... Kir: Two of the leading cities of Moab.

15:2 high places: Pagan shrines (16:12). **baldness ... shorn:** Ancient expressions of mourning (22:12; Jer 48:37; Mic 1:16).

15:4 Heshbon and Elealeh: Near the northern border of Moabite territory.

15:5 Zoar: Just south of the Dead Sea in Edomite territory.

15:6 waters of Nimrim: An oasis or seasonal stream near the southeastern end of the Dead Sea.

15:7 Brook of the Willows: Often identified with the Brook Zered, which marks the southern border of Moab (Wadi el-Hesa).

---

[a] One ancient Ms Vg: Heb *he*.
[b] Cn: Heb *the house and Dibon*.

⁹For the waters of Di′bon^c are full of blood;
  yet I will bring upon Dibon^c even more,
a lion for those of Moab who escape,
  for the remnant of the land.

16 They have sent lambs
  to the ruler of the land,
from Se′la, by way of the desert,
  to the mount of the daughter of Zion.
²Like fluttering birds,
  like scattered nestlings,
so are the daughters of Moab
  at the fords of the Arnon.
³"Give counsel,
  grant justice;
make your shade like night
  at the height of noon;
hide the outcasts,
  betray not the fugitive;
⁴let the outcasts of Moab
  sojourn among you;
be a refuge to them
  from the destroyer.
When the oppressor is no more,
  and destruction has ceased,
and he who tramples under foot
  has vanished from the land,
⁵then a throne will be established in steadfast love
  and on it will sit in faithfulness
  in the tent of David
one who judges and seeks justice
  and is swift to do righteousness."

⁶We have heard of the pride of Moab,
  how proud he was;

of his arrogance, his pride, and his insolence—
  his boasts are false.
⁷Therefore let Moab wail,
  let every one wail for Moab.
Mourn, utterly stricken,
  for the raisin-cakes of Kir′-har′eseth.

⁸For the fields of Heshbon languish,
  and the vine of Sibmah;
the lords of the nations
  have struck down its branches,
which reached to Ja′zer
  and strayed to the desert;
its shoots spread abroad
  and passed over the sea.
⁹Therefore I weep with the weeping of Ja′zer
  for the vine of Sibmah;
I drench you with my tears,
  O Heshbon and E″lea′leh;
for upon your fruit and your harvest
  the battle shout has fallen.
¹⁰And joy and gladness are taken away
  from the fruitful field;
and in the vineyards no songs are sung,
  no shouts are raised;
no treader treads out wine in the presses;
  the vintage shout is hushed.^d
¹¹Therefore my soul moans like a lyre for Moab,
  and my heart for Kirhe′res.

12 And when Moab presents himself, when he wearies himself upon the high place, when he comes to his sanctuary to pray, he will not prevail.

13 This is the word which the Lᴏʀᴅ spoke concerning Moab in the past. ¹⁴But now the Lᴏʀᴅ says, "In three years, like the years of a hireling,

---

15:9 a lion: Bloodshed throughout the land attracts carnivores, posing new dangers for survivors.

16:1 lambs: A gift of tribute to the king of Judah (cf. 2 Kings 3:4). It suggests that Moab offers to subjugate itself to Judah's rule in exchange for protection. **Sela:** A rock fortress or hideout from which Moabite survivors send envoys to Jerusalem. Sela is also the name of a location in Edom (2 Kings 14:7). **the daughter of Zion:** See note on 1:8.

16:2 the Arnon: Flows westward through Moab into the center of the Dead Sea.

16:4 the destroyer: The invading army, most likely from Assyria. See note on 16:13–14.

16:5 the tent of David: An image of the kingdom of David (Amos 9:11), which was founded on God's promissory oath to establish David's throne forever (2 Sam 7:12–16; Ps 89:3–4). Israel's hope for a coming Messiah, expected to be an ideal ruler, was anchored in the Lord's covenant of kingship with David. The embassy from Moab invokes this future hope when it speaks of one who **judges**, seeks **justice**, and does **righteousness**. Isaiah used this language to describe the Davidic Immanuel child earlier in the book (9:1–6; 11:1–9).

16:6 pride: The reason for Moab's downfall (Zeph 2:8–9). Pride was the reason for Babylon's downfall as well (14:12–

15). Moab's conceit and false assurance of strength may be linked to its agricultural abundance.

16:7–11 Moab is compared to a sprawling grapevine that is ravaged by war.

16:7 raisin-cakes: An ancient delicacy (Song 2:5), sometimes given as a food offering to idols (Hos 3:1).

16:8 Heshbon ... Sibmah: Neighboring cities in northern Moab. **the desert:** The north Arabian desert, bordering Moab on the east. **the sea:** The Dead Sea, bordering Moab on the west.

16:9 I weep: Isaiah himself mourns the calamities that have come to Moab.

16:10 vintage shout: The celebratory shout of farmers who tread the grapes after a bountiful harvest (Jer 25:30).

16:12 the high place: An idol shrine, perhaps dedicated to Chemosh, the national god of the Moabites. Prayers to the deity are futile in lifting God's judgment from the land, since Chemosh is no god at all.

16:13–14 Isaiah predicts that Moab will be devastated in **three years**. The background is probably Moab's alliance with Egypt, Ethiopia, and Philistia in revolting against Assyrian rule ca. 715–712 ʙ.ᴄ. Following this period, the Assyrian king Sargon II likely conducted a punitive campaign against Moab for its partnership in the rebellion. Judah is warned not to join the league of states asserting independence from Assyria. The covenant people are to trust in God, not in foreign policy schemes that seek security in earthly arrangements apart from the Lord.

---

^cOne ancient Ms Vg Compare Syr: Heb *Dimon.*
^dGk: Heb *I have hushed.*

the glory of Moab will be brought into contempt, in spite of all his great multitude, and those who survive will be very few and feeble."

An Oracle concerning Damascus

17 An oracle concerning Damascus.

Behold, Damascus will cease to be a city,
and will become a heap of ruins.
²Her cities will be deserted for ever;ᵉ
they will be for flocks,
which will lie down, and none will make them
afraid.
³The fortress will disappear from E'phraim,
and the kingdom from Damascus;
and the remnant of Syria will be
like the glory of the children of Israel,
says the LORD of hosts.

⁴And in that day
the glory of Jacob will be brought low,
and the fat of his flesh will grow lean.
⁵And it shall be as when the reaper gathers
standing grain
and his arm harvests the ears,
and as when one gleans the ears of grain
in the Valley of Reph'aim.
⁶Gleanings will be left in it,
as when an olive tree is beaten—
two or three berries
in the top of the highest bough,
four or five
on the branches of a fruit tree,
says the LORD God of Israel.

7 In that day men will regard their Maker, and their eyes will look to the Holy One of Israel; ⁸they will not have regard for the altars, the work of their hands, and they will not look to what their own fingers have made, either the Ashe'rim or the altars of incense.

9 In that day their strong cities will be like the deserted places of the Hi'vites and the Am'orites,ᶠ which they deserted because of the children of Israel, and there will be desolation.

¹⁰For you have forgotten the God of your
salvation,
and have not remembered the Rock of your
refuge;
therefore, though you plant pleasant plants
and set out slips of an alien god,
¹¹though you make them grow on the day that you
plant them,
and make them blossom in the morning that
you sow;
yet the harvest will flee away
in a day of grief and incurable pain.

¹²Ah, the thunder of many peoples,
they thunder like the thundering of the sea!
Ah, the roar of nations,
they roar like the roaring of mighty waters!
¹³The nations roar like the roaring of many
waters,
but he will rebuke them, and they will flee
far away,

17:1–3: Jer 49:23–27; Amos 1:3–5; Zech 9:1.

17:1–11 An oracle against Damascus (Syria) and Ephraim (Israel). The historical backdrop is the Syro-Ephraimite conflict of 735 B.C., the same crisis that stands behind chaps. 7–8. Isaiah contends that Judah need not fear the threats of these northern neighbors, for God is about to bring them low at the hands of the Assyrians. On the positive side, the catastrophe will prompt some survivors in Israel to forsake their idols and return to the Lord (17:7–8).

17:1 Damascus: The capital of the Aramean kingdom of Syria. It fell to the Assyrians in 732 B.C.

17:3 Ephraim: Refers to the Northern Kingdom of Israel, founded by Jeroboam I of the tribe of Ephraim (1 Kings 11:26; 12:20). **remnant of Syria:** Only a small portion of the population will escape destruction and deportation. Syria's humiliation will be similar to Israel's drastic reduction in population when the Assyrians ravaged Galilee and the Transjordan in 734–733 B.C. (2 Kings 15:29; 1 Chron 5:26).

17:4–9 Three prophecies revealing events that will take place **in that day,** which is the day of God's judgment (17:4, 7, 9). See note on 2:12.

17:5 gleans: I.e., gathers what is left in the fields after farmers have harvested the season's crop. Here the thoroughness of devastation is emphasized. **Valley of Rephaim:** The location of fertile lands southwest of Jerusalem (2 Sam 5:18).

17:6 two or three berries: All that is left on the tree after harvesters knocked most of the olives off the branches with a high-reaching stick.

17:7 their Maker: A reference to the Lord as Creator (51:13; 54:5). Repentance among the survivors is one of the positive outcomes of the judgments that befell the Northern Kingdom of Israel (as in 10:20–21). **the Holy One of Israel:** See note on 1:4.

17:8 work of their hands: Idols, and the altars used to serve them, are nothing but human creations (44:9–20). **Asherim:** Trees or wooden poles, dedicated to the Canaanite goddess Asherah, that stood erect in idol sanctuaries (Judg 3:7; 2 Kings 17:10).

17:9 Hivites ... Amorites: Two of the Gentile peoples that occupied Canaan before Israel's conquest and settlement of the land (Deut 7:1).

17:10 you have forgotten: I.e., you have forsaken your covenant with God, which forbids the worship of other gods (Deut 8:19). **plants ... slips:** Cultivating shoots may be linked with a pagan fertility cult.

17:12 Ah: Or "Woe", a cry of distress or lamentation. See word study: *Woe* at 28:1. **the thunder of many peoples:** Refers initially to the Assyrians, who will face God's wrath after they have executed God's judgment on Syria and Ephraim (10:5–34; 14:24–27). At the same time, Isaiah indicates that Assyria is just one of many nations who will plan to assault God's people but will be driven away (17:14).

17:13 he will rebuke them: God will put the Assyrians to flight once they have engulfed the land like a flood (see 8:7–8). They will retreat just as the waters at creation drew back from the dry land at God's command (Gen 1:9; Ps 104:6–7). Isaiah thus prophesies the deliverance of Jerusalem in 701 B.C. (see 37:33–37).

ᵉ Cn Compare Gk: Heb *the cities of Aroer are deserted.*
ᶠ Cn Compare Gk: Heb *the wood and the highest bough.*

chased like chaff on the mountains before the
   wind
   and whirling dust before the storm.
¹⁴At evening time, behold, terror!
   Before morning, they are no more!
   This is the portion of those who despoil us,
   and the lot of those who plunder us.

18 Ah, land of whirring wings
   which is beyond the rivers of Ethiopia;
²which sends ambassadors by the Nile,
   in vessels of papyrus upon the waters!
   Go, you swift messengers,
   to a nation, tall and smooth,
   to a people feared near and far,
   a nation mighty and conquering,
   whose land the rivers divide.

³All you inhabitants of the world,
   you who dwell on the earth,
   when a signal is raised on the mountains, look!
   When a trumpet is blown, hear!
⁴For thus the Lord said to me:
   "I will quietly look from my dwelling
   like clear heat in sunshine,
   like a cloud of dew in the heat of harvest."
⁵For before the harvest, when the blossom is
      over,
   and the flower becomes a ripening grape,
   he will cut off the shoots with pruning hooks,
   and the spreading branches he will hew
      away.

⁶They shall all of them be left
   to the birds of prey of the mountains
   and to the beasts of the earth.
   And the birds of prey will summer upon them,
   and all the beasts of the earth will winter upon
      them.

7 At that time gifts will be brought to the Lord
of hosts
   from a people tall and smooth,
   from a people feared near and far,
   a nation mighty and conquering,
   whose land the rivers divide,
to Mount Zion, the place of the name of the Lord of
hosts.

An Oracle concerning Egypt

19 An oracle concerning Egypt.
   Behold, the Lord is riding on a swift cloud
   and comes to Egypt;
   and the idols of Egypt will tremble at his
      presence,
   and the heart of the Egyptians will melt within
      them.
²And I will stir up Egyptians against Egyptians,
   and they will fight, every man against his
      brother
   and every man against his neighbor,
   city against city, kingdom against
      kingdom;
³and the spirit of the Egyptians within them will
      be emptied out,
   and I will confound their plans;

18: Zeph 2:12.   **19:** Jer 46; Ezek 29–32; Zech 14:18–19.

18:1—20:6 Oracles against Ethiopia and Egypt. The historical setting is probably between 715 and 712 b.c., when these
nations along the Nile conspired with Philistia and Moab to
throw off the yoke of Assyrian rule. Eventually the conspiracy
would backfire and bring Assyrian reprisals. Isaiah foresees this
coming catastrophe but also looks beyond it to the conversion
of the Ethiopians and Egyptians, who will one day serve the
God of Israel (18:7; 19:19-25; 45:14).
   18:1 Ah: Or "Woe", as in 17:12. **whirring wings:** Flying
insects that infest the Nile valley. **Ethiopia:** Cush, the land
south of Egypt (modern Sudan and part of Ethiopia).
   18:2 ambassadors: Diplomats from Ethiopia seek Judah's
partnership in the alliance against Assyria. They are sent back
with a prediction that war is coming and that their plans will
fail (18:3-6). Judah refused to participate in the revolt. **vessels
of papyrus:** Boats made of papyrus reeds tied together and
waterproofed with pitch (cf. Ex 2:3).
   18:3 inhabitants of the world: Called to recognize that
the judgment of entire nations is the Lord's doing. **signal:** A
banner or flag used to summon troops into battle (5:26; 13:2).
   18:4 I will quietly look: The Lord will do nothing to stop
the oncoming Assyrian hordes but will allow them to fulfill
his plans.
   18:5 he will cut off: The Lord is pictured as a vinedresser
who prunes away tendrils and offshoots that bear no fruit (Jn
15:1-2).
   18:6 birds ... beasts: Heavy casualties will mean a feast
for carnivores and carrion birds (cf. Ezek 39:17-24).

   18:7 gifts will be brought: Ethiopia is one of the nations
that will make pilgrimage to Zion (2:2) to seek the Davidic
Messiah (11:10-11) and serve the Lord with gifts (60:4-7).
   19:1 riding on a swift cloud: The Lord thunders toward
Egypt in his battle chariot (see Ps 104:3). The passage draws on the imagery of Canaanite mythology, which
describes Baal, the storm and fertility god, as a rider of the
clouds. Only in this case, the Lord approaches in a storm of
judgment, not to bring needed rainfall. For additional uses
of this imagery, see note on Dan 7:13. • The Lord "riding on
a swift cloud" refers either to the body of the Virgin Mary,
which was not weighed down by human seed, or to Christ's
body, which was conceived by the Holy Spirit. He came
into the Egypt of this world so that the deceit of idolatry
would realize it had been conquered. Even magi from the
East, knowing that the Son of God came to destroy their
arts, traveled to Bethlehem to worship this child (St. Jerome,
Commentary on Isaiah 7, 12). According to the prophecy,
the Lord comes to Egypt, not without a body, but in a cloud,
signifying his Incarnation. It thus calls him "a savior" who will
"deliver them" (Is 19:20). There is no doubt these prophecies
foretold the Lord's coming (Eusebius of Caesarea, *Demonstration of the Gospel* 8, 5). **idols of Egypt:** Stand helpless
and afraid before the God of Israel, who executed his judgments on them at the time of the Exodus (Ex 12:12; Num
33:4).
   19:2 they will fight: Domestic and societal strife are the
initial pangs of judgment (cf. Mt 24:7-8; Mk 13:12).

and they will consult the idols and the
  sorcerers,
    and the mediums and the wizards;
⁴and I will give over the Egyptians
  into the hand of a hard master;
and a fierce king will rule over them,
  says the Lord, the Lᴏʀᴅ of hosts.

⁵And the waters of the Nile will be dried up,
  and the river will be parched and dry;
⁶and its canals will become foul,
  and the branches of Egypt's Nile will diminish
    and dry up,
    reeds and rushes will rot away.
⁷There will be bare places by the Nile,
  on the brink of the Nile,
and all that is sown by the Nile will dry up,
  be driven away, and be no more.
⁸The fishermen will mourn and lament,
  all who cast hook in the Nile;
and they will languish
  who spread nets upon the water.
⁹The workers in combed flax will be in despair,
  and the weavers of white cotton.
¹⁰Those who are the pillars of the land will be
  crushed,
    and all who work for hire will be grieved.

¹¹The princes of Zoan are utterly foolish;
  the wise counselors of Pharaoh give stupid
    counsel.
How can you say to Pharaoh,
  "I am a son of the wise,
  a son of ancient kings"?

¹²Where then are your wise men?
  Let them tell you and make known
    what the Lᴏʀᴅ of hosts has purposed against
      Egypt.
¹³The princes of Zoan have become fools,
  and the princes of Memphis are deluded;
those who are the cornerstones of her tribes
  have led Egypt astray.
¹⁴The Lᴏʀᴅ has mingled within her a spirit of
  confusion;
and they have made Egypt stagger in all her
  doings
    as a drunken man staggers in his vomit.
¹⁵And there will be nothing for Egypt
  which head or tail, palm branch or reed, may do.

16 In that day the Egyptians will be like women, and tremble with fear before the hand which the Lᴏʀᴅ of hosts shakes over them. ¹⁷And the land of Judah will become a terror to the Egyptians; every one to whom it is mentioned will fear because of the purpose which the Lᴏʀᴅ of hosts has purposed against them.

18 In that day there will be five cities in the land of Egypt which speak the language of Canaan and swear allegiance to the Lᴏʀᴅ of hosts. One of these will be called the City of the Sun.

19 In that day there will be an altar to the Lᴏʀᴅ in the midst of the land of Egypt, and a pillar to the Lᴏʀᴅ at its border. ²⁰It will be a sign and a witness to the Lᴏʀᴅ of hosts in the land of Egypt; when they cry to the Lᴏʀᴅ because of oppressors he will send them a savior, and will defend and deliver them. ²¹And the Lᴏʀᴅ will make himself known to the Egyptians;

19:4 a fierce king: Identity uncertain. The king may be Shabako, an Ethiopian who came to power in Egypt around 715 B.C., or Esarhaddon, an Assyrian monarch who subdued Egypt a few decades later (681–669 B.C.).

19:5–10 The Nile River is the lifeblood of Egypt, which receives too little rain to support life. Any disruption in its flow spells disaster for the civilization that depends on it.

19:6 its canals: Irrigation channels that make farming along the Nile possible. **branches:** A reference to the Delta region of northern Egypt, where the Nile splits into multiple streams before emptying into the Mediterranean Sea.

19:9 flax: Its fibers are stripped by a combing process and used to make linen.

19:10 the pillars: Represent the ruling class.

19:11 Zoan: A prominent city in the eastern Delta, also known as Tanis.

19:12 your wise men?: Egypt was renowned for its sages and abundant wisdom literature (1 Kings 4:30). Isaiah taunts them for being ignorant of the Lord's designs for Egypt.

19:13 Memphis: A prominent city along the Nile, just south of the Delta region.

19:14 spirit of confusion: A form of divine judgment. It is compared to a state of moral and spiritual drunkenness that is induced by the Lord (as in 29:9–10).

19:16–24 A sequence of events scheduled to begin on **that day**, which is a day of judgment and fear followed by a time of salvation and conversion (19:16, 18, 19, 23, 24).

This particular oracle stands out from its surroundings: in the midst of chaps. 13–21, an extended section announcing judgment on Gentiles, Isaiah sounds a note of redemption and reconciliation. It shows that the Lord's ultimate aim is not the destruction of the nations beyond Israel but their conversion (see 2:2–4).

19:17 terror: Egypt will fear, not the tiny state of Judah, but the awesome power of Judah's God.

19:18 five cities: Jewish settlements in Egypt (Jer 44:1). **language of Canaan:** Hebrew. **swear allegiance:** Suggests that Gentile conversions are in view, as with the oaths sworn in Josh 2:8–14 (Rahab the Canaanite) and Ruth 1:16–17 (Ruth the Moabitess). **City of the Sun:** The city of On, later called Heliopolis, which was home to the cult of Re, the Egyptian sun god.

19:19 altar to the Lᴏʀᴅ: A place of sacrificial worship in Egypt (19:21). Jewish colonies in Egypt constructed temples in OT times, one in Elephantine (5th century B.C.) and another in Leontopolis (second century B.C.). However, since the laws of Deuteronomy prohibit sacrifice outside the central sanctuary (i.e., the Temple in Jerusalem), Isaiah must be looking beyond the restrictions of Deuteronomy to a time when the nations beyond Israel will worship the Lord by sacrifice. A similar prophecy appears in Mal 1:11. **pillar to the Lᴏʀᴅ:** A monument to Egypt's newfound faith in the only true God (cf. Gen 28:18–22).

19:20 a savior: Like one of the judges who delivered Israel in days past (Judg 2:18; 3:9).

and the Egyptians will know the Lord in that day and worship with sacrifice and burnt offering, and they will make vows to the Lord and perform them. ²²And the Lord will strike Egypt, striking and healing, and they will return to the Lord, and he will heed their supplications and heal them.

23 In that day there will be a highway from Egypt to Assyria, and the Assyrian will come into Egypt, and the Egyptian into Assyria, and the Egyptians will worship with the Assyrians.

24 In that day Israel will be the third with Egypt and Assyria, a blessing in the midst of the earth, ²⁵whom the Lord of hosts has blessed, saying, "Blessed be Egypt my people, and Assyria the work of my hands, and Israel my heritage."

The Conquest of Egypt and Ethiopia

20 In the year that the commander in chief, who was sent by Sargon the king of Assyria, came to Ash'dod and fought against it and took it,—²at that time the Lord had spoken by Isai'ah the son of A'moz, saying, "Go, and loose the sackcloth from your loins and take off your shoes from your feet," and he had done so, walking naked and barefoot—³the Lord said, "As my servant Isai'ah has walked naked and barefoot for three years as a sign and a portent against Egypt and Ethiopia, ⁴so shall the king of Assyria lead away the Egyptians captives and the Ethiopians exiles, both the young and old, naked and barefoot, with buttocks uncovered, to the shame of Egypt. ⁵Then they shall be dismayed

and confounded because of Ethiopia their hope and of Egypt their boast. ⁶And the inhabitants of this coastland will say in that day, 'Behold, this is what has happened to those in whom we hoped and to whom we fled for help to be delivered from the king of Assyria! And we, how shall we escape?'"

Oracles concerning Babylon, Edom, and Arabia

21 The oracle concerning the wilderness of the sea.

As whirlwinds in the Neg'eb sweep on,
  it comes from the desert,
  from a terrible land.
²A stern vision is told to me;
  the plunderer plunders,
  and the destroyer destroys.
Go up, O E'lam,
  lay siege, O Med'ia;
all the sighing she has caused
  I bring to an end.
³Therefore my loins are filled with anguish;
  pangs have seized me,
  like the pangs of a woman with labor pains;
I am bowed down so that I cannot hear,
  I am dismayed so that I cannot see.
⁴My mind reels, horror has appalled me;
  the twilight I longed for
  has been turned for me into trembling.
⁵They prepare the table,
  they spread the rugs,
  they eat, they drink.

19:22 striking and healing: Divine chastisement encourages repentance. It has a remedial purpose that may be compared to the discipline that a father administers to his misbehaving children, the aim of which is not their condemnation, but their correction and improvement (Deut 8:5; Job 5:17–18; Prov 3:12).

19:23 a highway: Unites peoples who are separated (11:16; 62:10). **Egyptians ... Assyrians:** Egypt and Assyria, the chief rival powers in Isaiah's day, represent all nations. The prophet foresees a future when animosities between nations are overcome. Sharing a common faith in the one true God, all peoples will be drawn together into a common worship (2:1–4, 11:10). This will finally be realized through the Church's mission to evangelize all nations (Mt 28:18–20), which creates a single covenant community in which Jews and Gentiles glorify the same Lord (Rom 15:7–12).

19:25 people ... work ... heritage: Conversion among the nations expands the membership of the covenant people, so that Gentiles will come to share in Israel's spiritual blessings (Rom 15:27). Prior to messianic times, only Israel is designated the Lord's special people (Lev 26:12), the work of his hands (29:23), and his heritage (Deut 32:9).

20:1 commander: Assyria's chief military officer, known as the Tartan (2 King 18:17). **Sargon:** Sargon II, king of Assyria (722–705 B.C.). **Ashdod:** One of the leading cities of the Philistines, over 30 miles west of Jerusalem. It fell to Assyrian forces in 711 B.C. The conquest of Ashdod is also attested in the *Annals of Sargon*. See note on 16:13–14.

20:2 sackcloth: A coarse, hair-spun fabric worn by penitents (Jon 3:5). In this case, however, it may be a hairy mantle worn by the prophet (cf. 2 Kings 1:8; Zech 13:4).

20:3 naked and barefoot: Stripped of clothing. Isaiah's startling appearance is a prophetic sign of the humiliation that is coming to Egypt and Ethiopia, as they will be taken

as captives of war (2 Sam 10:4–5; 2 Chron 28:14–15). **three years:** Probably during the anti-Assyrian revolt of 715–712 B.C. (16:14). **sign ... portent:** As announced in 8:18.

20:5–6 The prophet's message for Judah is made clear: trust in a political alliance with Egypt is foolish in view of God's intention to bring defeat and disgrace upon the Egyptians.

21:1–10 The fall of Babylon is foretold. The historical background is disputed by scholars. Some relate the oracle to Assyrian campaigns against Babylon in 702 B.C. and especially 689 B.C., when the city was destroyed by Sennacherib. Others see a reference to the Medo-Persian victory over Babylon in 539 B.C. Elam and Media, mentioned in 21:2, were allies of Babylon in the early seventh century, but they became enemies who sacked the city under Cyrus II in the sixth century.

21:1 the wilderness of the sea: Perhaps a reference to the Babylonian homeland, covering the southern Mesopotamian plain bordering the Persian Gulf. Another possibility is that "the sea" refers to the city of Babylon, which the Lord will bring to judgment by reducing it to a barren wilderness (see Jer 51:36–37). **whirlwinds in the Negeb:** The strong gusts that blow into Israel from the Sinai Peninsula (Jer 13:24; Zech 9:14).

21:2 Elam: East of Babylon. **Media:** Northeast of Babylonia. Once an independent kingdom, the Medes were absorbed into the Persian kingdom about 550 B.C. For their role in God's plan to overthrow the Babylonians in 539 B.C., see 13:17 and Jer 51:11.

21:3 woman with labor pains: An image of one seized by sudden distress (13:8; 26:17; Jn 16:21; 1 Thess 5:3). Isaiah is doubled over in pain and dread at the prospect of the coming calamity.

21:5 they eat, they drink: Vividly portrayed in Dan 5:1–4. **oil the shield:** Leather shields were rubbed with oil to slick the surface and perhaps to make them resistant to puncture (2 Sam 1:21).

Arise, O princes,
  oil the shield!
[6]For thus the Lord said to me:
"Go, set a watchman,
  let him announce what he sees.
[7]When he sees riders, horsemen in pairs,
  riders on donkeys, riders on camels,
let him listen diligently,
  very diligently."
[8]Then he who saw[g] cried:
"Upon a watchtower I stand, O Lord,
  continually by day,
and at my post I am stationed whole nights.
[9]And, behold, here come riders,
  horsemen in pairs!"
And he answered,
  "Fallen, fallen is Babylon;
and all the images of her gods
  he has shattered to the ground."
[10]O my threshed and winnowed one,
  what I have heard from the Lord of hosts,
  the God of Israel, I announce to you.
[11]The oracle concerning Du'mah.
One is calling to me from Se'ir,
  "Watchman, what of the night?
  Watchman, what of the night?"
[12]The watchman says:
"Morning comes, and also the night.
  If you will inquire, inquire;
  come back again."

[13]The oracle concerning Arabia.
In the thickets in Arabia you will lodge,
  O caravans of De'danites.
[14]To the thirsty bring water,
  meet the fugitive with bread,
  O inhabitants of the land of Te'ma.
[15]For they have fled from the swords,
  from the drawn sword,
from the bent bow,
  and from the press of battle.

16 For thus the Lord said to me, "Within a year, according to the years of a hireling, all the glory of Ke'dar will come to an end; [17]and the remainder of the archers of the mighty men of the sons of Ke'dar will be few; for the Lord, the God of Israel, has spoken."

An Oracle concerning the Valley of Vision

22 The oracle concerning the valley of vision.
What do you mean that you have gone
  up,
all of you, to the housetops,
[2]you who are full of shoutings,
  tumultuous city, exultant town?
Your slain are not slain with the sword
  or dead in battle.
[3]All your rulers have fled together,
  without the bow they were captured.
All of you who were found were captured,
  though they had fled far away.[h]

21:6 **watchman:** A friend or fellow prophet who reports to Isaiah on the signs of Babylon's demise. Others described as watchmen include Ezekiel (Ezek 3:17) and Habakkuk (Hab 2:1).

21:9 **Fallen, fallen is Babylon:** An announcement of total defeat, which includes the destruction of Babylon's useless idols (Jer 50:2; 51:8, 44). In Isaiah's day, the vision serves to discourage Judah from making a political alliance with Babylon, which it was sorely tempted to do (see 39:1-8). In the sixth century, however, Babylon's fall was happy news for Judah, which had seen the Babylonians destroy Jerusalem in 586 B.C. and take thousands into exile. • Twice in the Book of Revelation, an angel recites these words to announce the demise of the harlot city that seduced the nations into sin and persecuted the earliest Christians (Rev 14:8; 18:2).

21:10 **threshed and winnowed one:** Judah, which was ravaged by the Assyrians in the eighth century B.C. and then by the Babylonians in the sixth century B.C.

21:11-17 Oracles naming four Arabian peoples whom the Bible identifies as descendants of Abraham through his wives Keturah (Dedan, Gen 25:1-3) and Hagar (Dumah, Tema, and Kedar, Gen 25:12-15). The background of these oracles is uncertain, but historical sources indicate that the Assyrian king Sennacherib's campaigns against the Chaldeans of Babylon in the late eighth century included raids on settlements in north Arabia.

21:11 **Dumah:** An oasis in northern Arabia. **Seir:** The hill country of Edom, south of the Dead Sea (Gen 32:3). **Watchman:** Refers to a night patrolman who keeps watch atop the walls of the city (62:6; Song 5:7). **the night:** Signifies the darkness of terror, which the speaker hopes will end soon.

21:13 **the thickets:** Hiding places off the main caravan trails. **Dedanites:** Desert traders (Ezek 27:20).

21:14 **water ... bread:** Traditional hospitality must be shown to persons fleeing war. **Tema:** An oasis settlement in northern Arabia.

21:16 **Kedar:** A tribe of nomadic tent dwellers (Ps 120:5). Later oracles in the book envision the Kedarites singing songs to the Lord and offering him gifts of sacrifice (42:10-11; 60:7).

21:17 **the archers:** Suggests that Kedarite warriors were proficient with the bow, just as their ancestor Ishmael had been (Gen 21:20). **the Lord ... has spoken:** Another reminder that the destiny of nations beyond Israel is determined, not by their idol gods, but by the plan of the one true God.

22:1-25 Two oracles of judgment, the first directed at Jerusalem (22:1-14) and the second at a senior member of Judah's royal government (22:15-25). Both are guilty of looking after their own interests without regard for their duties as servants of the Lord. Including these oracles within a collection of texts that announce judgment on foreign nations (chaps. 13-23) hints that Judah and Jerusalem, despite being set apart for God's purposes, have become no different from Gentile peoples who fail to seek the Lord.

22:1 **The oracle:** The historical occasion is likely the late eighth century, when Sennacherib began to punish Babylon and its allies, including Judah, for revolting against Assyria after the death of Sargon II in 705 B.C. Assyrian forces eventually invaded Judah, which was all but overrun in 701 B.C. Jerusalem, however, was miraculously spared destruction, thanks to the Lord's intervention (36:1—37:38). See note on 1:7-9. **valley of vision:** Perhaps a location near Jerusalem is meant, such as the Hinnom valley, southwest of the city. Another possibility is that Isaiah is speaking sarcastically: Jerusalem, though built on a high mountain, is as blind and vulnerable as a city seated in a valley, which cannot see danger coming in the distance. For the notion of spiritual blindness, see 6:9-10.

22:2 **exultant town:** Jerusalem celebrates the end of Sennacherib's siege of 701 B.C., even though death and destruction

---

[g] One ancient Ms: Heb *a lion.*
[h] Gk Syr Vg: Heb *from far away.*

⁴Therefore I said:
"Look away from me,
   let me weep bitter tears;
do not labor to comfort me
   for the destruction of the daughter of my
      people."

⁵For the Lord God of hosts has a day
   of tumult and trampling and confusion
   in the valley of vision,
a battering down of walls
   and a shouting to the mountains.
⁶And E'lam bore the quiver
   with chariots and horsemen,ⁱ
   and Kir uncovered the shield.
⁷Your choicest valleys were full of chariots,
   and the horsemen took their stand at the gates.
⁸He has taken away the covering of Judah.

In that day you looked to the weapons of the House of the Forest, ⁹and you saw that the breaches of the city of David were many, and you collected the waters of the lower pool, ¹⁰and you counted the houses of Jerusalem, and you broke down the houses to fortify the wall. ¹¹You made a reservoir between the two walls for the water of the old pool. But you did not look to him who did it, or have regard for him who planned it long ago.

¹²In that day the Lord God of hosts
   called to weeping and mourning,
   to baldness and putting on of sackcloth;
¹³and behold, joy and gladness,
   slaying oxen and killing sheep,
   eating flesh and drinking wine.
"Let us eat and drink,
   for tomorrow we die."
¹⁴The Lord of hosts has revealed himself in my
      ears:
"Surely this iniquity will not be forgiven you
   till you die,"
   says the Lord God of hosts.

Denunciation of Self-Seeking Officials

15 Thus says the Lord God of hosts, "Come, go to this steward, to Shebna, who is over the household, and say to him: ¹⁶What have you to do here and whom have you here, that you have hewn here a tomb for yourself, you who hew a tomb on the height, and carve a habitation for yourself in the rock? ¹⁷Behold, the Lord will hurl you away violently, O you strong man. He will seize firm hold on you, ¹⁸and whirl you round and round, and throw you like a ball into a wide land; there you shall die, and there shall be your splendid chariots, you shame of your master's house. ¹⁹I will thrust you from your office, and you will be cast down from your station. ²⁰In that day I will call my servant Eli'akim the son of Hilki'ah,

---

litter the land of Judah (36:1). **not slain:** May mean that some inhabitants of the city died in the siege or surrendered without a fight.

22:4 Look away: Isaiah is overcome with grief at the severity of God's judgment.

22:5 the Lord . . . has a day: See note on 2:12.

22:6 Elam: East of Babylon. Elam's connection to the siege of Jerusalem is obscure, although it will join forces with Media to conquer Babylon in the sixth century B.C. (21:2). **Kir:** Location uncertain. It was the original homeland of the Syrians according to Amos 9:7.

22:8 covering: The divine protection that shields Judah when its people remain faithful to the Lord. **House of the Forest:** The armory (39:2) that Solomon built as part of his palace complex in Jerusalem (1 Kings 7:1–5; 10:17).

22:9–13 Isaiah rebukes Jerusalem for trusting its own ability to protect itself apart from faithful reliance on the Lord. Preoccupied with defensive preparations (weapons, walls, and water supply), the city failed to "get right" with God by acts of repentance (22:12).

22:9 the lower pool: A reservoir in south Jerusalem that collected water from the Gihon spring. Hezekiah's engineers channeled this water into the city through a rock-hewn tunnel that still exists today (2 Kings 20:20).

22:11 the old pool: Perhaps the same as the "upper pool" mentioned in 7:3. **to him who did it:** Or "to its Maker", referring to the Lord as the founder of Jerusalem.

22:12 baldness: Cutting or shaving one's hair is a traditional gesture of mourning (15:2; Mic 1:16). **sackcloth:** A coarse fabric worn by penitents (Jon 3:5). Jerusalem declined to repent in sackcloth and failed to seek God's help during the Assyrian siege; however, a few of its leaders, including King Hezekiah, were not so unwise (see 37:1–2).

22:13 Let us eat and drink: Expresses in words the foolishness of celebrating rather than repenting on the eve of disaster. Judah could not see that sinful revelry and a prideful self-trust invite divine judgments. • Paul cites this verse to parody those who, denying the resurrection of the dead, give themselves a moral excuse to indulge in the pleasures of the flesh as long as time permits (1 Cor 15:32).

22:15–25 Judah's royal steward (Shebna) is stripped of his office and replaced by another (Eliakim). According to 36:3 and 37:2, Eliakim, son of Hilkiah, was the royal steward when the Assyrians besieged Jerusalem in 701 B.C., in which case this episode must have taken place before that date. The account shows that corruption of faith and life prevails, not only among the common people in Judah, as indicated in 1:1–14, but also at the highest levels of the government.

22:15 Shebna: Royal steward (= prime minister) of the kingdom of Judah under Hezekiah, making him second in rank to the king. He is expelled from office for excessive self-concern and, by implication, for neglect of government duties. He may be the same individual called "Shebna the secretary" in chaps. 36–37, but this is uncertain. **over the household:** Part of a title borne by prime ministers in ancient Israel. See word study: *Over the Household* in 1 Kings 16:9.

22:16 a tomb for yourself: Insinuates that Shebna did more to prepare for his own future than to promote the welfare of the kingdom. Archaeologists have discovered a rock-cut tomb in the village of Silwan, east of Jerusalem, that dates back to the eighth century B.C. and was dedicated to a royal steward of Judah named *Shebnayahu*. This may well be the tomb that is mentioned in Isaiah.

22:18 your splendid chariots: Perhaps a stately retinue that escorted the steward around from place to place (cf. 2 Sam 15:1).

22:20 my servant: An honorary designation for persons who are faithful to the Lord (see 20:3; Josh 1:1; Ps 89:3). **Eliakim:** Once installed in office as Shebna's successor, he will play

---

ⁱ The Hebrew of this line is obscure.

²¹and I will clothe him with your robe, and will bind your belt on him, and will commit your authority to his hand; and he shall be a father to the inhabitants of Jerusalem and to the house of Judah. ²²And I will place on his shoulder the key of the house of David; he shall open, and none shall shut; and he shall shut, and none shall open. ²³And I will fasten him like a peg in a sure place, and he will become a throne of honor to his father's house. ²⁴And they will hang on him the whole weight of his father's house, the offspring and issue, every small vessel, from the cups to all the flagons. ²⁵In that day, says the Lᴏʀᴅ of hosts, the peg that was fastened in a sure place will give way; and it will be cut down and fall, and the burden that was upon it will be cut off, for the Lᴏʀᴅ has spoken."

An Oracle concerning Tyre

23 The oracle concerning Tyre.

Wail, O ships of Tar'shish,
  for Tyre is laid waste, without house or haven!
From the land of Cyprus
  it is revealed to them.
²Be still, O inhabitants of the coast,
  O merchants of Si'don;
your messengers passed over the sea ʲ
³ and were on many waters;
your revenue was the grain of Shihor,
  the harvest of the Nile;
you were the merchant of the nations.

⁴Be ashamed, O Si'don, for the sea has
    spoken,
  the stronghold of the sea, saying:
"I have neither endured labor pains nor given
    birth,
  I have neither reared young men nor brought
    up virgins."
⁵When the report comes to Egypt,
  they will be in anguish over the report about
    Tyre.
⁶Pass over to Tar'shish,
  wail, O inhabitants of the coast!
⁷Is this your exultant city
  whose origin is from days of old,
 whose feet carried her
  to settle afar?
⁸Who has purposed this
  against Tyre, the bestower of crowns,
 whose merchants were princes,
  whose traders were the honored of the
    earth?
⁹The Lᴏʀᴅ of hosts has purposed it,
  to defile the pride of all glory,
  to dishonor all the honored of the
    earth.
¹⁰Overflow your land like the Nile,
  O daughter of Tar'shish;
  there is no restraint any more

22:22: Rev 3:7. **23:** Ezek 26:1– 28:19; Joel 3:4–8; Amos 1:9–10; Zech 9:3–4.

---

a leading role in Jerusalem's negotiations with the Assyrians in 701 B.C. (chaps. 36–37).

22:21 your robe ... your belt: Outward symbols of the royal steward's authority (Gen 41:41–44). **a father:** A paternal figurehead who is to act in the best interests of the people.

22:22 shoulder: Bears the weight of government responsibility, as in 9:6. Perhaps this alludes to a ceremony that involved placing a very large wooden key on the shoulder of the steward at his installation. **the key of the house of David:** Symbolic of the royal authority entrusted to the chief steward, who serves directly under the Davidic king. Being the king's representative, the steward is authorized to **open** and **shut** in his name, i.e., to make binding decisions bearing on the administration of the kingdom. • In the NT, Jesus is the messianic King from David's line who holds "the key of David" and thus wields full authority over his kingdom (Rev 3:7). At the same time, he elevates Peter to be his chief steward by entrusting him with "the keys of the kingdom", thereby investing him with the authority to bind and loose in matters pertaining to his kingdom on earth. See note on Mt 16:19.

22:23 like a peg: One that is hammered securely into a wall. **his father's house:** Either his extended family or possibly a reference to the royal house of David that he serves (22:22).

22:25 will give way: Eventually even the admirable Eliakim will break under the weight of his family's failings and come to judgment.

23:1–18 An oracle about the downfall (23:1–14) and recovery of Tyre (23:15–18). It is the last in the collection of Isaiah's oracles concerning the nations (chaps. 13–23). Just as this collection begins with divine judgment on Babylon, which took pride in its military might (13:11; 14:4), so it ends with

divine judgment on Tyre, which took pride in its commercial wealth (23:9). The lesson for Judah is that security is found only in the Lord, not in alliances with powerful nations, which, if God so wills it, can quickly come to nothing despite their material strength.

23:1 Tyre: The leading port city of Phoenicia, a coastal region north of Israel, and the center of a lucrative trading empire in ancient times. Sennacherib, king of Assyria, attacked the city of Tyre around 701 B.C. **ships of Tarshish:** Large merchant vessels built for shipping cargo over long distances. Poetically speaking, the ships mourn the financial losses that result from Tyre's demise. See note on 23:10.

23:2 Sidon: Another coastal city of Phoenicia, north of Tyre.

23:3 grain of Shihor: The food that Tyre imported from Egypt on grain ships. News of Tyre's fall is bad news for her many business partners around the Mediterranean (23:5). **merchant of the nations:** For Tyre's fame as a commercial tycoon, see Ezek 27:12–25.

23:7 to settle afar: The Phoenicians founded multiple colonies within sailing distance (e.g., in Cyprus, Sardinia, North Africa, Spain).

23:9 The Lᴏʀᴅ of hosts: See note on 1:9. **the pride of all glory:** The besetting sin of nations who imagine themselves secure on the basis of their resources and accomplishments economic, military, or otherwise—apart from reliance on the one true God. Human pride and earthly glory are often singled out as the targets of God's judgment in Isaiah's oracles against the nations (13:11, 19; 14:4, 12–15; 16:6; 17:4; 21:16).

23:10 daughter: Language that Isaiah uses to personify ancient cities (e.g., Sidon, 23:12; Jerusalem, 37:22; Babylon, 47:1). **Tarshish:** Perhaps Tartessos in southern Spain, where the Phoenicians had established a mining colony in the second millennium B.C. Another possibility is that Tarshish is a reference to Tarsus in Asia Minor (Josephus, *Antiquities of the Jews* 1, 127).

ʲ One ancient Ms: Heb *who passed over the sea, they replenished you.*

¹¹He has stretched out his hand over the sea,
he has shaken the kingdoms;
the LORD has given command concerning
Canaan
to destroy its strongholds.
¹²And he said:
"You will no more exult,
O oppressed virgin daughter of Si′don;
arise, pass over to Cyprus,
even there you will have no rest."

13 Behold the land of the Chalde′ans! This is the people; it was not Assyria. They destined Tyre for wild beasts. They erected their siege towers, they razed her palaces, they made her a ruin.ᵏ
¹⁴Wail, O ships of Tar′shish,
for your stronghold is laid waste.
¹⁵In that day Tyre will be forgotten for seventy years, like the days of one king. At the end of seventy years, it will happen to Tyre as in the song of the harlot:
¹⁶"Take a harp,
go about the city,
O forgotten harlot!
Make sweet melody,
sing many songs,
that you may be remembered."

¹⁷At the end of seventy years, the LORD will visit Tyre, and she will return to her hire, and will play the harlot with all the kingdoms of the world upon the face of the earth. ¹⁸Her merchandise and her hire will be dedicated to the LORD; it will not be stored or hoarded, but her merchandise will supply abundant food and fine clothing for those who dwell before the LORD.

Impending Judgment on the Earth

24 Behold, the LORD will lay waste the earth and make it desolate,
and he will twist its surface and scatter its
inhabitants.
²And it shall be, as with the people, so with the
priest;
as with the slave, so with his master;
as with the maid, so with her mistress;
as with the buyer, so with the seller;
as with the lender, so with the borrower;
as with the creditor, so with the debtor.
³The earth shall be utterly laid waste and utterly
despoiled;
for the LORD has spoken this word.
⁴The earth mourns and withers,
the world languishes and withers;
the heavens languish together with the
earth.

23:17: Rev 17:2.

23:11 stretched out his hand: The Lord is ready to strike a devastating blow. See note on 5:25. **Canaan:** Its northernmost extent included Tyre and Sidon (Gen 10:19).

23:13 Chaldeans ... not Assyria: The RSV2CE translates and punctuates this verse to say that the Chaldeans (= Babylonians) are the conquerors of Tyre rather than a people conquered by others. Scholars who understand the passage this way suggest the historical background is the Babylonian siege of Tyre under Nebuchadnezzar (605–562 B.C.). However, the verse can also be translated: "Behold the land of the Chaldeans, the people who are not. Assyria destined Tyre for wild beasts." On this reading, the prophet recalls Assyria's subjugation of Babylon in 703 B.C. to warn that the same fate awaits Tyre, which was subdued by Assyria around 701 B.C.

23:15 seventy years: Stands for a temporary period (ca. 700–630 B.C.) when Tyre is brought low and forced out of business by the judgments of God. Afterward, Tyre will again pursue her partners in trade like a prostitute seeking clients. It is Tyre's idolatrous drive to amass wealth that is met with God's disapproval. **the harlot:** An image used earlier of sinful Jerusalem (1:21).

23:18 dedicated to the LORD: The conversion of Tyre appears to be in view. Initially it will resume its old ways; but eventually its wealth will stream into Israel. Similar prophecies in 45:14 and 60:4–14 portray Gentiles acknowledging the God of Israel and bringing their riches to his people and Temple. Since Deut 23:18 forbids dedicating a prostitute's income to the Lord's sanctuary, Tyre's riches cannot be deposited in the Temple but will be used to purchase **food** and **clothing**.

24:1—27:13 The Isaiah Apocalypse, a collection of oracles that envision universal judgment and final salvation. Expanding beyond the horizons of chaps. 13–23, which stress the Lord's sovereignty over individual nations, chaps. 24–27 affirm his sovereignty over the world. **(1)** *Literarily*, the chapters may be called proto-apocalyptic, i.e., they employ images and themes that reappear in more developed form in later Jewish and Christian writings classified as apocalyptic (such as Daniel and Revelation). The chapters are also interspersed with songs of praise and celebration sung by the redeemed (25:1–5, 9; 26:1–21; 27:2–5). **(2)** *Historically*, these prophecies concern the fall of Babylon in the sixth century B.C. The city that wrought devastation throughout the Near East (13:5, 9) will itself be brought to judgment (13:11–13). At the center of the drama stand two unnamed cities, most likely Babylon (24:10; 25:2; 26:5) and Jerusalem (26:1; 27:10). **(3)** *Eschatologically*, Isaiah also looks beyond the sixth century B.C. to a time when the Lord will establish his kingdom in Jerusalem (24:23), a time when Gentiles will glorify the God of Israel (25:3) and learn righteousness (26:9). On an even more distant horizon, the prophet glimpses the final end of death and sorrow (25:8), the resurrection of the dead (26:19), and God's punishment of all wicked powers in heaven and earth (24:21–22; 27:1). **(4)** *Theologically*, although these prophecies are firmly anchored in history, the events envisioned function as typology. Babylon, in addition to being a city of the past, represents the arrogance of mankind in general, which will one day face the Lord's humbling judgment. Jerusalem, by contrast, represents the people who trust in the Lord and praise him for salvation.

24:1 lay waste the earth: A universal judgment that has an impact on the lives of everyone at every level of society (24:2).

24:4–6 Creation suffers the effects of human sin (Gen 3:17; Hos 4:1–3). • The prophet describes the coming judgment by alluding to the story of Noah, only this time the world is not drowned in a flood but scorched by a severe drought. Parallels with the story of the flood include **(1)** pollution of **the earth** by violence (24:5; 26:21; Gen 6:11);

ᵏThe Hebrew of this verse is obscure.

⁵The earth lies polluted
  under its inhabitants;
for they have transgressed the laws,
  violated the statutes,
  broken the everlasting covenant.
⁶Therefore a curse devours the earth,
  and its inhabitants suffer for their guilt;
therefore the inhabitants of the earth are
    scorched,
  and few men are left.
⁷The wine mourns,
  the vine languishes,
  all the merry-hearted sigh.
⁸The mirth of the timbrels is stilled,
  the noise of the jubilant has ceased,
  the mirth of the lyre is stilled.
⁹No more do they drink wine with singing;
  strong drink is bitter to those who drink it.
¹⁰The city of chaos is broken down,
  every house is shut up so that none can enter.
¹¹There is an outcry in the streets for lack of wine;
  all joy has reached its eventide;
  the gladness of the earth is banished.
¹²Desolation is left in the city,
  the gates are battered into ruins.
¹³For thus it shall be in the midst of the earth
  among the nations,
as when an olive tree is beaten,
as at the gleaning when the vintage is done.

¹⁴They lift up their voices, they sing for joy;
  over the majesty of the Lord they shout from
    the west.
¹⁵Therefore in the east give glory to the Lord;
  in the islands of the sea, to the name of the
    Lord, the God of Israel.

¹⁶From the ends of the earth we hear songs of
    praise,
  of glory to the Righteous One.
But I say, "I pine away,
  I pine away. Woe is me!
For the treacherous deal treacherously,
  the treacherous deal very treacherously."
¹⁷Terror, and the pit, and the snare are upon you,
  O inhabitant of the earth!
¹⁸He who flees at the sound of the terror
  shall fall into the pit;
and he who climbs out of the pit shall be caught
  in the snare.
For the windows of heaven are opened,
  and the foundations of the earth tremble.
¹⁹The earth is utterly broken,
  the earth is torn apart,
  the earth is violently shaken.
²⁰The earth staggers like a drunken man,
  it sways like a hut;
its transgression lies heavy upon it,
  and it falls, and will not rise again.

²¹On that day the Lord will punish
  the host of heaven, in heaven,
  and the kings of the earth, on the earth.
²²They will be gathered together
  as prisoners in a pit;
they will be shut up in a prison,
  and after many days they will be punished.
²³Then the moon will be confounded,
  and the sun ashamed;
for the Lord of hosts will reign
  on Mount Zion and in Jerusalem
and before his elders he will manifest his
  glory.

24:8: Rev 18:22.

---

(2) mention of God's **everlasting covenant** (24:5; Gen 9:16); **(3)** the **curse** that afflicts the land (24:6; Gen 8:21); **(4)** a remnant of **few** survivors (24:6; Gen 7:23); and **(5)** a reference to the opening of **the windows of heaven** (24:18; Gen 7:11).

24:5 transgressed the laws: Especially the law against bloodshed (26:21; Gen 9:5–6). **the everlasting covenant:** The covenant that God established with Noah (Gen 9:11), which is a renewed form of the covenant that God established with creation in the beginning. See notes on Gen 1:1–2:4 and 6:18.

24:10 The city of chaos: Babylon in the throes of divine judgment.

24:13 beaten … done: Survivors will be as scarce as the small amount of fruit that remains after orchards and vineyards have been harvested.

24:14 lift up their voices: I.e., praising and glorifying God, the response of Israelite exiles scattered among the nations (27:12–13) as well as Gentile converts from among the nations (25:3).

24:16 Woe is me!: Isaiah uttered the same cry when he saw the Lord in heavenly majesty (6:5).

24:17–18 The prophet Jeremiah speaks in similar terms in Jer 48:43–44.

24:18 opened … tremble: A torrential downpour that coincides with an earthquake.

24:21 On that day: The day of the Lord's judgment and salvation. Several oracles in this section of Isaiah are given this time stamp (25:9; 26:1; 27:1, 2, 12). See note on 2:12. **host of heaven:** The sun, moon, and stars, which Israel's neighbors worshiped as astral deities (Deut 4:19; Jer 8:2; 19:13).

24:22 prisoners in a pit: Rebel spirits and kings will be detained in the netherworld to await their final sentencing. This vision seemingly gave rise to a later Jewish tradition regarding disobedient angels, known as the Watchers, being imprisoned in the gloom of the underworld until the full measure of their punishment is imposed (*1 Enoch* 14, 5; 18:14). • Several passages of the NT also have links with Isaiah's vision, e.g., those that depict Satan and the fallen angels as captives in the netherworld of Hades, also called the abyss (2 Pet 2:4; Jude 6; Rev 20:1–3).

24:23 the moon will be confounded: Upheaval in the heavens appears in several prophetic and apocalyptic texts that foretell the ominous "day of the Lord" (13:9–10; 34:4; Ezek 32:7–8; Joel 2:30–31; Amos 8:9). **the Lord of hosts will reign:** God will establish his kingdom in connection with his coming cosmic judgment (Rev 11:15–18). **before his elders:** Alludes to the messianic banquet on Mount Zion, described in 25:6–8. The feast will recall the covenant meal shared by the elders of Israel on Mount Sinai (Ex 24:9–11).

51

Praise for Deliverance from Oppression

25 O Lord, you are my God;
    I will exalt you, I will praise your name;
for you have done wonderful things,
    plans formed of old, faithful and sure.
²For you have made the city a heap,
    the fortified city a ruin;
the palace of strangers is a city no more,
    it will never be rebuilt.
³Therefore strong peoples will glorify you;
    cities of ruthless nations will fear you.
⁴For you have been a stronghold to the poor,
    a stronghold to the needy in his distress,
    a shelter from the storm and a shade from the
        heat;
for the blast of the ruthless is like a storm against
    a wall,
⁵   like heat in a dry place.
You subdue the noise of the strangers;
    as heat by the shade of a cloud,
    so the song of the ruthless is stilled.

6 On this mountain the Lord of hosts will make for all peoples a feast of fat things, a feast of choice wines—of fat things full of marrow, of choice wines well refined. ⁷And he will destroy on this mountain the covering that is cast over all peoples, the veil that is spread over all nations. ⁸He will swallow up death for ever, and the Lord God will wipe away tears from all faces, and the reproach of his people he will take away from all the earth, for the Lord has spoken.

9 It will be said on that day, "Behold, this is our God; we have waited for him, that he might save us. This is the Lord; we have waited for him; let us be glad and rejoice in his salvation."

10 For the hand of the Lord will rest on this mountain, and Moab shall be trodden down in his place, as straw is trodden down in a dung-pit. ¹¹And he will spread out his hands in the midst of it as a swimmer spreads his hands out to swim; but the Lord will lay low his pride together with the skill[1] of his hands. ¹²And the high fortifications of his walls he will bring down, lay low, and cast to the ground, even to the dust.

Judah's Song of Praise to God

26 In that day this song will be sung in the land of Judah:

25:8: 1 Cor 15:54; Rev 7:17; 21:4.　**25:10–12:** Is 15–16; Jer 48; Ezek 25:8–11; Amos 2:1–3; Zeph 2:8–11.

25:1 you are my God: Salvation is experienced in a truly personal way, in addition to being a blessing for entire peoples and nations. **plans formed of old:** History unfolds according to the Lord's purposes determined long ago, as described in 14:24–27.

25:2 the city a heap: Babylon is brought low (13:19; 21:9). Isaiah's vision of total conquest may encompass several events beginning with the Persian takeover of Babylon under Cyrus II in 539 B.C. and culminating with the Greek overthrow of the city by Alexander the Great in 332 B.C.

25:4 the poor ... needy: The afflicted of Israel, whether captives in exile or survivors who remain behind in the land (14:32). **shelter ... shade:** God protects his people from the hostile forces of the world, here depicted as a thunderstorm and sweltering heat (4:6).

25:5 the song of the ruthless: The victory chants of the Babylonians fall silent, just as all celebratory music falls silent in 24:8–9.

📖🕊 **25:6–8** A banquet on Mount Zion to which the entire world is invited. The Lord is the host of this eschatological feast, which is a grand celebration of his kingship (24:23). It will feature an extravagant spread of **fat things** (meat from well-fed animals) and **choice wines** (well-aged and finely strained vintage), and the guests at table are given a share in everlasting life and happiness when the Lord swallows up death forever (25:8). The future banquet on Zion is one aspect of Isaiah's teaching that Jerusalem will be glorified (4:5) and will become a place to which all nations will flow (2:1–2). It is also related to promises that God will feed his people (40:11) with an abundance of food and drink (23:18; 55:1–2; 62:8–9). Isaiah's vision inspired later Jewish writings that link the joys of the world to come with foods that confer immortality on those who eat them (e.g., *1 Enoch* 25, 3–7; *Joseph and Asenath* 16, 8–16). • Jesus evokes this vision when he depicts the kingdom of God as both a pilgrimage banquet (Mt 8:11; Lk 13:29) and a wedding banquet (Mt 22:1–14; Lk 14:15–

24). His teaching on the Eucharist even describes sacramental communion—eating the flesh and drinking the blood of the Son of Man—as a means of receiving eternal life (Jn 6:53–58). The Book of Revelation evokes Isaiah's prophecy when it envisions the demise of death, the wiping away of every tear, and the wedding supper of the Lamb (Rev 7:17; 19:7–9; 21:4). • The Lord will make for all peoples, not just for the people of Israel, a feast of wine and joy. The joy is founded on our hope in Christ, since we will reign with him and enjoy spiritual delights that surpass understanding. By wine is meant the mystical sacrament, the unbloody sacrifice we celebrate in the churches (St. Cyril of Alexandria, *Commentary on Isaiah* 25, 6–7).

25:6 all peoples: The prophecy is all-inclusive, referring to "all peoples" and "all nations" (25:7) as well as "all faces" and "all the earth" (25:8).

25:7 the covering: A burial shroud, which was spread over the nations by God's judgments in chaps. 13–23. Doing away with this covering is tantamount to a promise of resurrection and new life. Others identify the covering as a garment worn by mourners or as a veil that restricts vision (cf. 2 Cor 3:14).

📖 **25:8 He will swallow up death:** The image of God swallowing death is a reversal of 5:14, where death manifests its power as an insatiable appetite for the living. • Paul, who proclaims God's triumph over death in Jesus (2 Tim 1:10), cites this passage as support for the resurrection of the saints to a state of glory and immortality (1 Cor 15:54). **the reproach of his people:** This language is often used for Gentiles mocking the Israelites in exile (Deut 28:37; Ps 44:13–16; Ezek 5:14–15). Here the Gentiles are included alongside Israel as the Lord's "people", as in 19:25.

25:10 the hand of the Lord: The Lord's power to save (25:9). **Moab:** A longstanding enemy of Judah, east of the Dead Sea. Utter humiliation awaits the Moabites for their pride (25:11; cf. 16:6–14).

26:1–6 A hymn of thanksgiving for the Lord's salvation (as in 12:1–6).

26:1 a strong city: A redeemed Jerusalem. **walls and bulwarks:** Saving protection for the city, unlike the "walls" and "fortifications" of Moab, which are thrown down (25:12).

---

[1] The meaning of the Hebrew word is uncertain.

"We have a strong city;
 he sets up salvation
 as walls and bulwarks.
²Open the gates,
 that the righteous nation which keeps faith
 may enter in.
³You keep him in perfect peace,
 whose mind is stayed on you,
 because he trusts in you.
⁴Trust in the Lord for ever,
 for the Lord God
 is an everlasting rock.
⁵For he has brought low
 the inhabitants of the height,
 the lofty city.
He lays it low, lays it low to the ground,
 casts it to the dust.
⁶The foot tramples it,
 the feet of the poor,
 the steps of the needy."

⁷The way of the righteous is level;
 you^m make smooth the path of the righteous.
⁸In the path of your judgments,
 O Lord, we wait for you;
your memorial name
 is the desire of our soul.
⁹My soul yearns for you in the night,
 my spirit within me earnestly seeks you.
For when your judgments are in the earth,
 the inhabitants of the world learn
 righteousness.
¹⁰If favor is shown to the wicked,
 he does not learn righteousness;
in the land of uprightness he deals perversely
 and does not see the majesty of the Lord.
¹¹O Lord, your hand is lifted up,
 but they see it not.

Let them see your zeal for your people, and be
 ashamed.
 Let the fire for your adversaries consume
 them.
¹²O Lord, you will ordain peace for us,
 you have wrought for us all our works.
¹³O Lord our God,
 other lords besides you have ruled over us,
 but your name alone we acknowledge.
¹⁴They are dead, they will not live;
 they are shades, they will not arise;
 to that end you have visited them with
 destruction
 and wiped out all remembrance of them.
¹⁵But you have increased the nation, O Lord,
 you have increased the nation; you are
 glorified;
 you have enlarged all the borders of the
 land.

¹⁶O Lord, in distress they sought you,
 they poured out a prayer^n
 when your chastening was upon them.
¹⁷Like a woman with child,
 who writhes and cries out in her pangs,
 when she is near her time,
 so were we because of you, O Lord;
¹⁸ we were with child, we writhed,
 but we gave birth only to wind.
 We have wrought no deliverance in the earth,
 and the inhabitants of the world have not
 fallen.
¹⁹Your dead shall live, their bodies^o shall rise.
 O dwellers in the dust, awake and sing for
 joy!
 For your dew is a dew of light,
 and on the land of the shades you will let it
 fall.

26:2 Open the gates: To welcome pilgrims who are streaming to Zion (Ps 118:19–20) in order to attend the Lord's banquet (25:6). **the righteous nation:** Not simply Israel or Judah, but any nation that comes to learn righteousness through the chastening of divine judgment (26:9).

26:4 Trust in the Lord: Patient reliance on the Lord, believing that his promises will be fulfilled, is a hallmark of Isaiah's preaching (see 7:9; 12:2; 33:2). **rock:** The Lord, pictured as a fortress of defense for those who take refuge in him (2 Sam 22:2).

26:5 the lofty city: The prideful city of Babylon, destined for humiliation and destruction (21:9; 24:10; 25:2).

26:10 the wicked: Sometimes need chastisement to come to repentance (26:9).

26:11 your hand is lifted up: The Lord is ready to strike a punishing blow.

26:12 you have wrought ... our works: An acknowledgment that Israel's successes are the result of God's powerful work among them. As such, the passage is an early expression of the theology of grace (cf. Ps 44:1–3).

26:13 other lords: Foreign kings who ruled over the Israelites in the past.

26:14 shades: The souls of the dead pictured as shadows in the darkness of the underworld, known as Sheol or the Pit.

26:17 Like a woman with child: The suffering of God's people is compared to the pangs of childbirth (Mic 4:9–10; Jn 16:21).

26:19 Your dead shall live: One of the clearest affirmations of bodily resurrection in the OT. Some interpret the language of this text as a metaphor signifying the restoration of Israel from exile among the nations, as in Ezek 37:1–14. More likely the point is that new life will come to the departed, reviving their spirits in the darkness of Sheol and reawakening their bodies from the dust of the grave, as in Dan 12:1–3. That Judaism came to believe in a future resurrection of the dead, see 2 Mac 7:9, 14. **their bodies shall rise:** The Hebrew expression is singular ("my body"), apparently intended as a collective ("my corpses"). The Greek LXX reads: "those in the tombs will be raised." **dust:** The human body reverts to this disintegrated state after death (Gen 3:19; Job 21:26; Ps 104:29). **dew:** A reviving source of life following the long night of death (cf. Ps 133:3).

---

^m Cn Compare Gk: Heb *thou (that art) upright.*
^n Heb uncertain.
^o Cn Compare Syr Tg: Heb *my body.*

²⁰Come, my people, enter your chambers,
  and shut your doors behind you;
 hide yourselves for a little while
  until the wrath is past.
²¹For behold, the LORD is coming forth out of his
   place
  to punish the inhabitants of the earth for their
   iniquity,
 and the earth will disclose the blood shed upon
   her,
  and will no more cover her slain.

Israel's Expiation

27 In that day the LORD with his hard and great
and strong sword will punish Levi′athan the
fleeing serpent, Leviathan the twisting serpent, and
he will slay the dragon that is in the sea.

²In that day:
 "A pleasant vineyard, sing of it!
³ I, the LORD, am its keeper;
  every moment I water it.
 Lest any one harm it,
  I guard it night and day;
⁴ I have no wrath.
 Would that I had thorns and briers to battle!
  I would set out against them,
  I would burn them up together.
⁵Or let them lay hold of my protection,
  let them make peace with me,
  let them make peace with me."

⁶In days to come^q Jacob shall take root,
  Israel shall blossom and put forth shoots,
  and fill the whole world with fruit.

⁷Has he struck them down as he struck those who
   struck them?
  Or have they been slain as their slayers were
   slain?
⁸Measure by measure,^r by exile you contended
   with them;
  he removed them with his fierce blast in the
   day of the east wind.
⁹Therefore by this the guilt of Jacob will be expiated,
  and this will be the full fruit of the removal of
   his sin:
 when he makes all the stones of the altars
  like chalkstones crushed to pieces,
 no Ashe′rim or incense altars will remain
  standing.
¹⁰For the fortified city is solitary,
  a habitation deserted and forsaken, like the
   wilderness;
 there the calf grazes,
  there he lies down, and strips its branches.
¹¹When its boughs are dry, they are broken;
  women come and make a fire of them.
 For this is a people without discernment;
  therefore he who made them will not have
   compassion on them,
 he that formed them will show them no favor.

26:20 the wrath: The divine judgment announced in 24:1.

27:1 In that day: The first verse of chap. 27 is the final verse of the judgment oracle in 26:20–21. The chapter divisions that appear in modern Bibles were devised in the Middles Ages and do not always correspond to the original author's intentions. **Leviathan:** A sea monster that represents primordial chaos in ancient Semitic mythology. The Bible depicts him as a serpent with multiple heads (Ps 74:14) that lives at the bottom of the sea (Amos 9:3) and that can be roused to bring curses upon the world (Job 3:8). Although a terrifying menace to mortals, Leviathan is no match for the Lord, who has the power to subdue him (Ps 104:26). In the NT, the multi-headed dragon is unmasked as the devil (Rev 12:3, 9). Some scholars hold that, in Isaiah's vision, Leviathan is a symbol of Babylon, the city that God will punish with a **sword** for its monstrous wickedness (see Jer 50:35–38). Perhaps such an event is foretold in this prophecy; if so, it is only a partial fulfillment of a more ultimate promise, namely, that God will destroy the devil and all the agents of evil at the end of time (Rev 20:7–10). See word study: *Leviathan* at Job 41:1.

27:2–6 A new Song of the Vineyard. It looks beyond the time of judgment announced in the first Song of the Vineyard in 5:1–7. In the earlier song, the vineyard of Israel produced wild grapes, and so God left it unprotected, allowed it to be overrun by briers and thorns, and deprived it of rain. In this song, the vineyard of Israel is restored. The Lord will water and

protect it (27:3), keep it free of briers and thorns (27:4), and cause it to fill the world with fruit (27:6).

27:3 its keeper: For the Lord as the Guardian of his people, see Ps 121:1–8.

27:4 Would that I: The Lord desires to prove his love by defending his beloved from attack. **thorns and briers:** Nations formerly hostile to Israel are now called to seek reconciliation with God (27:5).

27:8 Measure by measure: The chastisement of Israel is carefully administered so as not to be more severe than necessary. Scripture teaches that God disciplines his people like a father disciplines a son whom he loves (Deut 8:5; Prov 3:11–12; Heb 12:5–11). **by exile:** Not stated explicitly in the Hebrew but implied by the language of "removal" from the land. According to the next verse, the suffering and scattering of Israel among foreign nations is meant to induce repentance, especially the repudiation of idolatry (as in 17:7–8). **the east wind:** The hot and dry wind that blows into Israel from Arabia. It symbolizes the onset of judgment.

27:9 this ... removal of his sin: The Greek LXX reads slightly differently, with the Lord saying: "this is his blessing, when I take away his sin." • Paul quotes this verse in Rom 11:27, in combination with Is 59:20–21 and Jer 31:33, to verify that Jesus offers forgiveness to Jacob (= Israel) through the New Covenant. **altars:** Used to make sacrifices to other gods. Israel was supposed to have destroyed these altars upon entering the Promised Land (Ex 34:13; Deut 7:5). **Asherim:** Wooden poles or trees dedicated to the Canaanite goddess Asherah. See note on 17:8.

27:10 the fortified city: Appears to be Babylon, which is described in this way in 25:2. Also, Isaiah stated earlier that God intended to make Babylon desolate (13:19–22).

---

^qHeb *Those to come.*
^rCompare Syr Vg Tg: The meaning of the Hebrew word is unknown.

¹²In that day from the river Euphra'tes to the Brook of Egypt the Lᴏʀᴅ will thresh out the grain, and you will be gathered one by one, O people of Israel. ¹³And in that day a great trumpet will be blown, and those who were lost in the land of Assyria and those who were driven out to the land of Egypt will come and worship the Lᴏʀᴅ on the holy mountain at Jerusalem.

Warning to Jerusalem

28 Woe to the proud crown of the drunkards of E'phraim,

and to the fading flower of its glorious beauty,
which is on the head of the rich valley of those
overcome with wine!
²Behold, the Lord has one who is mighty and strong;
like a storm of hail, a destroying tempest,

like a storm of mighty, overflowing waters,
he will cast down to the earth with violence.
³The proud crown of the drunkards of E'phraim
will be trodden under foot;
⁴and the fading flower of its glorious beauty,
which is on the head of the rich valley,
will be like a first-ripe fig before the summer:
when a man sees it, he eats it up
as soon as it is in his hand.

⁵In that day the Lᴏʀᴅ of hosts will be a crown of glory,
and a diadem of beauty, to the remnant of his people;
⁶and a spirit of justice to him who sits in judgment,

27:13: Mt 24:31; 1 Cor 15:52; 1 Thess 4:16.

27:12–13 The conclusion to the Isaiah Apocalypse (= chaps 24–27). It restates the promise of 11:11–12 that the Lord will recover the lost exiles of Israel and Judah from their dispersion among foreign nations. Isaiah views this as the ingathering of a grain harvest that stretches throughout the Near East from Egypt to Assyria (cf. Jer 50:17–20).

27:12 Euphrates to the Brook of Egypt: The full extent of the land promised to Abraham (Gen 15:18) and ruled for a time by Solomon (1 Kings 4:21). Beyond these outer limits lie the lands of exile, Egypt and Assyria. Even the Gentiles among them will join Israel in worshiping the Lord as members of his covenant people (19:23–25).

27:13 great trumpet: Signals a Jubilee release from captivity (as in Lev 25:8–10) and a summons for God's people to assemble for worship (as in Num 29:1–6 and Joel 2:15). See word study: *Trumpet* at Judg 6:34. • Isaiah's prophecy informs select NT prophecies. Jesus foretells the ingathering of God's elect at the sound of a great trumpet (Mt 24:31), and Paul speaks of a trumpet call that announces the resurrection of the saints from the dead (1 Cor 15:52; 1 Thess 4:16). **the holy mountain:** Zion, the center of the coming kingdom of God (24:23) and the focal point of salvation and worship for Israel and the nations (2.2–4, 25:6–8; 66:18–20).

28:1–39:8 The central section of Isaiah shifts from prophetic visions of the future (chaps. 13–27) to the historical setting of the prophet's ministry in the eighth century B.C. Judah and Jerusalem, threatened by the rise of Assyria, face the dilemma of choosing between reliance on the Lord and putting trust in a political alliance with Egypt (30:1–2; 31:1).

Hezekiah of Judah stands out in this section as a faithful king whose trust in God results in the miraculous deliverance of Jerusalem in 701 B.C. (33:20–22; 37:14–37).

28:1–33:24 Chapters 28–33 are a collection of "woe" oracles (28:1; 29:1, 15; 30:1; 31:1; 33:1).

28:1–13 A message that Isaiah delivered against the Northern Kingdom of Israel prior to the fall of Samaria in 722 B.C. It functions in this context as a warning to the Southern Kingdom of Judah, which is committing the same sins that brought ruin on the north. In terms of focus, the prophet scolds both ruling and religious authorities for failing to provide trustworthy leadership for God's people.

28:1 proud crown: A flowery or leafy head garland that represents the festive atmosphere in Samaria, the capital of the Northern Kingdom. **drunkards:** Includes the religious leaders, i.e., the priests and prophets (28:7). **Ephraim:** Another name for the Northern Kingdom of Israel, its dominant tribe being the tribe of Ephraim. **rich valley:** The city of Samaria sits in a fertile valley.

28:2 one who is mighty: Assyria, the nation that God will use to bring judgment on Samaria (10:5–6; 2 Kings 17:1–6). **overflowing waters:** Recalls the description of Assyria in 8:7–8.

28:4 like a first-ripe fig: Samaria, ripe for destruction, will be easily conquered.

28:5 a crown of glory: The glorious kingship of the Lord (33:22) in contrast to the prideful and corrupt monarchy in Samaria (28:1). **remnant:** The few survivors of the north who will escape death and deportation when Samaria falls.

WORD STUDY

Woe (28:1)

Hôy (Heb.): An interjection that appears roughly 50 times in the OT. The word is variously translated "Woe", "Alas", "Ah", or "Ho". It originated as a cry of anguish and lament uttered by persons mourning the dead (1 Kings 13:30; Jer 34:5). In some cases, however, death is not a fact of the recent past but a future prospect. Thus, when a prophet utters a "woe" on himself, he seems to despair for his life (Is 6:5). Ordinarily, prophets pronounce "woes" as warnings that God's judgments (= the curses of the covenant) are ready to fall on sinful cities or nations (Is 10:5; Jer 48:1; Ezek 13:3; Amos 5:18; Mic 2:1; Nah 3:1; Zech 11:17). These sayings function as denunciations of evildoing as well as urgent appeals for repentance. The underlying idea is that recipients of a woe oracle are following a path that leads to death. At times the "woes" of the prophets are strung together into a tight sequence of warnings and threats (Hab 2:6, 9, 12, 15, 19). In Isaiah, one encounters both a succession of woe oracles (Is 5:8, 11, 18, 20, 21, 22) as well as a larger collection of sayings punctuated by intermittent pronouncements of woe (Is 28:1; 29:1, 15; 30:1; 31:1; 33:1).

and strength to those who turn back the battle
  at the gate.

⁷These also reel with wine
  and stagger with strong drink;
the priest and the prophet reel with strong drink,
  they are confused with wine,
  they stagger with strong drink;
they err in vision,
  they stumble in giving judgment.
⁸For all tables are full of vomit,
  no place is without filthiness.

⁹"Whom will he teach knowledge,
  and to whom will he explain the message?
Those who are weaned from the milk,
  those taken from the breast?
¹⁰For it is precept upon precept, precept upon
    precept,
  line upon line, line upon line,
  here a little, there a little."

¹¹No, but by men of strange lips
  and with an alien tongue
the Lord will speak to this people,
¹² to whom he has said,
"This is rest;
  give rest to the weary;

and this is repose";
  yet they would not hear.
¹³Therefore the word of the Lord will be to them
  precept upon precept, precept upon precept,
  line upon line, line upon line,
  here a little, there a little;
that they may go, and fall backward,
  and be broken, and snared, and taken.

¹⁴Therefore hear the word of the Lord, you
    scoffers,
  who rule this people in Jerusalem!
¹⁵Because you have said, "We have made a
    covenant with death,
  and with Sheol we have an agreement;
when the overwhelming scourge passes through
  it will not come to us;
for we have made lies our refuge,
  and in falsehood we have taken shelter";
¹⁶therefore thus says the Lord God,
  "Behold, I am laying in Zion for a foundation
    a stone, a tested stone,
  a precious cornerstone, of a sure foundation:
  'He who believes will not be in haste.'
¹⁷And I will make justice the line,
  and righteousness the plummet;
and hail will sweep away the refuge of lies,
  and waters will overwhelm the shelter."

28:11–12: 1 Cor 14:21.   **28:12:** Mt 11:29.   **28:16:** Rom 9:33; 10:11; 1 Pet 2:4–6.

28:7 they err ... they stumble: Ephraim's religious leaders are caught up in the drunken revelry. Isaiah views this as a symptom of God's judgment, which he compares to a spiritual stupor in 29:9.

28:10 precept upon precept, line upon line: The Hebrew is a string of gibberish. Sounds such as these were apparently uttered in mockery of Isaiah, and perhaps of other prophets, whose warnings against Samaria were dismissed as childish babble. The Lord's punishment will thus fit the crime: Samaria and the kingdom of Israel, unwilling to hear the word of God, will be overrun by foreign conquerors speaking a foreign language (28:11–13). • Rejecting divine instruction, the drunkards of Ephraim will be forced to suffer the curses of the covenant spelled out in Deut 28:49–51.

28:11 men of strange lips: Assyrians, who speak a language unknown to the common folk in Judah (Aramaic, 36:11). • Paul cites this passage in 1 Cor 14:21 to make a point about the charismatic gift of tongues. Although speaking in tongues is a gift of the Spirit, it brings limited benefit to the worshiping congregation unless someone is present to interpret what is said (1 Cor 14:1–5). Furthermore, as in Isaiah's prophecy, speaking in tongues that no one understands can be a sign of judgment for unbelievers (or "the unfaithful"), i.e., for those who are unwilling to heed clear instruction (1 Cor 14:22).

28:13 fall ... broken ... snared ... taken: The language of defeat and exile, as in 8:15.

28:14 scoffers: Those who ridicule the wisdom of trusting in God.

28:15 a covenant with death: An alliance that Judah made with Egypt in order to protect itself from an Assyrian assault (see 30:1–5; 31:1–3). Isaiah warns that such a treaty, which is based on human calculations apart from any spiritual discernment or trust in the Lord, is doomed to failure (28:18). **Sheol:** Hebrew name for the netherworld of the dead. See word study: *Sheol* at Num 16:30. **the overwhelming scourge:** Assyria's invasion of Judah, which will come when Hezekiah refuses to pay tribute (2 Kings 18:7–8). The term "overwhelming" can also be translated "overflowing", suggesting the image of a catastrophic flood, as in 8:8.

28:16 I am laying in Zion: The Lord lays a foundation for true security in contrast to the false "refuge" and "shelter" constructed by Jerusalem's leaders (28:15). This is done on Mount Zion, the twin center of Davidic rule and divine worship in Israel. Here the Lord will accomplish a new work, pictured as the building of a new Temple and a new fulfillment of God's covenant with David (2 Sam 7:12–16). Like the sanctuary built by David's son, Solomon, this one will rest on a costly stone foundation (1 Kings 5:17). **cornerstone:** Seems to represent the Davidic monarchy, which the Lord established on Zion (Ps 2:6) and for the sake of which he will defend Zion from destruction by the Assyrians (37:35). The Davidic covenant is also the foundation of Israel's hope for a coming Messiah (9:1–6; 11:1–10). In the Aramaic *Targum of Isaiah*, the stone is identified as "a strong king" (= the Messiah). **He who believes:** An inscription on the cornerstone, indicating that the Zion stone is a secure basis for Israel's faith. **will not be in haste:** I.e., will have no reason to panic. The Greek LXX reads: "will not be put to shame". • Isaiah 28:16 is a messianic prophecy about Jesus. He is the stone in Zion who offers salvation to all who believe in him (Rom 9:33; 10:11) and the cornerstone of a new and living Temple made of believers indwelt by the Holy Spirit (Eph 2:19–22; 1 Pet 2:4–6). • Faith is the foundation of justice, and the just man builds justice on faith, as when he professes the truth. The Lord says through Isaiah: "I am laying in Zion a stone for a foundation", indicating that Christ is the foundation of the Church. He is the foundation, so that we may build on him the works of justice (St. Ambrose, *On the Duties of the Clergy* 1, 29, 142).

¹⁸Then your covenant with death will be annulled,
  and your agreement with Sheol will not stand;
when the overwhelming scourge passes through
  you will be beaten down by it.
¹⁹As often as it passes through it will take you;
  for morning by morning it will pass through,
  by day and by night;
and it will be sheer terror to understand the
  message.
²⁰For the bed is too short to stretch oneself on it,
  and the covering too narrow to wrap oneself
  in it.
²¹For the LORD will rise up as on Mount Pera′zim,
  he will rage as in the valley of Gib′eon;
to do his deed—strange is his deed!
  and to work his work—alien is his work!
²²Now therefore do not scoff,
  lest your bonds be made strong;
for I have heard a decree of destruction
  from the Lord GOD of hosts upon the whole land.

²³Give ear, and hear my voice;
  listen, and hear my speech.
²⁴Does he who plows for sowing plow continually?
  does he continually open and harrow his
  ground?
²⁵When he has leveled its surface,
  does he not scatter dill, sow cummin,
and put in wheat in rows
  and barley in its proper place,
  and spelt as the border?
²⁶For he is instructed rightly;
  his God teaches him.

²⁷Dill is not threshed with a threshing sledge,
  nor is a cart wheel rolled over cummin;
but dill is beaten out with a stick,
  and cummin with a rod.

²⁸Does one crush bread grain?
  No, he does not thresh it for ever;
when he drives his cart wheel over it
  with his horses, he does not crush it.
²⁹This also comes from the LORD of hosts;
  he is wonderful in counsel,
  and excellent in wisdom.

The Siege of Jerusalem

29 Ho Ar′iel, Ariel,
  the city where David encamped!
Add year to year;
  let the feasts run their round.
²Yet I will distress Ar′iel,
  and there shall be moaning and lamentation,
  and she shall be to me like an Ariel.
³And I will encamp against you round about,
  and will besiege you with towers
  and I will raise siegeworks against you.
⁴Then deep from the earth you shall speak,
  from low in the dust your words shall come;
your voice shall come from the ground like the
  voice of a ghost,
  and your speech shall whisper out of the dust.

⁵But the multitude of your foes ˢ shall be like small
  dust,
  and the multitude of the ruthless like passing
  chaff.
And in an instant, suddenly,
⁶   you will be visited by the LORD of hosts
with thunder and with earthquake and great noise,
  with whirlwind and tempest, and the flame of
  a devouring fire.
⁷And the multitude of all the nations that fight
  against Ar′iel,
  all that fight against her and her stronghold
  and distress her,
shall be like a dream, a vision of the night.

28:18 beaten down by it: For Assyria's devastation of Judah in 701 B.C., see note on 1:7–9.

28:20 too short . . . too narrow: Judah will get no comfort from its reliance on Egypt.

28:21 Perazim: The place where David defeated the Philistines with the Lord's help in 2 Sam 5:17–20. **Gibeon:** The place where Joshua defeated the Canaanites with the Lord's help in Josh 10:6–10. **strange is his deed:** It seems strange that God would rouse foreign armies to fight against his people instead of defending them from attack. Yet Israel was forewarned of this possibility. Among the curses of the covenant, which are triggered by rebellion, is the threat of foreign conquest (Deut 28:47–52).

28:23–29 A parable about a simple farmer who is more receptive to God's instruction than the rulers of Jerusalem, since at least he acts on the practical wisdom that is given to him. The orderly planting and processing of his harvest stand in contrast to the disorder that reigns in Judah because of the foolishness of its leaders.

28:23 Give ear: An appeal to listen and learn God's counsel (Jer 13:15).

28:25 dill . . . cummin: Seasoning herbs.

29:1–8 Jerusalem will be humiliated but not annihilated (29:1–4), for God will rescue Zion suddenly and unexpectedly (29:5–8). The prophecy foretells the Lord's deliverance of the city from the Assyrian siege of 701 B.C. A report of the event appears in chaps. 36–37.

29:1 Ho: The Hebrew term, which is a cry of lamentation, is translated "woe" in 28:1; 29:15; 30:1; 31:1; 33:1. See word study: *Woe* at 28:1. **Ariel:** A poetic name for Jerusalem. It can be translated "lion of God" (i.e., the seat of kingship, Gen 49:9; Rev 5:5) or "altar hearth" (as in Ezek 43:16). Jerusalem is coming to judgment for its pride—either for being the center of royal government in Israel or for being the center of divine worship in Israel. **where David encamped:** For David's capture of Jerusalem, see 2 Sam 5:6–10.

29:3 I will encamp: I.e., by summoning the Assyrians to lay siege to the city.

29:5 dust . . . chaff: Easily blown away by the Lord (17:13).

29:6 thunder . . . earthquake . . . fire: Depictions of the overwhelming power of God, recalling the dramatic events at Mount Sinai (Ex 19:16–19). Isaiah is speaking symbolically, since the Lord will save Jerusalem by a silent plague of death (37:36).

ˢ Cn: Heb *strangers*

⁸As when a hungry man dreams he is eating
  and awakes with his hunger not satisfied,
or as when a thirsty man dreams he is drinking
  and awakes faint, with his thirst not quenched,
so shall the multitude of all the nations be
  that fight against Mount Zion.

⁹Stupefy yourselves and be in a stupor,
  blind yourselves and be blind!
Be drunk, but not with wine;
  stagger, but not with strong drink!
¹⁰For the Lord has poured out upon you
  a spirit of deep sleep,
and has closed your eyes, the prophets,
  and covered your heads, the seers.

11 And the vision of all this has become to you like the words of a book that is sealed. When men give it to one who can read, saying, "Read this," he says, "I cannot, for it is sealed." ¹²And when they give the book to one who cannot read, saying, "Read this," he says, "I cannot read."

¹³And the Lord said:
"Because this people draw near with their mouth
  and honor me with their lips,
while their hearts are far from me,
  and their fear of me is a commandment of men
    learned by rote;
¹⁴therefore, behold, I will again
  do marvelous things with this people,
  wonderful and marvelous;
and the wisdom of their wise men shall perish,
  and the discernment of their discerning men
    shall be hidden."

¹⁵Woe to those who hide deep from the Lord their
    counsel,
  whose deeds are in the dark,
  and who say, "Who sees us? Who knows
    us?"
¹⁶You turn things upside down!
  Shall the potter be regarded as the clay;
that the thing made should say of its maker,
  "He did not make me";
or the thing formed say of him who formed it,
  "He has no understanding"?

¹⁷Is it not yet a very little while
  until Lebanon shall be turned into a fruitful
    field,
  and the fruitful field shall be regarded as a
    forest?
¹⁸In that day the deaf shall hear the words of a
    book,
  and out of their gloom and darkness
    the eyes of the blind shall see.
¹⁹The meek shall obtain fresh joy in the Lord,
  and the poor among men shall exult in the
    Holy One of Israel.
²⁰For the ruthless shall come to nothing and the
    scoffer cease,
  and all who watch to do evil shall be cut
    off,
²¹who by a word make a man out to be an
    offender,
  and lay a snare for him who reproves in the
    gate,
  and with an empty plea turn aside him who is
    in the right.

29:13: Mt 15:8–9; Mk 7:6–7. **29:14:** 1 Cor 1:19. **29:16:** Is 45:9; Rom 9:20. **29:18–19:** Mt 11:5.

29:8 not satisfied: Victory over Jerusalem will seem assured to the Assyrians (36:10–13), only to vanish like a dream upon waking in the morning (37:36–37).

29:10 a spirit of deep sleep: The Lord brings spiritual blindness and deafness upon Judah as foretold in 6:9–10. Because the Southern Kingdom refused the word of God spoken by Isaiah (30:9–11), the purposes of God are incomprehensible to it, like a scroll that is unreadable (29:11–12). See note on 63:17. • Paul cites this verse in Rom 11:8 to speak of divine judgment on unbelieving Israel in his own day. Though some of his kin accepted the gospel, many did not, for God sent a hardening upon part of Israel in order to bring salvation to the Gentiles (Rom 11:7, 25). **prophets ... seers:** Normally expected to understand God's actions and purposes in history.

29:11 a book that is sealed: A scroll that is rolled up and kept closed with a wax seal along its outside edge. The image implies that Judah's educated scribes are no better off than the illiterate masses.

29:13 Because this people ... honor me: Judah's leaders are charged with hypocrisy, i.e., with going through the motions of serving God but refusing to consult or rely on him when framing national policy. Instead, they chart a course for the nation on the basis of purely human calculations (forging a diplomatic alliance with Egypt, 30:1–5). Their worship is thus shallow and insincere, coming from the **lips** but not from the **heart**. • Jesus cites this passage in his criticism of the Pharisees in Mt 15:8–9 and Mk 7:6–7. He faults them for giving greater weight to human traditions devised by Pharisaic elders than to the commandments of God. Thus, despite appearances of piety, their leadership is untrustworthy.

29:14 the wisdom of their wise men: The worldly plans of Judah's politicians, which are destined to fail. • Paul quotes this passage (in a form similar to the Greek LXX) to say that God will confound the wisdom of the wise. He thus warns the Corinthians, who highly esteem philosophers and sages, that the gospel of Christ is the highest form of wisdom, to the point of making worldly wisdom look foolish in comparison.

29:16 Shall the potter ... as the clay: Isaiah rebukes the upside-down thinking of the rulers of Judah, who foolishly act as if creatures can outsmart their Creator and devise more intelligent plans than God does for the welfare of his people. For the metaphor of God as a potter and Israel as the clay, see also 45:9 and Jer 18:1–11. • Paul alludes to this passage in Rom 9:20–21 to insist that God has the sovereign right to shape history according to his plan, and creatures have no grounds to protest either his wisdom or his justice in doing so.

29:17–24 Isaiah looks beyond the divine judgments of 29:9–11 to a time when Israel will be blessed with renewed vision, understanding, and joy.

29:17 Lebanon: Its mighty cedars represent the prideful and powerful (2:13), who will be felled by the judgments of God (10:18–19, 33–34).

Hope for the Future

22 Therefore thus says the LORD, who redeemed Abraham, concerning the house of Jacob:
"Jacob shall no more be ashamed,
  no more shall his face grow pale.
²³For when he sees his children,
  the work of my hands, in his midst,
  they will sanctify my name;
they will sanctify the Holy One of Jacob,
  and will stand in awe of the God of Israel.
²⁴And those who err in spirit will come to understanding,
  and those who murmur will accept instruction."

A Rebellious People

30 "Woe to the rebellious children," says the LORD,
  "who carry out a plan, but not mine;
and who make a league, but not of my spirit,
  that they may add sin to sin;
²who set out to go down to Egypt,
  without asking for my counsel,
to take refuge in the protection of Pharaoh,
  and to seek shelter in the shadow of Egypt!
³Therefore the protection of Pharaoh shall turn to your shame,
  and the shelter in the shadow of Egypt to your humiliation.
⁴For though his officials are at Zoan
  and his envoys reach Han'es,
⁵every one comes to shame
  through a people that cannot profit them,
that brings neither help nor profit,
  but shame and disgrace."

⁶An oracle on the beasts of the Neg'eb.
Through a land of trouble and anguish,
  from where come the lioness and the lion,
  the viper and the flying serpent,
they carry their riches on the backs of donkeys,
  and their treasures on the humps of camels,
to a people that cannot profit them.
⁷For Egypt's help is worthless and empty,
  therefore I have called her
  "Ra'hab who sits still."

⁸And now, go, write it before them on a tablet,
  and inscribe it in a book,
that it may be for the time to come as a witness
  for ever.
⁹For they are a rebellious people,
  lying sons,
sons who will not hear
  the instruction of the LORD;
¹⁰who say to the seers, "See not";
  and to the prophets, "Prophesy not to us what is right;
speak to us smooth things,
  prophesy illusions,
¹¹leave the way, turn aside from the path,
  let us hear no more of the Holy One of Israel."
¹²Therefore thus says the Holy One of Israel,
  "Because you despise this word,
  and trust in oppression and perverseness,
  and rely on them;
¹³therefore this iniquity shall be to you
  like a break in a high wall, bulging out, and about to collapse,
  whose crash comes suddenly, in an instant;
¹⁴and its breaking is like that of a potter's vessel
  which is smashed so ruthlessly
that among its fragments not a shard is found
  with which to take fire from the hearth,
  or to dip up water out of the cistern."

¹⁵For thus said the Lord GOD, the Holy One of Israel,
  "In returning and rest you shall be saved;
  in quietness and in trust shall be your strength."

29:22 redeemed Abraham: God rescued him from idolatry (Josh 24:23) and reckoned his faith as righteousness (Gen 15:6).

29:23 sanctify my name: Jacob's children will reverence the Lord's name as holy (Mt 6:9; Lk 1:49).

30:1-17 Isaiah reprimands the rulers of Judah for rejecting God's word (30:12) and trusting instead in Egypt and its military might (30:2). Judah stands in need of protection since King Hezekiah rebelled against Assyrian rule (2 Kings 18:7). In the prophet's view, the Lord alone has the power to defend Judah, if only his people will trust in him (30:15).

30:1 Woe: A cry of lamentation. See word study: *Woe* at 28:1. **rebellious children:** The faithless of Israel, who became the Lord's sons and daughters by covenant (Deut 14:1). Children who rebel against their parents are subject to the death penalty according to the Mosaic Law (Deut 21:18-21). **a league:** A treaty in which Judah places itself under Egyptian vassalage in exchange for military protection against Assyria. **add sin to sin:** The result of forsaking God's way.

30:4 Zoan ... Hanes: Cities in the Nile Delta where the treaty was negotiated and ratified.

30:6 Negeb: The wilderness in the deep south of Judah. The embassy from Jerusalem will have to pass through this region on the way to Egypt. **the flying serpent:** Perhaps a winged cobra such as those that appear in Egyptian artwork (14:29). **riches:** The tribute offering that Judah will use to "buy" security from the Pharaoh.

30:7 Rahab: Another name for Leviathan, the sea dragon representing the forces of chaos in Near Eastern mythology (51:9; Job 26:12; Ps 89:10). For Rahab as a symbol of Egypt, see Ezek 29:2-5. See note on 27:1. **who sits still:** I.e., who will do nothing to help Judah.

30:8 a witness for ever: Isaiah is told to document Judah's course of action so that, when it fails, his prophecies will be vindicated and future generations will learn to trust in the Lord more than in purely human, political strategies (cf. 8:16).

30:9 sons who will not hear: Recalls the opening indictment of the book (1:2-4).

30:10 Prophesy not: Judah's rulers pressure the prophets to keep quiet about the Lord's opposition to their alliance with Egypt. Normally prophets would be consulted before such an undertaking (see 1 Kings 22:5-28). **smooth things:** False assurances that the treaty will benefit Judah.

30:11 the Holy One of Israel: See note on 1:4.

30:15 In returning: An idiom for repentance. **We will speed ... you shall speed:** The Lord's punishment will fit the

And you would not, ¹⁶but you said,
"No! We will speed upon horses,"
    therefore you shall speed away;
and, "We will ride upon swift steeds,"
    therefore your pursuers shall be swift.
¹⁷A thousand shall flee at the threat of one,
    at the threat of five you shall flee,
till you are left
        like a flagstaff on the top of a mountain,
        like a signal on a hill.

¹⁸Therefore the Lord waits to be gracious to you;
    therefore he exalts himself to show mercy to
        you.
For the Lord is a God of justice;
    blessed are all those who wait for him.

God's Promise to Zion

19 Yes, O people in Zion who dwell at Jerusalem; you shall weep no more. He will surely be gracious to you at the sound of your cry; when he hears it, he will answer you. ²⁰And though the Lord give you the bread of adversity and the water of affliction, yet your Teacher will not hide himself any more, but your eyes shall see your Teacher. ²¹And your ears shall hear a word behind you, saying, "This is the way, walk in it," when you turn to the right or when you turn to the left. ²²Then you will defile your silver-covered graven images and your gold-plated molten images. You will scatter them as unclean things; you will say to them, "Begone!"

23 And he will give rain for the seed with which you sow the ground, and grain, the produce of the ground, which will be rich and plenteous. In that day your flock will be given pasture, and the lamb will graze in open fields; ²⁴and the oxen and the donkeys that till the ground will eat salted food, which has been winnowed with shovel and fork. ²⁵And upon every lofty mountain and every high hill there will be brooks running with water, in the day of the great slaughter, when the towers fall. ²⁶Moreover the light of the moon will be as the light of the sun, and the light of the sun will be sevenfold, as the light of seven days, in the day when the Lord binds up the hurt of his people, and heals the wounds inflicted by his blow.

²⁷Behold, the name of the Lord comes from far,
    burning with his anger, and in thick rising
        smoke;
his lips are full of indignation,
    and his tongue is like a devouring fire;
²⁸his breath is like an overflowing stream
    that reaches up to the neck;
to sift the nations with the sieve of destruction,
    and to place on the jaws of the peoples a bridle
        that leads astray.

Judgment on Assyria

29 You shall have a song as in the night when a holy feast is kept; and gladness of heart, as when one sets out to the sound of the flute to go to the mountain of the Lord, to the Rock of Israel. ³⁰And the Lord will cause his majestic voice to be heard and the descending blow of his arm to be seen, in furious anger and a flame of devouring fire, with a cloudburst and tempest and hailstones. ³¹The Assyrians will be terror-stricken at the voice of the Lord, when he strikes with his rod. ³²And every stroke of the staff of punishment which the Lord lays upon them will be to the sound of timbrels and lyres; battling with brandished arm he will fight with them. ³³For a burning place^t has long been prepared; yes, for the king^u it is made ready,

---

crime: since Judah hurried into a foolish alliance with a foreign nation (Egypt), it will hurriedly flee from another foreign nation (Assyria).

30:17 like a flagstaff: Implies that Judah will be isolated and vulnerable.

30:18–26 Isaiah's impassioned appeal to Jerusalem. He is adamant that God wants nothing more than to answer the prayers of his people in Zion (30:19), to send blessings upon them (30:23), and to heal their wounds (30:26). They have only to put their trust in him (30:18) and to discard their worthless idols (30:22) to receive these mercies.

30:18 waits to be gracious: The Lord is patient with his erring people, allowing them time to repent of their sins (Rom 2:4; 2 Pet 3:9). They finally cry out for God to be gracious in 33:2.

30:20 your Teacher: The Lord, who knows how to discipline his children and to lead them back to living by the covenant (Deut 8:5; Prov 3:5-6, 11-12).

30:23–26 A symbolic description of Jerusalem's recovery following the siege of 701 B.C. This will be a time when the Lord provides an abundance of water, food, and light for the remnant of his people who are left.

30:23 he will give rain: One of the blessings of the covenant (Deut 11:13-14; 28:12).

30:25 day of the great slaughter: The day of Jerusalem's deliverance in 701 B.C., when an angel slays 185,000 Assyrian soldiers in a single night (37:36). **towers:** An image of the proud (2:15).

30:27–33 Assyria will face the wrath of God, as noted earlier in 10:12-19, 33-34.

30:29 song ... night ... feast: Alludes to Passover, a nighttime feast that celebrated Israel's deliverance from bondage in Egypt (Ex 12:1-42). **go to the mountain of the Lord:** Passover is one of three festivals that required pilgrims to worship in Jerusalem (Deut 16:1-17). **the Rock of Israel:** The Lord, whose faithfulness makes him a secure refuge for his people (17:10; 26:4; Deut 32:4; Ps 92:15).

30:32 sound of timbrels: The sound of God's people rejoicing over their deliverance. It recalls the celebration that followed the crossing of the sea and the destruction of Pharaoh's army during the Exodus (Ex 15:19-21).

30:33 a burning place: Topheth, a cultic site in the valley directly south of Jerusalem where children were sacrificed by fire to the pagan god Molech (2 Kings 23:10; Jer 7:31). A similar fate awaits all who rebel against the Lord (66:24). **king:** Sennacherib of Assyria, who is destined for a funeral pyre. The king will die by assassination in Nineveh (37:37-38).

---

^t Or *Topheth.*
^u Or *Molech.*

its pyre made deep and wide, with fire and wood in abundance; the breath of the Lord, like a stream of brimstone, kindles it.

Help from Egypt Is Futile

31 Woe to those who go down to Egypt for help
and rely on horses,
who trust in chariots because they are many
and in horsemen because they are very strong,
but do not look to the Holy One of Israel
or consult the Lord!
²And yet he is wise and brings disaster,
he does not call back his words,
but will arise against the house of the evildoers,
and against the helpers of those who work
iniquity.
³The Egyptians are men, and not God;
and their horses are flesh, and not spirit.
When the Lord stretches out his hand,
the helper will stumble, and he who is helped
will fall,
and they will all perish together.

⁴For thus the Lord said to me,
As a lion or a young lion growls over his prey,
and when a band of shepherds is called forth
against him
is not terrified by their shouting
or daunted at their noise,
so the Lord of hosts will come down
to fight upon Mount Zion and upon its hill.
⁵Like birds hovering, so the Lord of hosts
will protect Jerusalem;

he will protect and deliver it,
he will spare and rescue it.

6 Turn to him from whom you[v] have deeply revolted, O people of Israel. ⁷For in that day every one shall cast away his idols of silver and his idols of gold, which your hands have sinfully made for you.
⁸"And the Assyrian shall fall by a sword, not of man;
and a sword, not of man, shall devour him;
and he shall flee from the sword,
and his young men shall be put to forced
labor.
⁹His rock shall pass away in terror,
and his officers desert the standard in panic,"
says the Lord, whose fire is in Zion,
and whose furnace is in Jerusalem.

A Reign of Righteousness and Justice

32 Behold, a king will reign in righteousness,
and princes will rule in justice.
²Each will be like a hiding place from the wind,
a covert from the tempest,
like streams of water in a dry place,
like the shade of a great rock in a weary land.
³Then the eyes of those who see will not be closed,
and the ears of those who hear will listen.
⁴The mind of the rash will have good judgment,
and the tongue of the stammerers will speak
readily and distinctly.
⁵The fool will no more be called noble,
nor the knave said to be honorable.

31:1–3 Isaiah rebukes Judah for reliance on Egypt instead of the Lord, as in 30:1–5.

31:1 Woe: A cry of lamentation. See word study: *Woe* at 28:1. **go down to Egypt:** To ratify a treaty. See note on 30:1. **rely on horses ... chariots:** Judah's diplomats seek a partnership with Egypt because of its military strength. They forget that God is infinitely more powerful, as shown when he drowned Egypt's horses and chariots at the time of the Exodus (Ex 14:23–28). **the Holy One of Israel:** See note on 1:4.

31:2 the house of the evildoers: The kingdom of Judah. **the helpers:** The Egyptians.

31:3 flesh, and not spirit: The weakness of mortal creatures is contrasted with the divine power of God. **stretches out his hand:** I.e., to strike a devastating blow.

31:4–5 Two similes that make the same point: like a hungry **lion** before its food, and like **birds** circling overhead, the Lord will keep watch over Jerusalem to ensure that others do not touch it.

31:4 the Lord of hosts: See note on 1:9. **upon Mount Zion:** Or, possibly, "against Mount Zion".

31:5 birds hovering: An image of divine protection, as in Deut 32:10–11.

31:6 Turn to him: A prophetic appeal for repentance. **deeply revolted:** More than just a failure to trust in the one true God, the people of Israel are guilty of worshiping false gods. Repentance thus requires them to rid their lives of idols (2:20; 17:7–8; 30:22).

31:8 a sword, not of man: Points to a divine intervention. Jerusalem will not have to defend itself with arms because the

Lord will send an angel to decimate the Assyrian army (37:36). **he shall flee:** Sennacherib of Assyria will abruptly withdraw from the city and return to Nineveh (37:37).

31:9 His rock: Implies a contrast with the Lord, "the Rock of Israel" (30:29). **the standard:** The banner that troops follow into battle. **fire:** The presence of God, who dwells in a special way in the Jerusalem Temple. He is a devouring fire (33:14) who purifies his people of their sins (4:4) and consumes their enemies (30:27).

32:1–20 Isaiah foresees a time when the house of David trusts in the Lord for the welfare of the nation. It will be a time of spiritual renewal that follows a time of purifying judgment. Judah's leaders must first come to see the futility of excluding God from their political planning; only then will Judah's spiritual numbness be lifted and clarity of sight be restored (32:3–4). These blessings coincide with the reign of an ideal king (32:1) and an outpouring of the Spirit from heaven (32:15).

32:1 king: Initially embodied in King Hezekiah, whose reliance on the Lord and prayer for divine help led to the deliverance of Jerusalem in 701 b.c. (chaps. 36–37). At the same time, Isaiah's description of this exemplary king, particularly his commitment to **righteousness** and **justice**, suggests a more ultimate fulfillment in the Messiah, the royal heir of David who will govern with "justice" and "righteousness" (9:7; 11:1–5). **princes:** Leaders in the restored Davidic kingdom. See note on 1:26.

32:3–4 A time of blessing following God's judgments on Judah, described earlier in the book as blindness and deafness to the word of God (6:9–10) and likened to a drunken stupor (29:9, 18).

[v] Heb *they*.

⁶For the fool speaks folly,
    and his mind plots iniquity:
to practice ungodliness,
    to utter error concerning the Lord,
to leave the craving of the hungry unsatisfied,
    and to deprive the thirsty of drink.
⁷The knaveries of the knave are evil;
    he devises wicked devices
to ruin the poor with lying words,
    even when the plea of the needy is right.
⁸But he who is noble devises noble things,
    and by noble things he stands.

⁹Rise up, you women who are at ease, hear my
      voice;
    you complacent daughters, give ear to my
      speech.
¹⁰In little more than a year
    you will shudder, you complacent women;
  for the vintage will fail,
    the fruit harvest will not come.
¹¹Tremble, you women who are at ease,
    shudder, you complacent ones;
strip, and make yourselves bare,
    and put sackcloth upon your loins.
¹²Beat upon your breasts for the pleasant fields,
    for the fruitful vine,
¹³for the soil of my people
    growing up in thorns and briers;
  yes, for all the joyous houses
    in the joyful city.
¹⁴For the palace will be forsaken,
    the populous city deserted;
  the hill and the watchtower

will become dens for ever,
    a joy of wild donkeys,
    a pasture of flocks;
¹⁵until the Spirit is poured upon us from on high,
    and the wilderness becomes a fruitful field,
    and the fruitful field is deemed a forest.
¹⁶Then justice will dwell in the wilderness,
    and righteousness abide in the fruitful field.
¹⁷And the effect of righteousness will be peace,
    and the result of righteousness, quietness and
      trust for ever.
¹⁸My people will abide in a peaceful habitation,
    in secure dwellings, and in quiet resting
      places.
¹⁹And the forest will utterly go down,ʷ
    and the city will be utterly laid low.
²⁰Happy are you who sow beside all waters,
    who let the feet of the ox and the donkey range
      free.

A Prophecy of Deliverance: The Lord, the Majestic King

33 Woe to you, destroyer,
    who yourself have not been destroyed;
you treacherous one,
    with whom none has dealt treacherously!
When you have ceased to destroy,
    you will be destroyed;
and when you have made an end of dealing
      treacherously,
    you will be dealt with treacherously.

²O Lord, be gracious to us; we wait for you.
    Be our arm every morning,
    our salvation in the time of trouble.

32:9–14 Isaiah urges the **women** of Jerusalem to repent before the coming judgment, as in 3:16–24. These ladies, undisturbed by the warnings of the prophet, typify the false sense of security that the general populace places in Judah's reliance on Egypt.

32:10 vintage will fail: Crop failure (or destruction) will bring an abrupt end to the festive and carefree atmosphere in Judah.

32:11 sackcloth: A coarse, hair-spun fabric worn next to the skin in times of mourning and repentance (Jon 3:8).

32:13 thorns and briers: Signs of God's judgment in several oracles of the book (see 5:6; 7:23–25; 10:17).

32:14 the populous city deserted: Jerusalem stands under a threat of destruction. However, it is not guaranteed this fate so long as time for repentance remains ("a little more than a year", 32:10). Isaiah's warning concerns the Assyrian siege of the city before it was divinely spared in 701 B.C., thanks to the prayers of Hezekiah (chaps. 36–37). Some think the prophecy looks beyond Isaiah's lifetime to the Babylonian conquest of Jerusalem in 586 B.C., an event that left the city abandoned for several decades (2 Kings 25:8–21). Isaiah forewarned Hezekiah of this calamity as well (see 39:5–7).

32:15 the Spirit: The future "blessing" that God will pour out on his people in the time of messianic fulfillment (44:3). • This is one of several OT passages that envision the Spirit of God being "poured out" from heaven like water, giving new life to the world (Ezek 39:29; Joel 2:28–29). It is ultimately fulfilled in the time of the gospel, beginning at the first Christian Pentecost (Acts 2:1–21).

32:16 justice … righteousness: The outpouring of the Spirit coincides with the reign of the ideal king in 32:1.

32:19 the forest: Assyria, destined to be felled by the axe of God's judgment (10:18, 33–34). **the city:** Jerusalem, destined to be humbled (1:21–31) and cleansed of iniquity (33:24).

33:1–24 Isaiah prophesies the fall of Assyria (33:1) as well as the restoration of Jerusalem (33:20–24).

33:1 Woe: A cry of lamentation previously directed against sinful Judah and Jerusalem but now directed to their enemies. See word study: *Woe* at 28:1. **destroyer … treacherous one:** Assyria, represented in its king, Sennacherib, who will be humiliated and later assassinated (37:36–38). Babylon is also described in these terms in 21:2 and 24:16, suggesting Isaiah has a typological view of history in which the Lord's victory over Assyria in 701 B.C. prefigures the overthrow of Babylonia in 539 B.C. **treacherously:** Sennacherib will besiege Jerusalem and demand its surrender, even after Hezekiah pays a heavy tribute to the king as an act of submission (2 Kings 18:13–16).

33:2 O Lord, be gracious: A turning point for Jerusalem. On the eve of disaster, the city turns to God in prayer, trusting in Isaiah's promise that God will be "gracious" to his people when they cry out to him in their need (30:19). **we wait for you:** A trustful reliance on God that brings a favorable answer to prayer. **our arm:** I.e., our strength (51:9).

ʷCn: Heb *And it will hail when the forest comes down.*

³At the thunderous noise peoples flee,
  at the lifting up of yourself nations are
    scattered;
⁴and spoil is gathered as the caterpillar gathers;
  as locusts leap, men leap upon it.

⁵The LORD is exalted, for he dwells on high;
  he will fill Zion with justice and righteousness;
⁶and he will be the stability of your times,
  abundance of salvation, wisdom, and
    knowledge;
  the fear of the LORD is his treasure.

⁷Behold, the valiant onesʸ cry without;
  the envoys of peace weep bitterly.
⁸The highways lie waste,
  the wayfaring man ceases.
 Covenants are broken,
  witnessesᶻ are despised,
  there is no regard for man.
⁹The land mourns and languishes;
  Lebanon is confounded and withers away;
 Sharon is like a desert;
  and Bashan and Carmel shake off their leaves.

¹⁰"Now I will arise," says the LORD,
  "now I will lift myself up;
  now I will be exalted.
¹¹You conceive chaff, you bring forth stubble;
  your breath is a fire that will consume you.
¹²And the peoples will be as if burned to lime,
  like thorns cut down, that are burned in the
    fire."

¹³Hear, you who are far off, what I have done;
  and you who are near, acknowledge my might.

¹⁴The sinners in Zion are afraid;
  trembling has seized the godless:
 "Who among us can dwell with the devouring
    fire?
  Who among us can dwell with everlasting
    burnings?"
¹⁵He who walks righteously and speaks uprightly,
  who despises the gain of oppressions,
 who shakes his hands, lest they hold a bribe,
  who stops his ears from hearing of bloodshed
  and shuts his eyes from looking upon evil,
¹⁶he will dwell on the heights;
  his place of defense will be the fortresses of
    rocks;
  his bread will be given him, his water will be
    sure.

¹⁷Your eyes will see the king in his beauty;
  they will behold a land that stretches afar.
¹⁸Your mind will muse on the terror:
 "Where is he who counted, where is he who
    weighed the tribute?
  Where is he who counted the towers?"
¹⁹You will see no more the insolent people,
  the people of an obscure speech which you
    cannot comprehend,
 stammering in a tongue which you cannot
    understand.
²⁰Look upon Zion, the city of our appointed
    feasts!
  Your eyes will see Jerusalem,
  a quiet habitation, an immovable tent,
 whose stakes will never be plucked up,
  nor will any of its cords be broken.
²¹But there the LORD in majesty will be for us
  a place of broad rivers and streams,

33:5 The LORD is exalted: As a divine King enthroned in majesty over all creation (6:1–3). His power will be shown when he protects Zion from Assyria, the most fearsome nation in the Near East in Isaiah's day. **justice and righteousness:** Points to a transformation of Zion that occurs when God raises up a faithful king (32:1) and sends down the Spirit (32:15).

33:6 wisdom ... knowledge ... fear of the LORD: Gifts imparted by the Spirit and possessed in their fullness by the Davidic Messiah (see 11:1–3).

33:7–9 Dire circumstances associated with Assyria's invasion of Judah. These also point to the moral and spiritual corruption of the people of Judah.

33:8 Covenants are broken: Perhaps an allusion to Judah's covenant with Egypt (28:15), which proved to be useless, just as Isaiah had foretold (30:1–7).

33:9 Lebanon: A forested region north of Israel. **Sharon:** The coastal plain of western Israel. **Bashan:** The fertile land northeast of the Sea of Galilee.

33:11 your breath is a fire: The Lord, like the Davidic Messiah in 11:4, brings judgment on the wicked by his powerful word (cf. 2 Thess 2:8).

33:14 afraid: The result of witnessing God's power against the ungodly. **the devouring fire:** The Lord himself, whose holy presence dwells on Zion. See note on 31:9.

33:15–16 A picture of genuine repentance (33:15) and a promise of the blessings that come with it (33:16).

33:17 the king in his beauty: A veiled reference either to King Hezekiah (as in 32:1) or to the Lord (as in 33:22). Isaiah was privileged to see God in royal splendor at his calling to be a prophet (6:1).

33:18 weighed the tribute: Those who sealed Judah's alliance with Egypt with an offering of tribute (30:6–7). **counted the towers:** Those who trusted in Jerusalem's defenses.

33:19 people of an obscure speech: The Assyrians, who spoke a language that was unintelligible to the common folk of Judah (28:11).

33:20–24 The future restoration and blessing of Jerusalem. Its inhabitants, who are weak and foolish and in need of forgiveness (33:24), cannot bring the city to its appointed destiny (33:23). Only the Lord can make it a **quiet habitation**, an **immovable tent** that is protected and secure (cf. 4:5–6). Poetically speaking, God can make the land-locked city of Jerusalem a place of **rivers** and **streams** that has all the advantages of Nineveh and Babylon, built along the Tigris and Euphrates rivers, but without exposure to enemy attacks by water.

ʸ The meaning of the Hebrew word is uncertain.
ᶻ One ancient Ms: Heb *cities.*

where no galley with oars can go,
nor stately ship can pass.
²²For the LORD is our judge, the LORD is our ruler,
the LORD is our king; he will save us.

²³Your tackle hangs loose;
it cannot hold the mast firm in its place,
or keep the sail spread out.

Then prey and spoil in abundance will be divided;
even the lame will take the prey.
²⁴And no inhabitant will say, "I am sick";
the people who dwell there will be forgiven
their iniquity.

The Wrath of the Lord

34 Draw near, O nations, to hear,
and listen, O peoples!
Let the earth listen, and all that fills it;
the world, and all that comes from it.
²For the LORD is enraged against all the nations,
and furious against all their host,
he has doomed them, has given them over for
slaughter.
³Their slain shall be cast out,
and the stench of their corpses shall rise;
the mountains shall flow with their blood.
⁴All the host of heaven shall rot away,
and the skies roll up like a scroll.
All their host shall fall,
as leaves fall from the vine,
like leaves falling from the fig tree.

⁵For my sword has drunk its fill in the heavens;
behold, it descends for judgment upon E′dom,
upon the people I have doomed.

⁶The LORD has a sword; it is sated with blood,
it is gorged with fat,
with the blood of lambs and goats,
with the fat of the kidneys of rams.
For the LORD has a sacrifice in Bozrah,
a great slaughter in the land of E′dom.
⁷Wild oxen shall fall with them,
and young steers with the mighty bulls.
Their land shall be soaked with blood,
and their soil made rich with fat.

⁸For the LORD has a day of vengeance,
a year of recompense for the cause of Zion.
⁹And the streams of E′dom[a] shall be turned into
pitch,
and her soil into brimstone;
her land shall become burning pitch.
¹⁰Night and day it shall not be quenched;
its smoke shall go up for ever.
From generation to generation it shall lie
waste;
none shall pass through it for ever and
ever.
¹¹But the hawk and the porcupine shall possess
it,
the owl and the raven shall dwell in it.
He shall stretch the line of confusion over it,
and the plummet of chaos over[b] its nobles.
¹²They shall name it No Kingdom There,
and all its princes shall be nothing.

¹³Thorns shall grow over its strongholds,
nettles and thistles in its fortresses.
It shall be the haunt of jackals,
an abode for ostriches.

34: Is 63:1–6; Jer 49:7–22; Ezek 25:12–14; 35; Amos 1:11–12; Obad; Mal 1:2–5. **34:4:** Rev 6:13–14. **34:9–10:** Rev 19:3.

33:22 judge ... ruler ... king: The Lord is the only stable foundation for just government and a flourishing society.

34:1—35:10 Oracles of judgment against Edom (chap. 34) and prophecies of salvation for Zion (chap. 35). Their historical background is uncertain, since these sayings show parallels with earlier and later parts of the book: as in chaps. 24–27, reference is made to a worldwide judgment (24:1–3; 34:1–3), apocalyptic upheaval in the sky (24:23; 34:4), and the Lord's avenging sword (27:1; 34:5–6); and, as in chaps. 40–66, reference is made to the Lord's day of vengeance (34:8; 63:4), a highway in the wilderness (35:1, 8; 40:3), and the joyful return of God's people to Zion (35:10; 51:11).

34:2 all the nations: Wicked nations that refuse to acknowledge the God of Israel as king and judge of the world (33:22). The obliteration of Edom envisioned in 34:5–17 anticipates this universal judgment. **doomed:** The Hebrew means "devoted to destruction".

34:4 the host of heaven: The sun, moon, and stars, worshiped as deities by various peoples in the biblical world (Deut 4:19). **like a scroll ... like leaves:** Celestial signs of God's cosmic judgment (13:10). • Isaiah's vision reappears in the Book of Revelation when the sixth seal is opened and the wrath of the Lamb is unleashed, causing the powerful and wealthy of the world to scramble for shelter in mountain caves (Rev 6:12–14).

34:5–17 God's judgment on Edom, the region south of the Dead Sea. The Edomites were longtime enemies of Israel (Num 20:14–21) as well as distant kin (i.e., descendants of Jacob's brother, Esau). Scholars sometimes infer from this and other passages that Edom took hostile action against Judah and Jerusalem in connection with the Babylonian conquest of 586 B.C. (see also Ps 137:7; Jer 49:7–22; Ezek 25:12–14; Obad 1–14). The Lord avenges the wrongs committed against Zion (34:8) by laying waste the land of Edom (34:5).

34:5 my sword: The Lord's power and justice unsheathed against the wicked. • The image of a sword that devours flesh with its "blood" (34:6) and brings both "vengeance" and "recompense" to the enemies of Israel (34:8) comes from the Song of Moses in Deut 32:35, 41–42.

34:6 Bozrah: A leading Edomite city.

34:9–10 Edom's fate is likened to that of Sodom and Gomorrah, as described in Gen 19:24–28 and Deut 29:23.

34:11 confusion ... chaos: The same Hebrew terms are translated "without form" and "void" in Gen 1:2. The allusion suggests that Edom will become as uninhabitable as the world in its original, unordered state.

---

[a] Heb *her streams.*
[b] Heb lacks *over.*

¹⁴And wild beasts shall meet with hyenas,
the satyr shall cry to his fellow;
yes, there shall the night creature alight,
and find for herself a resting place.

¹⁵There shall the owl nest and lay
and hatch and gather her young in her
shadow;
yes, there shall the kites be gathered,
each one with her mate.
¹⁶Seek and read from the book of the Lᴏʀᴅ:
Not one of these shall be missing;
none shall be without her mate.
For the mouth of the Lᴏʀᴅ has commanded,
and his Spirit has gathered them.
¹⁷He has cast the lot for them,
his hand has portioned it out to them with the
line;
they shall possess it for ever,
from generation to generation they shall dwell
in it.

The Lord Will Come to Save

35 The wilderness and the dry land shall be
glad,
the desert shall rejoice and blossom;
like the lily ²it shall blossom abundantly,
and rejoice with joy and singing.
The glory of Lebanon shall be given to it,
the majesty of Car′mel and Sharon.
They shall see the glory of the Lᴏʀᴅ,
the majesty of our God.

³Strengthen the weak hands,
and make firm the feeble knees.
⁴Say to those who are of a fearful heart,
"Be strong, fear not!
Behold, your God
will come with vengeance,
with the recompense of God.
He will come and save you."

⁵Then the eyes of the blind shall be opened,
and the ears of the deaf unstopped;
⁶then shall the lame man leap like a deer,
and the tongue of the mute sing for joy.
For waters shall break forth in the wilderness,
and streams in the desert;
⁷the burning sand shall become a pool,
and the thirsty ground springs of water;
the haunt of jackals shall become a swamp,ᶜ
the grass shall become reeds and rushes.

⁸And a highway shall be there,
and it shall be called the Holy Way;
the unclean shall not pass over it,ᵈ
and fools shall not err therein.
⁹No lion shall be there,
nor shall any ravenous beast come up
on it;
they shall not be found there,
but the redeemed shall walk there.
¹⁰And the ransomed of the Lᴏʀᴅ shall return,
and come to Zion with singing;

35:3: Heb 12:12. **35:5–6:** Mt 11:5; Lk 7:22.

34:14 satyr ... night creature: Thought to be demons that haunted desolate places, the first under the appearance of a goat and the second named "Lilith".

34:16 the book of the Lᴏʀᴅ: Some identify this with the book that Scripture describes as a register kept in heaven of all people and their deeds (see Ex 32:32; Ps 69:28; Rev 20:12); others see a reference to the Torah, which includes the account of every animal and its mate boarding Noah's ark (Gen 6:19–20).

34:17 cast the lot: The Promised Land was apportioned by lot to the twelve tribes of Israel (Josh 14:1–5).

35:1 wilderness: The arid lands of north Arabia that stood between Babylon and Zion and symbolized Judah's spiritual state in exile. Visions of the wilderness bursting into bloom and flowing with abundant water also appear in 41:18–19; 43:19–20. According to 51:3, the Lord wants to return his languishing people to the blessings of the garden of Eden.

35:2 The glory of Lebanon: Either its majestic cedar trees or possibly the snow-capped Mount Hermon. **the majesty of Carmel:** The lush growth that covers Mount Carmel, which rises along the Mediterranean coast of northern Israel. **Sharon:** The fertile coastal plain of western Israel. **They:** The redeemed of Israel (35:10). **see the glory of the Lᴏʀᴅ:** I.e., they witness firsthand God's greatness and saving love (40:5).

35:3 Strengthen ... hands ... knees: A message of encouragement meant to lift the spirits of the covenant people in exile. The good news is that God himself is coming

to release them from captivity and bring them home (40:9–11; 41:13–14; 52:1–2). • The Book of Hebrews alludes to the LXX version of this passage when it reassures Christians that God allows his children to undergo the discipline of suffering because it leads to righteousness (Heb 12:12).

35:4 He will come and save you: A reference to Israel's divine deliverance. • This passage points to a great mystery, namely, that Christ was to come in the flesh. Not just anybody, not an angel, not an ambassador, but "He" will come to save you. Who is showing this humility? One who is highly exalted. How exalted? Make no search on earth but rise above the stars, beyond the heavenly company of angels, even beyond all creation, and by faith arrive at the Creator (St. Augustine, *Sermons* 293, 5).

35:5–6 Miracles of healing that announce God's salvation. • Jesus draws from this text, as well as 61:1, to reassure John the Baptist that his identity as the coming Messiah is verified by his healing ministry (Mt 11:2–5; Lk 7:18–23).

35:8 highway: A way of returning to God, pictured as a straight and level road through the wilderness (40:3–4). It leads from captivity back to Zion (35:10). **the Holy Way:** The way that brings the redeemed to the Lord, who is "holy" in the highest degree (6:3). • The earliest Christians viewed adherence to the gospel as following "the Way" foretold by Isaiah (Acts 9:2; 19:23; 22:4; 24:14, 22). Perhaps Jesus himself had this theme from Isaiah in mind when he described himself as "the way" to the Father (Jn 14:6).

35:9 the redeemed: See word study: *Redeem* at Lev 25.

35:10 come to Zion with singing: A vision of exiles celebrating as they return home to praise the Lord for his deliverance. The same vision appears in 51:11. • The Book

---

ᶜCn: Heb *in the haunt of jackals is her resting place.*
ᵈHeb *it and he is for them a wayfarer.*

everlasting joy shall be upon their heads;
they shall obtain joy and gladness,
and sorrow and sighing shall flee away.

Sennacherib Threatens Jerusalem

36 In the fourteenth year of King Hezeki'ah, Sennach'erib king of Assyria came up against all the fortified cities of Judah and took them. ²And the king of Assyria sent the Rab'shakeh from La'chish to King Hezeki'ah at Jerusalem, with a great army. And he stood by the conduit of the upper pool on the highway to the Fuller's Field. ³And there came out to him Eli'akim the son of Hilki'ah, who was over the household, and Shebna the secretary, and Jo'ah the son of A'saph, the recorder.

4 And the Rab'shakeh said to them, "Say to Hezeki'ah, 'Thus says the great king, the king of Assyria: On what do you rest this confidence of yours? ⁵Do you think that mere words are strategy and power for war? On whom do you now rely, that you have rebelled against me? ⁶Behold, you are relying on Egypt, that broken reed of a staff, which will pierce the hand of any man who leans on it. Such is Pharaoh king of Egypt to all who rely on him. ⁷But if you say to me, "We rely on the LORD our God," is it not he whose high places and altars Hezeki'ah has removed, saying to Judah and to Jerusalem, "You shall worship before this altar"? ⁸Come now, make a wager with my master the king of Assyria: I will give you two thousand horses, if you are able on your part to set riders upon them. ⁹How then can you repulse a single captain among the least of my master's servants, when you rely on Egypt for chariots and for horsemen? ¹⁰Moreover, is it without the LORD that I have come up against this land to destroy it? The LORD said to me, Go up against this land, and destroy it.'"

11 Then Eli'akim, Shebna, and Jo'ah said to the Rab'shakeh, "Please, speak to your servants in Arama'ic, for we understand it; do not speak to us in the language of Judah within the hearing of the people who are on the wall." ¹²But the Rab'shakeh said, "Has my master sent me to speak these words to your master and to you, and not to the men sitting on the wall, who are doomed with you to eat their own dung and drink their own urine?"

13 Then the Rab'shakeh stood and called out in a loud voice in the language of Judah: "Hear the words of the great king, the king of Assyria! ¹⁴Thus says the king: 'Do not let Hezeki'ah deceive you, for he will not be able to deliver you. ¹⁵Do not let Hezeki'ah make you rely on the LORD by saying, "The LORD will surely deliver us; this city will not be given into

---

36:1—38:8, 21–22: 2 Kings 18:13—20:11; 2 Chron 32:1–24.

---

of Hebrews reveals that Zion, the city of God, is a historical image of an eternal reality: the heavenly Mount Zion, the final destination of God's people, where angels and saints forever celebrate the salvation won by Jesus (Heb 12:22–24).

36:1—39:8 A collection of stories about King Hezekiah and his interactions with Isaiah. **(1)** *Historically*, the setting is the end of the eighth century B.C., when Assyria's threat to Jerusalem reached its climax. **(2)** *Chronologically*, the stories are presented out of order, so that events of 701 B.C. are narrated first (chaps. 36–37), followed by events dated around 703 B.C. (chaps. 38–39). The reason for this is thematic: the author wants to turn his focus from Assyria (the dominant world power in the preceding chapters) to Babylonia (the dominant world power in the following chapters), and this transition is helped by narrating an Assyrian crisis before announcing a future Babylonian crisis. **(3)** *Canonically*, these chapters parallel the account in 2 Kings 18:13—20:19. Since the non-chronological sequence of events in these chapters fits the thematic interests of Isaiah rather than 2 Kings, it seems more likely that the author of 2 Kings derived his account from the Book of Isaiah (or an early form of it) rather than vice versa. **(4)** *Theologically*, the Lord features prominently in these events, working miracles of deliverance (37:30–36), a retreating shadow (38:7–8), and healing from fatal sickness (38:5, 21).

36:1 the fourteenth year: 701 B.C. **Hezekiah:** The twelfth Davidic king of Judah from ca. 729 to 686 B.C. He is admired in Scripture for his religious reforms (2 Kings 18:1–8) and his efforts to reunite the divided tribes of Israel as a single worshiping community (2 Chron 30:1–27). It appears that Hezekiah was co-regent for many years alongside his father, Ahaz, before the start of his independent reign in 715 B.C. **Sennacherib:** King of Assyria from 705 to 681 B.C. He invaded Judah in 701 B.C. to punish Hezekiah for discontinuing mandatory payments of tribute to Assyria (2 Kings 18:13–16). The surviving *Annals of Sennacherib* describe how this king ravaged

the countryside of Judah, captured 46 towns and fortifications, deported more than 200,000 exiles, and cooped up Hezekiah within the walls of Jerusalem "like a bird in a cage". These events fulfill Isaiah's prophetic warnings in 7:14–25 and 8:6–8.

36:2 Rabshakeh: The title of a senior Assyrian official. He is the spokesman of the embassy sent to Jerusalem to demand Hezekiah's submission. **Lachish:** Over 25 miles southwest of Jerusalem (Tell el-Duweir). It served as Sennacherib's command center during his campaign in Palestine. **conduit of the upper pool:** Part of ancient Jerusalem's water supply system. Its location is uncertain but likely near the northwestern wall of the city. This is the same place where Isaiah challenged Ahaz, Hezekiah's father, to trust the Lord for protection from enemy threats (7:3).

36:3 Eliakim ... Shebna ... Joah: Senior officials of the ruling court in Judah. Eliakim, the royal steward, is also mentioned in 22:20. For the nature of his position, see word study: *Over the Household* at 1 Kings 16:9.

36:4–20 Sennacherib's spokesman engages in psychological warfare. Intimidation tactics include mocking Judah's alliance with Egypt (36:6), ridiculing Hezekiah's reliance on the Lord (36:7), and boasting that no god or nation has withstood the advance of the Assyrians (36:18–20). The enemy wants the citizens of Jerusalem to doubt the wisdom of Hezekiah's leadership, which may be described as a quiet trust in the Lord (see 30:15).

36:4 the great king: The customary title for Assyrian monarchs at this time.

36:6 relying on Egypt: Judah sought to gain military support from Egypt against Assyria, a move that Isaiah denounced (30:1–5; 31:1–3).

36:11 Aramaic: The language of diplomacy in the western Assyrian Empire. The request to hold negotiations in Aramaic is a request to halt negotiations in Judean Hebrew, lest the arrogant threats of Sennacherib cause panic in the city.

the hand of the king of Assyria." ¹⁶Do not listen to Hezeki′ah; for thus says the king of Assyria: Make your peace with me and come out to me; then every one of you will eat of his own vine, and every one of his own fig tree, and every one of you will drink the water of his own cistern; ¹⁷until I come and take you away to a land like your own land, a land of grain and wine, a land of bread and vineyards. ¹⁸Beware lest Hezeki′ah mislead you by saying, "The LORD will deliver us." Has any of the gods of the nations delivered his land out of the hand of the king of Assyria? ¹⁹Where are the gods of Ha′math and Arpad? Where are the gods of Sepharva′im? Have they delivered Samar′ia out of my hand? ²⁰Who among all the gods of these countries have delivered their countries out of my hand, that the LORD should deliver Jerusalem out of my hand?' "

21 But they were silent and answered him not a word, for the king's command was, "Do not answer him." ²²Then Eli′akim the son of Hilki′ah, who was over the household, and Sheb′na the secretary, and Jo′ah the son of A′saph, the recorder, came to Hezeki′ah with their clothes torn, and told him the words of the Rab′shakeh.

Hezekiah Consults Isaiah

37 When King Hezeki′ah heard it, he tore his clothes, and covered himself with sackcloth, and went into the house of the LORD. ²And he sent Eli′akim, who was over the household, and Shebna the secretary, and the senior priests, clothed with sackcloth, to the prophet Isai′ah the son of A′moz. ³They said to him, "Thus says Hezeki′ah, 'This day is a day of distress, of rebuke, and of disgrace; children have come to the birth, and there is no strength to bring them forth. ⁴It may be that the LORD your God heard the words of the Rab′shakeh, whom his master the king of Assyria has sent to mock the living God, and will rebuke the words

which the LORD your God has heard; therefore lift up your prayer for the remnant that is left.' "

5 When the servants of King Hezeki′ah came to Isai′ah, ⁶Isai′ah said to them, "Say to your master, 'Thus says the LORD: Do not be afraid because of the words that you have heard, with which the servants of the king of Assyria have reviled me. ⁷Behold, I will put a spirit in him, so that he shall hear a rumor, and return to his own land; and I will make him fall by the sword in his own land.' "

8 The Rab′shakeh returned, and found the king of Assyria fighting against Libnah; for he had heard that the king had left La′chish. ⁹Now the king heard concerning Tirha′kah king of Ethiopia, "He has set out to fight against you." And when he heard it, he sent messengers to Hezeki′ah, saying, ¹⁰"Thus shall you speak to Hezeki′ah king of Judah: 'Do not let your God on whom you rely deceive you by promising that Jerusalem will not be given into the hand of the king of Assyria. ¹¹Behold, you have heard what the kings of Assyria have done to all lands, destroying them utterly. And shall you be delivered? ¹²Have the gods of the nations delivered them, the nations which my fathers destroyed, Gozan, Haran, Rezeph, and the people of Eden who were in Telas′sar? ¹³Where is the king of Ha′math, the king of Arpad, the king of the city of Sepharva′im, the king of He′na, or the king of Ivvah?' "

Hezekiah's Prayer

14 Hezeki′ah received the letter from the hand of the messengers, and read it; and Hezekiah went up to the house of the LORD, and spread it before the LORD. ¹⁵And Hezeki′ah prayed to the LORD: ¹⁶"O LORD of hosts, God of Israel, who are enthroned above the cherubim, you are the God, you alone, of all the kingdoms of the earth; you have made heaven and earth. ¹⁷Incline your ear, O LORD, and hear; open your eyes, O LORD, and see;

36:16 vine ... fig tree: Images of a peaceful life undisturbed by war (1 Kings 4:25; Mic 4:4).

36:17 a land like your own: A claim that the lands of the Assyrian exile have all the blessings of the Promised Land (Deut 8:7–9).

36:19 Samaria: The capital of the Northern Kingdom of Israel, overthrown by the Assyrians in 722 B.C.

36:22 their clothes torn: A sign of extreme distress (1 Kings 21:27; 2 Kings 6:30).

37:1 sackcloth: A coarse, hair-spun fabric worn next to the skin in times when prayer and repentance are matters of urgency (2 Kings 6:30; Joel 1:13).

37:2 Eliakim ... Shebna: Hezekiah's delegates. See note on 36:3. **the prophet Isaiah:** Isaiah of Jerusalem, whose oracles are preserved in the present book (1:1). Several hallmarks of Isaiah's distinctive language and style appear in this chapter, e.g., the assurance that Judah need not be "afraid" of the Assyrians (37:6; cf. 10:24); the mention of Assyria's "arrogance" (37:29; cf. 10:12); the description of Jerusalem as the "daughter of Zion" (37:22; cf. 1:8; 10:32); the reference to the Lord as the "Holy One of Israel" (37:23; cf. 1:4); the promise of a "remnant" (37:31–32; cf. 1:9); the announcement of a "sign" that confirms a divine message (37:30; cf. 7:14; 8:18). Sending delegates to Isaiah is an act of faith for

Hezekiah, who wisely turns to prophets rather than politicians in times of national crisis.

37:4 your prayer: Israel's prophets are known for being powerful intercessors (Jer 15:1).

37:7 return: A prophecy that Sennacherib will disengage and order his troops back home to Assyria. Jerusalem has nothing to fear (37:6), for God will rise up and defend the city (37:34–35). **fall by the sword:** Sennacherib will be assassinated by his sons in 681 B.C. (37:37–38).

37:8 Libnah: Southwest of Jerusalem, not far from Lachish on the Judah-Philistia border.

37:9 Tirhakah: An Egyptian pharaoh who ruled Ethiopia, which at this time included part of southern Egypt. His reign as king did not begin until 690 B.C., which means that he was still a military commander when Egypt planned this strike against Assyrian forces in Palestine.

37:12–13 Sennacherib boasts that neither "gods" nor "kings" have withstood the advance of the Assyrian war machine.

37:16 O LORD of hosts: See note on 1:9. **the cherubim:** Images of angels whose wings form the Lord's throne above the Ark of the Covenant. See note on Ex 25:18. **you alone:** Hezekiah affirms the monotheistic belief of Israel (Deut 4:35, 39; 6:4).

and hear all the words of Sennach'erib, which he has sent to mock the living God. ¹⁸Of a truth, O LORD, the kings of Assyria have laid waste all the nations and their lands, ¹⁹and have cast their gods into the fire; for they were no gods, but the work of men's hands, wood and stone; therefore they were destroyed. ²⁰So now, O LORD our God, save us from his hand, that all the kingdoms of the earth may know that you alone are the LORD."

21 Then Isai'ah the son of A'moz sent to Hezeki'ah, saying, "Thus says the LORD, the God of Israel: Because you have prayed to me concerning Sennach'erib king of Assyria, ²²this is the word that the LORD has spoken concerning him:
    'She despises you, she scorns you—
        the virgin daughter of Zion;
    she wags her head behind you—
        the daughter of Jerusalem.

²³'Whom have you mocked and reviled?
    Against whom have you raised your voice
and haughtily lifted your eyes?
    Against the Holy One of Israel!
²⁴By your servants you have mocked the Lord,
    and you have said, With my many chariots
I have gone up the heights of the mountains,
    to the far recesses of Lebanon;
I felled its tallest cedars,
    its choicest cypresses;
I came to its remotest height,
    its densest forest.
²⁵I dug wells
    and drank waters,
and I dried up with the sole of my foot
    all the streams of Egypt.

²⁶'Have you not heard
    that I determined it long ago?
I planned from days of old
    what now I bring to pass,

that you should make fortified cities
    crash into heaps of ruins,
²⁷while their inhabitants, shorn of strength,
    are dismayed and confounded,
and have become like plants of the field
    and like tender grass,
like grass on the housetops,
    blighted* before it is grown.

²⁸I know your sitting down
    and your going out and coming in,
    and your raging against me.
²⁹Because you have raged against me
    and your arrogance has come to my ears,
I will put my hook in your nose
    and my bit in your mouth,
and I will turn you back on the way
    by which you came.'

30 "And this shall be the sign for you: this year eat what grows of itself, and in the second year what springs of the same; then in the third year sow and reap, and plant vineyards, and eat their fruit. ³¹And the surviving remnant of the house of Judah shall again take root downward, and bear fruit upward; ³²for out of Jerusalem shall go forth a remnant, and out of Mount Zion a band of survivors. The zeal of the LORD of hosts will accomplish this.

33 "Therefore thus says the LORD concerning the king of Assyria: He shall not come into this city, or shoot an arrow there, or come before it with a shield, or cast up a siege mound against it. ³⁴By the way that he came, by the same he shall return, and he shall not come into this city, says the LORD. ³⁵For I will defend this city to save it, for my own sake and for the sake of my servant David."

Sennacherib's Defeat and Death

36 And the angel of the LORD went forth, and slew a hundred and eighty-five thousand in the camp of the Assyrians; and when men arose early

---

37:19 **the work of men's hands:** A standard critique of pagan idols. The Bible declares them to be lifeless, man-made statues that have no real power to influence the world (44:9–20; Ps 115:4–8; Jer 10:1–5).

37:21–35 The Lord's reply to Hezekiah delivered by Isaiah. The message is twofold: 37:21–29 consists of words of judgment against the arrogant Assyrians, and 37:30–35 offers words of comfort to a frightened Jerusalem.

37:22 **daughter of Zion:** A poetic title for Jerusalem, personified as a young woman under the watchful protection of her father (1:8).

37:23 **the Holy One of Israel:** See note on 1:4.

37:26 **I planned from days of old:** The Assyrians wrongly suppose that their status as a mighty empire is their own doing (10:12–14). To the contrary, the God of Israel—who is the God of all nations—predetermined this as part of his providential plan for salvation history. Isaiah insists that God is the

sovereign Lord of history who foreknew and foreordained the destiny of nations long ago (41:4; 44:6–8; 46:8–11).

37:30 **the sign:** The people of Judah will harvest food for two years without planting crops, despite the fact that Assyrian forces ravaged much of the land. The miracle of the harvest signifies how the surviving remnant of God's people will again flourish (37:31).

37:35 **for the sake of ... David:** By defending the city and royal government of Jerusalem, the Lord defends his covenant of kingship with David, as promised to Hezekiah in 38:6. See note on 1 Kings 11:36 and essay: *The Davidic Covenant* at 2 Sam 7.

37:36 **the angel of the LORD:** An executor of divine judgment sent from heaven to inflict mass casualties in the Assyrian camp (Sir 48:21). It is not specified exactly how the enemy soldiers died, but perhaps the angel unleashed a plague (as in 2 Sam 24:15–16 and Ps 78:49–50). See word study: *Angel of the LORD* at Gen 16:7. **a hundred and eighty-five thousand:** For a discussion of large numbers in the Bible, see note on Num 1:46.

---

*With 2 Kings 19:26: Heb *field*.

in the morning, behold, these were all dead bodies. [37]Then Sennach'erib king of Assyria departed, and went home and dwelt at Nin'eveh. [38]And as he was worshiping in the house of Nis'roch his god, Adram'melech and Share'zer, his sons, slew him with the sword, and escaped into the land of Ar'arat. And E'sar-had'don his son reigned in his stead.

Hezekiah's Sickness

38 In those days Hezeki'ah became sick and was at the point of death. And Isai'ah the prophet the son of A'moz came to him, and said to him, "Thus says the LORD: Set your house in order; for you shall die, you shall not recover." [2]Then Hezeki'ah turned his face to the wall, and prayed to the LORD, [3]and said, "Remember now, O LORD, I beseech you, how I have walked before you in faithfulness and with a whole heart, and have done what is good in your sight." And Hezeki'ah wept bitterly. [4]Then the word of the LORD came to Isai'ah: [5]"Go and say to Hezeki'ah, Thus says the LORD, the God of David your father: I have heard your prayer, I have seen your tears; behold, I will add fifteen years to your life. [6]I will deliver you and this city out of the hand of the king of Assyria, and defend this city.

7 "This is the sign to you from the LORD, that the LORD will do this thing that he has promised: [8]Behold, I will make the shadow cast by the declining sun on the dial of A'haz turn back ten steps." So the sun turned back on the dial the ten steps by which it had declined.[f]

9 A writing of Hezeki'ah king of Judah, after he had been sick and had recovered from his sickness:
[10]I said, In the noontide of my days
   I must depart;
I am consigned to the gates of Sheol
   for the rest of my years.

[11]I said, I shall not see the LORD
   in the land of the living;
I shall look upon man no more
   among the inhabitants of the world.
[12]My dwelling is plucked up and removed from me
   like a shepherd's tent;
like a weaver I have rolled up my life;
   he cuts me off from the loom;
from day to night you bring me to an end;[g]
13 I cry for help[h] until morning;
like a lion he breaks all my bones;
   from day to night you bring me to an end.[g]

[14]Like a swallow or a crane[i] I clamor,
   I moan like a dove.
My eyes are weary with looking upward.
   O Lord, I am oppressed; be my security!
[15]But what can I say? For he has spoken to me,
   and he himself has done it.
All my sleep has fled[j]
   because of the bitterness of my soul.

[16]O Lord, by these things men live,
   and in all these is the life of my spirit.[k]
Oh, restore me to health and make me live!
[17]Behold, it was for my welfare
   that I had great bitterness;
but you have held back[l] my life
   from the pit of destruction,
for you have cast all my sins behind your back.
[18]For Sheol cannot thank you,
   death cannot praise you;
those who go down to the pit cannot hope
   for your faithfulness.
[19]The living, the living, he thanks you,
   as I do this day;
the father makes known to the children
   your faithfulness.

37:37 Nineveh: The capital city of Assyria on the upper Tigris River.

37:38 Nisroch: A deity not yet identified. **slew him:** The assassination of Sennacherib took place in 681 B.C., as foretold by Isaiah twenty years earlier in 701 B.C. (37:7). **Ararat:** North of Assyria in modern Armenia. **Esarhaddon:** Successor to Sennacherib as king of Assyria (ca. 681 to 669 B.C.).

38:1 In those days: The time reference is nonspecific. This is because the events of chap. 38 took place *before* the events narrated in chaps. 36–37. Notice that Jerusalem's deliverance is still a future event in 38:6, and yet the miracle was described in 37:36–37. See note on 36:1–39:8. **you shall not recover:** A conditional prophecy that is subject to revision, as shown by 38:5.

38:3 Remember now, O LORD: The king prays for recovery from a terminal illness. He seeks this blessing by appealing to

his faithfulness to the Lord's covenant, i.e., his efforts to rid the kingdom of Judah of idols (2 Kings 18:1–8). **wept bitterly:** Tears of penitent sorrow (2 Cor 7:10).

38:5 fifteen years: Hezekiah died about 686 B.C., fifteen years after the Lord's deliverance of Jerusalem in 701 B.C.

38:7 the sign: Announcing signs that reinforce divine promises is a characteristic feature of Isaiah's ministry (7:14; 8:18; 37:30).

38:8 back ten steps: A miracle of sunlight and shadow. It takes place on a time-keeping device, presumably a rooftop sundial that utilized one or more flights of stairs to mark the hours of the day. Hezekiah witnesses the shadow mysteriously retreat backward in a "counterclockwise" direction. For another miracle in the Bible linked with the sun, see note on Josh 10:13.

38:9–20 Hezekiah's psalm of thanksgiving. It recounts the trials faced by the king during his sickness and expresses gratitude to God for rescuing him from death (cf. Jon 2:2–9). The psalm serves as an illustration of the power of prayer. In view of the larger context, one can see a parallel between the personal fate of Hezekiah and the collective fate of Jerusalem: both are brought to the brink of death, yet both are preserved by the saving intervention of God (see 38:6).

---

f The Hebrew of this verse is obscure.
g Heb uncertain.
h Cn: Heb obscure.
i Heb uncertain.
j Cn Compare Syr: Heb *I will walk slowly all my years.*
k Heb uncertain.
l Cn Compare Gk Vg: Heb *loved.*

20The Lord will save me,
and we will sing to stringed instruments[m]
all the days of our life,
at the house of the Lord.

21Now Isai′ah had said, "Let them take a cake of figs, and apply it to the boil, that he may recover." 22Hezeki′ah also had said, "What is the sign that I shall go up to the house of the Lord?"

Envoys from Babylon Welcomed

39 At that time Mer′odachbal′adan the son of Bal′adan, king of Babylon, sent envoys with letters and a present to Hezeki′ah, for he heard that he had been sick and had recovered. 2And Hezeki′ah welcomed them; and he showed them his treasure house, the silver, the gold, the spices, the precious oil, his whole armory, all that was found in his storehouses. There was nothing in his house or in all his realm that Hezekiah did not show them. 3Then Isai′ah the prophet came to King Hezeki′ah, and said to him, "What did these men say? And from where did they come to you?" Hezekiah said, "They have come to me from a far country, from Babylon." 4He said, "What have they seen in your house?" Hezeki′ah answered, "They have seen all that is in my house; there is nothing in my storehouses that I did not show them."

5 Then Isai′ah said to Hezeki′ah, "Hear the word of the Lord of hosts: 6Behold, the days are coming, when all that is in your house, and that which your fathers have stored up till this day, shall be carried to Babylon; nothing shall be left, says the Lord. 7And some of your own sons, who are born to you, shall be taken away; and they shall be eunuchs in the palace of the king of Babylon." 8Then said Hezeki′ah to Isai′ah, "The word of the Lord which you have spoken is good." For he thought, "There will be peace and security in my days."

God Comforts His People

40 *Comfort, comfort my people, says your God. 2Speak tenderly to Jerusalem,
and cry to her
that her warfare[n] is ended,
that her iniquity is pardoned,
that she has received from the Lord's hand
double for all her sins.

3A voice cries:
"In the wilderness prepare the way of the Lord,
make straight in the desert a highway for our God.

39:1–8: 2 Kings 20:12–19; 2 Chron 32:31.   **40:3:** Mt 3:3; Mk 1:3; Lk 3:4; Jn 1:23.

38:21 cake of figs: Dried figs were believed to have healing properties. **boil:** An infection or blistering of the skin that some have diagnosed as Pemphigus.

39:1 At that time: The time reference is nonspecific. See note on 38:1. **Merodachbaladan:** Merodachbaladan II, king of Babylon from ca. 721 to 710 B.C. He regained the throne briefly in 704 B.C. until the Assyrians ousted him from power in 703 B.C. Many scholars contend that his envoys come to Jerusalem with more than a "get well" message for Hezekiah. Merodach is probably seeking a political alliance with Judah in opposition to Assyria. Hezekiah leads the Babylonian dignitaries on a tour of his royal treasures as a way of showing that Judah would make a wealthy and worthy ally (39:2).

39:5–7 Isaiah foretells the Babylonian conquest of Jerusalem more than a century before its occurrence (2 Kings 25:8–17). He warns that a partnership with Babylon will backfire when the empire drags Hezekiah's riches and relatives into exile. Isaiah often advised faith in the Lord over foreign policies that put the covenant people at risk by giving them a false sense of security in other nations (see Is 7–8; 30–31).

40:1—55:13 Chapters 40–55 proclaim a message of comfort and hope to the Judean exiles in Babylon around the midpoint of the sixth century B.C. Isaiah's prophecy of the conquest of Jerusalem in 39:5–7 is now a painful memory of the past. The historical vantage point of the book thus jumps forward to address circumstances long after the lifetime of Isaiah. The prophet's message centers on the approaching end of the Babylonian Exile (539 B.C.) and the return of Jewish captives to Jerusalem with the help of one named "Cyrus" (44:28; 45:1, 13; 48:20). In the meantime, the covenant people must

exercise patient trust in the Lord (40:27–31). These chapters emphasize that the God of Israel is not merely a national deity but the almighty Creator and sovereign Lord of all nations and their destinies.

40:1 Comfort, comfort: The Lord consoles his people after decades of suffering in exile. Oracles of consolation feature prominently in chaps. 40–66, just as oracles of confrontation dominated chaps. 1–39. This shift in tone and emphasis corresponds with Moses' promise that God, after humbling his people and making them powerless, will have "compassion" on them (Deut 32:36). **my people ... your God:** This language indicates that, despite the chastisements of defeat and exile, Israel's covenant relationship with the Lord endures (Lev 26:12; Jer 31:33).

40:2 warfare: Or "time of service", the idea being that God's people were sold into captivity as debt slaves (50:1). Underlying this notion is the belief that sin creates a spiritual debt with God that is paid off by means of temporal suffering (cf. Mt 18:23–35). **double for all her sins:** A way of stressing that the Judean exiles have paid off their debts in full.

📖✝ **40:3–5** The Lord will deliver his people from Babylon, just as he delivered them from Egypt, only this time he will lead them to Zion instead of Sinai. • The Gospels identify the **voice** in the **wilderness** with John the Baptist, the herald of the Messiah (Mt 3:1–3; Mk 1:2–4; Lk 3:1–6; Jn 1:19–23; CCC 719). Release from Babylon not only replicates the former exodus from Egypt but anticipates a greater salvation in the future, when God will come in the flesh to deliver the world from sin and death. It is through the Incarnation of the Word in Jesus Christ that **the glory of the Lord** is more fully revealed (Jn 1:14). • Those who received the baptism of John were not regenerated. But they were prepared by the ministry of the forerunner, who cried out to prepare the way for Christ, in whom alone they could be regenerated. For his Baptism is not by water only, as John's was, but is also by the Holy Spirit (St. Augustine, *On Faith, Hope, and Love* 14, 49).

---

[m] Heb *my stringed instruments.*
[n] Or *time of service.*
*40:1: Here begins the "Book of the Consolation of Israel," as it has been beautifully called. It was written to comfort and console the people in their exile in Babylonia.

⁴Every valley shall be lifted up,
    and every mountain and hill be made low;
the uneven ground shall become level,
    and the rough places a plain.
⁵And the glory of the LORD shall be revealed,
    and all flesh shall see it together,
    for the mouth of the LORD has spoken."

⁶A voice says, "Cry!"
    And I said, "What shall I cry?"
All flesh is grass,
    and all its beauty is like the flower of the field.
⁷The grass withers, the flower fades,
    when the breath of the LORD blows upon it;
    surely the people is grass.
⁸The grass withers, the flower fades;
    but the word of our God will stand for ever.
⁹Get you up to a high mountain,
    O Zion, herald of good tidings;°
lift up your voice with strength,
    O Jerusalem, herald of good tidings,ᵖ
lift it up, fear not;
say to the cities of Judah,
    "Behold your God!"
¹⁰Behold, the Lord GOD comes with might,
    and his arm rules for him;
behold, his reward is with him,
    and his recompense before him.

¹¹He will feed his flock like a shepherd,
    he will gather the lambs in his arms,
he will carry them in his bosom,
    and gently lead those that are with young.

¹²Who has measured the waters in the hollow of his
        hand
    and marked off the heavens with a span,
enclosed the dust of the earth in a measure
    and weighed the mountains in scales
    and the hills in a balance?
¹³Who has directed the Spirit of the LORD,
    or as his counselor has instructed him?
¹⁴Whom did he consult for his enlightenment,
    and who taught him the path of justice,
and taught him knowledge,
    and showed him the way of understanding?
¹⁵Behold, the nations are like a drop from a bucket,
    and are accounted as the dust on the scales;
behold, he takes up the isles like fine dust.
¹⁶Lebanon would not suffice for fuel,
    nor are its beasts enough for a burnt offering.
¹⁷All the nations are as nothing before him,
    they are accounted by him as less than nothing
        and emptiness.

¹⁸To whom then will you liken God,
    or what likeness compare with him?

40:4–5: Lk 3:5–6.   **40:6–8:** 1 Pet 1:24–25.   **40:9:** Is 52:7; Nah 1:15; Acts 10:36; Rom 10:15.
40:10: Rev 22:7, 12.   **40:13:** Rom 11:34; 1 Cor 2:16.

40:4 Every valley ... plain: The clearing and construction of a new highway in the wilderness signifies how God will remove all obstacles to his people's return from exile.

40:6–8 Isaiah's message of good news is more certain and lasting than anything on earth, including the Babylonian Empire, which at this point in history had reached its full strength and appeared to be indestructible. Even still, despite appearances, the prophetic word of God can be trusted to reach its fulfillment. • Peter relates this passage to the gospel, which imparts to those who believe an imperishable life that outlasts the perishable things of this world (1 Pet 1:23–25). • When you look at something grassy or a flower, think about human nature and remember Isaiah's comparison, which signifies the shortness of life and the brevity of pleasure. Today one is vigorous, healthy, and eager. Tomorrow one is run down by age and weakened by illness (St. Basil of Caesarea, *On the Six Days of Creation* 5, 2).

40:6 And I said, "What shall I cry?": Similar to Isaiah's initial responses to the Lord in 6:8 and 6:11. These resemblances suggest that the prophet receives a new commission to deliver a new message—not words of judgment for his own generation, but words of comfort for a future generation (40:1). **All flesh:** All living things on earth (Gen 9:14–17).

40:9 O Zion ... O Jerusalem: It is unclear whether the city is the bearer of the message or its intended recipient (see textual notes o and p). **herald of good tidings:** A messenger tasked with bringing news to others—in this case, the welcome announcement that God is about to lead his people back to Zion (41:27). The Greek LXX renders the

Hebrew with an expression that could be translated "one who evangelizes".

40:10 might ... arm: Represent the power of God to deliver his people.

40:11 a shepherd: An OT image for kings and other rulers (Num 27:17; 2 Sam 5:2; Ps 78:71), most notably for God (Ps 23:1; 80:1) and his Messiah (Ezek 34:23; Mic 5:4). The same image carries over into the NT (Mt 25:31–33; Jn 10:11; Heb 13:20; 1 Pet 2:25).

40:12–31 Rhetorical questions and claims meant to strengthen the faith of God's people and dispel their doubts about his intention to save them.

40:12 Who has measured ...?: Implied answer: no one, except the Lord God, who designed and constructed the universe like an artisan in his workshop (cf. Job 38–41). **a span:** A hand measurement (= the distance between the tips of the thumb and little finger when the fingers are spread apart).

40:13 Who ... his counselor ...?: Implied answer: no one, since God's wisdom surpasses all. • Paul quotes the LXX version of this passage twice in the NT: once in Rom 11:34, where he marvels at the wisdom of God manifest in his plan to save all nations, including Israel, and again in 1 Cor 2:16, where he affirms that God's wisdom is unknowable apart from the Spirit, who imparts a spiritual knowledge of God and his ways to believers in Christ.

40:15 a drop from a bucket: The collective might of all nations add up to practically nothing in comparison with the Lord's power, as explained in 40:17.

40:16 Lebanon: North of Israel and famous for its massive cedar trees.

40:18–20 A prophetic critique of idols. Far from being rivals of the true God, they are nothing more than handmade images (44:9–20; Jer 10:1–15).

° Or *O herald of good tidings to Zion.*
ᵖ Or *O herald of good tidings to Jerusalem.*

19 The idol! a workman casts it,
and a goldsmith overlays it with gold,
and casts for it silver chains.
20 He who is impoverished[q] chooses for an offering
wood that will not rot;
he seeks out a skilful craftsman
to set up an image that will not move.

21 Have you not known? Have you not heard?
Has it not been told you from the beginning?
Have you not understood from the foundations
of the earth?
22 It is he who sits above the circle of the earth,
and its inhabitants are like grasshoppers;
who stretches out the heavens like a curtain,
and spreads them like a tent to dwell in;
23 who brings princes to nought,
and makes the rulers of the earth as nothing.

24 Scarcely are they planted, scarcely sown,
scarcely has their stem taken root in the
earth,
when he blows upon them, and they wither,
and the tempest carries them off like
stubble.

25 To whom then will you compare me,
that I should be like him?
says the Holy One.
26 Lift up your eyes on high and see:
who created these?
He who brings out their host by number,
calling them all by name;
by the greatness of his might,
and because he is strong in power
not one is missing.

27 Why do you say, O Jacob,
and speak, O Israel,
"My way is hidden from the LORD,
and my right is disregarded by my
God"?
28 Have you not known? Have you not heard?
The LORD is the everlasting God,
the Creator of the ends of the earth.
He does not faint or grow weary,
his understanding is unsearchable.
29 He gives power to the faint,
and to him who has no might he increases
strength.
30 Even youths shall faint and be weary,
and young men shall fall exhausted;
31 but they who wait for the LORD shall renew their
strength,
they shall mount up with wings like eagles,
they shall run and not be weary,
they shall walk and not faint.

Israel Assured of God's Help

41 Listen to me in silence, O islands;
let the peoples renew their strength;
let them approach, then let them speak;
let us together draw near for judgment.

2 Who stirred up one from the east
whom victory meets at every step?
He gives up nations before him,
so that he tramples kings under foot;
he makes them like dust with his sword,
like driven stubble with his bow.
3 He pursues them and passes on safely,
by paths his feet have not trod.
4 Who has performed and done this,
calling the generations from the beginning?

40:19 chains: May refer to silver wiring used as decorative inlay on idol images.

40:22 sits above: The Lord is enthroned in the heavens (66:1). This belief was represented in the sanctuaries of Israel by the lid of the Ark of the Covenant, where angelic figures called cherubim extended their wings to form a throne for the Lord (37:16; Ps 80:1). **the circle of the earth:** This could refer **(1)** to the earth itself, imagined as a circular disc; **(2)** to the vault of the sky, pictured as a dome arching over the earth; or **(3)** to the surrounding horizon, where the dome of the heavens was thought to rest on the earth. For the firmament of heaven, see note on Gen 1:6. **stretches out the heavens:** The work of creation, with the sky suspended over the earth, is compared to pitching a tent (42:5; 44:24; 45:12). This reflects ancient Israel's belief that the world is a cosmic sanctuary, just as the wilderness Tabernacle and the Jerusalem Temple were viewed as replicas of the cosmos on an architectural scale. See note on Ex 40:33 and essay: *The Theology of the Temple* at 2 Chron 5.

40:27–31 Words of encouragement for the exiles, who are tempted to think that God has forgotten them. In reality, the exiles have forgotten the Lord's goodness and love. Isaiah announces that God is ready to take strength from the mighty (Babylonians) and give it to the weak and weary who rely on him (faithful Jewish exiles).

40:31 wings like eagles: Brings to mind the Exodus from Egypt, when the Lord brought his people to Mount Sinai "on eagle's wings" (Ex 19:4).

41:1–29 The Lord puts the nations and their gods on trial, questioning them and challenging them to produce evidence of their ability to shape the course of history. Predictably, no such evidence is forthcoming; only the God of Israel, who manages earthly powers and rulers as instruments of his will, controls the direction of world events.

41:2 stirred up: The same expression is used in 13:17 to prophesy the fall of Babylon to Medo-Persia (see also 41:25 and Ezra 1:1). **one from the east:** Cyrus II the Great, named in 44:28 and 45:1. He founded the Persian Empire about 550 B.C. when he overtook Media and rapidly expanded his domain into Asia Minor and west India. Babylon surrendered to Persian forces in 539 B.C., at which time its foreign captives, including exiles from Judah, were allowed to return to their homelands (Ezra 1:1–4). Isaiah stresses that Cyrus' remarkable rise to power is the Lord's doing. See note on 41:25.

41:4 the first ... the last: God is the sovereign Lord of history from beginning to end as well as the origin and destiny of all creation (44:6; 48:12). • Jesus speaks of himself in these terms when he reveals his glory in the Book of Revelation (Rev 1:17; 22:13).

[q] Heb uncertain.

I, the Lord, the first,
    and with the last; I am He.
⁵The islands have seen and are afraid,
    the ends of the earth tremble;
    they have drawn near and come.
⁶Every one helps his neighbor,
    and says to his brother, "Take courage!"
⁷The craftsman encourages the goldsmith,
    and he who smooths with the hammer him
        who strikes the anvil,
  saying of the soldering, "It is good";
    and they fasten it with nails so that it cannot
      be moved.

⁸But you, Israel, my servant,
    Jacob, whom I have chosen,
    the offspring of Abraham, my friend;
⁹you whom I took from the ends of the earth,
    and called from its farthest corners,
  saying to you, "You are my servant,
    I have chosen you and not cast you off";
¹⁰fear not, for I am with you,
    be not dismayed, for I am your God;
I will strengthen you, I will help you,
    I will uphold you with my victorious right hand.

¹¹Behold, all who are incensed against you
    shall be put to shame and confounded;
  those who strive against you
    shall be as nothing and shall perish.
¹²You shall seek those who contend with you,
    but you shall not find them;
  those who war against you
    shall be as nothing at all.
¹³For I, the Lord your God,
    hold your right hand;

it is I who say to you, "Fear not,
    I will help you."

¹⁴Fear not, you worm Jacob,
    you men of Israel!
I will help you, says the Lord;
    your Redeemer is the Holy One of Israel.
¹⁵Behold, I will make of you a threshing sledge,
    new, sharp, and having teeth;
you shall thresh the mountains and crush
      them,
    and you shall make the hills like chaff;
¹⁶you shall winnow them and the wind shall carry
      them away,
    and the tempest shall scatter them.
And you shall rejoice in the Lord;
    in the Holy One of Israel you shall glory.

¹⁷When the poor and needy seek water,
    and there is none,
    and their tongue is parched with thirst,
I the Lord will answer them,
    I the God of Israel will not forsake them.
¹⁸I will open rivers on the bare heights,
    and fountains in the midst of the
      valleys;
I will make the wilderness a pool of water,
    and the dry land springs of water.
¹⁹I will put in the wilderness the cedar,
    the acacia, the myrtle, and the olive;
I will set in the desert the cypress,
    the plane and the pine together;
²⁰that men may see and know,
    may consider and understand together,
that the hand of the Lord has done this,
    the Holy One of Israel has created it.

41:8: Jas 2:23. **41:8–9:** Lk 1:54; Heb 2:16. **41:10:** Acts 18:10.

41:5–7 Uncertain times lead foolish nations to calm their fears by making more idols, as if the future could be influenced by the lifeless creations of a craftsman (cf. 19:3).

41:7 fasten it with nails: A reference to securing idol images in place (Jer 10:4).

41:8 Israel, my servant: Israel is the object of God's special love and election (Deut 7:6–8; Ps 135:4). With the Lord as their Defender, the exiles of Judah need not fear the political and military developments that unsettle other nations (41:5); God is coming to help them (41:10, 13–14) and bring them joy (41:16). The people of Israel are designated the Lord's servant in several passages in Isaiah (see 44:1, 21; 45:4). **offspring of Abraham:** The twelve tribes of Israel are descended from Abraham's grandson Jacob. **my friend:** Or "my beloved".

41:9 from the ends of the earth: Abraham lived in the city of Ur in southern Mesopotamia before God called him to the land of Canaan (Gen 11:31; 12:1). The return of the Judean exiles from Babylon in southern Mesopotamia will replicate Abraham's migration to the Promised Land. **not cast you off:** Israel's election as the Lord's covenant people has not been undone by the Exile. They are humbled but not forsaken (1 Sam 12:22; Rom 11:1).

41:11 put to shame: Beginning with Babylon, which is soon to fall, as announced in 13:19–22 and 21:9.

41:14 worm: Something despised as insignificant (Job 25:6; Ps 22:6). **Redeemer:** The term in Hebrew is *go'el* and refers to one who rescues a blood relative from servitude. The idea is that God is a divine Father (63:16; 64:8) who is coming to the aid of his first-born son in captivity (Ex 4:22; Jer 31:9). Use of this language hints that deliverance from Babylon will resemble Israel's Exodus from Egypt (Ex 6:6; 15:13). See word study: *Redeem* at Lev 25:25. **the Holy One of Israel:** See note on 1:4.

41:15 threshing sledge: A harvesting implement with a studded underside. It was dragged over grain to separate the kernels from their husks. **mountains ... hills:** Obstacles to the fulfillment of God's purposes will be cleared away, as in 40:4.

41:17–20 Isaiah sees the desert highway from Babylon to Zion (40:3) having plenty of drinking water and shade trees (43:19–20)—images that symbolize the blessings that God will bestow on the exiles returning home from Babylon. • These provisions evoke memories of Israel's journey from Egypt to Sinai at the time of the Exodus (Ex 15:27; 17:1–7).

41:20 the hand of the Lord: The same supernatural power that performed signs and wonders at the time of the Exodus from Egypt (Ex 3:19–20; 7:4–5; 15:6, 11–12).

²¹Set forth your case, says the Lord;
  bring your proofs, says the King of Jacob.
²²Let them bring them, and tell us
  what is to happen.
 Tell us the former things, what they are,
  that we may consider them,
 that we may know their outcome;
  or declare to us the things to come.
²³Tell us what is to come hereafter,
  that we may know that you are gods;
 do good, or do harm,
  that we may be dismayed and terrified.
²⁴Behold, you are nothing,
  and your work is nought;
  an abomination is he who chooses you.

²⁵I stirred up one from the north, and he has come,
  from the rising of the sun, and he shall call on
  my name;
 he shall trample^r on rulers as on mortar,
  as the potter treads clay.
²⁶Who declared it from the beginning, that we
  might know,
 and beforetime, that we might say, "He is
  right"?

There was none who declared it, none who
  proclaimed,
 none who heard your words.
²⁷I first have declared it to Zion,^s
  and I give to Jerusalem a herald of good tidings.
²⁸But when I look there is no one;
  among these there is no counselor
 who, when I ask, gives an answer.
²⁹Behold, they are all a delusion;
  their works are nothing;
  their molten images are empty wind.

The Lord's Servant; and Israel's Disobedience

42 *Behold my servant, whom I uphold,
  my chosen, in whom my soul delights;
 I have put my Spirit upon him,
  he will bring forth justice to the nations.
²He will not cry or lift up his voice,
  or make it heard in the street;
³a bruised reed he will not break,
  and a dimly burning wick he will not quench;
 he will faithfully bring forth justice.
⁴He will not fail^t or be discouraged^u
  till he has established justice in the earth;
  and the islands wait for his law.

42:1–4: Mt 12:18–21.

41:21-29 The gods of the nations are summoned to testify before God the Judge. At issue is whether idols can predict the future and thereby demonstrate their claims to deity. They are challenged to cite prophecies delivered in the past that have since been fulfilled (**the former things**, 41:22) or to utter new predictions about the future that can be tested in the days ahead (**what is to come**, 41:23). None of these gods responds (41:28) because none actually exists (41:29).

41:21 King of Jacob: The Lord's kingship was impressed upon Isaiah at his call to prophetic ministry (6:5) and is reiterated several times in the book (33:22; 43:15; 52:7).

41:23 do good, or do harm: Idols can do neither, and so they need not be feared as forces influencing the outcome of history.

41:24 you are nothing: The nonexistence of gods other than the Lord is asserted several times in Isaiah (43:10; 45:5, 21; 46:9). See note on 44:6-8. **abomination:** The degraded spiritual state of an idol worshiper.

41:25 one from the north: Cyrus II of Persia, identified in 41:2 as "one from the east". The difference between these two descriptions is not simply a poetical variation. Persia lies east of ancient Babylonia, but when the Persians finally captured Babylon, they took the city from the north. See note on 41:2. **call on my name:** Seems to indicate that Cyrus will acknowledge publicly that the Lord is behind his rise to power. For an account of his words, see Ezra 1:2.

41:27 I . . . declared it to Zion: Only Israel's God foretold the triumph of the Medo-Persian Empire over the Babylonian Empire in the sixth century B.C., something he did through the prophet Isaiah in the eighth century B.C. (13:1—14:23; 21:1-10). **herald of good tidings:** Seems to mean Isaiah himself. See note on 40:9.

📖 **42:1-9** The first of four "Servant Songs" in Isaiah, followed by 49:1-7, 50:4-11, 52:13—53:12. At one level, the Servant appears to be the nation of Israel (41:8), whose mission is to bring God's justice and light to a world living in darkness (42:4). However, the covenant people cannot give sight to the "blind" (42:7), because they themselves have become "blind" (42:19); they cannot free "prisoners" (42:7), for they themselves are confined to "prisons" (42:22); and they are unsuited to teach the nations the "law" of God (42:4), because they themselves have rebelled against the "law" (42:24). The Servant thus appears to be an exemplary Israelite—a figure who represents Israel as a people and is chosen by the Lord to fulfill Israel's vocation. Embodying what Israel is called to be, the Servant will bring salvation to Israel and the nations alike (49:5-6; 53:10-12). • The NT identifies Jesus as "the servant of the Lord" prophesied by Isaiah. This first Servant Song is referenced in connection with Christ's infancy (Lk 2:30-32), Baptism (Mk 1:9-11), and ministry (Mt 12:15-21).

✝ **42:1 my chosen:** The language of divine election (Deut 7:6-8). **my Spirit:** Instructs the Servant in divine wisdom (40:13) and empowers him to fulfill his mission (61:1), just as the Spirit endows the Davidic Messiah in 11:2. The statement here stands in contrast to 41:29, which describes powerless idols as "empty wind". **justice:** The Hebrew *mishpat* denotes a right ordering of human life, personal and societal, in accord with God's will. • The Word born of the Virgin received the Spirit according to the limits of his humanity. Being divine, he was not sanctified by the Spirit, since he is the one who sanctifies; but being human through the Incarnation, he is sanctified and anointed to justify the Gentiles with holy judgment (St. Cyril of Alexandria, *Commentary on Isaiah* 42, 1).

42:3 will not break: The Servant's ministry is marked by gentleness (40:11).

42:4 discouraged: Can also be translated "bruised" or "crushed", indicating that the Servant will undergo suffering

---

^r Cn: Heb *come.*
^s Cn: Heb *first to Zion, Behold, behold them.*
^t Or *burn dimly.*
^u Or *bruised.*
*42:1-4: The "Servant of Yahweh" is here introduced. This and three other prophecies (49:1-6; 50:4-9; 52:13—53:12) depict the Messiah in a new light, giving details of his meekness and suffering.

⁵Thus says God, the Lord,
 who created the heavens and stretched them
  out,
 who spread forth the earth and what comes
  from it,
 who gives breath to the people upon it
 and spirit to those who walk in it:
⁶"I am the Lord, I have called you in
  righteousness,
 I have taken you by the hand and kept you;
 I have given you as a covenant to the people,
 a light to the nations,
⁷ to open the eyes that are blind,
 to bring out the prisoners from the dungeon,
  from the prison those who sit in darkness.
⁸I am the Lord, that is my name;
 my glory I give to no other,
 nor my praise to graven images.
⁹Behold, the former things have come to pass,
 and new things I now declare;
 before they spring forth
 I tell you of them."

¹⁰Sing to the Lord a new song,
 his praise from the end of the earth!
Let the sea roarᵛ and all that fills it,
 the islands and their inhabitants.
¹¹Let the desert and its cities lift up their voice,
 the villages that Ke′dar inhabits;
let the inhabitants of Se′la sing for joy,
 let them shout from the top of the mountains.
¹²Let them give glory to the Lord,
 and declare his praise in the islands.

¹³The Lord goes forth like a mighty man,
 like a man of war he stirs up his fury;
he cries out, he shouts aloud,
 he shows himself mighty against his foes.

¹⁴For a long time I have held my peace,
 I have kept still and restrained myself;
now I will cry out like a woman with labor pains,
 I will gasp and pant.
¹⁵I will lay waste mountains and hills,
 and dry up all their herbage;
I will turn the rivers into islands,
 and dry up the pools.
¹⁶And I will lead the blind
 in a way that they know not,
in paths that they have not known
 I will guide them.
I will turn the darkness before them into light,
 the rough places into level ground.
These are the things I will do,
 and I will not forsake them.
¹⁷They shall be turned back and utterly put to
  shame,
 who trust in graven images,
who say to molten images,
 "You are our gods."

¹⁸Hear, you deaf;
 and look, you blind, that you may see!
¹⁹Who is blind but my servant,
 or deaf as my messenger whom I send?
Who is blind as my dedicated one,
 or blind as the servant of the Lord?

42:5: Acts 17:24–25. **42:6:** Is 49:6; Lk 2:32; Acts 13:47; 26:23. **42:7, 16:** Acts 26:18.

(53:5, 10). **the islands:** The peoples of the Mediterranean, which together represent all distant nations.

 42:5 stretched them out: Like a tent. See note on 40:22. **breath:** The "breath of life" (Gen 2:7).

 42:6 a covenant: A formal means of creating bonds of kinship between persons unrelated. In a way not explained, the Servant will accomplish this in himself: he will create relationships of covenantal kinship when he draws both the disgraced **people** of Israel and the unenlightened **nations** into the family of God, who reveals himself as Father (63:16; 64:8). The Servant's work is connected with prophetic expectations for a new and everlasting covenant that will surpass those made previously (55:3; Jer 31:31–34; Ezek 37:26–27). See essay: *What Is a Covenant?* at Deut 5. **a light:** A source of wisdom and salvation for the tribes of Israel and faraway nations (49:5–6). In essence, the Servant fulfills the national vocation of Israel to be a channel of God's blessing to the world (Gen 22:17–18) and a witness to the righteousness of God's Law (Deut 4:5–8). See note on Ex 19:6. • The Lord foretells the sending and exaltation of his Son, in order that he might be just and fulfill his promise. In taking his hand, the Father works through him; and in keeping him safe, he does not allow him to be detained by death or allow his body to see corruption. He also speaks of his Son's office as a covenant

mediator and as one who illuminates others (St. Thomas Aquinas, *Commentary on Isaiah 42, 6*).

 42:7 bring out the prisoners: Also the mission of the Lord's anointed in 61:1–3.

 42:9 former things: Prophecies given in the past that have since come true. The reference is probably to the predictions in Is 1–39, so that fulfillment of these oracles establishes a firm basis for trusting in the **new things** that God is announcing in Is 40–66. **I tell you:** God is addressing the people of Israel (the "you" is plural).

 42:10 new song: Sung to commemorate the "new things" (42:9) that God will do for his people when he leads them home (40:3–5). The salvation in view reaches to **the end of the earth**, as in 49:6.

 42:11 Kedar: A tribal people of northern Arabia. **Sela:** A city in Edom later known as Petra.

 42:13 a man of war: Perhaps an allusion to Ex 15:3, a line from the Song of the Sea in which Moses and the Israelites praise the Lord as the divine Warrior who vanquished the Egyptians (Ex 15:1–18). Other expressions from this song appear in 12.2, 5.

 42:16 the blind: Those who lack an understanding of the Lord's purposes in history.

 42:18 deaf ... blind: The spiritual condition of Israel, owing in part to the judgments of God enacted through Isaiah's ministry (6:9–10). Despite being the Lord's messenger, Israel has the same need for mercy and grace as the nations

---

ᵛCn Compare Ps 96:11; 98:7: Heb *Those who go down to the sea.*

²⁰He sees^w many things, but does not observe them;
  his ears are open, but he does not hear.
²¹The Lᴏʀᴅ was pleased, for his righteousness'
    sake,
  to magnify his law and make it glorious.
²²But this is a people robbed and plundered,
  they are all of them trapped in holes
  and hidden in prisons;
  they have become a prey with none to rescue,
  a spoil with none to say, "Restore!"
²³Who among you will give ear to this,
  will attend and listen for the time to come?
²⁴Who gave up Jacob to the spoiler,
  and Israel to the robbers?
  Was it not the Lᴏʀᴅ, against whom we have
    sinned,
  in whose ways they would not walk,
  and whose law they would not obey?
²⁵So he poured upon him the heat of his anger
  and the might of battle;
  it set him on fire round about, but he did not
    understand;
  it burned him, but he did not take it to heart.

The Lord Is Redeemer of Israel

43 But now thus says the Lᴏʀᴅ, he who created you, O Jacob,
  he who formed you, O Israel:
  "Fear not, for I have redeemed you;
  I have called you by name, you are mine.
²When you pass through the waters I will be with
    you;
  and through the rivers, they shall not
    overwhelm you;

when you walk through fire you shall not be
    burned,
  and the flame shall not consume you.
³For I am the Lᴏʀᴅ your God,
  the Holy One of Israel, your Savior.
  I give Egypt as your ransom,
  Ethiopia and Seba in exchange for you.
⁴Because you are precious in my eyes,
  and honored, and I love you,
  I give men in return for you,
  peoples in exchange for your life.
⁵Fear not, for I am with you;
  I will bring your offspring from the east,
  and from the west I will gather you;
⁶I will say to the north, Give up,
  and to the south, Do not withhold;
  bring my sons from afar
  and my daughters from the end of the earth,
⁷every one who is called by my name,
  whom I created for my glory,
  whom I formed and made."

⁸Bring forth the people who are blind, yet have
    eyes,
  who are deaf, yet have ears!
⁹Let all the nations gather together,
  and let the peoples assemble.
  Who among them can declare this,
  and show us the former things?
  Let them bring their witnesses to justify them,
  and let them hear and say, It is true.
¹⁰"You are my witnesses," says the Lᴏʀᴅ,
  "and my servant whom I have chosen,

43:5: Acts 18:10.

42:24 Who gave up Jacob ...?: The Lord, who surrendered his faithless people to foreign conquerors as punishment for sin. He handed the kingdom of Israel over to the Assyrians in the eighth century B.C. and then the kingdom of Judah over to the Babylonians in the sixth century B.C. Theologically, the point is that God is the sovereign Lord of history, and so even calamities that befall his beloved Israel are part of his overall plan of salvation.
42:25 did not understand: Israel failed to learn repentance from its suffering (as in 1:5).
43:1-7 Words of tender affection that reassure the Israelites of God's love. The exiles have not been abandoned by the Lord in the midst of their suffering. The Creator of the covenant people (43:15) will also be their Redeemer (43:14) (CCC 218-20, 287). See note on 41:14.
43:1 formed you: Israel's calling is viewed as a divine act of creation (44:2). The Hebrew verb *yaṣar*, which also describes Adam's creation in Gen 2:7, suggests the image of a potter giving shape to a lump of clay. The Lord's relationship to Israel is depicted in precisely these terms in 29:16 and 45:9 (CCC 287). **I have redeemed you:** See note on 41:14. **called you by name:** Points to an intimate personal relationship between God and Israel. **you are mine:** Reaffirms Israel's election as the Lord's "own possession" (Ex 19:5; Deut 7:6).
43:2 waters ... fire: Represent the adversities and trials of the exiled community (Ps 66:12).

43:3 the Holy One of Israel: See note on 1:4. **Egypt ... Ethiopia ... Seba:** Kingdoms in Africa and Arabia that God will hand over to the Persians as a reward for releasing Israel from captivity in Babylon.
43:5-7 Israel's restoration from exile, portrayed as an ingathering of God's children from the four points of the compass (11:11-12). The Israelites became sons and daughters of the Lord by virtue of the covenant (Deut 14:1). • Jesus probably alludes to this passage when he foretells that "men will come from east and west, and from north and south, and sit at table in the kingdom of God" (Lk 13:29).
43:8 blind ... deaf: The captives of Israel (42:18-19).
43:9 Who ... can declare this: A challenge to the nations to cite prophecies of their gods that foretold the rise of Cyrus and the fall of Babylon. None can testify to this, since only the God of Israel can announce the future before it happens (41:21-24; 44:6-8). The prophet envisions this interrogation taking place in a public assembly.
43:10 You are my witnesses: Israel, entrusted with divine revelation, can testify that the Lord announces future events before they happen and then brings them to pass (e.g., the fall of Babylon, foretold in 13:1—14:23). Unlike other nations, Israel was in a unique position to **know** and **believe** in the God who determines the course of history. • Jesus draws from this passage when he commissions the apostles to be his "witnesses" among all nations (Lk 24:48; Acts 1:8). The gospel of salvation was a message announced by the Lord in ancient times and is now coming to fulfillment in messianic times (Lk

---

^w Heb *you see.*

that you may know and believe me
and understand that I am He.
Before me no god was formed,
nor shall there be any after me.
[11]I, I am the LORD,
and besides me there is no savior.
[12]I declared and saved and proclaimed,
when there was no strange god among you;
and you are my witnesses," says the LORD.
[13]"I am God, and also henceforth I am He;
there is none who can deliver from my hand;
I work and who can hinder it?"

[14]Thus says the LORD,
your Redeemer, the Holy One of Israel:
"For your sake I will send to Babylon
and break down all the bars,
and the shouting of the Chalde′ans will be
turned to lamentations.*
[15]I am the LORD, your Holy One,
the Creator of Israel, your King."
[16]Thus says the LORD,
who makes a way in the sea,
a path in the mighty waters,
[17]who brings forth chariot and horse,
army and warrior;
they lie down, they cannot rise,
they are extinguished, quenched like a wick:
[18]"Remember not the former things,
nor consider the things of old.
[19]Behold, I am doing a new thing;
now it springs forth, do you not perceive it?
I will make a way in the wilderness and rivers in
the desert.
[20]The wild beasts will honor me,
the jackals and the ostriches;

for I give water in the wilderness,
rivers in the desert,
to give drink to my chosen people,
[21] the people whom I formed for myself
that they might declare my praise.

[22]"Yet you did not call upon me, O Jacob;
but you have been weary of me, O Israel!
[23]You have not brought me your sheep for burnt
offerings,
or honored me with your sacrifices.
I have not burdened you with offerings,
or wearied you with frankincense.
[24]You have not bought me sweet cane with money,
or satisfied me with the fat of your sacrifices.
But you have burdened me with your sins,
you have wearied me with your iniquities.

[25]"I, I am He
who blots out your transgressions for my own
sake,
and I will not remember your sins.
[26]Put me in remembrance, let us argue together;
set forth your case, that you may be proved
right.
[27]Your first father sinned,
and your mediators transgressed against me.
[28]Therefore I profaned the princes of the sanctuary,
I delivered Jacob to utter destruction
and Israel to reviling.

God's Blessing on Israel

44 "But now hear, O Jacob my servant,
Israel whom I have chosen!
[2]Thus says the LORD who made you,
who formed you from the womb and will help
you:

24:44-47; Acts 3:18-26). **I am He:** I.e., the only God that actually exists (44:6; CCC 212).

43:13 none ... from my hand: As stated in the Song of Moses (Deut 32:39). **who can hinder it?:** Implies that no power in heaven or on earth can frustrate the Lord's purposes or prevent the fulfillment of his will (Job 9:12; Rom 9:19).

43:14 Babylon: The city will surrender to the Persians in 539 B.C.

43:15-21 Deliverance from exile is poetically described as a new exodus. God will open a path **in the sea** (43:16; Ex 14:21), overthrow the **chariot** and **horse** of the enemy (43:17; Ex 15:1, 4), lead his people on **a way in the wilderness** (43:19; Ex 13:21), and give them **water** to drink (43:20; Ex 17:1-7). The Exodus from Egypt is the foremost example of divine salvation in Israel's early history, inspiring a lasting confidence in the Lord's power to rescue his people from captivity (CCC 1363). See essay: *The New Exodus in Isaiah.*

43:15 your King: See note on 41:21.

43:19 a new thing: A new act of deliverance, to be celebrated with a "new song" (42:10).

43:20 I give water: Not merely drinking water, as in the Exodus from Egypt, but the blessing of salvation. Isaiah links

this with an outpouring of the divine "Spirit" in 44:3 (cf. Jn 7:37-39; 1 Cor 12:13).

43:22 weary of me: The Jewish community in Babylon struggles with spiritual apathy. Serving the Lord has come to feel like a burden, even though exile has made it impossible to perform the ministries of the Temple. As a result, God is wearied with them (43:24).

43:24 sweet cane: Used to make incense (Jer 6:20).

43:25 I will not remember your sins: The same promise is made in Jeremiah's prophecy of the New Covenant (Jer 31:34).

43:27 Your first father: The patriarch Jacob (Hos 12:2-3). **your mediators:** Spiritual leaders such as priests and prophets. Moses and Aaron may be specifically in mind.

43:28 I delivered Jacob: God himself is behind the humiliation of Israel (42:24; 47:6).

44:1-5 God's promises in 43:1-28 culminate in a prophecy of divine blessing and renewal. The exiles in Babylon had grown weary of serving the Lord (43:22), but the day approaches when they will be refreshed by the Spirit (44:3) and reinvigorated in faith (44:5).

44:1 Jacob my servant: The people of Israel (41:8-9; 43:1; 44:21). **chosen:** Reaffirms the election of Israel. See note on 43:1.

44:2 formed you: See note on 43:1. **Jeshurun:** An ancient name for Israel. It probably means "upright one" (Deut 32:15; 33:5, 26).

---

*Heb obscure.

Fear not, O Jacob my servant,
  Jesh'urun whom I have chosen.
³For I will pour water on the thirsty land,
  and streams on the dry ground;

I will pour my Spirit upon your descendants,
  and my blessing on your offspring.
⁴They shall spring up like grass amid waters,ʸ
  like willows by flowing streams.

 44:3 my Spirit: Pictured as life-giving water poured out from heaven on the People of God. The same expectation appears in 32:15; Ezek 39:29; Joel 2:28–29; Zech 12:10. • These oracles find their fulfillment in the outpouring of the Holy Spirit on the Church at Pentecost (Acts 2:14–18) and subsequently in Baptism (Acts 2:38; Rom 5:5).

ʸ Gk Compare Tg: Heb *They shall spring up in among grass.*

The New Exodus in Isaiah

The Book of Isaiah is full of expectations for the People of God. Prominent among these is the anticipation of a "new exodus". Frequently we hear of God's plan to save his people in ways that bring to mind how he delivered Israel from bondage in Egypt. The epic story of the Exodus is thus viewed as a pattern for a new act of salvation to come. Only now the covenant people find themselves, not as slaves living in Egypt, but as captives exiled among foreign nations. Isaiah's message is that the Lord intends to rescue his people again, just as he did in the days of Moses.

At the same time, this is only part of the promise. Deliverance from exile, while clearly a sign of God's love and commitment to his people, points beyond itself to something deeper and more ultimate. Israel's exile from its homeland is symptomatic of its spiritual condition, namely, its exile from God and the fullness of his blessings. The promise of a new exodus is ultimately about a restoration to full covenant communion with the Lord. At the end of the day, the People of God need more than a land to call their own; they need deliverance from the sins that separate them from God. Isaiah uses exodus imagery to speak about both of these issues, creating expectations of a return from exile as well as a spiritual reconciliation with the Lord.

(1) In the first exodus, the Lord *redeemed* the Israelites enslaved in Egypt (Ex 6:6; 15:13). In the new exodus, he will act again as the *Redeemer* of his people (Is 41:14; 43:1; 48:20; 52:3–4, 9–10; 63:9).

(2) In the first exodus, the Lord *led* the Israelites from bondage on a *way* through the *wilderness* (Ex 13:21). In the new exodus, he will *lead* his people again out of captivity on a *way* or *highway* through the *wilderness* (Is 11:16; 35:8–9; 40:3–5; 42:16; 43:19; 49:11; 63:11–14).

(3) In the first exodus, the Lord *led* the Israelites through the *waters* of the sea to safety (Ex 14:12–22). In the new exodus, he will *lead* his people through *waters* unharmed once again (Is 11:15; 43:16; 51:9–10).

(4) In the first exodus, the Lord *protected* the Israelites with his *glory*, appearing as *cloud by day* and a *fire by night* (Ex 14:19-20; 40:36–38; Num 9:15–23). In the new exodus, he will protect his people again as their *rear guard*, sheltering them with the *cloud* and *fire* of his *glory* (Is 4:5–6; 52:12; 58:8).

(5) In the first exodus, the Lord supplied *water* for the Israelites to *drink* in the wilderness (Ex 17:1–7; Num 20:2-9) and gave them rest under *shade trees* (Ex 15:27). In the new exodus, he will again refresh his people with *water* and *shade trees* (Is 35:6–7; 41:17–19; 43:20; 48:21).

(6) In the first exodus, the Lord *fought* for the Israelites as a *divine warrior* (Ex 14:14; 15:3). In the new exodus, he will *fight* again for his people as a *divine warrior* (Is 10:26; 42:13).

(7) In the first exodus, the Lord led the Israelites to a holy *mountain* (Sinai, Ex 19:1–2, 16–17) and there made a *covenant* with them (Ex 24:8). In the new exodus, he will bring his people to another holy *mountain* (Zion, Is 35:10; 51:11) and ratify another *covenant* with them (Is 54:10; 59:21; 61:8).

The return of God's people from Babylon in the sixth and fifth centuries B.C. marks the beginning of this new exodus but not its completion. Indeed, the period of Judean restoration fell woefully short of the grand expectations expressed in Isaiah. Even the Jewish people who returned to the homeland had a sense that more was expected, since they continued to live as "slaves" beholden to foreign rulers (Neh 9:36–37).

According to the New Testament, the new exodus finds its completion in the work of the Messiah. John the Baptist announces this turning point by preparing the Lord's *way* in the *wilderness* (Mt 3:3; Mk 1:3; Jn 1:23). Jesus accomplishes the awaited deliverance through his *exodus* in Jerusalem (Lk 9:31), his dying and rising again, which ratifies a new *covenant* (Lk 22:20) and secures an eternal *redemption* (Heb 9:12). Thereafter believers experience the new exodus by passing through the *waters* of Baptism and receiving the spiritual *drink* of the Eucharist (1 Cor 10:1–11). Set free from the *slavery of sin* (Rom 6:17–18), they are led to the heavenly *Mount Zion* (Heb 12:22). Eventually they will see the Lord come as a *divine warrior* against their persecutors (Rev 19:11–16), and they will be forever *refreshed* and *sheltered* by the Lord's glorious presence (Rev 7:15–17).

⁵This one will say, 'I am the Lᴏʀᴅ's,'
　　another will call himself by the name of Jacob,
and another will write on his hand, 'The Lᴏʀᴅ's,'
　　and surname himself by the name of Israel."

⁶Thus says the Lᴏʀᴅ, the King of Israel
　　and his Redeemer, the Lᴏʀᴅ of hosts:
"I am the first and I am the last;
　　besides me there is no god.
⁷Who is like me? Let him proclaim it,
　　let him declare and set it forth before me.
Who has announced from of old the things to come?ᶻ
　　Let them tell usᵃ what is yet to be.
⁸Fear not, nor be afraid;
　　have I not told you from of old and declared it?
　　And you are my witnesses!
Is there a God besides me?
　　There is no Rock; I know not any."

The Folly of Idol Worship

⁹ All who make idols are nothing, and the things they delight in do not profit; their witnesses neither see nor know, that they may be put to shame. ¹⁰Who fashions a god or casts an image, that is profitable for nothing? ¹¹Behold, all his fellows shall be put to shame, and the craftsmen are but men; let them all assemble, let them stand forth, they shall be terrified, they shall be put to shame together.

12 The ironsmith fashions itᵇ and works it over the coals; he shapes it with hammers, and forges it with his strong arm; he becomes hungry and his strength fails, he drinks no water and is faint. ¹³The carpenter stretches a line, he marks it out with a pencil; he fashions it with planes, and marks it with a compass; he shapes it into the figure of a man, with the beauty of a man, to dwell in a house. ¹⁴He cuts down cedars; or he chooses a holm tree or an oak and lets it grow strong among the trees of the forest; he plants a cedar and the rain nourishes it. ¹⁵Then it becomes fuel for a man; he takes a part of it and warms himself, he kindles a fire and bakes bread; also he makes a god and worships it, he makes it a graven image and falls down before it. ¹⁶Half of it he burns in the fire; over the half he eats flesh, he roasts meat and is satisfied; also he warms himself and says, "Aha, I am warm, I have seen the fire!" ¹⁷And the rest of it he makes into a god, his idol; and falls down to it and worships it; he prays to it and says, "Deliver me, for you are my god!"

Israel Is Not Forgotten

18 They know not, nor do they discern; for he has shut their eyes, so that they cannot see, and their minds, so that they cannot understand. ¹⁹No one considers, nor is there knowledge or discernment to say, "Half of it I burned in the fire, I also baked bread on its coals, I roasted flesh and have eaten; and shall I make the residue of it an abomination? Shall I fall down before a block of wood?" ²⁰He feeds on ashes; a deluded mind has led him astray, and he cannot deliver himself or say, "Is there not a lie in my right hand?"

²¹Remember these things, O Jacob,
　　and Israel, for you are my servant;

44:6: Is 48:12; Rev 1:17; 2:8; 22:13.

44:5 I am the Lᴏʀᴅ's: A reversal of the situation in 43:22. Divine blessing will bring about a renewed zeal for the Lord. **Jacob:** The name will be honored once again after the disgrace of the exile is over. **write on his hand:** May allude to the ancient practice of slave owners marking the hands of their slaves with identifying tattoos. • Isaiah's promise is echoed in Rev 3:12, where Jesus says of the faithful Christian: "I will write on him the name of my God."

44:6–8 Strong assertions of monotheism, the belief that no god exists in the world except one: the God of Israel (43:10–13). The Bible acknowledges that pagan nations worshiped a pantheon of other gods and goddesses in their idolatrous religions (Ex 20:3); it also warns that Israel must not follow their example (Ex 23:32–33; 34:14). But alongside this practical reality stood the theological conviction, attributed to Moses, that the Lord alone is God in the truest sense of the word (Deut 4:35, 39; 6:4). Scripture identifies false gods, represented by idols, with demons, in which case idol worship is not just foolish but spiritually dangerous (Deut 32:16–17; Ps 96:5 LXX; 1 Cor 10:14–22) (CCC 212).

44:6 the King of Israel: See note on 41:21. **his Redeemer:** I.e., Israel's. See note on 41:14. **the first ... the last:** The God of Israel is the sovereign Lord of history from beginning to end. See note on 41:4.

44:7 Who has announced ...?: The question implies that no god except the Lord can reveal the future and bring about the fulfillment of prophecy (41:21–24).

44:8 my witnesses: See note on 43:10. **Rock:** An image of God as a place of protection and salvation for his people (17:10; 26:4; 30:29; Ps 19:14; 89:26).

44:9–20 Isaiah pokes fun at idols, their makers, and their worshipers. Both the craftsmen who fashion these images and those who treat them as gods suffer from a "deluded mind" (44:20). He finds it tragically ironic that people should create gods to worship instead of worshiping the God who created them. The prophet stresses these points to strengthen the exiles in Babylon against the temptations of an idolatrous culture. Similar examples of prophetic satire against idolatry appear in 40:18–20; 46:5–7; Jer 10:1–10.

44:9 their witnesses: Idol worshipers, who are set in contrast to the people of Israel, who are the "witnesses" who "know" the one true God (43:10; 44:8).

44:13 the figure of a man: It is ironic that God made man in his image (Gen 1:26–27) and yet idolaters make gods in the image of men (Ezek 16:17).

44:15 becomes fuel: The same material used to fashion a "god" is also used as firewood.

44:18 he has shut their eyes: The Lord's judgment on idolaters makes them as blind to reality as the images they worship (Ps 115:4–8). See note on 63:17.

44:20 a lie: Idolatry is a deception, a masking of spiritual truth behind falsehood. • Paul makes this point when he denounces foolish Gentiles who "exchanged the truth about God for a lie and worshiped and served the creature rather than the Creator" (Rom 1:25).

44:21 Remember these things: An appeal for repentance follows the polemic against idols. **my servant:** The people of Israel (41:8–9; 43:10; 44:1). **I formed you:** See note on 43:1.

ᶻCn: Heb *from my placing an eternal people and things to come.*
ᵃTg: Heb *them.*
ᵇCn: Heb *an axe.*

I formed you, you are my servant;
 O Israel, you will not be forgotten by me.
[22]I have swept away your transgressions like a
   cloud,
 and your sins like mist;
 return to me, for I have redeemed you.

[23]Sing, O heavens, for the Lord has done it;
 shout, O depths of the earth;
 break forth into singing, O mountains,
 O forest, and every tree in it!
 For the Lord has redeemed Jacob,
 and will be glorified in Israel.

[24]Thus says the Lord, your Redeemer,
 who formed you from the womb:
 "I am the Lord, who made all things,
 who stretched out the heavens alone,
 who spread out the earth—Who was with
   me?[c]—
[25]who frustrates the omens of liars,
 and makes fools of diviners;
 who turns wise men back,
 and makes their knowledge foolish;
[26]who confirms the word of his servant,
 and performs the counsel of his messengers;
 who says of Jerusalem, 'She shall be inhabited,'
 and of the cities of Judah, 'They shall be built,
 and I will raise up their ruins';

[27]who says to the deep, 'Be dry,
 I will dry up your rivers';
[28]who says of Cyrus, 'He is my shepherd,
 and he shall fulfil all my purpose';
 saying of Jerusalem, 'She shall be built,'
 and of the temple, 'Your foundation shall be
   laid.'"

Cyrus, God's Instrument

45 Thus says the Lord to his anointed, to Cyrus,
   whose right hand I have grasped,
 to subdue nations before him
 and uncover the loins of kings,
 to open doors before him
 that gates may not be closed:
[2]"I will go before you
 and level the mountains,[d]
 I will break in pieces the doors of bronze
 and cut asunder the bars of iron,
[3]I will give you the treasures of darkness
 and the hoards in secret places,
 that you may know that it is I, the Lord,
 the God of Israel, who call you by your name.
[4]For the sake of my servant Jacob,
 and Israel my chosen,
 I call you by your name,
 I surname you, though you do not know me.
[5]I am the Lord, and there is no other,
 besides me there is no God;
 I clothe you, though you do not know me,

44:23: Jer 51:48; Rev 12:12; 18:20.   **44:25:** 1 Cor 1:20.

44:22 I have swept away ... your sins: Reaffirms the announcement of divine forgiveness in 40:2. **like mist:** Like a morning haze that disappears after sunrise. **return to me:** A call to repentance and renewed faith. See word study: *Return* at Jer 3:1.

44:23 Sing, O heavens: All creation will burst out in song when the Lord overthrows mighty Babylon and delivers his people (Jer 51:48).

44:24-28 The restoration of Judah, Jerusalem, and the Temple is assured. These had fallen to Babylonian conquerors in 586 B.C. The word delivered by the prophet is trustworthy, for it comes from the Creator of all things and the Lord of all history. Historically, the first wave of exiles returned to Judah ca. 538 B.C., and the Temple was rebuilt by ca. 515 B.C. (CCC 215).

44:24 your Redeemer: See note on 41:14. **stretched out the heavens:** Like a tent. See note on 40:22. **alone:** Unlike other gods or goddesses (CCC 317).

44:28 Cyrus: Cyrus II, founder of the Persian Empire, whose forces seized control of Babylon in 539 B.C. Cyrus will be the Lord's instrument of deliverance when he releases the Jews from captivity (45:13) and commissions the rebuilding of the Temple in Jerusalem (Ezra 4:1-3). Reference was made to him earlier as "one from the east" (41:2). Because it is unusual for prophets to identify persons to come in the future by name, the appearance of Cyrus' name in this verse and 45:1 has contributed to the controversy over the authorship and date of the latter chapters of Isaiah. **(1)** Some take the presence of his name as evidence that chaps. 40-55 were written in the time of Cyrus in the sixth century B.C., meaning they were not written by Isaiah himself, who prophesied in the eighth century B.C. **(2)** Others find the reference to Cyrus' name compatible with

the tradition of Isaiah's authorship, so long as the possibility of predictive prophecy is admitted, e.g., Josiah, king of Judah, was prophesied by name about 300 years before his time (1 Kings 13:1-2). For additional considerations, see introduction: *Author and Date*. **my shepherd:** Like Moses, who was called from the pasture to liberate the captives of Israel. Cyrus will initiate a new exodus of God's people from Babylon, sending them through the desert back to the Promised Land. See note on 43:15-21.

45:1-6 Cyrus' military victories are proof that the one true God empowers and prospers his way, although Cyrus himself does not know the Lord (45:4). See note on 44:28.

45:1 anointed: The Hebrew is *mashiah*, which is the basis of the English word "Messiah". It is applied to the priests (Lev 4:3; 8:12), prophets (Ps 105:15), and kings of Israel (1 Sam 2:10; 24:6). This is the only place where the title is given to a Gentile in the OT, although Jeremiah similarly described Nebuchadnezzar of Babylon as a "servant" of the Lord, insofar as he administered God's judgment on the land of Judah (Jer 25:9; 27:6). The title "anointed" signals that Cyrus is chosen and empowered by the Lord to deliver the Jewish community in Babylon from exile (45:13). Perhaps it also signals that Cyrus, who is tasked with rebuilding the Temple in Jerusalem, is given a responsibility that normally rested with the Davidic king, since at this stage in history the Davidic monarchy had gone into eclipse.

45:2 doors of bronze ... bars of iron: The fortified gates of Persia's enemies.

45:3 by your name: Literally, since the name Cyrus appears in 44:28 and 45:1.

45:4 my servant Jacob: The people of Israel (41:8-9; 43:1; 44:21).

45:5 there is no other: The doctrine of monotheism. See note on 44:6-8.

---

[c]Another reading is *who spread out the earth by myself.*
[d]One ancient Ms Gk: Heb *the swellings.*

⁶that men may know, from the rising of the sun
  and from the west, that there is none besides
    me;
  I am the LORD, and there is no other.
⁷I form light and create darkness,
  I make well-being and create woe,
  I am the LORD, who do all these things.

⁸"Shower, O heavens, from above,
  and let the skies rain down righteousness;
  let the earth open, that salvation may sprout
    forth,ᵉ
  and let it cause righteousness to spring up
    also;
  I the LORD have created it.

⁹"Woe to him who strives with his Maker,
  an earthen vessel with the potter!ᶠ
  Does the clay say to him who fashions it, 'What
    are you making?'
  or 'Your work has no handles'?
¹⁰Woe to him who says to a father, 'What are you
    begetting?'
  or to a woman, 'With what are you suffering
    labor pains?'"
¹¹Thus says the LORD,
  the Holy One of Israel, and his Maker:
  "Will you question meᵍ about my children,
  or command me concerning the work of my
    hands?
¹²I made the earth,
  and created man upon it;
  it was my hands that stretched out the heavens,
  and I commanded all their host.
¹³I have aroused him in righteousness,
  and I will make straight all his ways;

he shall build my city
  and set my exiles free,
not for price or reward,"
  says the LORD of hosts.

¹⁴Thus says the LORD:
  "The wealth of Egypt and the merchandise of
    Ethiopia,
  and the Sabe′ans, men of stature,
  shall come over to you and be yours,
    they shall follow you;
  they shall come over in chains and bow down
    to you.
  They will make supplication to you, saying:
  'God is with you only, and there is no other,
    no god besides him.'"
¹⁵Truly, you are a God who hide yourself,
  O God of Israel, the Savior.
¹⁶All of them are put to shame and confounded,
  the makers of idols go in confusion
    together.
¹⁷But Israel is saved by the LORD
  with everlasting salvation;
  you shall not be put to shame or confounded
    to all eternity.

¹⁸For thus says the LORD,
  who created the heavens
    (he is God!),
  who formed the earth and made it
    (he established it;
  he did not create it a chaos,
    he formed it to be inhabited!):
  "I am the LORD, and there is no other.
¹⁹I did not speak in secret,
  in a land of darkness;

45:9: Is 29:16; Rom 9:20. **45:14:** 1 Cor 14:25 **45:17:** Heb 5:9.

45:7 well-being … woe: All circumstances of life and history, times of blessing and abundance as well as times of difficulty and want, are within the providential plan of God.

45:9 Woe: A cry of lamentation. See word study: *Woe* at 28:1. **potter … clay:** Images of the relationship between God and Israel, the people he formed for himself. Here the sovereign freedom of the potter is defended in view of God's decision to use a foreign ruler (Cyrus) to accomplish his plan for Israel. See notes on 29:16 and 43:1. **What are you making? … Your work has no handles:** The Judean exiles, perplexed and offended by the promise of a pagan deliverer, question the Lord's wisdom and even criticize his work.

45:11 the Holy One of Israel: See note on 1:4. **my children:** The people of Israel, who are sons and daughters of the Lord by covenant (1:2; Deut 14:1; 32:19).

45:12 stretched out the heavens: Like a tent. See note on 40:22.

45:13 I have aroused him: The Lord has summoned Cyrus to save his people (44:28; 45:1). **my city:** Jerusalem. **my exiles:** The displaced Judeans in Babylon.

45:14–17 Peoples of the Nile River valley embrace monotheism and join the community of Israel. They have come to see that idolaters are put to shame, while the covenant people are blessed with salvation. For a similar prophecy of Egyptians coming to know and worship the Lord, see 19:16–25.

45:14 wealth: The rich tribute that foreigners bring to Jerusalem, as in the days of Solomon (1 Kings 4:21; 10:23–25).

45:15 the Savior: The Lord is the real Deliverer of his people, even when he employs human instruments such as Cyrus to accomplish his will. Moreover, he is entirely unlike the idols of the nations, which cannot save at all (45:20).

45:17 everlasting salvation: The chief benefit of God's "everlasting love" for Israel (Jer 31:3). • Paul reaffirms the truth of this statement when he declares that "all Israel will be saved" in the days of the New Covenant (Rom 11:26). See essay: *The Salvation of All Israel* at Rom 11.

45:18 chaos: An allusion to Gen 1:2, where the same term is translated "without form" (Heb., *tohu*). God created the world to be a place of order and beauty, not a place of formless disarray that cannot support life.

45:19 I the LORD speak the truth: The Lord can be trusted to keep his promises, since he is incapable of lying, deceiving, or proving false in what he says (Num 23:19; Titus 1:2; Heb 6:18). On the contrary, God's word is perfect, sure, and true (Ps 19:7–9; 119:160; Jn 17:17).

ᵉ One ancient Ms: Heb *that they may bring forth salvation.*
ᶠ Cn: Heb *potsherds* or *potters.*
ᵍ Cn: Heb *Ask me of things to come.*

I did not say to the offspring of Jacob,
  'Seek me in chaos.'
I the Lord speak the truth,
  I declare what is right.

20"Assemble yourselves and come,
  draw near together,
  you survivors of the nations!
They have no knowledge
  who carry about their wooden idols,
and keep on praying to a god
  that cannot save.
21Declare and present your case;
  let them take counsel together!
Who told this long ago?
  Who declared it of old?
Was it not I, the Lord?
  And there is no other god besides me,
a righteous God and a Savior;
  there is none besides me.

22"Turn to me and be saved,
  all the ends of the earth!
For I am God, and there is no other.
23By myself I have sworn,
  from my mouth has gone forth in
    righteousness
a word that shall not return:
  'To me every knee shall bow,
  every tongue shall swear.'

24"Only in the Lord, it shall be said of me,
  are righteousness and strength;
to him shall come and be ashamed,
  all who were incensed against him.

25In the Lord all the offspring of Israel
  shall triumph and glory."

Idols Cannot Save

46 Bel bows down, Nebo stoops,
  their idols are on beasts and cattle;
these things you carry are loaded
  as burdens on weary beasts.
2They stoop, they bow down together,
  they cannot save the burden,
  but themselves go into captivity.

3"Listen to me, O house of Jacob,
  all the remnant of the house of Israel,
who have been borne by me from your birth,
  carried from the womb;
4even to your old age I am He,
  and to gray hairs I will carry you.
I have made, and I will bear;
  I will carry and will save.

5"To whom will you liken me and make me
    equal,
  and compare me, that we may be alike?
6Those who lavish gold from the purse,
  and weigh out silver in the scales,
hire a goldsmith, and he makes it into a god;
  then they fall down and worship!
7They lift it upon their shoulders, they carry it,
  they set it in its place, and it stands there;
  it cannot move from its place.
If one cries to it, it does not answer
  or save him from his trouble.

8"Remember this and consider,
  recall it to mind, you transgressors,

45:21: Acts 15:18. **45:23:** Rom 14:11; Phil 2:10–11.

45:21 no other god: The doctrine of monotheism. See note on 44:6–8.

45:22 Turn to me: The Lord invites the Gentiles to acknowledge him as the one true God.

45:23 By myself I have sworn: A divine oath in which the Lord invokes his own name to guarantee the fulfillment of his pledge (Gen 22:16; Heb 6:13–18). **a word that shall not return:** Words spoken by God are not ineffectual but powerful in accomplishing all that he wills (55:11; Ps 33:6, 9). **every knee shall bow:** Envisions all people and nations appearing before the throne of God and acknowledging his lordship over the world. **every tongue shall swear:** The Greek LXX reads: "every tongue shall confess to God" (i.e., the words of 45:24–25). • Paul twice draws from this vision in his letters. He quotes the verse in Rom 14:11 to remind believers who are passing judgment on one another that each one of us will give an account of our actions to God the Judge. He likewise alludes to it in Phil 2:10–11, when he says that God has exalted the crucified and risen Jesus as Lord over creation, so that all will bow and make confession before him. Paul thereby identifies Jesus with the divine Lord of Isaiah's prophecy, implying that salvation will reach "the ends of the earth" (45:22) as well as "the offspring of Israel" (45:25) in Christ Jesus.

46:1 Bel: Another name for Marduk, chief god of the city of Babylon (Jer 50:2). **Nebo:** Son of Marduk and the patron god of the city of Borsippa. Forms of his name are included in the names of several Babylonian kings such as Nebuchadnezzar and Nabonidus. **you carry:** The idol images of Bel and Nebo were carried in procession through Babylon as part of the city's annual New Year's festival (46:7). Whereas the lifeless gods of Babylon must be carried by their worshipers (45:20), the God of Israel will "carry" his people to salvation (46:4).

46:2 They stoop, they bow: Epitomizes how idols, far from helping their devotees in times of need, are nothing but an onerous burden (46:7). **into captivity:** Babylon's gods will be seized and humiliated by conquerors.

46:3–4 The Lord's commitment to caring for Israel is a lifelong commitment.

46:3 remnant: The survivors of the Babylonian conquest of Judah in 586 B.C., most of whom went into exile.

46:4 I will carry you: An image that also appears in 40:11 and 63:9. • It calls to mind the Exodus of Israel from Egypt, when the Lord carried his people like a father carries his son (Deut 1:31) or an eagle its young (Ex 19:4; Deut 32:11). See essay: *The New Exodus in Isaiah* at Is 43.

46:5–7 A prophetic critique of idols. See note on 44:9–20.

46:7 it does not answer: Prayer to an idol is utterly futile.

46:8–13 The Lord seeks repentance by rebuking his people for their rebelliousness (46:8) and stubbornness (46:12).

⁹   remember the former things of old;
   for I am God, and there is no other;
     I am God, and there is none like me,
¹⁰declaring the end from the beginning
     and from ancient times things not yet done,
   saying, 'My counsel shall stand,
     and I will accomplish all my purpose,'
¹¹calling a bird of prey from the east,
     the man of my counsel from a far country.
   I have spoken, and I will bring it to pass;
     I have planned, and I will do it.

¹²"Listen to me, you stubborn of heart,
     you who are far from deliverance:
¹³I bring near my deliverance, it is not far off,
     and my salvation will not tarry;
   I will put salvation in Zion,
     for Israel my glory."

The Humiliation of Babylon

47 Come down and sit in the dust,
     O virgin daughter of Babylon;
   sit on the ground without a throne,
     O daughter of the Chalde'ans!
   For you shall no more be called
     tender and delicate.
²Take the millstones and grind meal,
     put off your veil,
   strip off your robe, uncover your legs,
     pass through the rivers.
³Your nakedness shall be uncovered,
     and your shame shall be seen.
   I will take vengeance,
     and I will spare no man.
⁴Our Redeemer—the LORD of hosts is his name—
     is the Holy One of Israel.

⁵Sit in silence, and go into darkness,
     O daughter of the Chalde'ans;
for you shall no more be called
     the mistress of kingdoms.
⁶I was angry with my people,
     I profaned my heritage;
   I gave them into your hand,
     you showed them no mercy;
   on the aged you made your yoke
     exceedingly heavy.
⁷You said, "I shall be mistress for ever,"
     so that you did not lay these things to
       heart
     or remember their end.

⁸Now therefore hear this, you lover of pleasures,
     who sit securely,
   who say in your heart,
     "I am, and there is no one besides me;
   I shall not sit as a widow
     or know the loss of children":
⁹These two things shall come to you
     in a moment, in one day;
   the loss of children and widowhood
     shall come upon you in full measure,
   in spite of your many sorceries
     and the great power of your enchantments.

¹⁰You felt secure in your wickedness,
     you said, "No one sees me";
   your wisdom and your knowledge
     led you astray,
   and you said in your heart,
     "I am, and there is no one besides me."
¹¹But evil shall come upon you,
     for which you cannot atone;
   disaster shall fall upon you,
     which you will not be able to expiate;
   and ruin shall come on you suddenly,
     of which you know nothing.

47: Is 13:1—14:23; Jer 50—51; Hab 1   2.   **47:8:** Rev 18:7.   **47:9:** Rev 18.8.

46:9 the former things: God's faithfulness to his promises in the past (41:22; 42:9; 43:18). **there is no other:** The doctrine of monotheism. See note on 44:6–8.

46:10 declaring the end: I.e., predicting the future. This is a truly divine ability that only the God of Israel possesses. See note on 41:21–29.

46:11 a bird of prey from the east: Cyrus II, king of Persia, similarly described in 41:2. See note on 44:28.

47:1–15 Judgment will fall on Babylon for its arrogance (47:8–11), its sorcery (47:12–13), and its merciless treatment of the Judean exiles (47:6). Its demise will be unanticipated and unstoppable, despite the army of wise men and astrologers who claim to predict the future. Figuratively, Babylon stands for all worldly powers that embrace the illusion of their permanence (47:7), despite presumptuous self-indulgence (47:8) and thinking themselves accountable to no one for their actions (47:10). For a similar prophetic taunt against Babylon, see 14:3–21.

47:1 virgin daughter: Babylon is a pampered royal lady who is about to be humiliated and reduced to the level of a common slave. **Chaldeans:** Babylonians.

47:3 I will take vengeance: Echoes the Lord's oath in the Song of Moses (Deut 32:40–42).

47:4 Redeemer: See note on 41:14. **the LORD of hosts:** See note on 1:9. **the Holy One of Israel:** See note on 1:4.

47:5 the mistress of kingdoms: The Neo-Babylonian Empire was the reigning superpower in the Near East in the early and middle decades of the sixth century B.C.

47:6 I gave them into your hand: God willed Babylon's conquest of Judah and Jerusalem as chastisement for his unfaithful people (43:28; 42:24).

47:8 I am ... no one besides me: Babylon's claim to divine supremacy is in direct opposition to God's revelation of himself in 45:5–6. Here and in 47:10, Babylon's arrogance has reached the heights of blasphemy, as in 14:13–14.

47:9 loss of children and widowhood: Babylon will be left destitute and without hope for the future. **sorceries:** Superstitious practices of the Babylonians, which include divination (inspecting animal organs to predict the future), astrology (searching the night sky for signs of destiny), and magic (reciting incantations to ward off evil influences).

47:11 you know nothing: The fall of Babylon will not be foreseen by its fortune-tellers.

¹²Stand fast in your enchantments
    and your many sorceries,
      with which you have labored from your
        youth;
    perhaps you may be able to succeed,
      perhaps you may inspire terror.
¹³You are wearied with your many counsels;
    let them stand forth and save you,
    those who divide the heavens,
      who gaze at the stars,
    who at the new moons predict
      what[h] shall befall you.

¹⁴Behold, they are like stubble,
    the fire consumes them;
    they cannot deliver themselves
      from the power of the flame.
    No coal for warming oneself is this,
      no fire to sit before!
¹⁵Such to you are those with whom you have
      labored,
    who have trafficked with you from your youth;
    they wander about each in his own direction;
      there is no one to save you.

Israel's Unfaithfulness to God the Creator and Redeemer

48 Hear this, O house of Jacob,
    who are called by the name of Israel,
    and who came forth from the loins[i] of Judah;
    who swear by the name of the Lord,
    and confess the God of Israel,
      but not in truth or right.
²For they call themselves after the holy city,
    and stay themselves on the God of Israel;
      the Lord of hosts is his name.

³"The former things I declared of old,
    they went forth from my mouth and I made
      them known;
    then suddenly I did them and they came to
      pass.

⁴Because I know that you are obstinate,
    and your neck is an iron sinew
    and your forehead brass,
⁵I declared them to you from of old,
    before they came to pass I announced them to
      you,
    lest you should say, 'My idol did them,
      my graven image and my molten image
      commanded them.'

⁶"You have heard; now see all this;
    and will you not declare it?
    From this time forth I make you hear new
      things,
    hidden things which you have not known.
⁷They are created now, not long ago;
    before today you have never heard of them,
    lest you should say, 'Behold, I knew them.'
⁸You have never heard, you have never known,
    from of old your ear has not been opened.
    For I knew that you would deal very
      treacherously,
    and that from birth you were called a rebel.

⁹"For my name's sake I defer my anger,
    for the sake of my praise I restrain it for you,
    that I may not cut you off.
¹⁰Behold, I have refined you, but not like[j] silver;
    I have tried you in the furnace of affliction.
¹¹For my own sake, for my own sake, I do it,
    for how should my name[k] be profaned?
    My glory I will not give to another.

¹²"Listen to me, O Jacob,
    and Israel, whom I called!
    I am He, I am the first,
    and I am the last.
¹³My hand laid the foundation of the earth,
    and my right hand spread out the heavens;
    when I call to them,
    they stand forth together.

48:12: Is 44:6; Rev 1:17; 2:8; 22:13.

47:14 they: Babylon's magicians, who will prove to be helpless when the Lord's judgment overtakes the city.

48:1–22 The end of the Babylonian Exile is not something God's people deserve, since they continue to be obstinate (48:4) and rebellious (48:8). It will come about, however, because God wishes to defend the honor of his name (48:9–11).

48:1 from the loins of Judah: The majority of the exiles are from the tribe of Judah, since the Babylonians took captives from the Southern Kingdom of Judah (see 2 Kings 24:10–17; 25:8–11). **not in truth:** The exiles maintain outward expressions of faith while being distant from God in their hearts. This was also a problem among Isaiah's contemporaries (1:12–17; 29:13).

48:2 the holy city: Jerusalem (Neh 11:1).

48:3 former things: Prophecies of the Lord that have since come true, as in 42:9.

48:4 your neck ... iron: The Jewish exiles remain stiff-necked, refusing to be guided by the yoke of God's Law (48:17–19). **your forehead brass:** An ancient way of saying "defiant" or "bull-headed".

48:6 new things: Things previously unimagined that God will reveal to his people.

48:8 rebel: The same was true of Isaiah's contemporaries (1:2).

48:10 I have refined you: Far from being pointless, undergoing suffering purified Israel's faith and loyalty to the Lord (Sir 2:4–5; 1 Pet 1:6–7).

48:12 the first ... the last: The God of Israel is the sovereign Lord of history from beginning to end. See note on 41:4.

---

[h] Gk Syr Compare Vg: Heb *from what.*
[i] Cn: Heb *waters.*
[j] Cn: Heb *with.*
[k] Gk Old Latin: Heb lacks *my name.*

¹⁴"Assemble, all of you, and hear!
  Who among them has declared these things?
The LORD loves him;
  he shall perform his purpose on Babylon,
  and his arm shall be against the Chalde′ans.
¹⁵I, even I, have spoken and called him,
  I have brought him, and he will prosper in his way.
¹⁶Draw near to me, hear this:
  from the beginning I have not spoken in secret,
  from the time it came to be I have been there."
And now the Lord GOD has sent me and his Spirit.

¹⁷Thus says the LORD,
  your Redeemer, the Holy One of Israel:
"I am the LORD your God, who teaches you to profit,
  who leads you in the way you should go.
¹⁸O that you had listened to my commandments!
  Then your peace would have been like a river,
  and your righteousness like the waves of the sea;
¹⁹your offspring would have been like the sand,
  and your descendants like its grains;
  their name would never be cut off
  or destroyed from before me."

²⁰Go forth from Babylon, flee from Chalde′a,
  declare this with a shout of joy, proclaim it,
  send it forth to the end of the earth;
  say, "The LORD has redeemed his servant Jacob!"
²¹They thirsted not when he led them through the deserts;
  he made water flow for them from the rock;
  he cleft the rock and the water gushed out.
²²"There is no peace," says the LORD, "for the wicked."

The Servant's Mission

49 Listen to me, O islands,
  and pay attention, you peoples from afar.
The LORD called me from the womb,
  from the body of my mother he named my name.
²He made my mouth like a sharp sword,
  in the shadow of his hand he hid me;
  he made me a polished arrow,
  in his quiver he hid me away.
³And he said to me, "You are my servant,
  Israel, in whom I will be glorified."
⁴But I said, "I have labored in vain,
  I have spent my strength for nothing and vanity;
  yet surely my right is with the LORD,
  and my recompense with my God."

⁵And now the LORD says,
  who formed me from the womb to be his servant,

49:1: Jer 1:5; Gal 1:15. **49:4:** Phil 2:16.

48:14 all of you: Addresses the Jewish exiles in Babylon. **them:** The idols and fortune-tellers of Babylon. **The LORD loves him:** Cyrus II, who will free the covenant people from captivity (44:28; 45:1, 13). The choice of Cyrus to act on God's behalf is grounded in God's love (Deut 7:6–8). **Chaldeans:** Babylonians.

48:16 And now: The speaker is not identified. Possible candidates include Cyrus (45:1), Isaiah (6:8–13), and the Lord's Servant (42:1). • Christian tradition detects a veiled reference to the Trinity in this verse, with **the Lord GOD** designating the Father, the one **sent** indicating the Son, and the **Spirit** being the Holy Spirit.

48:17 Redeemer: See note on 41:14. **the Holy One of Israel:** See note on 1:4. **teaches you to profit:** I.e., teaches you how to obtain divine blessings.

48:18–19 Disobedience prevents God's people from flourishing as he intends.

48:20–22 Departure from Babylon will be like a new exodus in which the Lord's people are **redeemed** from captivity (Ex 15:13), led through various **deserts** (Ex 15:22; 16:1; 19:1; Num 10:12), and given **water** to drink from a wilderness **rock** (Ex 17:1–7; Num 20:2–13). See essay: *The New Exodus in Isaiah* at Is 43.

48:22 no peace ... for the wicked: A warning, not primarily for the Babylonians, but for the Judean exiles who persist in rebellion (48:8; 57:21).

49:1–7 The second "Servant Song" in Isaiah. Here the Servant is closely identified with the people of Israel (49:3); at the same time, he is distinguished from the people as a whole, since he acts as the deliverer of Israel (49:5). The Servant thus appears to be an ideal or exemplary Israelite—a representative of the covenant people whose mission is to restore the family of Jacob to new life (49:6). Whereas Cyrus is granted the political power to bring exiles back to Jerusalem (44:28; 45:1, 13), the Servant is armed with the power of God's word (49:2) to reunite the tribes of Israel with the Lord (49:5) and to bring salvation to the rest of the world (49:6). The prophet thus envisions an event much larger than the end of the Babylonian Exile. From earliest Christian times, the Servant of the Lord has been identified with Jesus, whose salvation is for "all nations" (Mt 28:19). See note on 42:1–9.

49:1 Listen to me: The Servant addresses the nations, among whom Israel is living in exile. **islands:** The peoples of the Mediterranean, which together represent all distant nations. **from the womb:** The Servant received his prophetic calling before birth. • The same is said of the prophet Jeremiah (Jer 1:5) and the Apostle Paul (Gal 1:15–16). In all three cases, the Lord's servant is entrusted with a divine message, not only for the people of Israel, but for other nations as well.

49:2 a sharp sword: A word of divine judgment that issues from the mouth of the Servant (51:16; Hos 6:5). The Davidic Messiah is described in similar terms in 11:4. For use of this imagery in the NT, see Eph 6:17; Heb 4:12; Rev 19:15. **he hid me:** The Servant was not yet revealed to the world at the time the prophet was speaking.

49:3 my servant, Israel: See note on 41:8.

49:4 labored in vain ... yet surely: The Servant bemoans the resistance he encounters (53:1–3), yet without losing faith in the Lord or his plan.

49:5 formed me: Like a potter shaping a vessel out of clay. See note on 43:1. **from the womb:** Even before birth, God is intimately involved in the life of each person (Ps 139:13). See notes on 49:1 and Jer 1:5. **back to him:** I.e., back into covenant communion with the Lord. The Servant has a spiritual mission of repairing Israel's relationship with God.

to bring Jacob back to him,
    and that Israel might be gathered to him,
for I am honored in the eyes of the Lord,
    and my God has become my strength—
[6]he says:
"It is too light a thing that you should be my
    servant
    to raise up the tribes of Jacob
    and to restore the preserved of Israel;
I will give you as a light to the nations,
    that my salvation may reach to the end of the
    earth."

[7]Thus says the Lord,
    the Redeemer of Israel and his Holy One,
to one deeply despised, abhorred by the nations,
    the servant of rulers:
"Kings shall see and arise;
    princes, and they shall prostrate themselves;
because of the Lord, who is faithful,
    the Holy One of Israel, who has chosen
    you."

[8]Thus says the Lord:
"In a time of favor I have answered you,
    in a day of salvation I have helped you;
I have kept you and given you
    as a covenant to the people,
to establish the land,
    to apportion the desolate heritages;
[9]saying to the prisoners, 'Come forth,'
    to those who are in darkness, 'Appear.'
They shall feed along the ways,
    on all bare heights shall be their pasture;
[10]they shall not hunger or thirst,
    neither scorching wind nor sun shall strike
    them,

for he who has pity on them will lead them,
    and by springs of water will guide them.
[11]And I will make all my mountains a way,
    and my highways shall be raised up.
[12]Behold, these shall come from afar,
    and behold, these from the north and from the
    west,
    and these from the land of Sye′ne."[1]
[13]Sing for joy, O heavens, and exult, O earth;
    break forth, O mountains, into singing!
For the Lord has comforted his people,
    and will have compassion on his afflicted.

[14]But Zion said, "The Lord has forsaken me,
    my Lord has forgotten me."
[15]"Can a woman forget her sucking child,
    that she should have no compassion on the son
    of her womb?
Even these may forget,
    yet I will not forget you.
[16]Behold, I have graven you on the palms of my
    hands;
    your walls are continually before me.
[17]Your builders outstrip your destroyers,
    and those who laid you waste go forth from you.
[18]Lift up your eyes round about and see;
    they all gather, they come to you.
As I live, says the Lord,
    you shall put them all on as an ornament,
    you shall bind them on as a bride does.

[19]"Surely your waste and your desolate places
    and your devastated land—
surely now you will be too narrow for your
    inhabitants,
    and those who swallowed you up will be far
    away.

49:6: Is 42:6; Lk 2:32; Acts 13:47; 26:23.   **49:8:** 2 Cor 6:2.   **49:10:** Rev 7:16.   **49:13:** Is 44:23; Jer 51:48; Rev 12:12; 18:20.

49:6 the tribes of Jacob: The twelve tribes descended from the patriarch Jacob, who was renamed Israel (Gen 32:28; 35:10). **a light to the nations:** The Servant embodies all that Israel was called to be, namely, God's moral and spiritual witness to a world living in the darkness of idolatry and sin (Deut 4:5-8; Rom 2:19). See note on Ex 19:6. **to the end of the earth:** The full extent of the Servant's mission. • Paul reads this passage as a mandate for the Church's mission to evangelize the Gentiles (Acts 1:8; 13:47).

49:7 one deeply despised: The Servant will endure rejection and abuse (50:6; 53:2-3).

49:8 day of salvation: Suggests that God will deliver the Servant from his adversaries. • Paul quotes the Greek LXX of this passage in 2 Cor 6:2, inviting readers to accept the grace of God and thus experience salvation in the present time. **a covenant to the people:** See note on 42:6.

49:10 he ... will lead them: As a gentle shepherd (40:11).

49:11 a way ... highways: God promises a new exodus of his people from captivity. See essay: *The New Exodus in Isaiah* at Is 43.

49:12 these shall come from afar: The exiles of Israel will return from distant lands. They were scattered throughout the ancient world by the Assyrians (2 Kings 15:29; 17:6; 1 Chron 5:26) and the Babylonians (2 Kings 25:7, 11). **Syene:** Aswan, Egypt, representing the lands south of Israel.

49:13 Sing for joy: The outpouring of God's mercy calls for celebration, yet the exiles remain despondent (49:14). **the Lord has comforted:** Recalls the consoling words in 40:1-2.

49:14 Zion: Jerusalem, personified as a bride (49:18) and mother of many children (49:20-22). Despite feeling abandoned, Zion is assured of the Lord's continued love and care (49:15, 18, 22, 25).

49:16 on the palms of my hands: Another way of saying "you will not be forgotten by me" (44:21). Marking the hands is a sign of ownership, as in 44:5. **your walls:** Jerusalem's defenses, which were broken down by the Babylonians in 586 B.C. Zion's walls and gates would not be rebuilt until the time of Nehemiah in 445 B.C. (Neh 3:1-32).

49:18 As I live: An oath formula (Deut 32:40).

49:19 too narrow: Because of great numbers returning home to Zion.

---

[1] Cn: Heb *Sinim*.

²⁰The children born in the time of your
   bereavement
      will yet say in your ears:
   'The place is too narrow for me;
      make room for me to dwell in.'
²¹Then you will say in your heart:
   'Who has borne me these?
I was bereaved and barren,
   exiled and put away,
      but who has brought up these?
Behold, I was left alone;
   from where then have these come?' "

²²Thus says the Lord GOD:
   "Behold, I will lift up my hand to the nations,
      and raise my signal to the peoples;
   and they shall bring your sons in their bosom,
      and your daughters shall be carried on their
         shoulders.
²³Kings shall be your foster fathers,
   and their queens your nursing mothers.
With their faces to the ground they shall bow
      down to you, and lick the dust of your feet.
Then you will know that I am the LORD;
   those who wait for me shall not be put to
      shame."

²⁴Can the prey be taken from the mighty,
   or the captives of a tyrant[m] be rescued?
²⁵Surely, thus says the LORD:
   "Even the captives of the mighty shall be taken,
      and the prey of the tyrant be rescued,

for I will contend with those who contend with
      you,
   and I will save your children.
²⁶I will make your oppressors eat their own flesh,
   and they shall be drunk with their own blood
      as with wine.
Then all flesh shall know
   that I am the LORD your Savior,
      and your Redeemer, the Mighty One of
         Jacob."

The Sufferings of the Servant

50 Thus says the LORD:
   "Where is your mother's bill of divorce,
      with which I put her away?
Or which of my creditors is it
   to whom I have sold you?
Behold, for your iniquities you were sold,
   and for your transgressions your mother was
      put away.
²Why, when I came, was there no man?
   When I called, was there no one to answer?
Is my hand shortened, that it cannot redeem?
   Or have I no power to deliver?
Behold, by my rebuke I dry up the sea,
   I make the rivers a desert;
their fish stink for lack of water,
   and die of thirst.
³I clothe the heavens with blackness,
   and make sackcloth their covering."

⁴The Lord GOD has given me
   the tongue of those who are taught,

49:20 The children: The generations of Israel born in exile.

49:21 bereaved and barren: Like a wife who lost her husband and has no children.

49:22 my signal: The Hebrew term designates a banner or military standard that serves as a rallying point. It is used in 11:10, 12 (translated "ensign") to speak of the Davidic Messiah, to whom the nations will gather, along with the dispersed of Israel (Northern Kingdom) and Judah (Southern Kingdom) living among them. **sons ... daughters:** The exiled children of Israel carried home to Zion.

49:23 bow down to you: For the nations serving the covenant people, see also 45:14; 60:10; 61:5. **those who wait for me:** I.e., those who trust in the Lord and believe that he will make good on his promises (30:15).

49:25 I will contend with: Recalls the ancient promise that God will bless those who bless the descendants of Abraham and curse those who curse them (Gen 12:3; 27:29).

49:26 eat their own flesh ... blood: The punishment of Israel's conquerors is likened to a city under siege, in which people who are desperate to stay alive resort to cannibalism (Deut 28:52-57) and consumption of blood (see note on Jud 11:12). **the Mighty One:** The One who is stronger than Babylon, who holds his people captive (49:24).

50:1-3 Israel went into exile because of its sin, not because the Lord decided to divorce his people or sell them into slavery to pay off a debt. The positive side of this is that God is free, able, and willing to bring his people home.

50:1 your mother's: A reference to Zion as the mother of the exiles (49:14-26). **bill of divorce:** Required to make a divorce legal. Because the necessary documentation is lacking in this case, the covenant remains binding and the Lord is free to reclaim his exiled bride (54:5-7). • The background is Deut 24:1-4, which disallows a man to marry the same woman twice if she married another man after her first husband divorced her. **which of my creditors ...?:** A rhetorical question that implies God is indebted to no one. In biblical times, the head of a household could pay off personal debts by selling his children to creditors as indentured servants or debt slaves (2 Kings 4:1-7). • Christ came for those to whom it was said, "for your iniquities you were sold", and he redeemed them by his blood. Yet Christ was sold because he took our condition upon himself rather than our fault. He is not forced to pay the price of sin, since he committed no sin, but he took away the bond of our debt and by himself paid what was owed by all (St. Ambrose, *On Joseph* 4, 19).

50:2-3 The Lord asserts his power to save by recalling the miracles of the Exodus, such as the parting of the sea (Ex 14:21-22) and the plague of darkness (Ex 10:21-23).

50:4-11 The third "Servant Song" in Isaiah. Here the Servant is a prophet who speaks God's word, even as he suffers at the hands of persecutors. Again, he represents the people of Israel and yet is distinct from them: unlike Israel in exile, whose "ear has not been opened" and who continues to be a "rebel" (48:8), the Servant says that "GOD has opened my ear, and I was not rebellious" (50:5). See note on 42:1-9. • Christian tradition sees these verses fulfilled in the Passion of Jesus. They are read on Palm Sunday in the Roman Lectionary

---

[m]One ancient Ms Syr Vg: Heb *righteous man.*

that I may know how to sustain with a word
 him that is weary.
Morning by morning he wakens,
 he wakens my ear
 to hear as those who are taught.
[5]The Lord GOD has opened my ear,
 and I was not rebellious,
 I turned not backward.
[6]I gave my back to those who struck me,
 and my cheeks to those who pulled out the
  beard;
 I hid not my face
  from shame and spitting.

[7]For the Lord GOD helps me;
 therefore I have not been confounded;
 therefore I have set my face like a flint,
 and I know that I shall not be put to shame;
[8] he who vindicates me is near.
 Who will contend with me?
 Let us stand up together.
 Who is my adversary?
 Let him come near to me.
[9]Behold, the Lord GOD helps me;
 who will declare me guilty?
 Behold, all of them will wear out like a garment;
 the moth will eat them up.

[10]Who among you fears the LORD
 and obeys the voice of his servant,

who walks in darkness
 and has no light,
yet trusts in the name of the LORD
 and relies upon his God?
[11]Behold, all you who kindle a fire,
 who set brands alight.[n]
Walk by the light of your fire,
 and by the brands which you have kindled!
This shall you have from my hand:
 you shall lie down in torment.

The Lord Will Comfort Zion

51 "Listen to me, you who pursue deliverance,
 you who seek the LORD;
look to the rock from which you were hewn,
 and to the quarry from which you were dug.
[2]Look to Abraham your father
 and to Sarah who bore you;
for when he was but one I called him,
 and I blessed him and made him many.
[3]For the LORD will comfort Zion:
 he will comfort all her waste places,
and will make her wilderness like Eden,
 her desert like the garden of the LORD;
joy and gladness will be found in her,
 thanksgiving and the voice of song.

[4]"Listen to me, my people,
 and give ear to me, my nation;
for a law will go forth from me,
 and my justice for a light to the peoples.

50:8–9: Rom 8:33; Heb 1:11.

(CCC 713). • When the Savior was struck, he endured it patiently; when he was reviled, he did not revile; when he suffered, he did not threaten. Instead, he gave his back to those who beat him, his cheeks to their blows, and his face he did not turn from their spitting. Finally, he accepted death, giving us an image of virtue and an example for conducting ourselves (St. Athanasius of Alexandria, *Festal Epistles* 10, 7).

50:4 sustain with a word: The Servant's task is to encourage his weary people.

50:5 opened my ear: I.e., enabled me to hear and understand his call.

50:6 my back ... my cheeks ... my face: The Servant's obedience to the Lord results in physical abuse from others. • Echoes of this passage can be heard in the Gospel accounts of Jesus' humiliation before Jewish (Mt 26:67; Mk 14:65; Lk 22:63) and Roman authorities (Mt 27:26, 30; Mk 15:15, 19; Jn 19:1).

50:7 set my face like a flint: An idiom for resolute determination (Jer 21:10; Ezek 3:8–9).

50:8 he who vindicates me: The Lord, who comes to the defense of his Servant when opponents charge him with wrongdoing. • Paul has this passage in mind when he asks: "Who shall bring any charge against God's elect? It is God who justifies; who is to condemn?" (Rom 8:33–34). Implicit in Paul's comments is the identification of Jesus with the innocent Servant of Isaiah and the believer's participation in his innocence through grace.

50:10–11 Addressed to the exiles, who can either trust in the Lord and find their way home or serve idols by lighting fires on pagan altars and bring torment upon themselves.

50:10 obeys: Just as the Servant heeds the Lord, as stated in 50:5, so the exiles are urged to hear and obey the Lord's Servant, no matter the suffering this might bring (51:7).

51:1–8 Three oracles addressed to the exiles. Each begins with a call from the Lord: "Listen to me" (51:1, 4, 7).

51:1 deliverance: Or, "righteousness". **seek the LORD:** Points to the efforts taken to deepen one's relationship with God (55:6; Deut 4:29; Ps 105:3–4).

51:2 Abraham ... Sarah: Ancestors of Israel by physical descent and by a shared faith in the one true God. They are held up as models of patient trust in the Lord's promises. The Jewish community in Babylon may be small, but the Lord can bless and multiply them, just as he did Abraham and Sarah (Gen 13:16; 15:5; 17:2).

51:3 comfort: One of the themes of Isaiah's later chapters (40:1; 49:13; 51:12; 52:9; etc.). The point here is that God will make the wasteland blossom with life. **Zion:** Jerusalem and the exiles who will return there (51:11). **like Eden:** The promise of a new paradise. In place of the barrenness and anguish of his people, the Lord will cause abundant life and joy to flourish, recalling the blissful conditions of Eden before sin entered the world (Gen 2:8–25). Ezekiel also foresees a new Eden awaiting God's faithful (Ezek 36:35). **like the garden:** I.e., well-watered and teeming with life (Gen 2:6, 10; 13:10).

51:4 a law will go forth: To instruct the nations in God's ways (2:3). **a light to the peoples:** The Servant of the Lord is described in this way in 42:6 and 49:6.

---

[n]Syr: Heb *gird yourselves with brands.*

⁵My deliverance draws near speedily,
    my salvation has gone forth,
    and my arms will rule the peoples;
the islands wait for me,
    and for my arm they hope.
⁶Lift up your eyes to the heavens,
    and look at the earth beneath;
for the heavens will vanish like smoke,
    the earth will wear out like a garment,
    and they who dwell in it will die like gnats;°
but my salvation will be for ever,
    and my deliverance will never be ended.

⁷"Listen to me, you who know righteousness,
    the people in whose heart is my law;
fear not the reproach of men,
    and be not dismayed at their revilings.
⁸For the moth will eat them up like a garment,
    and the worm will eat them like wool;
but my deliverance will be for ever,
    and my salvation to all generations."

⁹Awake, awake, put on strength,
    O arm of the Lᴏʀᴅ;
awake, as in days of old,
    the generations of long ago.
Was it not you who cut Ra′hab in pieces,
    who pierced the dragon?
¹⁰Was it not you who dried up the sea,
    the waters of the great deep;
who made the depths of the sea a way
    for the redeemed to pass over?
¹¹And the ransomed of the Lᴏʀᴅ shall return,
    and come to Zion with singing;

everlasting joy shall be upon their heads;
    they shall obtain joy and gladness,
    and sorrow and sighing shall flee away.

¹²"I, I am he who comforts you;
    who are you that you are afraid of man who
      dies,
    of the son of man who is made like grass,
¹³and have forgotten the Lᴏʀᴅ, your Maker,
    who stretched out the heavens
    and laid the foundations of the earth,
and fear continually all the day
    because of the fury of the oppressor,
when he sets himself to destroy?
    And where is the fury of the oppressor?
¹⁴He who is bowed down shall speedily be
      released;
    he shall not die and go down to the Pit,
    neither shall his bread fail.
¹⁵For I am the Lᴏʀᴅ your God,
    who stirs up the sea so that its waves roar—
    the Lᴏʀᴅ of hosts is his name.
¹⁶And I have put my words in your mouth,
    and hid you in the shadow of my hand,
stretching outᴾ the heavens
    and laying the foundations of the earth,
    and saying to Zion, 'You are my people.'"

¹⁷Rouse yourself, rouse yourself,
    stand up, O Jerusalem,
you who have drunk at the hand of the Lᴏʀᴅ
    the cup of his wrath,
who have drunk to the dregs
    the bowl of staggering.

51:6: Heb 1:11.

51:5 the islands: The peoples of the Mediterranean, which together represent all distant nations who wait for salvation. **my arm:** An image of the Lord's power to save and to judge, already revealed in the events of the Exodus (Ex 6:6; 15:16; Deut 4:34; 26:8). The arm of the Lord is mentioned numerous times in Isaiah (30:30, 32; 40:10; 48:14; 51:9; 52:10; 53:1; 59:16; 63:5, 12). Descriptions of God as if he had a body, called anthropomorphisms, are figurative expressions that should not be taken literally, since God is not flesh but "spirit" (31:3; Jn 4:24).
51:6 my salvation: More enduring than the visible cosmos (24:21–23; 40:6–8; Ps 102:26).
51:7 righteousness: The path of covenant faithfulness marked out by God's commandments (Deut 4:8; 6:25). **the people:** The faithful of Israel who treasure the Torah in their hearts (Deut 6:6; Ps 37:31; 119:10–11).
51:8 the moth will eat them: Those who persecute the exiles will perish (50:9).
51:9–11 Deliverance from Babylon will be a new exodus, recalling how God **dried up the sea** and made **a way** of escape for the **redeemed** of Israel. See essay: *The New Exodus in Isaiah* at Is 43.
51:9 Awake, awake: The prophet implores God to rise up and rescue his people (cf. 52:1). **Rahab:** A fearsome sea

dragon in Semitic mythology, also known as Leviathan (27:1; Ps 74:13–14). He represents the powerful forces of evil that the Lord holds in check (Job 26:12; Ps 89:9–10). The Lord demonstrated his mastery over the sea at creation (Gen 1:9) and again when he parted the sea during the Exodus (Ex 14:21). Rahab sometimes represents the evil power of Egypt (30:7; cf. Ezek 29:3–5).
51:11 And the ransomed: The entire verse is identical to 35:10.
51:13 the oppressor: The Babylonians.
51:14 the Pit: The netherworld of the dead, also called Sheol.
51:15–16 Reassurance that the Lord has not rejected his covenant people. This is achieved by using the expressions **I am the Lᴏʀᴅ your God** (51:15) and **You are my people** (51:16), which allude to the traditional covenant formula of Lev 26:12.
51:16 hid you in ... my hand: Recalls the Servant's words in 49:2.
51:17 the cup of his wrath: An image of divine judgment in Scripture (Ps 75:8; Jer 25:15–29; Ezek 23:31–34). Its effects are likened to a state of drunkenness that causes people to become spiritually blind and stumble toward destruction (29:9–10). Judah and Jerusalem drank this cup at the time of the Babylonian conquest in the early sixth century B.C. but have since received the Lord's forgiveness after several decades of exile (40:1–2). Now it is Babylon's turn to taste the bitterness of God's wrath (51:22–23).

°Or *in like manner.*
ᴾSyr: Heb *plant.*

¹⁸There is none to guide her
  among all the sons she has borne;
there is none to take her by the hand
  among all the sons she has brought up.
¹⁹These two things have befallen you—
  who will condole with you?—
devastation and destruction, famine and sword;
  who will comfort you?^q
²⁰Your sons have fainted,
  they lie at the head of every street
  like an antelope in a net;
they are full of the wrath of the Lord,
  the rebuke of your God.

²¹Therefore hear this, you who are afflicted,
  who are drunk, but not with wine:
²²Thus says your Lord, the Lord,
  your God who pleads the cause of his
    people:
"Behold, I have taken from your hand
  the cup of staggering;
the bowl of my wrath
  you shall drink no more;
²³and I will put it into the hand of your tormentors,
  who have said to you,
'Bow down, that we may pass over';
and you have made your back like the ground
  and like the street for them to pass over."

Awake to Good Tidings of Redemption

52 Awake, awake,
  put on your strength, O Zion;
put on your beautiful garments,
  O Jerusalem, the holy city;
for there shall no more come into you
  the uncircumcised and the unclean.
²Shake yourself from the dust, arise,
  O captive^r Jerusalem;
loose the bonds from your neck,
  O captive daughter of Zion.

3 For thus says the Lord: "You were sold for nothing, and you shall be redeemed without money. ⁴For thus says the Lord God: My people went down at the first into Egypt to sojourn there, and the Assyrian oppressed them for nothing. ⁵Now therefore what have I here, says the Lord, seeing that my people are taken away for nothing? Their rulers wail, says the Lord, and continually all the day my name is despised. ⁶Therefore my people shall know my name; therefore in that day they shall know that it is I who speak; here am I."

⁷How beautiful upon the mountains
  are the feet of him who brings good tidings,
who publishes peace, who brings good tidings of
    good,
  who publishes salvation,
  who says to Zion, "Your God reigns."
⁸Listen, your watchmen lift up their voice,
  together they sing for joy;
for eye to eye they see
  the return of the Lord to Zion.

52:1: Rev 21:27. **52:5:** Rom 2:24. **52:7:** Acts 10:36; Rom 10:15; Eph 6:15.

51:18 the sons: The children of mother Zion (49:14–26).

52:1–12 Isaiah announces the end of Babylonian Exile and the Lord's return to Zion (40:9–11). He urges the captives in Babylon to ready themselves for the journey home.

52:1 Awake, awake: I.e., from the spiritual stupor induced by the "cup" of the Lord's wrath (51:17–22). **beautiful garments:** Festal attire, perhaps for a bride (49:18; 54:4–8). The city was stripped of its adornments by Babylonian conquerors (Ezek 23:26). **the holy city:** An epithet for Jerusalem (48:2; Neh 11:1, 18). **uncircumcised ... unclean:** Those who are ritually impure and thus unfit to enter the sanctified precincts of Jerusalem (Joel 3:17). Restrictions for protecting the holiness of the Temple are here applied to the whole city (see 2 Chron 23:19; Ezek 44:6–7).

52:2 from the dust, arise: Echoes the resurrection prophecy in 26:19. Israel's return from exile is also described as rising from the dead in Ezek 37:1–14. • Creation groans with birth pangs awaiting the redemption of the children of God from the corruption of the flesh. At our resurrection, we will shake off the mortality of the flesh, according to the passage "shake off the dust and arise, O Jerusalem" (St. Methodius, *On the Resurrection* 1, 8).

52:3 sold: Into temporary slavery. See note on 40:2. **for nothing:** No actual sale was made, implying that God never relinquished Israel and is therefore entitled to take his people back without a ransom payment.

52:4 My people: Israel remains the Lord's people, despite its history of captivity under the Egyptians, the Assyrians, and now the Babylonians. They are not forsaken or disowned (Ps 94:14; Rom 11:1). See note on 51:15–16.

52:5 my name is despised: The Greek LXX translation of this passage reads: "Because of you my name is always blasphemed among the nations." • Paul cites this Greek version in Rom 2:24 to show that Jewish disobedience to the Law brings dishonor to the Lord. This is particularly so when the covenant people find themselves scattered to foreign lands as punishment for their sins (Ezek 36:20–21).

52:6 shall know my name: By experiencing the steadfast love and mercy signified by the name "Lord" (Ex 34:5–7). See word study: *Know* at Judg 19:22.

52:7 How beautiful upon the mountains: The mountains of Israel (Nah 1:15). **him who brings good tidings:** A messenger, such as one who brings news of victory from the battlefront (2 Sam 18:24–27). Isaiah envisions a herald racing to Jerusalem to announce that the Lord is King and is bringing his people home from captivity. • Paul cites this passage to say that the good news of salvation requires preachers to be sent out with the message (Rom 10:15). **Your God reigns:** The essence of the good news proclaimed to Zion. The redemption of Israel, first from the bondage of Egypt and now from Babylon, is a demonstration of the Lord's kingship over the powers of this world (Ex 15:13–18). The *Targum on Isaiah* renders this statement: "the kingdom of your God is revealed".

52:8 your watchmen: Sentinels in Zion on the lookout for news from abroad. **the return of the Lord:** The firecloud of God's glory departed from Jerusalem before the destruction of the city and the exile of Judah to Babylon (Ezek 11:23). For a similar prophecy, see Zech 8:3.

---

^qOne ancient Ms Gk Syr Vg: Heb *how may I comfort you.*
^rCn: Heb *sit.*

⁹Break forth together into singing,
　　you waste places of Jerusalem;
for the Lᴏʀᴅ has comforted his people,
　　he has redeemed Jerusalem.
¹⁰The Lᴏʀᴅ has bared his holy arm
　　before the eyes of all the nations;
and all the ends of the earth shall see
　　the salvation of our God.

¹¹Depart, depart, go out from there,
　　touch no unclean thing;
go out from the midst of her, purify yourselves,
　　you who bear the vessels of the Lᴏʀᴅ.
¹²For you shall not go out in haste,
　　and you shall not go in flight,
for the Lᴏʀᴅ will go before you,
　　and the God of Israel will be your rear guard.

¹³Behold, my servant shall prosper,
　　he shall be exalted and lifted up,
　　and shall be very high.
¹⁴As many were astonished at him ˢ—
　　his appearance was so marred, beyond human
　　　semblance,
　　and his form beyond that of the sons of men—
¹⁵so shall he startle ᵗ many nations;
　　kings shall shut their mouths because of him;
for that which has not been told them they shall
　　see,
　　and that which they have not heard they shall
　　understand.

The Lord's Suffering Servant

53 Who has believed what we have heard?
　　And to whom has the arm of the Lᴏʀᴅ been
　　revealed?

52:10: Lk 2:30; 3:6.　**52:11:** 2 Cor 6:17.　**52:15:** Rom 15:21.　**53:1:** Jn 12:38; Rom 10:16.

52:9 comforted: See note on 40:1.

✝ **52:10 his holy arm:** The Lord's saving power (40:10; 53:1). See note on 51:5. • The arm of the Lord is made known to the nations, and the ends of the earth see his salvation, when the Church, which is the spiritual Jerusalem, is built by the apostles. This gives us two options for interpretation: either the Father reveals his arm to the nations, or the Son reveals his might. Many passages in Scripture indicate that the Son of God is the Father's arm and right hand (St. Jerome, *Commentary on Isaiah* 14, 19).

📖 **52:11–12** An exodus from Babylon, only this time the people will not depart **in haste** as they did from Egypt (Ex 12:33; Deut 16:3). God will again protect them as he once did, going **before** them as a pillar of cloud and fire (Ex 13:21–22) and standing as their **rear guard** (Ex 14:19–20). See essay: *The New Exodus in Isaiah* at Is 43.

📖 **52:11 go out from there:** I.e., depart from Babylon (Jer 50:8; 51:45). The phrase "from there" (Heb., *mishsham*) may imply that the prophet writing these words was not himself in Babylon. An interpretation along these lines is consistent with views that place the author of the book (or at least chaps. 40-55) in Jerusalem but is problematic for hypotheses that locate the prophet among the exiles in Babylon. For issues surrounding authorship of the book, see introduction: *Author and Date*. • Paul cites this verse to dissuade believers from having close associations with unbelievers (2 Cor 6:17). **touch no unclean thing:** Lest the exiles defile themselves, since this would disqualify them from worshiping at the Temple. **the vessels of the Lᴏʀᴅ:** The sacred furnishings of the Temple, which conquerors carted off to Babylon in stages (2 Kings 24:10-13; 25:13-16; Dan 1:1-2). The Lord promised the return of these items in Jer 27:21-22.

📖✝ **52:13—53:12** The fourth "Servant Song" in Isaiah. Here the Servant appears as a priestly figure that offers sacrifice (53:10) and makes intercession for others (53:12). He is faithful in doing the Lord's will ("righteous", 53:11) in spite of the suffering that it brings him ("a man of sorrows", 53:3). He is rejected (53:3), abused (53:5, 7), killed (53:8), and buried (53:9), yet he pours out his life to make atonement for the sins of others (53:10-12). In the end, tragedy turns to triumph, for the Lord exalts his Servant (52:13) in a way that prolongs "his days" (53:10). Theologically, the Servant is closely associated with the people of Israel; at the same time, he appears as an individual who acts for the benefit of Israel. The vicarious sacrifice of one (who is innocent) on behalf of many (who are guilty) is the central mystery of the song (53:5-6). Rhetorically, several voices speak in the song about the Servant and what he accomplished: the Lord (52:13-15; 53:11-12), witnesses from Israel (53:1-6), and the prophet (53:7-10). See note on 42:1-9. • The NT reads the fourth Servant Song as a messianic prophecy, following the lead of Jesus himself, who declared that it must be fulfilled in him (Lk 22:37). Jesus is thus proclaimed as the Lord's exalted "servant" (Acts 3:13; Phil 2:7-9); as one who takes away infirmities (Mt 8:17); as one who heals others by his wounds (1 Pet 2:21-25); as one who is slaughtered like a lamb (Acts 8:30-35); as one who gives his life for many (Mk 10:45; 14:24); and as one who makes many righteous (Rom 5:19). He is also proclaimed among Gentiles (Rom 15:20-21) as well as Jews (Jn 12:37-38; Rom 10:16-17) • The fourth Servant Song is read on Good Friday in the Roman Lectionary (CCC 713).

📖 **52:13 my servant:** Often identified in Jewish tradition as the people of Israel, as in 41:8; 44:1, 21; 45:4. Some ancient Jews, however, viewed this figure as the Messiah who intercedes with God to win mercy for the remnant of Israel (e.g., *Targum on Isaiah*). Christian tradition is unanimous in viewing the Lord's Servant as the Messiah (Jesus), not as opposed to Israel, but as an ideal representative who embodies and fulfills the vocation of Israel. **exalted and lifted up:** Isaiah described the Lord God in this way in 6:1. • The Greek LXX reads, "lifted up and glorified", which is the background for Peter's words in Acts 3:13. Paul presents Jesus as the exalted Servant in Phil 2:9.

52:14 beyond human semblance: The result of bodily disfigurement.

📖✝ **52:15 startle:** Or "sprinkle", an alternative translation suggesting the Servant will cleanse the nations of defilement as a Levitical priest sprinkles those who are unclean (Lev 14:6-7; cf. Ezek 36:25). **shut their mouths:** People will be stunned and rendered speechless (Job 21:5). **they shall see ... understand:** Things the nations never imagined would be made known to them. • Paul quotes the Greek LXX of this verse in Rom 15:21 as inspiration for his mission to evangelize Gentiles who have never heard the gospel. • The prophet foretells the remission of sins by the sprinkling of Christ's blood and the water of baptism. Kings will venerate him, listening silently, while the Gentiles, who were not told of him by the prophets and had not heard his preaching firsthand, will come to know the truth (St. Thomas Aquinas, *Commentary on Isaiah* 52, 15).

53:1-6 Witnesses from Israel recount **(1)** their initial reaction to the Servant and **(2)** what they came to understand about him in retrospect.

📖 **53:1 Who has believed:** Many refused to believe that the suffering Servant was God's chosen deliverer. **we:**

ˢ Syr Tg: Heb *you.*
ᵗ The meaning of the Hebrew word is uncertain.

²For he grew up before him like a young plant,
  and like a root out of dry ground;
he had no form or comeliness that we should look
    at him,
  and no beauty that we should desire him.
³He was despised and rejectedᵘ by men;
  a man of sorrows,ᵛ and acquainted with
    grief;ʷ
and as one from whom men hide their faces
  he was despised, and we esteemed him not.

⁴Surely he has borne our griefsˣ
  and carried our sorrows;ʸ
yet we esteemed him stricken,
  struck down by God, and afflicted.
⁵But he was wounded for our transgressions,
  he was bruised for our iniquities;
upon him was the chastisement that made us
    whole,
  and with his stripes we are healed.
⁶All we like sheep have gone astray;
  we have turned every one to his own way;

and the Lᴏʀᴅ has laid on him
  the iniquity of us all.*

⁷He was oppressed, and he was afflicted,
  yet he opened not his mouth;
like a lamb that is led to the slaughter,
  and like a sheep that before its shearers is
    silent,
  so he opened not his mouth.
⁸By oppression and judgment he was taken
    away;
  and as for his generation, who considered
that he was cut off out of the land of the living,
  stricken for the transgression of my
    people?
⁹And they made his grave with the wicked
  and with a rich man in his death,
although he had done no violence,
  and there was no deceit in his mouth.

¹⁰Yet it was the will of the Lᴏʀᴅ to bruise him;
  he has put him to grief;ᶻ

53:4: Mt 8:17. **53:5–6:** 1 Pet 2:24–25. **53:7–8:** Acts 8:32–33. **53:9:** 1 Pet 2:22.

The people of Israel, as distinct from "they" (= the nations and their rulers, 52:15). • According to the Gospel of John, this prophecy is fulfilled when the crowds in Jerusalem refuse to believe in Jesus despite the many signs he performed (Jn 12:38). Paul also sees in this verse a reference to Jewish unbelief in the gospel (Rom 10:16). **the arm of the Lᴏʀᴅ:** An image of the Lord's saving power (40:10; 52:10). See note on 51:5.

53:2 he grew up: Begins an extended flashback on the Servant's life of hardship before his exaltation (52:13). **a young plant:** A sapling planted in parched soil, which would not be expected to achieve great stature. • When Isaiah says "he had no form or comeliness", he is either comparing the humanity of the Son with the glory of his divinity, which surpasses all description, or he is speaking about his Passion and the dishonor he endured on the Cross (St. John Chrysostom, *Homilies on Matthew* 27, 3).

53:4 borne: Sin and suffering are viewed as onerous burdens carried through life. The Lord willed that the Servant should carry this load (53:5-6). **our griefs:** Or "our infirmities". • According to the Gospel of Matthew, this verse is fulfilled in Jesus, whose miracles of healing restored the sick to health (Mt 8:17). **struck down by God:** Initially, people thought the Servant was a godless man under a curse (Deut 21:22-23). Only later was it realized that his suffering won salvation for others (53:5-6). • Paul teaches that Jesus became a curse for us insofar as he bore the curse of the covenant (= death) in order to release its blessings (Gal 3:13).

53:5 wounded: Or "pierced" (as in 51:9). **his stripes:** The welts and lacerations made on the Servant's body. • Peter cites this verse to say that believers are healed through the Passion of Jesus (1 Pet 2:24).

53:6 the Lᴏʀᴅ ... iniquity of us all: The Greek LXX reads: "the Lord handed him over for our sins". • Paul appears to have this passage in mind when he teaches that Jesus "was put to death [literally, 'handed over'] for our trespasses" (Rom 4:25) and that he "died for our sins in accordance with the Scriptures" (1 Cor 15:3).

53:7-10 The testimony of the prophet, who refers to fellow Israelites as "my people" (53:8).

53:7 opened not his mouth: A sign of submission, i.e., the Servant refuses to protest the injustices perpetrated against him. • Silent submission is fulfilled in Jesus when he makes no answer to the charges brought against him at his trials (Mt 27:12; Mk 14:60-61; Lk 23:9). **a lamb:** An innocent victim persecuted and plotted against (Ps 44:22; Jer 11:19). • The NT uses this image to describe Jesus as a spotless lamb who takes away sin (Jn 1:29; 1 Pet 1:19).

53:8 who considered ... ?: The Servant's assailants did not understand what they were doing when they took his life (see Lk 23:34; Acts 3:17-18).

53:9 with the wicked: As if the Servant were a criminal. **a rich man:** Often connected with Mt 27:57, which identifies Joseph of Arimathea, who buried the body of Jesus, as "a rich man". **no violence ... no deceit:** The Greek LXX reads: "he committed no lawlessness, nor was deceit found in his mouth." • Peter applies this passage to Jesus in 1 Pet 2:22.

53:10 it was the will of the Lᴏʀᴅ: The suffering and death of the Servant was not an accident of history; rather, it was part of God's definite plan (Acts 2:23) to save his people from their sins (Mt 1:21). **an offering for sin:** Known in Levitical law as a "guilt offering" (Heb., *'asham*). In ancient Israel, a person who profaned something holy or consecrated to the Lord was required to make restitution, to pay a fine, and to offer a sacrifice of reparation in order to atone for his guilt and receive forgiveness (Lev 5:14–6:7; 19:22). The Greek LXX translates this "a sin offering" (Gk., *peri hamartias*), an expression Paul uses to speak of the sacrifice of Jesus (Rom 8:3). **shall prolong his days:** A mysterious statement in view of the Servant's death and burial (53:9). From a Christian standpoint, it hints at the Servant rising to new life.

ᵘOr *forsaken*.
ᵛOr *pains*.
ʷOr *sickness*.
ˣOr *sicknesses*.
ʸOr *pains*.
ᶻHeb *made him sick*.
*53:4–6: The doctrine of vicarious atonement is the unique characteristic of this prophecy. We find it in the New Testament in all its fulness.

when he makes himself[a] an offering for sin,
 he shall see his offspring, he shall prolong his
  days;
 the will of the Lord shall prosper in his hand;
11 he shall see the fruit of the travail of his soul
  and be satisfied;
 by his knowledge shall the righteous one, my
  servant,
  make many to be accounted righteous;
 and he shall bear their iniquities.
12Therefore I will divide him a portion with the
  great,
 and he shall divide the spoil with the
  strong;
because he poured out his soul to death,
 and was numbered with the transgressors;
yet he bore the sin of many,
 and made intercession for the transgressors.

Mercy and Comfort Offered

54 "Sing, O barren one, who did not bear;
 break forth into singing and cry aloud,
 you who have not had labor pains!
For the children of the desolate one will be
 more
 than the children of her that is married, says
  the Lord.
2Enlarge the place of your tent,
 and let the curtains of your habitations be
  stretched out;

hold not back, lengthen your cords
 and strengthen your stakes.
3For you will spread abroad to the right and to the
  left,
 and your descendants will possess the
  nations
 and will people the desolate cities.

4"Fear not, for you will not be ashamed;
 be not confounded, for you will not be put to
  shame;
 for you will forget the shame of your youth,
  and the reproach of your widowhood you will
   remember no more.
5For your Maker is your husband,
 the Lord of hosts is his name;
 and the Holy One of Israel is your Redeemer,
  the God of the whole earth he is called.
6For the Lord has called you
 like a wife forsaken and grieved in spirit,
 like a wife of youth when she is cast off,
  says your God.
7For a brief moment I forsook you,
 but with great compassion I will gather you.
8In overflowing wrath for a moment
 I hid my face from you,
 but with everlasting mercy I will have
  compassion on you,
 says the Lord, your Redeemer.

53:12: Lk 22:37.   **54:1:** Gal 4:27.

53:11 make ... righteous: The Servant will accomplish a reconciliation that brings many into a right relationship with God. • This passage underlies Paul's teaching on justification in Rom 5, where he contends that Christ's gift of righteousness, won by his obedience, abounds for "many" (Rom 5:15) and ensures that "many will be made righteous" (Rom 5:19).

53:12 divide the spoil: Like a conqueror who shares the rewards of conquest with his soldiers. **numbered with the transgressors:** The Servant is considered a criminal. • Jesus cites these words on the night of his arrest as words that must be fulfilled in him (Lk 22:37). **he bore the sin:** Like the scapegoat that carries the burden of Israel's iniquities into the wilderness on the Day of Atonement (Lev 16:22). See note on 53:4. **many:** Includes the "many nations" of 52:15.

54:1–17 The glorification of Jerusalem following the exile. The city is described as **(1)** a barren women who suddenly becomes the mother of a multitude of children (54:1), **(2)** a tent that must expand to accommodate a growing family (54:2–3), **(3)** an abandoned bride who is reunited with her husband (54:5–8), and **(4)** a city rebuilt of gemstones (54:11–12). In these ways, Jerusalem will experience God's compassion (54:7–8, 10) in place of its shame (54:4). • The NT draws from this vision to describe, not the capital city of Israel's history, but the heavenly Jerusalem above. Paul quotes the Greek translation of 54:1 to say that believers, whether Jews or Gentiles, have been freed by the mercy of Christ to become the children of this maternal city in heaven. The Book of Revelation also draws from this chapter to describe the celestial Jerusalem as a bridal city adorned for her husband and built with gems and other precious materials (Rev 21:2, 10–21).

54:1 O barren one: Jerusalem, a city left childless since its inhabitants went into exile. In view of 54:3, it is likely that Zion, the barren city, is being compared to Sarah, the barren wife of Abraham (Gen 11:30), who was made fruitful by God to become "a mother of nations" (Gen 17:15–16).

54:2 your tent: Too small to shelter the great multitude of its future children.

54:3 possess the nations: May allude to the divine oath in Gen 22:16–18, where God swore that Abraham's descendants will "possess" the gates of their enemies and become a blessing to "all the nations".

54:4 your widowhood: The period of the exile, during which time God allowed his people to suffer the bitter consequences of their disobedience.

54:5 your husband: The Lord, who wed himself to Israel in the wilderness of Sinai (Jer 2:2), although he was often provoked to jealousy by the infidelities of his people (Jer 3:1–14; Ezek 16:8–52; Hos 1–3). Isaiah underscores God's enduring commitment to his bride (62:4–5; Hos 2:19–20). **the Lord of hosts:** See note on 1:9. **the Holy One of Israel:** See note on 1:4. **Redeemer:** See note on 41:14.

54:7 I forsook you: God permitted the Babylonians to destroy Jerusalem in 586 B.C.

54:8 I hid my face: An idiom for the experience of divine judgment (57:17; 59:2; 64:7). It is the opposite of God showing his face to his people as a sign of favor (Num 6:25). **everlasting mercy:** The basis for Israel's election as the chosen people (Deut 7:7–8). It is a strong and forgiving love that is more enduring than the mountains (54:10; Jer 31:3).

---

[a] Vg: Heb *thou makest his soul.*

⁹"For this is like the days of Noah to me:
　as I swore that the waters of Noah
　should no more go over the earth,
　so I have sworn that I will not be angry with you
　and will not rebuke you.
¹⁰For the mountains may depart
　and the hills be removed,
　but my mercy shall not depart from you,
　and my covenant of peace shall not be removed,
　says the Lᴏʀᴅ, who has compassion on you.

¹¹"O afflicted one, storm-tossed, and not comforted,
　behold, I will set your stones in antimony,
　and lay your foundations with sapphires.ᵇ
¹²I will make your pinnacles of agate,
　your gates of carbuncles,
　and all your wall of precious stones.
¹³All your sons shall be taught by the Lᴏʀᴅ,
　and great shall be the prosperity of your
　　sons.
¹⁴In righteousness you shall be established;
　you shall be far from oppression, for you shall
　　not fear;
　and from terror, for it shall not come near you.
¹⁵If any one stirs up strife,
　it is not from me;
　whoever stirs up strife with you
　shall fall because of you.

¹⁶Behold, I have created the smith
　who blows the fire of coals,
　and produces a weapon for its purpose.
I have also created the ravager to destroy;
¹⁷　no weapon that is fashioned against you shall
　　prosper,
　and you shall confute every tongue that rises
　　against you in judgment.
This is the heritage of the servants of the Lᴏʀᴅ
　and their vindication from me, says the Lᴏʀᴅ."

An Invitation to Abundant Life

55 "Ho, every one who thirsts,
　come to the waters;
and he who has no money,
　come, buy and eat!
Come, buy wine and milk
　without money and without price.
²Why do you spend your money for that which is
　　not bread,
　and your labor for that which does not satisfy?
Listen diligently to me, and eat what is good,
　and delight yourselves in rich food.
³Incline your ear, and come to me;
　hear, that your soul may live;
　and I will make with you an everlasting covenant,
　my steadfast, merciful love for David.
⁴Behold, I made him a witness to the peoples,
　a leader and commander for the peoples.

54:11–12: Rev 21:19.　**54:13:** Jn 6:45.　**55:1:** Rev 21:6; 22:17.　**55:3:** Acts 13:34; Heb 13:20.

54:9–17 Jerusalem is assured of the Lord's mercy, peace, and protection for the future.

54:9 the days of Noah: A time of overwhelming judgment followed by a new beginning for God's people in a time of peace. The biblical story of the flood illustrates that manifestations of divine wrath in history are of limited duration. **I swore:** Refers to the covenant that God made with Noah (Gen 9:8–17).

54:10 my mercy: The Lord's enduring commitment to his people. See word study: *Steadfast Love* at Ex 34:6. **covenant of peace:** An "everlasting covenant" that crowns Israel's long history of living in covenant with the Lord (55:3; 61:8). This new covenant will bring the forgiveness of sins (Jer 31:31–34) and the rule of the Davidic Messiah (Ezek 34:24–25).

54:11–12 The Lord is the Builder of the glorified Jerusalem (**I will set ... I will make**). Using precious stones as building materials signifies the lavish abundance of God's future blessings.

54:13 your sons: Zion's future children (54:1). **taught by the Lᴏʀᴅ:** One of the signs of the New Covenant foretold in Scripture (Jer 31:34).

54:17 This is the heritage: Refers to the promises in chap. 54. **the servants of the Lᴏʀᴅ:** Those who walk in the footsteps of the Servant mentioned in earlier chapters (42:1–9; 49:1–9; 50:4–11; 52:13—53:12). As the messianic Servant was afflicted (53:4), vindicated (50:8), and taught by the Lord (50:4), so the servants who follow his path are afflicted (54:11), vindicated (54:17), and taught by the Lord (54:13). This community of servants will include Gentiles (56:6) alongside the tribes of Israel (63:17; 65:8–9).

55:1–2 The Lord invites all to a feast that is free of charge. He offers, not ordinary food and drink, but the blessings of his life-sustaining word (Deut 8:3). The passage builds on 25:6–8, the feast for all nations on Mount Zion, and resembles the invitation to Wisdom's banquet in Prov 9:1–6; Sir 24:19–21.

55:3–5 A new covenant is promised that fulfills the Lord's covenant with David, which was an "everlasting covenant" (2 Sam 23:5) founded on God's sure oath to establish David's throne and kingdom for all time (see 2 Sam 7:8–17; Ps 89:1–4, 25–37; 132:11). Some interpret these verses to promise a *transfer* of God's commitments from David's line to the whole nation of Israel. More likely, the prophet foresees an *extension* of the Davidic covenant that allows the whole covenant people to benefit from God sending an ideal king from David's line. Prophecies of a royal Davidic Messiah appear earlier in the book (9:6–7; 11:1–10) and elsewhere in the OT (see Jer 23:5–6; Ezek 34:23–24; Hos 3:5). • Paul connects this passage with the Resurrection of Jesus (Acts 13:34). Having been raised immortal, forever immune to corruption and death, Jesus is uniquely qualified to reign over the everlasting kingdom that God promised to David and his descendants. • This covenant shall not be brief, confined to a single period of time, but shall abide forever, so that the true David may come and the things that God promised may be fulfilled in the gospel. At a time when David was already asleep, Ezekiel calls him a shepherd, saying, "I will raise up for you one shepherd, my servant David" (St. Jerome, *Commentary on Isaiah* 15, 12).

55:3 my steadfast, merciful love: The Lord's faithfulness to his covenant commitments.

55:4 a leader ... for the peoples: Recalls how David extended his kingship, not only over the twelve tribes of Israel (2 Sam 5:1–5), but over several regional states surrounding Israel (2 Sam 8:1–15). The Lord thus made David "head of the nations", so that peoples unknown to him paid him homage and became his servants (2 Sam 22:44–45). The same

---

ᵇ Or *lapis lazuli.*

⁵Behold, you shall call nations that you know not,
    and nations that knew you not shall run to
        you,
  because of the Lᴏʀᴅ your God, and of the Holy
        One of Israel,
    for he has glorified you.

⁶"Seek the Lᴏʀᴅ while he may be found,
    call upon him while he is near;
⁷let the wicked forsake his way,
    and the unrighteous man his thoughts;
  let him return to the Lᴏʀᴅ, that he may have
        mercy on him,
    and to our God, for he will abundantly pardon.
⁸For my thoughts are not your thoughts,
    neither are your ways my ways, says the Lᴏʀᴅ.
⁹For as the heavens are higher than the earth,
    so are my ways higher than your ways
    and my thoughts than your thoughts.

¹⁰"For as the rain and the snow come down from
        heaven,
    and do not return there but water the earth,
  making it bring forth and sprout,
    giving seed to the sower and bread to the eater,
¹¹so shall my word be that goes forth from my
        mouth;
    it shall not return to me empty,

but it shall accomplish that which I intend,
    and prosper in the thing for which I sent it.

¹²"For you shall go out in joy,
    and be led forth in peace;
  the mountains and the hills before you
    shall break forth into singing,
    and all the trees of the field shall clap their
        hands.
¹³Instead of the thorn shall come up the cypress;
    instead of the brier shall come up the myrtle;
  and it shall be to the Lᴏʀᴅ for a memorial,
    for an everlasting sign which shall not be cut
        off."

Rewards of Righteousness

56 *Thus says the Lᴏʀᴅ:
"Keep justice, and do righteousness,
  for soon my salvation will come,
    and my deliverance be revealed.
²Blessed is the man who does this,
    and the son of man who holds it fast,
  who keeps the sabbath, not profaning it,
    and keeps his hand from doing any evil."

³Let not the foreigner who has joined himself to
        the Lᴏʀᴅ say,
    "The Lᴏʀᴅ will surely separate me from his
        people";

55:10: 2 Cor 9:10.

---

pattern of international rule under the headship of Israel's king is expected to play out in the messianic fulfillment of the Davidic covenant (55:5).

55:5 nations that you know not: Gentile peoples who have no covenant relationship with the Davidic king. **he has glorified you:** Words spoken to Zion and those who belong to it (60:9).

55:6–8 An appeal to seek the Lord and his forgiveness as the Babylonian Exile comes to an end. Now that deliverance is near at hand, this is a prime opportunity for Israel to repent and to return its hearts to the God who is rich in mercy (Ex 34:5–6). The need to seek the Lord in exile was foreseen in Deut 4:27–29.

55:8 my thoughts ... my ways: Drastically different from the "way" of the wicked man and the "thoughts" of the unrighteous man mentioned in 55:7. The mercies of the all-holy God are too abundant and too marvelous for sinful people to comprehend.

55:10–11 God's word is the instrument of his will. Once spoken, it never fails to achieve his purpose of bringing life to the world. Far from being powerless or ineffective, the divine word "stands for ever" (40:8) and should cause his people to "tremble" (66:2).

📖 **55:10 the rain ... the snow:** The word of God is likened to precipitation, as in Deut 32:2. **seed ... bread:** Things that sustain life, which are signs of God's blessing.

55:12 you shall go out: From captivity in Babylon (52:11–12). **clap their hands:** For scenes of creation rejoicing, see 44:23; 49:13; Ps 98:8.

55:13 the thorn ... the brier: Things that grow in desolate places, which are signs of God's judgment (5:6; 7:23–25; 34:13).

56:1—66:24 Prophecies about the salvation of God still to come—at a time in history *after* the deliverance of the exiles from Babylon. Isaiah 56–66 is designated Third Isaiah in part because these chapters address, not Isaiah's contemporaries (First Isaiah, chaps. 1–39) or the Jewish exiles in Babylon (Second Isaiah, chaps. 40–55), but the community who returned to Judah from Babylon and began rebuilding the nation (ca. fifth century B.C.). It was a time of high expectation and low morale as the thrill of starting a new life was dampened by practical difficulties and local opposition. The community at this time was divided into the faithful and those who opted for compromise. See introduction: *Author and Date.*

56:1 justice ... righteousness: Ideals exemplified by the Lord (5:16) but frequently elusive to his wayward people (1:21; 5:7). Ultimately, the Davidic Messiah will establish the "justice" and "righteousness" that God seeks (9:7; 16:5), partly by means of an outpouring of the Spirit (32:15–16; 33:5). **my salvation:** Not restricted to the deliverance of the Jewish exiles from Babylon. It is a salvation the Lord's Servant (= Messiah) will extend to "the end of the earth" (49:6).

56:2 the sabbath: A holy day (58:13) and the sign of God's covenant at creation (Ex 31:12–17). Observance of this weekly day of rest is an acknowledgment that all human life and work must be consecrated to God. Keeping the sabbath was an especially serious concern in the postexilic period, since profaning the sacred day of rest was one of the chief sins that led Judah and Jerusalem into exile in the first place (Neh 13:15–22; Jer 17:27).

📖 **56:3–8** The salvation to come is marked by the Lord's acceptance of persons formerly outside the covenant.

---

*56 to the end: These prophecies were probably uttered in the difficult days of the return from exile, about the year 538 B.C.

and let not the eunuch say,
"Behold, I am a dry tree."
[4]For thus says the Lord:
"To the eunuchs who keep my sabbaths,
who choose the things that please me
and hold fast my covenant,
[5]I will give in my house and within my walls
a monument and a name
better than sons and daughters;
I will give them an everlasting name
which shall not be cut off.

[6]"And the foreigners who join themselves to the
Lord,
to minister to him, to love the name of the
Lord,
and to be his servants,
every one who keeps the sabbath, and does not
profane it,
and holds fast my covenant—
[7]these I will bring to my holy mountain,
and make them joyful in my house of prayer;
their burnt offerings and their sacrifices
will be accepted on my altar;
for my house shall be called a house of prayer
for all peoples.
[8]Thus says the Lord God,
who gathers the outcasts of Israel,
I will gather yet others to him
besides those already gathered."[c]

[9]All you beasts of the field, come to devour—
all you beasts in the forest.
[10]His watchmen are blind,
they are all without knowledge;
they are all mute dogs,
they cannot bark;
dreaming, lying down,
loving to slumber.
[11]The dogs have a mighty appetite;
they never have enough.
The shepherds also have no understanding;
they have all turned to their own way,
each to his own gain, one and all.
[12]"Come," they say, "let us[d] get wine,
let us fill ourselves with strong drink;
and tomorrow will be like this day,
great beyond measure."

Idolatry Condemned

57 The righteous man perishes,
and no one lays it to heart;
devout men are taken away,
while no one understands.
For the righteous man is taken away from
calamity,
[2] he enters into peace;
they rest in their beds
who walk in their uprightness.
[3]But you, draw near to here,
sons of the sorceress,
offspring of the adulterer and the harlot.

56:7: Mt 21:13; Mk 11:17; Lk 19:46.

He will include **foreigners** having no genealogical ties with Israel as well as **eunuchs** (= emasculated males) who are incapable of fathering children. Acceptance by the Lord is based on keeping the **covenant** and doing what pleases him (56:4, 6). Isaiah thus looks beyond the days of the Mosaic covenant, which forbade both eunuchs and foreign enemies to join the worshiping assembly of Israel (Deut 23:1–6), restrictions that were still in force in the postexilic period (Neh 13:1–3). • The fulfillment of this prophecy is signaled in Acts 8:26–40, where a royal servant from Ethiopia, who was both a foreigner and a eunuch, came to believe in the scriptural words of Isaiah and was baptized. Jesus may allude to this passage when he describes celibate disciples as those who make themselves "eunuchs for the sake of the kingdom of heaven" (Mt 19:12).
56:4 the eunuchs: Isaiah had foreseen that some of the exiles would become "eunuchs" in Babylon (39:7).
56:5 my house: The Temple. **a monument and a name:** A memorial set up for one who had no children to preserve his family name (as in 2 Sam 18:18).
56:7 my holy mountain: The glorified Mount Zion, where the Lord promises to gather all nations for worship and instruction (2:2–3; 25:6–8; 66:18–21). **their sacrifices:** Those formerly excluded from participation in the Temple liturgy will finally bring their offerings to the Temple altar. **house of prayer for all peoples:** Solomon had envisioned foreigners coming to Jerusalem and praying toward the Temple (1 Kings 8:41–43). Isaiah foresees this taking place on a universal scale, as all nations gather before the Lord in his sanctuary. • Jesus quotes this passage when he expels the merchants

and moneychangers from the Temple, in part because their business was conducted in the Court of the Gentiles—the one area of the (Herodian) Temple where non-Jews were allowed to enter and pray (Mt 21:13; Mk 11:17).
56:8 I will gather yet others: An indication that the restoration of Israel has only begun with the return of Jewish exiles from Babylon. Most of the twelve tribes of Israel would be lost among the nations until the Messiah comes to restore them, along with the Gentiles (11:10–12). Jesus seems to allude to this passage in Jn 10:16.
56:9—57:2 A shift from oracles of salvation to oracles of judgment on Israel's leaders. Their failures have left the **righteous** endangered and victims of injustice (57:1). Isaiah speaks of **watchmen** (56:10) and **shepherds** (56:11) to designate prophets (Ezek 3:16–21; Hab 2:1) and rulers respectively (Jer 25:34–35; Ezek 34:1–16).
56:9 beasts: Represent foreign nations that God uses to chastise Israel (5:26–30).
56:10 without knowledge: See note on 5:13.
56:12 let us get wine: Isaiah witnessed this type of foolish self-indulgence among his own generation as well (5:11; 22:13).
57:2 enters into peace: The righteous dead will escape the pangs of judgment destined for sinners. **their beds:** I.e., their tombs.
57:3–13 The divine Judge summons his people and indicts them for their crimes. Despite the Lord's goodness to the returnees in Jerusalem, they **did not remember** him (57:11) but instead turned to **idols** (57:13) and engaged in cultic fornication and child sacrifice (57:5). Many failed to heed the call to repentance in 55:6–7, so that even as Judah's restoration is underway, pagan religion is making a comeback.

---

[c] Heb *his gathered ones.*
[d] One ancient Ms Syr Vg Tg: Heb *me.*

⁴Of whom are you making sport?
  Against whom do you open your mouth
    wide
  and put out your tongue?
  Are you not children of transgression,
    the offspring of deceit,
⁵you who burn with lust among the oaks,
    under every green tree;
  who slay your children in the valleys,
    under the clefts of the rocks?
⁶Among the smooth stones of the valley is your
    portion;
  they, they, are your lot;
  to them you have poured out a drink offering,
    you have brought a cereal offering.
  Shall I be appeased for these things?
⁷Upon a high and lofty mountain
    you have set your bed,
  and from there you went up to offer sacrifice.
⁸Behind the door and the doorpost
    you have set up your symbol;
  for, deserting me, you have uncovered your bed,
    you have gone up to it,
    you have made it wide;
  and you have made a bargain for yourself with
    them,
    you have loved their bed,
    you have looked on nakedness.ᵉ
⁹You journeyed to Mo'lechᶠ with oil
    and multiplied your perfumes;
  you sent your envoys far off,
    and sent down even to Sheol.
¹⁰You were wearied with the length of your way,
    but you did not say, "It is hopeless";
  you found new life for your strength,
    and so you were not faint.

¹¹Whom did you dread and fear,
    so that you lied,
  and did not remember me,
    did not give me a thought?
  Have I not held my peace, even for a long time,
    and so you do not fear me?
¹²I will tell of your righteousness and your doings,
    but they will not help you.
¹³When you cry out, let your collection of idols
    deliver you!
  The wind will carry them off,
    a breath will take them away.
  But he who takes refuge in me shall possess the
    land,
  and shall inherit my holy mountain.

¹⁴And it shall be said,
  "Build up, build up, prepare the way,
    remove every obstruction from my people's
      way."
¹⁵For thus says the high and lofty One
    who inhabits eternity, whose name is Holy:
  "I dwell in the high and holy place,
    and also with him who is of a contrite and
      humble spirit,
  to revive the spirit of the humble,
    and to revive the heart of the contrite.
¹⁶For I will not contend for ever,
    nor will I always be angry;
  for from me proceeds the spirit,
    and I have made the breath of life.
¹⁷Because of the iniquity of his covetousness I was
    angry,
  I struck him, I hid my face and was angry;
  but he went on backsliding in the way of his
    own heart.

57:15: Mt 5:3.

57:5 burn with lust: Idol shrines in Canaan had sacred groves where immoral sexual rites took place (Hos 4:13–14). **slay your children:** Child sacrifice was practiced in the Canaanite cult of Molech (Lev 18:21; 20:1–5) and even by sinful Israelites in OT times (2 Kings 23:10; Jer 7:31; Ezek 23:36–39). **in the valleys:** Children were immolated by fire in the Hinnom valley, south of Jerusalem (Jer 19:4–6).
  57:6 smooth stones: The Lord's judgment is compared to storm waters that sweep sinners into rocky ravines to die unburied. The Israelites considered lack of burial a great indignity, even a curse (Deut 28:26; Jer 7:33).
  57:8 your symbol: An idol image. **uncovered your bed:** An invitation to commit sexual sin.
  57:9 Molech: A deity worshiped by child sacrifice. See note on 57:5. **your envoys:** The sons and daughters who perished in the pagan ritual. **Sheol:** Hebrew term for the netherworld of the dead. See note on 5:14.
  57:11 dread and fear: The people should fear none but the Lord, as Isaiah taught in 8:13.

57:13 deliver you!: The prophet uses satire to mock idols. See note on 44:9–20. **refuge in me:** Patient reliance on the Lord is central to the message of the book (30:15; 32:17; 33:2). **my holy mountain:** If the wicked are doomed to die in the valleys (57:6), the righteous will dwell with the Lord on the heights of Zion. See note on 56:7.
  57:14–21 A promise of comfort and peace for those who repent.
  57:14 prepare the way: The same image in 40:3–4 describes the journey home to Jerusalem after the Babylonian Exile. It signifies that the road to repentance and restoration is clear, with no obstacles remaining to prevent sinners from making their way back to God.
  57:15 high and lofty: Isaiah used this language in 6:1, when he saw a vision of the Lord at his calling to be a prophet (6:1). **contrite and humble:** Divine blessings are for those who lament their sins and practice humility (66:2), for God will not despise "a broken and contrite heart" (Ps 51:17).
  57:16 the breath of life: The life that God gives to the earth's creatures (Gen 2:7; 6:17; 7:22).
  57:17 I struck him: An instance of divine chastisement, which aims to restore the order of justice. **backsliding:** The opposite of making progress toward a goal. The image is probably that of someone losing his footing while climbing uphill.

ᵉ The meaning of the Hebrew is uncertain.
ᶠ Or *the king*.

¹⁸I have seen his ways, but I will heal him;
  I will lead him and repay him with comfort,
    creating for his mourners the fruit of the lips.
¹⁹Peace, peace, to the far and to the near, says the
      Lord;
  and I will heal him.
²⁰But the wicked are like the tossing sea;
  for it cannot rest,
    and its waters toss up mire and dirt.
²¹There is no peace, says my God, for the wicked."

True and False Fasting and Worship

58 "Cry aloud, spare not,
    lift up your voice like a trumpet;
  declare to my people their transgression,
    to the house of Jacob their sins.
²Yet they seek me daily,
    and delight to know my ways,
  as if they were a nation that did righteousness
    and did not forsake the ordinance of their God;
  they ask of me righteous judgments,
    they delight to draw near to God.
³'Why have we fasted, and you see it not?
    Why have we humbled ourselves, and you
      take no knowledge of it?'
  Behold, in the day of your fast you seek your own
    pleasure,ᵍ
    and oppress all your workers.
⁴Behold, you fast only to quarrel and to fight
    and to hit with wicked fist.
  Fasting like yours this day
    will not make your voice to be heard on high.

⁵Is such the fast that I choose,
    a day for a man to humble himself?
  Is it to bow down his head like a rush,
    and to spread sackcloth and ashes under
      him?
  Will you call this a fast,
    and a day acceptable to the Lord?

⁶"Is not this the fast that I choose:
    to loose the bonds of wickedness,
    to undo the thongs of the yoke,
  to let the oppressed go free,
    and to break every yoke?
⁷Is it not to share your bread with the hungry,
    and bring the homeless poor into your house;
  when you see the naked, to cover him,
    and not to hide yourself from your own flesh?
⁸Then shall your light break forth like the dawn,
    and your healing shall spring up speedily;
  your righteousness shall go before you,
    the glory of the Lord shall be your rear guard.
⁹Then you shall call, and the Lord will answer;
    you shall cry, and he will say, Here I am.

"If you take away from the midst of you the yoke,
    the pointing of the finger, and speaking
      wickedness,
¹⁰if you pour yourself out for the hungry
    and satisfy the desire of the afflicted,
  then shall your light rise in the darkness
    and your gloom be as the noonday.

57:19: Acts 2:39; Eph 2:13, 17. **58:6:** Acts 8:23.

57:18 comfort: The consolation of God's mercy that follows his humbling judgment, as in 12:1 and 40:1–2. **fruit of the lips:** The praise of God's grateful people (Heb 13:15).

📖 **57:19 Peace:** A blessing of the covenant for those reconciled with God (Rom 5:1). **the far ... the near:** Peace is proclaimed to all the penitents of Israel, whether in the homeland or dispersed in the lands of exile. It is also possible that Isaiah means Israelites and Gentiles, i.e., those who are near to God (Ps 148:14) and those who wait for salvation from afar (49:6). • Paul alludes to this verse in Eph 2:17 in explaining how the Cross brings a peace that unites Jews and Gentiles, the circumcised and the uncircumcised, into a single covenant community in Christ.

57:21 no peace ... for the wicked: Serves as a warning for those who persist in rebellion (48:22).

58:1–14 The Lord explains why his people do not enjoy his blessings. The problem is religious hypocrisy—the sin of adhering to outward forms of religion (58:2) while tolerating injustice, strife, and neglect of the poor (58:3–4, 7). Serving the Lord cannot be separated from serving other members of the covenant community (Lev 19:13–18; 25:35–38).

58:2 they seek me: By prayer, worship, and fasting—actions that are hypocritical and vain apart from doing good and attending to the needs of others (1:10–17).

58:3 fasted: Fasting can be done for different reasons, e.g., as a way of expressing repentance or subduing the crav-

ings of the flesh. Here it is a form of supplication in which the discomfort of denying oneself food is offered to God as a prayer to grant a request (58:4). The prophet's polemic is not against fasting per se; it is aimed at the hypocrisy of fasting while exploiting and fighting with others. Jesus affirms the importance of fasting as a spiritual practice, even as he criticizes those who make a show of it for selfish reasons (Mt 6:16–18).

58:4 your voice ... heard: The people's prayers are unanswered. Their petitions to the Lord are hindered by sin (Ps 66:18; 1 Pet 3:7), in this case, by oppression and disregard for those in need (58:6–7; 59:1–2).

58:5 sackcloth and ashes: Wearing coarse fabric next to the skin and sitting in the soot of an extinguished fire was an ancient mourning ritual that accompanied fasting (Joel 1:13–14; Jon 3:5–6; Jud 8:5–6; 9:1).

58:6 the fast that I choose: The Lord calls for depriving ourselves of food and comforts in a way that benefits those who lack them (58:7).

📖 **58:7 hungry ... homeless ... naked:** True religion requires easing the burdens of others and providing them with life's necessities (Jas 1:27). • These are works of mercy and charity practiced in the OT by persons such as Job (Job 31:16–23) and Tobit (Tob 1:16–17). They are endorsed by Jesus as conditions for salvation (Mt 25:31–46) (CCC 2447).

58:8 rear guard: Just as God protected the Exodus pilgrims at the sea in Ex 14:19–20. See note on 52:11–12.

58:9 pointing of the finger: Probably false accusations against others (Prov 6:13).

ᵍ Or *pursue your own business.*

¹¹And the Lord will guide you continually,
    and satisfy your desire with good things,[h]
    and make your bones strong;
and you shall be like a watered garden,
    like a spring of water,
    whose waters do not fail.
¹²And your ancient ruins shall be rebuilt;
    you shall raise up the foundations of many
        generations;
you shall be called the repairer of the breach,
    the restorer of streets to dwell in.

¹³"If you turn back your foot from the sabbath,
    from doing your pleasure[i] on my holy day,
and call the sabbath a delight
    and the holy day of the Lord honorable;
if you honor it, not going your own ways,
    or seeking your own pleasure,[j] or talking idly;
¹⁴then you shall take delight in the Lord,
    and I will make you ride upon the heights of
        the earth;
I will feed you with the heritage of Jacob your
        father,
    for the mouth of the Lord has spoken."

Injustice and Oppression
to Be Punished

59 Behold, the Lord's hand is not shortened, that
    it cannot save,
    or his ear dull, that it cannot hear;
²but your iniquities have made a separation
    between you and your God,
and your sins have hidden his face from you
    so that he does not hear.
³For your hands are defiled with blood
    and your fingers with iniquity;
your lips have spoken lies,
    your tongue mutters wickedness.

⁴No one enters suit justly,
    no one goes to law honestly;
they rely on empty pleas, they speak lies,
    they conceive mischief and bring forth
        iniquity.
⁵They hatch adders' eggs,
    they weave the spider's web;
he who eats their eggs dies,
    and from one which is crushed a viper is
        hatched.
⁶Their webs will not serve as clothing;
    men will not cover themselves with what they
        make.
Their works are works of iniquity,
    and deeds of violence are in their hands.
⁷Their feet run to evil,
    and they make haste to shed innocent blood;
their thoughts are thoughts of iniquity,
    desolation and destruction are in their
        highways.
⁸The way of peace they know not,
    and there is no justice in their paths;
they have made their roads crooked,
    no one who goes in them knows peace.

⁹Therefore justice is far from us,
    and righteousness does not overtake us;
we look for light, and behold, darkness,
    and for brightness, but we walk in gloom.
¹⁰We grope for the wall like the blind,
    we grope like those who have no eyes;
we stumble at noon as in the twilight,
    among those in full vigor we are like dead men.
¹¹We all growl like bears,
    we moan and moan like doves;
we look for justice, but there is none;
    for salvation, but it is far from us.

59:7–8: Rom 3:15–17.

58:11 satisfy your desire: The Lord's fitting reward for those who "satisfy the desire of the afflicted" (58:10).

58:13 the sabbath: Its proper observance is a condition for renewed blessings, as shown by the "If . . . then . . . " relationship between this and the following verse. See note on 56:2.

58:14 ride upon the heights: Signifies prosperity and success (Deut 32:13; cf. Hab 3:19).

59:1–21 The prophet's indictment of the returnees from Babylon in chap. 58 continues with further accusations of sin (59:1–8) and a national confession of sin (59:9–19). These are followed by scenes of divine judgment (59:16–19) and future redemption (59:20–21).

59:1 the Lord's hand: His power to intervene and set matters right.

59:2 he does not hear: The Lord is not answering the prayers of his people, not because he is unable, but because their transgressions have made him unwilling. This section stresses that sin delays the arrival of a fuller salvation for God's people. See note on 58:4.

59:3 hands . . . fingers . . . lips . . . tongue: Specifying parts of the body related to the mouth and hands illustrates that Israel's speech and action are swayed by the power of sin. Paul employs a similar device when he links together OT quotations in Rom 3:10–18. **defiled with blood:** Results from their "deeds of violence" (59:6) perpetrated against the "innocent" (59:7). **lies:** Deceptive and untruthful speech is noted several times in the context, suggesting this was a common problem in the postexilic community.

59:4 No one: The entire nation is engulfed in social sins, so much so that even the few who remain faithful and shun evil become targets of persecution (59:15; Ps 14:4; Amos 5:10).

59:5 eggs . . . web: Evil and treachery. **viper:** The wicked man (Ps 140:1–3; Mt 23:33).

59:7–8 Peace with God and others is impossible so long as the Lord's commandments are broken in thought and deed. • Paul cites this passage in Rom 3:15–17 to assist in showing that sin has taken hold of all people, Gentiles and Jews alike.

59:9 light: Signifies the salvation and grace of God dawning upon the world (see 9:2; 42:6, 16; 49:6; 60:1–3, 19–20).

59:10 like the blind: I.e., lacking any perception of the Lord's purposes in history (42:16).

---

[h] The meaning of the Hebrew word is uncertain.
[i] Or *business.*
[j] Or *pursuing your own business.*

¹²For our transgressions are multiplied before you,
and our sins testify against us;
for our transgressions are with us,
and we know our iniquities:
¹³transgressing, and denying the Lord,
and turning away from following our God,
speaking oppression and revolt,
conceiving and uttering from the heart lying
words.
¹⁴Justice is turned back,
and righteousness stands afar off;
for truth has fallen in the public squares,
and uprightness cannot enter.
¹⁵Truth is lacking,
and he who departs from evil makes himself a
prey.

The Lord saw it, and it displeased him
that there was no justice.
¹⁶He saw that there was no man,
and wondered that there was no one to
intervene;
then his own arm brought him victory,
and his righteousness upheld him.
¹⁷He put on righteousness as a breastplate,
and a helmet of salvation upon his head;
he put on garments of vengeance for clothing,
and wrapped himself in fury as a mantle.
¹⁸According to their deeds, so will he repay,
wrath to his adversaries, repayment to his
enemies;

to the islands he will render repayment.
¹⁹So they shall fear the name of the Lord from the
west,
and his glory from the rising of the sun;
for he will come like a rushing stream,
which the wind of the Lord drives.

²⁰"And he will come to Zion as Redeemer,
to those in Jacob who turn from transgression,
says the Lord.
²¹"And as for me, this is my covenant with them,
says the Lord: my spirit which is upon you, and my
words which I have put in your mouth, shall not
depart out of your mouth, or out of the mouth of
your children, or out of the mouth of your children's
children, says the Lord, from this time forth and for
evermore."

The Lord Will Come as a Light and Will Gather His People

60 Arise, shine; for your light has come,
and the glory of the Lord has risen upon
you.
²For behold, darkness shall cover the earth,
and thick darkness the peoples;
but the Lord will arise upon you,
and his glory will be seen upon you.
³And nations shall walk by your light,
and kings in the brightness of your rising.

⁴Lift up your eyes round about, and see;
they all gather together, they come to you;

59:17: Eph 6:14, 17; 1 Thess 5:8.   **59:19:** Mt 8:11; Lk 13:29.   **59:20–21:** Rom 11:26–27.

59:12–13 Sins committed against the Lord (**transgressing, denying, turning away**) and one another (**oppression, revolt, lying words**).

59:14–15 When sin and dishonesty thrive in the community, the cause of justice is thwarted.

59:16 no man: See note on 59:4. **his own arm:** Equivalent to "the Lord's hand" in 59:1. The point is that God intervenes to do for his people what they cannot do for themselves.

59:17 breastplate ... helmet: The Lord appears as a divine Warrior suited up for battle against his enemies (63:1–6). • The imagery of God's armor reappears in Wis 5:17–20, which draws on this verse, and again in Eph 6:13–17, where Paul urges believers to arm themselves for spiritual warfare against the devil and his hosts.

59:18 According to their deeds: Judgment according to works is a universal teaching of the Bible, appearing in the OT (Ps 62:12; Prov 24:12; Jer 17:10) and the NT (Mt 16:27; Rom 2:6–10; 2 Cor 5:10; 1 Pet 1:17). **the islands:** The peoples of the Mediterranean, which together represent all distant nations.

59:20–21 The Lord will make a new covenant with his people (54:10), offering redemption to all who **turn from transgression** and placing his word in their mouths (cf. Jer 31:31–34). • Paul cites this prophecy in Rom 11:26–27 in reference to Jesus, the founder of a new covenant, who takes away the sins of all who come to faith in him. It is a redemption that embraces all Israel as well as all nations.

59:20 to Zion: The Greek LXX reads "for the sake of Zion", whereas Paul quotes it as saying "from Zion" (Rom 11:26). **Redeemer:** See note on 41:14.

59:21 my spirit: Or "my Spirit", the gift that God promised to pour down upon his people in 32:15 and 44:3 (cf. Joel 2:28–29). **in your mouth:** Perhaps an allusion to Deut 6:6–7.

60:1–22 A vision of Zion, a city that radiates with divine glory (60:2, 19–20), draws the nations to worship the one true God (60:7), is enriched by the wealth of the world (60:5, 11), and is honored by foreigners bowing down before it (60:14). Several images and themes in chap. 60 appear in other parts of the book (see 2:2–4; 4:2–6; 9:2; 25:6–8). • The Book of Revelation draws from this vision to describe the new Jerusalem that comes down from heaven (Rev 21:2). Both passages speak of a city where mourning has ceased (60:20; Rev 21:4), where the gates are always open (60:11; Rev 21:25), where the abundance of the nations pours in (60:4; Rev 21:26), and where the sun and moon are no more (60:19–20; Rev 21:23) because the glory of the Lord is its light (60:1–2; Rev 21:23–24).

60:1 your light: The glory of the Lord, often depicted as a fiery and luminous sign of his presence (Deut 5:23–26; Ezek 1:4–28; Lk 2:9). Here it shines through the darkness of sin and ignorance that covers the rest of the world (60:2).

60:4 sons ... daughters: The exiled children of Israel, whose mother is the glorified Zion (43:5–6; 49:14–21). **carried in the arms:** Envisions the Gentiles participating in Israel's restoration by bringing the family of Jacob back home to the Lord (49:22; 60:9; 66:18–20). • It is the Church whose children come from all directions after the resurrection. She rejoices in receiving the light that shines forever and in being clothed with the brilliance of the Word. There is no more precious ornament befitting the Lord's bride

your sons shall come from far,
  and your daughters shall be carried in the arms.
[5]Then you shall see and be radiant,
  your heart shall thrill and rejoice;[k]
because the abundance of the sea shall be turned
    to you,
  the wealth of the nations shall come to you.
[6]A multitude of camels shall cover you,
  the young camels of Mid′ian and E′phah;
all those from Sheba shall come.
  They shall bring gold and frankincense,
  and shall proclaim the praise of the LORD.
[7]All the flocks of Ke′dar shall be gathered to you,
  the rams of Nebai′oth shall minister to you;
they shall come up with acceptance on my altar,
  and I will glorify my glorious house.

[8]Who are these that fly like a cloud,
  and like doves to their windows?
[9]For the islands shall wait for me,
  the ships of Tar′shish first,
to bring your sons from far,
  their silver and gold with them,
for the name of the LORD your God,
  and for the Holy One of Israel,
  because he has glorified you.

[10]Foreigners shall build up your walls,
  and their kings shall minister to you;
for in my wrath I struck you,
  but in my favor I have had mercy on you.
[11]Your gates shall be open continually;
  day and night they shall not be shut;

that men may bring to you the wealth of the
    nations,
  with their kings led in procession.
[12]For the nation and kingdom
  that will not serve you shall perish;
  those nations shall be utterly laid waste.
[13]The glory of Lebanon shall come to you,
  the cypress, the plane, and the pine,
to beautify the place of my sanctuary;
  and I will make the place of my feet glorious.
[14]The sons of those who oppressed you
  shall come bending low to you;
and all who despised you
  shall bow down at your feet;
they shall call you the City of the LORD,
  the Zion of the Holy One of Israel.

[15]Whereas you have been forsaken and hated,
  with no one passing through,
I will make you majestic for ever,
  a joy from age to age.
[16]You shall suck the milk of nations,
  you shall suck the breast of kings;
and you shall know that I, the LORD, am your
    Savior
  and your Redeemer, the Mighty One of Jacob.

[17]Instead of bronze I will bring gold,
  and instead of iron I will bring silver;
instead of wood, bronze,
  instead of stones, iron.
I will make your overseers peace
  and your taskmasters righteousness.

60:6: Mt 2:11.   **60:11:** Rev 21:25–26.   **60:14:** Rev 3:9.

---

than a garment of light (St. Methodius, *Banquet of the Ten Virgins* 8, 5).

60:5 wealth of the nations: Tribute given to the Lord's sanctuary to be used for its services (60:13). The influx of goods includes aromatic spices (frankincense, 60:6), sacrificial animals (flocks and rams, 60:7), precious metals (gold and silver, 60:9), and high-quality lumber (cypress, 60:13).

60:6–9 Peoples flock to Zion from Arabia (east and south of Judah) as well as Phoenicia and the Mediterranean (north and west of Judah). The nations thus converge on Jerusalem from the four points of the compass (cf. 43:5–6).

60:6 Midian and Ephah: Descendants of Abraham by his wife Keturah that dwelt in northwest Arabia (Gen 25:1–4). **Sheba:** A trading empire from the southern Arabian Peninsula (modern Yemen) and known for its exotic spices (Jer 6:20). • Caravans of **camels** bearing **gold and frankincense** call to mind the retinue and gifts that the queen of Sheba brought to Solomon in Jerusalem at the height of his glory (1 Kings 10:1–2). The vision also relates to magi from the east bringing gifts of gold, frankincense, and myrrh to Jesus as the infant King (Mt 2:1–11). • Isaiah 60:1–6 is read on the Feast of the Epiphany in the Roman Lectionary.

60:7 Kedar ... Nebaioth: Locations in northern Arabia (and modern Jordan) that are linked with tribal peoples descended from Abraham's son Ishmael (Gen 25:13). **accep-**

tance on my altar: Envisions a time when all peoples, even descendants of Abraham who are outside the covenant people, can participate in Israel's worship. Similar scenarios appear in 19:21 and 56:6–7. **my glorious house:** The Lord's Temple.

60:9 the islands: The peoples of the Mediterranean, which together represent all distant nations. **ships of Tarshish:** Merchant vessels. Some scholars identify Tarshish with "Tartessos" in southern Spain; others think it refers to "Tarsus" in Asia Minor. **the Holy One of Israel:** See note on 1:4.

60:10 Foreigners: Gentile nations and their rulers will help to finance the building of Zion.

60:11 Your gates ... open: To accommodate the continuous inflow of riches. Open gates is also a sign of peacetime, when Zion fears no enemy attack (60:17–18).

60:13 The glory of Lebanon: The mighty forests of Phoenicia, north of Israel, whose trees are ideally suited for monumental construction projects. **the place of my feet:** The whole earth is the Lord's footstool (66:1), but this is especially true of the sanctuary in Jerusalem, where the Ark of the Covenant was kept (1 Chron 28:2; Ps 132:7). The place of his feet is the place where the Lord dwells in a special way (Ezek 43:7).

60:15 forsaken: Refers to the decades of desolation and ruin that followed the Babylonian conquest of Jerusalem in 586 B.C.

60:16 Redeemer: See note on 41:14.

60:17 gold ... silver: Building with precious metals, much like building with precious stones in 54:11–12, signifies the abundance of God's blessings on the future Zion.

---

[k]Heb *be enlarged.*

18Violence shall no more be heard in your land,
    devastation or destruction within your borders;
  you shall call your walls Salvation,
    and your gates Praise.

19The sun shall no longer be
    your light by day,
  nor for brightness shall the moon
    give light to you by night;[1]
  but the Lord will be your everlasting light,
    and your God will be your glory.
20Your sun shall no more go down,
    nor your moon withdraw itself;
  for the Lord will be your everlasting light,
    and your days of mourning shall be ended.
21Your people shall all be righteous;
    they shall possess the land for ever,
  the shoot of my planting, the work of my hands,
    that I might be glorified.
22The least one shall become a clan,
    and the smallest one a mighty nation;
  I am the Lord;
    in its time I will hasten it.

Good Tidings for the Afflicted

61 *The Spirit of the Lord God is upon me,
    because the Lord has anointed me

to bring good tidings to the afflicted;[m]
  he has sent me to bind up the brokenhearted,
    to proclaim liberty to the captives,
  and the opening of the prison[n] to those who
    are bound;
2to proclaim the year of the Lord's favor,
    and the day of vengeance of our God;
  to comfort all who mourn;
3to grant to those who mourn in Zion—
    to give them a garland instead of ashes,
  the oil of gladness instead of mourning,
    the mantle of praise instead of a faint spirit;
  that they may be called oaks of righteousness,
    the planting of the Lord, that he may be
      glorified.
4They shall build up the ancient ruins,
    they shall raise up the former devastations;
  they shall repair the ruined cities,
    the devastations of many generations.

5Aliens shall stand and feed your flocks,
    foreigners shall be your plowmen and
      vinedressers;
6but you shall be called the priests of the Lord,
    men shall speak of you as the ministers of our
      God;

60:19: Rev 21:23; 22:5.   **61:1-2:** Mt 11:5; Lk 4:18–19; 7:22.   **61:6:** Ex 19:6; 1 Pet 2:5; Rev 1:6; 5:10; 20:6.

60:18 Violence ... no more: In stark contrast to postexilic Jerusalem (59:6–7).

60:19 your everlasting light: The fiery presence of divine glory (60:1–2). • The image of God's glory outshining the brightness of the sun and moon reappears in Rev 21:23 in a description of the heavenly Jerusalem, a city illumined by the glory of God and the Lamb.

60:21 righteous: Faithful to the covenant (Deut 6:25). **the shoot of my planting:** An image of God's people as a branch or shoot (4:2) that grows into a forest of oaks (61:3).

60:22 a mighty nation: The Lord can make even the tiny, beleaguered community in Judah into a strong, flourishing people. • As in 51:2, Isaiah alludes to Abraham, one man whom God made into a great nation (Gen 12:2; 18:18).

61:1-11 Three oracles spoken by three different voices: the first is the Lord's anointed one (61:1–7); the second is the Lord himself (61:8–9); and the third appears to be the city of Zion personified (61:10–11).

61:1-3 The one who speaks claims to be **anointed** by the **Spirit** for a ministry of mercy and **good tidings** to those who suffer. He is not further identified, but earlier verses in Isaiah show that he has features in common with the Davidic Messiah (11:1–5) and the Servant of the Lord (42:1–4, 7). Contextually, he appears as God's anointed agent in bringing about the glorification of Zion (e.g., compare 61:3 with 60:21). • Jesus, after reading this passage in the synagogue at Nazareth, declares it fulfilled in his own ministry of preaching and healing (Lk 4:16–21). Anointed by the Spirit at his Baptism, he claims to be the Messiah foretold in Isaiah (cf. Acts 10:38).

61:1 liberty: The Hebrew term *deror* means "release", referring to the liberation of persons or property from the control of another (Lev 25:10; Jer 34:8–9; Ezek 46:17).

61:2 the year of the Lord's favor: The Jubilee year, which the Mosaic Law mandates every fiftieth year as a means of reversing temporarily the effects of poverty in Israel (Lev 25:8–55). It began with a proclamation of release, announcing that debts must be cancelled, indentured servants must be set free, and family property that was sold in times of hardship must be restored to its original owners. See notes on Lev 25:8–55 and Lk 4:18–19. **the day of vengeance:** When God executes his justice against his enemies (Deut 32:35). **comfort:** One of the hallmarks of Isaiah's message to exilic and postexilic Israel (40:1–2). • The Book of Sirach echoes this and the following verse when it describes Isaiah as one who "comforted those who mourned in Zion" (Sir 48:24).

61:3 ashes: Mourners sometimes sat in ashes (Jon 3:6) or sprinkled them on their heads (Jud 9:1). **oaks of righteousness:** A people firmly established in the covenant that God will make with them (61:8; cf. 55:3; 59:21). **planting of the Lord:** Related to the image of Israel as the Lord's vineyard (5:1–7; 27:2–6).

61:4 the ancient ruins: Jerusalem and the cities of Judah, which the Babylonians reduced to rubble in 586 b.c.

61:5 Aliens ... foreigners: Israel's former oppressors will become its servants.

61:6 the priests of the Lord: A renewal of Israel's national vocation to be a "kingdom of priests" (Ex 19:6). For much of biblical history, the priesthood was restricted to the Levitical family of Aaron, the brother of Moses (Ex 40:12–15). Isaiah foresees a dramatic expansion of priestly privileges in the future, so that all the tribes of Israel and even the Gentiles will have a share in this ministry. See note on 66:18–21. **you shall eat:** Just as Aaronic priests were entitled to food portions from various Temple offerings (Num 18:8–19). **the wealth of the nations:** The tribute that Gentile peoples bring to Israel, which includes animals to be used for sacrifices at the Lord's altar (60:7).

---

[1] One ancient Ms Gk Old Latin Tg: Heb lacks *by night*.
[m] Or *poor*.
[n] Or *the opening of the eyes*: Heb *the opening*.
* 61:1–4: cf. Lk 4:18–19.

you shall eat the wealth of the nations,
and in their riches you shall glory.
7 Instead of your shame you shall have a double portion,
instead of dishonor you[o] shall rejoice in your[p] lot;
therefore in your[p] land you[o] shall possess a double portion;
yours[q] shall be everlasting joy.

8 For I the LORD love justice,
I hate robbery and wrong;[r]
I will faithfully give them their recompense,
and I will make an everlasting covenant with them.
9 Their descendants shall be known among the nations,
and their offspring in the midst of the peoples;
all who see them shall acknowledge them,
that they are a people whom the LORD has blessed.

10 I will greatly rejoice in the LORD,
my soul shall exult in my God;
for he has clothed me with the garments of salvation,
he has covered me with the robe of righteousness,
as a bridegroom decks himself with a garland,
and as a bride adorns herself with her jewels.
11 For as the earth brings forth its shoots,
and as a garden causes what is sown in it to spring up,
so the Lord GOD will cause righteousness and praise
to spring forth before all the nations.

The Vindication and Salvation of Zion

62 For Zion's sake I will not keep silent,
and for Jerusalem's sake I will not rest,
until her vindication goes forth as brightness,
and her salvation as a burning torch.
2 The nations shall see your vindication,
and all the kings your glory;
and you shall be called by a new name
which the mouth of the LORD will give.
3 You shall be a crown of beauty in the hand of the LORD,
and a royal diadem in the hand of your God.
4 You shall no more be termed Forsaken,[s]
and your land shall no more be termed Desolate;[t]
but you shall be called My delight is in her,[u]
and your land Married;[v]
for the LORD delights in you,
and your land shall be married.
5 For as a young man marries a virgin,
so shall your sons marry you,
and as the bridegroom rejoices over the bride,
so shall your God rejoice over you.

62:2: Rev 2:17.

61:7 double portion: The inheritance of a first-born son (Deut 21:15–17). Israel is the first-born of the Lord, the divine Father, while other nations are viewed as younger siblings (Ex 4:22; Jer 31:9; Sir 36:12). This double inheritance is also fitting because it corresponds to the double chastisement that God's people endured in exile (40:2).

61:8 I hate robbery: Corresponds to the commandment "You shall not steal" (Ex 20:15). For other things hated by God, see Prov 8:13; Jer 44:4–5, Zech 8:17; Mal 2:16. **an everlasting covenant:** Some of the features of this new covenant are related in 54:10; 55:3–5; 59:21.

61:10 salvation ... righteousness: The gifts that adorn Zion like luxurious clothing (60:17–18; Rev 19:8). **bridegroom ... bride:** I.e., as a couple dresses in their finest attire and jewelry for their wedding day.

62:1–12 Another announcement of Zion's salvation. The glorified city will be vindicated in the eyes of the world (62:2), given a new name (62:4), wedded to the Lord as a bride (62:5), and established in peace and security (62:6–7) by a divinely sworn oath (62:8–9). The key idea, introduced at the outset, is that God will act "for the sake of" his people (62:1).

62:1 I will not keep silent: The words of the prophet. Like the watchmen in 62:6–7, he will not cease to declare the Lord's purposes until they are fulfilled. **her vindication:** Or "her righteousness". **brightness:** Zion will gleam with divine glory (60:1–3, 19–20).

62:2 a new name: Revealed in 62:4 as "My delight is in her." Zion's new name is one of the "new things" announced in 42:9; 43:19; 48:6. • Christ grants all believers to bear his name. Earthly kings have titles that are not shared with others, but Jesus Christ saw fit that we should be called Christians. Some will object that this is a new name, unknown before now, but the prophet anticipated this when he said, "my servants shall be called by a new name" (St. Cyril of Jerusalem, *Catechesis* 10, 6). • All things are made new in Christ: worship, life, and law. We do not cling to shadows and types but worship God in spirit and truth. We are not named after one of the ancestors of Israel, such as Ephraim or Manasseh, but we receive Christ, and taking his name like a crown, we are called Christians (St. Cyril of Alexandria, *Commentary on Isaiah* 65, 16).

62:3 crown of beauty: A poetic depiction of Jerusalem perched on a mountain and encircled by an impressive outer wall.

62:4 Forsaken: Zion's old name. Its replacement by a "new name" (62:2) signals that God will not abandon his redeemed city to conquest as he did with Jerusalem in 586 B.C. (54:6–7; 60:15).

62:5 your sons: Earlier this meant Zion's children returning from exile (49:22; 54:13; 60:4). Here, however, it introduces the odd notion of sons marrying their mother. Others prefer to translate the Hebrew not as "your sons" but as "your builder". Support for this alternative can be found elsewhere (Ps 147:2; Heb 11:10), including the latter half of the verse, where it is the Lord who weds himself to his people as a **bridegroom** to a **bride**. On this reading, Zion is compared to a forsaken wife whose divine husband takes her back (as in 54:5–8).

[o] Heb *they*.
[p] Heb *their*.
[q] Heb *theirs*.
[r] Or *robbery with a burnt offering*.
[s] Heb *Azubah*.
[t] Heb *Shemamah*.
[u] Heb *Hephzibah*.
[v] Heb *Beulah*.

⁶Upon your walls, O Jerusalem,
  I have set watchmen;
all the day and all the night
  they shall never be silent.
You who put the LORD in remembrance,
  take no rest,
⁷and give him no rest
  until he establishes Jerusalem
  and makes it a praise in the earth.
⁸The LORD has sworn by his right hand
  and by his mighty arm:
"I will not again give your grain
  to be food for your enemies,
and foreigners shall not drink your wine
  for which you have labored;
⁹but those who garner it shall eat it
  and praise the LORD,
and those who gather it shall drink it
  in the courts of my sanctuary."

¹⁰Go through, go through the gates,
  prepare the way for the people;
build up, build up the highway,
  clear it of stones,
  lift up an ensign over the peoples.
¹¹Behold, the LORD has proclaimed
  to the end of the earth:
Say to the daughter of Zion,
  "Behold, your salvation comes;
behold, his reward is with him,
  and his recompense before him."
¹²And they shall be called The holy people,
  The redeemed of the LORD;

and you shall be called Sought out,
  a city not forsaken.

Vengeance on Enemies; God's Mercy Recounted and Sought

63 Who is this that comes from E'dom,
  in crimsoned garments from Bozrah,
he that is glorious in his apparel,
  marching in the greatness of his strength?

"It is I, announcing vindication,
  mighty to save."

²Why is your apparel red,
  and your garments like his who treads in the
    wine press?

³"I have trodden the wine press alone,
  and from the peoples no one was with me;
I trod them in my anger
  and trampled them in my wrath;
their lifeblood is sprinkled upon my garments,
  and I have stained all my clothing.
⁴For the day of vengeance was in my heart,
  and my year of redemption^w has come.
⁵I looked, but there was no one to help;
  I was appalled, but there was no one to
    uphold;
so my own arm brought me victory,
  and my wrath upheld me.
⁶I trod down the peoples in my anger,
  I made them drunk in my wrath,
and I poured out their lifeblood on the
  earth."

63:1–6: Is 34; Jer 49:7–22; Ezek 25:12–14; 35; Amos 1:11–12; Obad; Mal 1:2–5. **63:3:** Rev 19:15.

62:6 watchmen: Prophets, who look for God's promises to be fulfilled (Ezek 3:17; Hab 2:1). **shall never be silent:** I.e., true prophets will always have a word from the Lord, unlike those who are "mute dogs" in 56:10.

62:8–9 The Lord swears an oath to protect the glorified Zion, similar to 54:9. He pledges to preserve it from the curses of the covenant that Jerusalem experienced in the past, one of which is conquest and plunder (Deut 28:30–34).

62:8 by his right hand: Raising the right hand is a ritual oath gesture (Deut 32:40; Dan 12:7; Rev 10:5–6).

62:10 the highway: The desert road leading from Babylon back to Jerusalem in 40:3–4 is here a figure of repentance, signifying the way back to the Lord's favor (as in 57:14–15). **an ensign:** A signal that summons the nations to bring Zion's exiled children home (49:22). This sign is also linked with the Davidic Messiah, who accomplishes a great ingathering of Israel and the Gentiles (11:10, 12).

62:11 Say to the daughter of Zion: The coming salvation is announced to Jerusalem. • Matthew cites these words in Mt 21:5, coupling them with the prophecy of Zech 9:9, to say that Jesus' entry into Jerusalem on a donkey fulfills prophetic expectations that salvation will come to the city in the form of a humble king.

62:12 they shall be called: Three more "new" names for Zion, in addition to those in 62:4.

63:1–6 The watchmen of 62:6 witness the Lord's triumphant return to Zion (52:8), posing questions (63:1–2) to which the Lord gives answers (63:3–6). It is an awesome spectacle of the Divine Warrior marching home as the victor over his enemies. For an image of God suiting up for battle, see 59:17.

63:1 Edom: The rugged highlands south of the Dead Sea. Its people, although related to the people of Israel (descendants of Esau, brother of Jacob), were longtime enemies of Israel (Mal 1:2–4) and targets of the Lord's judgment (see 34:1–12). Here Edom appears to represent all nations that fight against God and his chosen ones. **Bozrah:** A leading Edomite city (34:6). **mighty to save:** Salvation for the People of God includes the defeat of their foes (Col 2:13–15).

63:3 wine press: A large stone trough where grapes were trampled by foot. The crushing of the fruit and the likeness of red juice to blood (Gen 49:11) made the wine press a potent image of divine judgment in Scripture (Lam 1:15; Joel 3:13; Rev 14:19–20). **alone:** God needs no one to help him accomplish the work of salvation and judgment.

63:4 day of vengeance … redemption: When the Lord acts to set matters right, it becomes a day of reckoning for the godless and a day of deliverance for the faithful. These two ideas are similarly correlated in 61:2. See note on 41:14.

63:5 my own arm: Represents the Lord's power (52:10). This verse repeats the thought of 59:16.

63:6 I made them drunk: The Lord made them drink from the cup of his wrath (51:17–20).

---

^wOr *the year of my redeemed.*

⁷I will recount the merciful love of the Lᴏʀᴅ,
   the praises of the Lᴏʀᴅ,
according to all that the Lᴏʀᴅ has granted us,
   and the great goodness to the house of Israel
which he has granted them according to his
      mercy,
   according to the abundance of his steadfast
      love.
⁸For he said, Surely they are my people,
   sons who will not deal falsely;
   and he became their Savior.
⁹In all their affliction he was afflicted,*
   and the angel of his presence saved them;
in his love and in his pity he redeemed them;
   he lifted them up and carried them all the days
      of old.

¹⁰But they rebelled
   and grieved his holy Spirit;
therefore he turned to be their enemy,
   and himself fought against them.
¹¹Then he remembered the days of old,
   of Moses his servant.
Where is he who brought up out of the sea
   the shepherds of his flock?
Where is he who put in the midst of them
   his holy Spirit,

¹²who caused his glorious arm
   to go at the right hand of Moses,
who divided the waters before them
   to make for himself an everlasting name,
¹³   who led them through the depths?
Like a horse in the desert,
   they did not stumble.
¹⁴Like cattle that go down into the valley,
   the Spirit of the Lᴏʀᴅ gave them rest.
So you led your people,
   to make for yourself a glorious name.

¹⁵Look down from heaven and see,
   from your holy and glorious habitation.
Where are your zeal and your might?
   The yearning of your heart and your
      compassion
   are withheld from me.
¹⁶For you are our Father,
   though Abraham does not know us
   and Israel does not acknowledge us;
you, O Lᴏʀᴅ, are our Father,
   our Redeemer from of old is your name.
¹⁷O Lᴏʀᴅ, why do you make us err from your ways
   and harden our heart, so that we fear you not?
Return for the sake of your servants,
   the tribes of your heritage.

63:11: Heb 13:20.

63:7–14 A recital of the Lord's saving deeds in the past. Attention is focused on the miracles of the Exodus from Egypt (63:11–12), the journey in the wilderness (63:13), and the settlement of Canaan (63:14).

63:7 steadfast love: The Hebrew is *ḥesed* in the plural, referring to God's covenant loyalty to Israel (as in Ps 89:1). Use of the plural might be a reference to God's repeated acts of love toward his people or a way of underlining the majesty or excellence of his love. See word study: *Merciful Love* at Ex 34:7. **the abundance:** Revealed to Moses in Ex 34:6.

63:8 sons who will not deal falsely: Disproved by Israel's history of infidelity (1:4).

63:9 angel of his presence: Recalls how the Lord, at the time of the Exodus, manifested his presence through an angel (Ex 3:2; 23:20; 33:2). **redeemed them:** From bondage in Egypt (Ex 15:13). **carried them:** To Mount Sinai (Ex 19:4).

63:10 they rebelled: By worshiping the golden calf idol (Ex 32:1–6). **grieved his holy Spirit:** Mention of the Lord's Spirit occurs several times in this context (63:11, 14). It is a reference to the pillar of cloud and fire that led Israel from Egypt to the Promised Land (Ex 13:21–22; Num 9:15–23) (CCC 697). • Paul adopts the language of this passage in Eph 4:30 to warn believers against grieving the Holy Spirit by various forms of evildoing. • Christian tradition infers from this and other passages the full personhood of the Spirit. An impersonal force cannot be saddened by another's faults—only a being with consciousness, intelligence, and a capacity for relationships with other rational beings. **fought against them:** By calling for the death of the idolaters (Ex 32:27) and sending a plague among the survivors (Ex 32:35).

63:12 divided the waters: The miracle of the sea crossing (Ex 14:21–22).

63:13 in the desert: The wilderness journeys in the Book of Numbers.

63:14 gave them rest: In the Promised Land of Canaan (Josh 1:13; 21:44).

63:15—64:12 An appeal to God to work saving miracles. The recital of the Lord's deeds in the past (63:7–14) inspires a prayer for his merciful intervention once again.

63:15 your holy ... habitation: The Lord's heavenly temple (Ps 11:4; Rev 11:19).

63:16 our Father: God is rarely addressed this way in the OT, although the appellation occurs three times in this prayer alone (twice in 63:16; 64:8). He is invoked as a divine Father also in Wis 14:3; Sir 23:1. The language of divine paternity in the OT is based on the covenant of kinship that the Lord forged with Israel, his first-born son (Ex 4:22; Sir 36:12). • A new dimension of God's fatherhood is opened up in the NT with the revelation of his eternal Son in Jesus, who teaches disciples to call upon the Lord in precisely this way (Mt 6:9–13; Lk 11:2–4). Thus, if invoking God as Father is rare in the OT, it becomes routine in the NT (Rom 8:15; Gal 4:6; Eph 1:3; Jas 1:17; 1 Pet 1:17; etc.). **Abraham ... Israel:** The founding fathers of Israel. Even if the venerable patriarchs should forget the plight of the covenant people, God himself will not (49:15). **Redeemer:** See note on 41:14.

63:17 harden our heart: Divine hardening is not an action of God that causes people to sin but a form of judgment in which the Lord allows brazen sinners to defy his will without the restraint of his mercy. This response to sin was first revealed at the time of the Exodus, when God hardened the heart of Pharaoh (Ex 9:12; 10:1; 11:10; 14:8). Divine hardening is likewise mentioned in the NT as a spiritual condition of unbelieving Israel that will endure until God's plan of salvation for the Gentiles is accomplished (Rom 11:25–26). Divine hardening remains a mystery because Scripture also insists on human free choice (Sir 15:11–17) as well as God's universal

---

* Another reading is *he did not afflict*.

¹⁸Your holy people possessed your sanctuary a
 little while;
 our adversaries have trodden it down.
¹⁹We have become like those over whom you have
 never ruled,
 like those who are not called by your name.

Prayer for Mercy

64 O that you would tear the heavens and come
 down,
 that the mountains might quake at your
 presence—
²ʸas when fire kindles brushwood
 and the fire causes water to boil—
to make your name known to your adversaries,
 and that the nations might tremble at your
 presence!
³When you did terrible things which we looked
 not for,
 you came down, the moun-tains quaked at
 your presence.
⁴From of old no one has heard
 or perceived by the ear,
no eye has seen a God besides you,
 who works for those who wait for him.
⁵You meet him that joyfully works righteousness,
 those that remember you in your ways.
Behold, you were angry, and we sinned;
 in our sins we have been a long time, and shall
 we be saved?ᶻ

⁶We have all become like one who is unclean,
 and all our righteous deeds are like a polluted
 garment.
We all fade like a leaf,
 and our iniquities, like the wind, take us away.
⁷There is no one that calls upon your name,
 that bestirs himself to take hold of you;
for you have hidden your face from us,
 and have deliveredᵃ us into the hand of our
 iniquities.

⁸Yet, O Lᴏʀᴅ, you are our Father;
 we are the clay, and you are our potter;
 we are all the work of your hand.
⁹Be not exceedingly angry, O Lᴏʀᴅ,
 and remember not iniquity for ever.
 Behold, consider, we are all your people.
¹⁰Your holy cities have become a wilderness,
 Zion has become a wilderness,
 Jerusalem a desolation.
¹¹Our holy and beautiful house,
 where our fathers praised you,
 has been burned by fire,
 and all our pleasant places have become ruins.
¹²Will you restrain yourself at these things, O Lᴏʀᴅ?
 Will you keep silent, and afflict us sorely?

The Righteousness of God's Judgment

65 I was ready to be sought by those who did
 not ask for me;

64:4: 1 Cor 2:9. **65:1–2:** Rom 10:20–21.

---

desire that all people repent of their sins and be saved (1 Tim 2:4; 2 Pet 3:9). Within the broader framework of biblical teaching, then, divine hardening does not override human free will or destroy human responsibility for sin; rather, it is a disciplinary measure that seeks the conversion of the sinner. See note on Ex 4:21.

64:1–4 A communal prayer for a divine theophany—a dramatic display of God's power and presence in the world. Images of **fire** and quaking **mountains** suggest petitioners have in mind the theophany at Mount Sinai, where God descended in fire and earthquake (Ex 19:17–18).

64:1 the heavens: Imagined as a tent stretched over the earth (40:22). The prayer is that God, who is hidden from our sight, will tear through this barrier and come down to work his wonders in the world. • This verse probably lies behind Mark's account of the Baptism of Jesus, in which the heavens are rent open and the Spirit descends upon him (Mk 1:10).

64:3 terrible things: The miracles remembered in 63:11–14.

64:4 no one has heard ... seen: The Lord is unique and his works unprecedented. • Paul paraphrases this verse to insist that no one has ever known or even thought of the wonderful things that God now reveals to believers through the Spirit (1 Cor 2:9). **a God ... who works:** God acts powerfully in the lives of his people, unlike the idols of the nations, which are lifeless and helpless (44:9–20). **who wait for him:** I.e., who rely upon the Lord for strength and trust that his promises of salvation will come to pass (30:15, 18; 33:2; 40:31).

64:5–7 A communal confession of sin.

64:6 one who is unclean: Such as a leper, who lives apart from others and is forbidden to enter the Lord's sanctuary (Lev 13:45–46; Num 5:1–4). **a polluted garment:** A menstrual cloth rendered unclean by blood (Lev 15:19–23).

64:7 no one: Indicates that sin prevails in the postexilic community of Judah, as does 59:4. **hidden your face:** A figurative description of divine displeasure. See note on 54:8.

64:8 our Father: See note on 63:16. **clay ... potter:** Israel's relationship with God, its Creator, as in 29:16 and 45:9.

64:9 remember not iniquity: The same promise is made in Jeremiah's prophecy of the New Covenant (Jer 31:34).

64:11 holy and beautiful house: The Solomonic Temple, burned down by the Babylonians in 586 ʙ.ᴄ. (2 Kings 25:8–9). This sanctuary was an architectural model of the Lord's "holy and glorious habitation" in heaven (63:15). See essay: *Theology of the Temple* at 2 Chron 5.

64:12 restrain yourself ...?: The question is whether the Lord will continue hiding his face and allowing his people to suffer the chastisements that their sins deserve.

65:1–7 God explains why his people suffer affliction: it is his just response to their return to paganism (64:12). Still, the Lord's eagerness to bestow his gifts will not be thwarted, for a remnant of the faithful will enjoy salvation (65:8–25).

65:1–2 A divine plea for repentance, which goes unheeded. The Lord is **ready** to reveal himself to the world beyond Israel, to the nations that neither **seek** nor **ask for** him; however, the people he has chosen to be "a light to the nations" (42:6) is a **rebellious people** who are stubbornly unresponsive to his appeals (65:12). • Paul quotes the Greek LXX of this passage in Rom 10:20–21. He sees the first line fulfilled in Gentiles coming to faith in Christ (65:1) and the second line in Jewish unbelief in Jesus (65:2). • The Lord

---

ʸ Ch 64:1 in Heb.
ᶻ Hebrew obscure.
ᵃ Gk Syr Old Latin Tg: Heb *melted*.

I was ready to be found by those who did not
  seek me.
I said, "Here am I, here am I,"
  to a nation that did not call on my name.
[2]I spread out my hands all the day
  to a rebellious people,
who walk in a way that is not good,
  following their own devices;
[3]a people who provoke me
  to my face continually,
sacrificing in gardens
  and burning incense upon bricks;
[4]who sit in tombs,
  and spend the night in secret places;
who eat swine's flesh,
  and broth of abominable things is in their
    vessels;
[5]who say, "Keep to yourself,
  do not come near me, for I am set apart from
    you."
These are a smoke in my nostrils,
  a fire that burns all the day.
[6]Behold, it is written before me:
  "I will not keep silent, but I will repay,
yes, I will repay into their bosom
[7] their[b] iniquities and their[b] fathers' iniquities
    together,

                                    says the Lord;
because they burned incense upon the mountains
  and reviled me upon the hills,
I will measure into their bosom
  payment for their former doings."

[8]Thus says the Lord:
"As the wine is found in the cluster,
  and they say, 'Do not destroy it,
  for there is a blessing in it,'

so I will do for my servants' sake,
  and not destroy them all.
[9]I will bring forth descendants from Jacob,
  and from Judah inheritors of my mountains;
my chosen shall inherit it,
  and my servants shall dwell there.
[10]Sharon shall become a pasture for flocks,
  and the Valley of A'chor a place for herds to
    lie down,
  for my people who have sought me.
[11]But you who forsake the Lord,
  who forget my holy mountain,
who set a table for Fortune
  and fill cups of mixed wine for Destiny;
[12]I will destine you to the sword,
  and all of you shall bow down to the slaughter;
because, when I called, you did not answer,
  when I spoke, you did not listen,
but you did what was evil in my eyes,
  and chose what I did not delight in."

[13]Therefore thus says the Lord God:
"Behold, my servants shall eat,
  but you shall be hungry;
behold, my servants shall drink,
  but you shall be thirsty;
behold, my servants shall rejoice,
  but you shall be put to shame;
[14]behold, my servants shall sing for gladness of
    heart,
  but you shall cry out for pain of heart,
  and shall wail for anguish of spirit.
[15]You shall leave your name to my chosen for a
    curse,
  and the Lord God will slay you;
  but his servants he will call by a different
    name.

---

denounces the fault of his people for their ungrateful response to his gifts. He spread forth his hands in giving many benefits over the centuries since he took them to himself and, mystically, when he spread forth his hands on the Cross for those who walk in a way that is not good (St. Thomas Aquinas, *Commentary on Isaiah 65*, 2).

65:3 provoke me: With idols (Deut 32:21). **sacrificing in gardens:** Worshiping other gods in outdoor cult shrines, contrary to the Mosaic Law (Ex 20:3-5).

65:4 sit in tombs: Either a metaphor for living in a state of uncleanness, which is contracted from the bodies and graves of the dead (Num 19:11-22), or a pagan ritual for communicating with the dead, which is forbidden (Deut 18:10-11). **eat swine's flesh:** Consumption of pork is contrary to the Mosaic Law, which classifies it as an unclean food for Israel (Lev 11:7-8).

65:5 I am set apart: The Lord is angered by the hypocrisy of his people, who are concerned to protect their consecration to God, all the while worshiping the idols of the Gentiles.

65:6 I will not keep silent: Answers the question posed in 64:12. Only instead of bringing the relief from suffering that his people desire, the Lord promises judgment.

65:7 mountains ... hills: The typical location of pagan worship sites.

65:8-25 The inheritance of the righteous remnant. Throughout this section, God addresses his faithful ones as **my servants** (65:8, 9, 13-15), **my chosen** (65:9, 15, 22), and **my people** (65:10, 19, 22). For the significance of the plural "servants", see note on 54:17.

65:9 from Jacob ... from Judah: From all the tribes of Israel, northern as well as southern, as in 11:12.

65:10 Sharon: The lush coastal plain of western Israel extending from Mount Carmel down to Joppa. **Valley of Achor:** In the western Jordan valley near Jericho. **who have sought me:** Unlike those in 65:1.

65:11 set a table: The Greek LXX reads: "preparing a table for a demon", which may be the background for Paul's remarks in 1 Cor 10:21. **Fortune ... Destiny:** Either pagan deities worshiped by the apostates of Israel or their superstitious concerns with luck and fate.

65:12 I will destine you: A play on the reference to "Destiny" in 65:11. The Lord promises a punishment that fits the crime.

65:13-16 Israel is divided between a faithful remnant and faithless rebels.

65:15 call by a different name: As indicated in 62:2, 4.

---

[b] Gk Syr: Heb *your*.

¹⁶So that he who blesses himself in the land
  shall bless himself by the God of truth,
and he who takes an oath in the land
  shall swear by the God of truth;
because the former troubles are forgotten
  and are hidden from my eyes.

¹⁷"For behold, I create new heavens
  and a new earth;
and the former things shall not be remembered
  or come into mind.
¹⁸But be glad and rejoice for ever
  in that which I create;
for behold, I create Jerusalem a rejoicing,
  and her people a joy.
¹⁹I will rejoice in Jerusalem,
  and be glad in my people;
no more shall be heard in it the sound of weeping
  and the cry of distress.
²⁰No more shall there be in it
  an infant that lives but a few days,
  or an old man who does not fill out his days,
for the child shall die a hundred years old,
  and the sinner a hundred years old shall be
  accursed.
²¹They shall build houses and inhabit them;
  they shall plant vineyards and eat their
  fruit.

²²They shall not build and another inhabit;
  they shall not plant and another eat;
for like the days of a tree shall the days of my
  people be,
  and my chosen shall long enjoy the work of
  their hands.
²³They shall not labor in vain,
  or bear children for calamity;ᶜ
for they shall be the offspring of the blessed of
  the Lᴏʀᴅ,
  and their children with them.
²⁴Before they call I will answer,
  while they are yet speaking I will hear.
²⁵The wolf and the lamb shall feed together,
  the lion shall eat straw like the ox;
  and dust shall be the serpent's food.
They shall not hurt or destroy
  in all my holy mountain,
                                says the Lᴏʀᴅ."

The Judgment of God

66 Thus says the Lᴏʀᴅ:
Heaven is my throne
  and the earth is my footstool;
what is the house which you would build for me,
  and what is the place of my rest?
²All these things my hand has made,
  and so all these things are mine,ᵈ
                                says the Lᴏʀᴅ.

65:17: Is 66:22; 2 Pet 3:13; Rev 21:1.   **65:25:** Is 11:6–9.   **66:1–2:** Mt 5:34; Acts 7:49–50.

65:16 God of truth: The Hebrew reads: "God of Amen". It indicates that God is faithful when he is called upon to bless his people and when he is invoked by his people as a witness of their oaths (CCC 1063).

65:17–25 A vision of God's new creation, focusing on the transformation of Jerusalem. Its language is highly poetic and draws sharp contrasts between the joys and delights to come with the disappointments of the present. The holy mountain will be a place of undisturbed peace where sadness (65:19–20), frustration (65:22–23), and war are things of the past (65:25). The righteous who dwell there will live in prayerful dialogue with the Lord, who is quick to attend to their every plea (65:24).

65:17 new heavens ... new earth: These will remain forever, unlike the form of the present creation, which will pass away (66:22). Other "new things" awaited by God's people (42:9; 48:6) include a "new name" (62:2) and a "new song" (42:10) to celebrate a new act of salvation (43:19). • Isaiah's prophecy of a new creation here and in 66:22 is utilized in NT descriptions of the world to come. It is linked with the final Day of the Lord, when the present creation dissolves in fire to make way for "new heavens and a new earth in which righteousness dwells" (2 Pet 3:13). The Book of Revelation likewise draws from this vision to describe the glorious dwelling of the saints following the Last Judgment (Rev 20:11–15). It is revealed as the heavenly Jerusalem, a place of unspeakable beauty and perpetual light in the presence of God and the Lamb (Rev 21:1–22:5) (CCC 1042–50). • Newness means an improvement of the elements, not their destruction. When the psalmist says that all things will grow old and be changed like a garment, it is shown that ruin and destruction signify improvement rather than annihilation. To take an example from our condition: when a baby becomes a child, and a child becomes an adolescent, and an adolescent becomes a man, and a man becomes an elderly man, the person does not perish as he moves through the phases of life (St. Jerome, *Commentary on Isaiah* 18, 13).

65:22 like the days of a tree: An image of longevity and strength, recalling how the faithful will be "oaks of righteousness" (61:3).

65:24 I will answer: In contrast to God's silence toward sinful Israel in previous chapters (58:4; 59:1–2; 64:12).

65:25 The wolf and the lamb: Peaceful conditions resulting from the work of the Davidic Messiah (11:1–9). **dust ... the serpent's food:** Alludes to the sentence of judgment that God pronounced on the Satanic tempter in Gen 3:14.

66:1–24 Addressed to the community in postexilic Jerusalem, where worship in the Temple has become deeply offensive to the Lord. There is a remnant of devout "servants" (66:14) who "tremble" at God's word (66:2, 5). But the majority, despite going through the motions of the sanctuary liturgy, are devoted in their hearts to the worship of other gods (66:3). The Lord thus promises to act, bringing comfort to the righteous (66:10–14) and fiery judgment on the rebels (66:15–16, 24).

66:1 throne ... footstool: The whole of creation is God's sanctuary (Ps 78:69). This mystery is artistically represented by the Ark of the Covenant: the Lord sits enthroned on the wings of the cherubim (37:16), while the lidded chest below serves as his footstool (1 Chron 28:2). See note on 60:13 and essay: *Theology of the Temple* at 2 Chron 5. **the house:** The Temple in Jerusalem, rebuilt by Jewish returnees from Babylon ca. 520–515 ʙ.ᴄ. Though a sign of God's presence in the world, it could never contain him, as Solomon recognized (1 Kings 8:27). His presence is more reliably located with the "humble and contrite in spirit" (66:2; 33:14–16). **the place of my rest:** A traditional designation for the Temple (Ps 132:14; 2 Chron 6:41).

ᶜ Or *sudden terror.*
ᵈ Gk Syr: Heb *came to be.*

But this is the man to whom I will look,
 he that is humble and contrite in spirit,
 and trembles at my word.

3"He who slaughters an ox is like him who kills a
  man;
 he who sacrifices a lamb, like him who breaks
  a dog's neck;
 he who presents a cereal offering, like him who
  offers swine's blood;
 he who makes a memorial offering of
  frankincense, like him who blesses an idol.
These have chosen their own ways,
 and their soul delights in their abominations;
4I also will choose affliction for them,
 and bring their fears upon them;
because, when I called, no one answered,
 when I spoke they did not listen;
but they did what was evil in my eyes,
 and chose that in which I did not delight."
5Hear the word of the LORD,
 you who tremble at his word:
"Your brethren who hate you
 and cast you out for my name's sake
have said, 'Let the LORD be glorified,
 that we may see your joy';
 but it is they who shall be put to shame.

6"Listen, an uproar from the city!
 A voice from the temple!
The voice of the LORD,
 rendering recompense to his enemies!

7"Before she was in labor
 she gave birth;
before her pain came upon her
 she was delivered of a son.
8Who has heard such a thing?
 Who has seen such things?
Shall a land be born in one day?
 Shall a nation be brought forth in one moment?

For as soon as Zion was in labor
 she brought forth her sons.
9Shall I bring to the birth and not cause to bring
  forth?
 says the LORD;
 shall I, who cause to bring forth, shut the womb?
 says your God.

10"Rejoice with Jerusalem, and be glad for her,
 all you who love her;
rejoice with her in joy,
 all you who mourn over her;
11that you may suck and be satisfied
 with her consoling breasts;
that you may drink deeply with delight
 from the abundance of her glory."

12For thus says the LORD:
"Behold, I will extend prosperity to her like a
  river,
 and the wealth of the nations like an
  overflowing stream;
and you shall suck, you shall be carried upon her
  hip,
 and fondled upon her knees.
13As one whom his mother comforts,
 so I will comfort you;
 you shall be comforted in Jerusalem.
14You shall see, and your heart shall rejoice;
 your bones shall flourish like the grass;
and it shall be known that the hand of the LORD is
  with his servants,
 and his indignation is against his enemies.

15"For behold, the LORD will come in fire,
 and his chariots like the stormwind,
to render his anger in fury,
 and his rebuke with flames of fire.
16For by fire will the LORD execute judgment,
 and by his sword, upon all flesh;
 and those slain by the LORD shall be many.

66:6: Rev 16:1, 17.   **66:7:** Rev 12:5.

66:3 He who ... is like: The word "like" is not in the Hebrew, suggesting the accusations are better read as identifications than comparisons, i.e., those who participate in the worship of the Temple are actually guilty of moral and idolatrous crimes. **kills a man:** Contrary to the Mosaic Law (Ex 20:13). **swine's blood:** The pig is classified as an unclean animal in the Law (Lev 11:7–8).

66:4 no one answered: Reiterates God's complaint in 65:12. **I did not delight:** Choosing things offensive to the Lord disqualifies sinners from being a part of the glorified Zion, which will be renamed: "My delight is in her" (62:4).

66:5 Your brethren: The evildoers in Jerusalem who persecute the righteous among them.

✦ **66:7–12** Mother Zion miraculously gives birth to all her children (the faithful remnant) in a single day and without the pangs of labor and delivery. On that day, she will comfort and suckle her little ones, so that their mourning gives way to joy. For Jerusalem as a mother city, see 49:14–23. • Mary conceived the Son of God, not by carnal union or by human seed, but by the will of the Father and the working of the Spirit. Although she gave birth at the normal time according to the law of pregnancy, it surpassed the normal laws of birth because it was painless. For where pleasure did not precede, pain did not follow, as the prophet declared, "Before she was in labor, she gave birth" (St. John of Damascus, *On the Orthodox Faith* 4, 14).

66:8 her sons: Zion's children are also mentioned in 49:22, 25; 51:18, 20; 54:13; 60:4, 9.

66:11 her glory: The glory of the Lord that envelopes her (60:1–2, 9).

66:13 I will comfort you: One of the great themes of the Book of Isaiah (12:1; 40:1; 51:12; 61:2). For the Lord's maternal tenderness, see also 49:15.

66:14 servants: For the significance of the plural, see note on 54:17.

66:15–16 Judgment by fire is frequently the lot of evildoers in Isaiah (10:17; 29:6; 30:30–33; 33:10–12; 47:14; 66:24).

17 "Those who sanctify and purify themselves to go into the gardens, following one in the midst, eating swine's flesh and the abomination and mice, shall come to an end together, says the Lord.

The New Heavens and New Earth

18 "For I know[e] their works and their thoughts, and I am [f] coming to gather all nations and tongues; and they shall come and shall see my glory, [19]and I will set a sign among them. And from them I will send survivors to the nations, to Tar'shish, Put,[g] and Lud, who draw the bow, to Tu'bal and Ja'van, to the islands afar off, that have not heard my fame or seen my glory; and they shall declare my glory among the nations. [20]And they shall bring all your brethren from all the nations as an offering to the Lord, upon horses, and in chariots, and in litters, and upon mules, and upon dromedaries, to my holy mountain Jerusalem, says the Lord, just as the sons of Israel bring their cereal offering in a clean vessel to the house of the Lord. [21]And some of them also I will take for priests and for Levites, says the Lord.

22 "For as the new heavens and the new earth
    which I will make
shall remain before me, says the Lord;
    so shall your descendants and your name
    remain.
[23]From new moon to new moon,
    and from sabbath to sabbath,
all flesh shall come to worship before me,
says the Lord.

24 "And they shall go forth and look on the dead bodies of the men that have rebelled against me; for their worm shall not die, their fire shall not be quenched, and they shall be an abhorrence to all flesh."

66:22: Is 65:17; 2 Pet 3:13; Rev 21:1. **66:24:** Mk 9:48.

66:17 gardens . . . swine's flesh: The same sins condemned in 65:3–4. **the abomination:** Food classified as unclean by the Mosaic Law (Lev 11:1–47).

66:18–21 The Lord will gather all nations to Mount Zion and reveal his glory to them. This grand event is expected to take place in stages: **(1)** The Lord makes an initial gathering of peoples of different nationalities and languages (66:18); **(2)** he sends out some of them to declare his glory in distant lands (66:19); **(3)** the messengers return home bringing the exiles of Israel back from the nations to which they were scattered (66:20); and **(4)** God chooses priests and ministers of worship from the assembled multitude (66:21). This passage is the most explicit missionary text in the OT. • Paul appears to have this prophecy in mind in Rom 15:14–29 as one that finds partial fulfillment in his own life. He outlines his missionary field along the same trajectory, extending from Jerusalem (Rom 15:19) to Spain at the far western end of the Mediterranean world (15:28). It is his mission to bring the gospel to nations that have never heard of God's glory in Christ (Rom 15:21), and those who believe become his priestly offering to God (Rom 15:16).

66:18 all nations and tongues: This expression, combined with the peoples and places named in 66:19, allude to the Table of Nations in Gen 10:1–32, which is an ancient inventory of population groups stemming from Noah and his three sons (Shem, Ham, and Japheth).

66:19 a sign: Perhaps the Davidic Messiah, who is the rallying point for all nations (11:10) and for the exiles of Israel (11:12; cf. 49:22; 62:10). **Tarshish:** Either Tartessos in southern Spain or Tarsus in eastern Asia Minor (= Japhethites, Gen 10:4). **Put:** In northern Africa (= Hamites, Gen 10:6). **Lud:** Lydia in Asia Minor (= Shemites, Gen 10:22). **Tubal:** In northern Asia Minor (= Japhethites, Gen 10:2). **Javan:** Greece (= Japhethites, Gen 10:2). **the islands afar:** The western extremity of the Mediterranean world as far as Spain.

66:20 all your brethren: The exiles of Israel, whose return is facilitated by the Gentiles, as in 49:22 and 60:9.

66:21 priests: An expansion of sacred ministry is prophesied. Under the Mosaic covenant, priesthood was a hereditary ministry confined to the family line of Aaron, the brother of Moses (Ex 40:12–15). Isaiah looks beyond this to a new era in covenant history when the Lord will choose priests and other ministers of worship from the multitudes of Israel and the Gentiles that he gathers to himself (as in 61:6). • From a Christian standpoint, the prophecy relates to the common priesthood of all believers in Christ (1 Pet 2:9) as well as the ministerial priesthood of the apostles and their successors (Rom 15:15–16) (CCC 1268, 1546–51). **Levites:** Priestly assistants from the tribe of Levi (Num 18:1–2).

66:22 new heavens . . . earth: See note on 65:17.

66:23 new moon: The first day of each month in Israel's calendar. **sabbath:** The seventh and last day of the week. The coupling of "new moon" and "sabbath" forms a literary inclusion, i.e., an outer frame that marks the beginning and end of the book (compare 66:23 with 1:13). **all flesh:** The whole human race. **worship:** The goal of God's redemptive plan for all nations (2:2–3; 19:21, 23; 27:13; 56:6–7; 60:1–14; Zech 14:16).

66:24 look on the dead bodies: The scene outside Jerusalem, recalling the time when God slew thousands of Assyrians in 37:36. **fire shall not be quenched:** A dreadful prospect of divine judgment by fire (66:15–16). • Jesus draws from this prophecy in Mk 9:43, 48 to describe the damnation of sinners by unquenchable fire (cf. Mt 25:41; Rev 20:10). See word study: *Hell* in Mk 9:23.

---

[e] Gk Syr: Heb lacks *know*.
[f] Gk Syr Vg Tg: Heb *it is*.
[g] Gk: Heb *Pul*.

Isaiah

Chapter 1

For understanding
1. **1:2–20.** What form does Isaiah's opening tirade have? What role does the prophet take? With what does Isaiah charge Israel? What are some of the parallels between these verses and the Song of Moses in Deut 32?
2. **1:4.** What is Isaiah's signature epithet for the Lord, and how often does it appear in the book? What revelation does it encapsulate? What gaping divide does it also underscore?
3. **1:10–17.** What attitude does the prophet denounce in these verses? In biblical teaching, what do liturgy and life form? If Isaiah's polemic is not against the rites of Mosaic worship themselves, what is it against?
4. **1:19–20.** What are the "two ways" of the covenant set before Jerusalem and between which it must choose? Although not apparent in translation, what does the Hebrew verb '*akal,* which appears in both verses, indicate?

For application
1. **1:2.** According to the note for this verse, rebellion against parents and their discipline was a capital offense (look up Deut 21:18–21). Why do you think the Mosaic Law was that harsh? How do parents in our culture tend to treat rebellious older children? Even though we are more lenient, what makes the kind of rebellion Deuteronomy describes still serious?
2. **1:10–15.** As you examine your conscience, what separation of your religious observance from your work, home, or recreational life do you detect? What effect does that separation have on your view of your faith? On your prayers? How do you think God views it?
3. **1:18–19.** Why does God urge you to repent of and confess your sins? What have you done that he cannot forgive? Who benefits from confession, you or he?
4. **1:25.** According to the analogy in this verse, who will cleanse with lye or smelt silver? How does lye clean household items or smelting purify metal? How does this serve as a metaphor for the purification from sin that suffering or mortification can accomplish?

Chapter 2

For understanding
1. **2:2–4.** What do these verses present? What is its focal point, and what will it become? With what era will it coincide? In the ancient world, how were mountains viewed?
2. **Word Study: The Latter Days (2:2).** What does the Hebrew phrase '*aharit hayyamim* mean? Occasionally, what does the expression foresee regarding judgment? In another instance, what does Jacob predict regarding the latter days? Because the phrase is thus linked to the eschatological hopes of Israel, what kind of time do the latter days mark? If they are not simply the "last days" of human history, to what do they point?
3. **2:3.** For what is Zion another name? Originally, how was the word "Zion" restricted in meaning? In the NT, how is the summit of Zion, crowned with the city of Jerusalem, viewed? When does Jesus seem to have this passage in mind? According to Eusebius of Caesarea, how should one identify the law going forth from Zion, which differs from the law of Sinai?
4. **2:12.** What was the "day of the Lord" as announced by the prophets? For whom is it sometimes a day of reckoning or settling of accounts? Theologically, what glimpse does every "day of the Lord" throughout history offer?

For application
1. **2:2.** What is your experience with mountains like the Rockies, the Sierra Nevadas, or the Smokies? What draws people to mountains? Where in nature do you feel closest to God?
2. **2:4.** Warfare and the stockpiling of weapons have been constants in the relations between groups of people throughout history. What are some reasons for this? According to this verse (and its context), from where will the desire to stop war and destroy weaponry come?
3. **2:9.** What is the difference between being *humbled* and being *humiliated*? Which would you rather have happen to you? How can being humiliated teach humility?
4. **2:22.** On what person or group of people do you depend for your security or happiness? How effective have they been in providing what you expect of them? Who looks to you for these things? What happens when you fail? If you decide to turn away from such support, to whom do you turn?

Chapters 3–4

For understanding
1. **3:1.** What does the expression "stay and staff" mean? What will be swept away in the coming distress? What was the deportation policy of the Assyrians and Babylonians?
2. **4:2.** To whom does the title "branch of the Lord" refer, as used by the prophets and also Isaiah? What meanings of the image in this passage are under dispute, and what might be their resolution? Of what is abundant vegetation a sign?
3. **4:4.** Who are the daughters of Zion referred to here? What does the Hebrew word *damim* mean, and to what may it refer? What is the purpose of a spirit of burning? According to St. Jerome, how will the remnant of Jerusalem be saved?
4. **4:5.** What do the images of the cloud by day and fire by night recall? What is the glory, and what is it called in rabbinic theology? How does the glory form a canopy over Zion, and what did it provide for the Exodus pilgrims fleeing Egypt? To what does the Hebrew word for canopy, *huppah,* refer?

Study Questions

For application

1. **3:5.** Have you ever made or heard complaints about the decline of civility in our culture or the lack of respect of youth toward parents, teachers, or elders? If you agree with such complaints, what do you think is the root cause for the decline? If you disagree, why do you think people make such complaints?
2. **3:6-7.** If you were asked to take charge of a clearly failing enterprise, such as a business or church scheduled to close, what would be your answer? What considerations would guide your decision?
3. **3:16-24.** What attitudes toward self or others can the ability to afford lavish goods such as those mentioned in these verses generate? To what extent have you been affected by a consumerist mentality? How does your possession of goods affect your attitude to the poor and homeless?
4. **4:4-6.** In recent years, speculation has emerged that Christianity will decline until a purified remnant remains. Since many Christians today appear to be abandoning the faith, what is your opinion? What significance do you see for the Church in the image of the protective "cloud by day" and "flaming fire by night"? Where does that image come from, and what did it mean for Israel at the time?

Chapter 5

For understanding

1. **5:1-7.** What kind of parable is the Song of the Vineyard? How is it similar to Nathan's parable in 2 Sam 12:1-7? What does this sad story of unrequited love announce? What does the parable stress? How does Jesus draw from Isaiah's Song of the Vineyard?
2. **5:8-24.** What does Isaiah decry in these verses? Prefacing his words with six "woes", what does he denounce? Where are the dreadful consequences wrought by these sins spelled out?
3. **5:14.** For what is Sheol the Hebrew name? How is it portrayed here?
4. **5:20.** About what does this verse speak? What is diminished the more a society descends into godlessness? What does wanton iniquity cause over time?

For application

1. **5:1-4.** What religious instruction for children and adults is available in your parish or church community? What has been the fruit in terms of conversion? If these efforts are not bearing the desired fruit, what do you think may be the cause?
2. **5:10.** What evangelistic efforts is your church or parish making, and what are the results? How have your expectations for the future been influenced by the results you are currently achieving?
3. **5:20.** How is our secular culture attempting to call good evil and evil good? What effects are these reversals having on the moral quality of our culture? What is the Church doing to oppose such views? What can you do about them?
4. **5:21.** How does one gain wisdom? What does being "wise in one's own eyes" mean? If that is as bad as the prophet says, what wisdom should one try to gain?

Chapter 6

For understanding

1. **6:2.** What are seraphim? As the Lord's angelic attendants, how do they behave? How are these heavenly spirits symbolically portrayed? How does Catholic tradition identify the seraphim?
2. **6:3.** With its threefold repetition, to what is the expression "Holy, holy, holy" probably equivalent, and what does this mean? What shows that this encounter with divine holiness had a deep impact on Isaiah? How does Catholic tradition explain the threefold acclamation as a form of address? According to St. John Chrysostom, from whom does the cry "Holy, holy, holy" come, and what does it accomplish? How is "the whole earth" represented in this passage?
3. **6:6.** According to St. Cyril of Alexandria, what does the burning coal taken from the altar by one of the seraphim signify? According to St. John of Damascus, how does the burning coal prepare one for the Eucharist?
4. **6:9-10.** How will Isaiah's preaching put the Lord's punitive sentence into effect? If divine hardening is not a cause of people's sin, what is it? Why does God harden the heart of the disobedient? What do the Lord's words to Isaiah, quoted several times in the NT, explain? Who refers to them this way?

For application

1. **6:1-3.** Have you ever had an experience of the holiness of God? How did it change your relationship with him? If you have not had such an experience, what might your response be if you did?
2. **6:8.** When the liturgy calls upon you to "go and announce the Gospel of the Lord", how eager are you to comply? Is your attitude "send me" or "send someone else"? If you sense no eagerness to spread the Gospel, what prevents it?
3. **6:9-10.** These verses are a good description of spiritual obtuseness. As you examine your own conscience, do you detect any spiritual sluggishness? For example, when you hear words of exhortation from the Scriptures or from the pulpit that call for personal change, do you shut your ears?
4. **6:11.** Isaiah asks how long his ministry is to continue. How long are you supposed to strive for holiness? How long are you supposed to encourage others toward that same holiness?

Chapter 7

For understanding

1. **7:1—9:7.** What does Isaiah address in these chapters? Historically, against what background do these events take place? Theologically, what seemed to be in jeopardy? What is Ahaz urged to believe?

2. **7:9.** What test is set before Ahaz? What is he invited to do, and what does he do instead? To what do his actions amount? To what does the expression "you shall not be established" probably allude? What proviso is included in this covenant?
3. **7:14–25.** How is this first Immanuel prophecy theologically significant, and what makes it difficult to interpret? What three interpretations have been proposed? According to Mt 1:23, how does the prophecy of Is 7:14 find its ultimate fulfillment? If this is not a denial of any preliminary fulfillment in Isaiah's time, how are the births of Immanuel and the Messiah intrinsically related? What does it mean to speak of a fulfillment in stages? According to St. Justin Martyr, why did God foretell that things beyond human ability would take place?
4. **Word Study: Virgin (7:14).** What does the Hebrew word 'almah, used nine times in the OT, mean? Although, strictly speaking, 'almah is not the technical term in Hebrew for a virgin, how is "virgin" defensible as an interpretive translation? Why is it significant that Matthew cites the Septuagint version of this passage in Mt 1:23?
5. **7:14.** What does the name "Immanuel" mean in Hebrew? According to St. Bede, how does the name of the Savior, whom the prophet calls "God with us", signify both of his natures in one person?

For application
1. **7:3.** Read the note for this verse. Why do you think the Lord told Isaiah to take his son Shearjashub with him to meet the king? What implicit message was the son's name meant to convey?
2. **7:9.** What are some ways your faith has been tested? How does faith in God stabilize your personal life? How does lack of faith destabilize it?
3. **7:10–11.** Isaiah challenges the king to ask God for a sign that his word is true, and the king declines. Why would an unbeliever wish *not* to have proof that God's word is true? What would knowing the truth require of him?
4. **7:14.** Throughout Scripture, God often directs the naming of newborn children. What are some examples of biblical figures whose names the Lord has either chosen initially or caused to be renamed? Why do you think the Lord is concerned with people's names?

Chapters 8–9

For understanding
1. **8:14–15.** How do these verses present contrasting images of the Lord in relation to Israel? How does Isaiah, speaking about 735 B.C., apply this to both houses of Israel? Historically, how will this application come about? How does the NT apply this depiction of the Lord as a stumbling stone to Jesus?
2. **9:2.** Of what is the "great light" a sign? How does Matthew see this prophecy fulfilled in Jesus' Galilean ministry, both in this passage and later ones? According to St. Jerome, why did Jesus begin his ministry in the lands of Zebulun and Naphtali in Galilee?
3. **9:6–7.** In Isaiah's second Immanuel prophecy, how is the "son" promised in 7:14 further identified? According to some scholars, from where do these verses come, and as what would the four titles given to the child in 9:6 thus function? When does the angel Gabriel allude to this oracle? Why is its ultimate fulfillment messianic? According to St. Irenaeus, in what twofold way do these things testify to Christ?
4. **9:6.** To what does placing the government "upon his shoulder" allude? How is the king a "Wonderful Counselor"? As a "divine warrior", how will the king represent the Lord, "the mighty God"? How will the king be an "Everlasting Father"? How is he the "Prince of Peace"?

For application
1. **8:5–8.** How would you rephrase the Lord's message to Isaiah in your own words? What is the analogy of the two streams—one, the gentle flow of water through a conduit; the other, the flood of a mighty river—trying to convey? Which flow of water does the Lord desire that the people receive?
2. **8:14.** How is the Lord of Hosts a stone of offense and a stumbling block to our culture? For whom is he a trap and a snare? How do you experience him?
3. **9:1–2.** Why do you think Jesus chose Galilee rather than Judah as the focal area of his ministry? If he were to have ministered in this country, in what region do you think he would have chosen to focus his light? What makes you think so?
4. **9:7.** This verse ends with a proclamation of God's zeal. How does he show his zeal for his Church? What zeal does he wish for you to have?

Chapters 10–12

For understanding
1. **10:20.** Who are the "remnant of Israel"? Following the demise of the Northern Kingdom in 722 B.C., with what was Jerusalem flooded, and what did it make the city? When judgment finally comes, what will the remnant do? What reversal will it mark?
2. **11:1.** What image does the "stump" recall? Of what does the oracle speak, and whose act brings about its preservation? Who is Jesse? What two things does the image of a shoot rising from the stump imply? How do the prophets describe the royal Messiah from David's line? When does Matthew show that he has this passage in mind, and what word play does it involve?
3. **11:2–3a.** Upon whom will the full measure of the Spirit rest, and for what will it equip him? Since only six gifts of the Holy Spirit, which inspire baptized believers to follow God's will in thought and action, are mentioned in the Hebrew text, how does Catholic tradition arrive at seven gifts? According to St. Gregory the Great, why are the sevenfold graces of the Spirit listed in descending order (from wisdom to fear)?
4. **11:10.** Paul cites the Greek LXX version of this passage in Rom 15:12. What does he do with this verse? What is an ensign, and for what is it used? What does Isaiah envision distant nations coming in search of? How does Jesus relate this ensign to his Cross?

5. **12:1–6.** What two psalms does this completion and climax of the Book of Immanuel feature? When will God's people sing these songs? How do Isaiah 11 and 12 compare with Exodus 14 and 15 in both theme and language?

For application
1. **10:14.** Do you have any experience with being bullied? If so, how did you respond when the bully threatened or attacked you? What caused the bullying to stop (if it did)? If you were the bully, how did you view your victims? What motivated you to start and later to stop?
2. **10:20.** What does it mean to lean on an oppressor? What motivates a victim of bullying to "lean on" or even depend on the bully? How can that dependence be overcome or broken? How does one "lean on" the Lord?
3. **11:2–3a.** These "seven gifts of the Holy Spirit" are discussed in preparation for the Sacrament of Confirmation. Compare them with the charisms listed by Paul in 1 Cor 12:4–11. What are the connections? What are they for? Whom do they benefit?
4. **11:6–9.** In the Christian understanding of these verses, who brings about the benefits of peace described here? What are the underlying causes of this peace? (Hint: Review the previous verses.)

Chapters 13–16

For understanding
1. **13:1—14:23.** What are these chapters about? As what will the Babylonians, like the Assyrians before them, serve? What does Isaiah single out as the main reason for Babylon's humiliation? What else does he show about the succession of powers in the ancient Near East?
2. **14:12.** To what does the Day Star refer, and how does it apply to Isaiah's prediction regarding Babylon? Because the Latin Vulgate translates the epithet "Day Star" as *Lucifer*, meaning "light bearer", how does Catholic tradition read this passage? How does Origen of Alexandria answer his question about why Lucifer, as a being of darkness, is called a bearer of light? How does St. Augustine compare the "body" of the devil with the Body of Christ?
3. **15:1—16:14.** What four parts does this oracle concerning Moab have? What other prophet will cite and expand parts of this oracle?
4. **16:5.** Of what is the "tent of David" an image, and on what was it founded? On what was Israel's hope for a coming Messiah anchored? How does the embassy from Moab invoke this future hope?
5. **16:13–14.** According to Isaiah's prediction, how soon will Moab's devastation come to pass? What is probably the background? What is Judah warned not to do, and why?

For application
1. **13:6.** How do the Lord's enemies experience the "day of the LORD"? How do his friends?
2. **14:2.** The toppling of the high and the exaltation of the low is a frequent theme in Scripture. In Mary's *Magnificat* (Lk 1:46–55), how does she describe it? How was that reversal revealed in her life? Have you ever seen it materialize in yours?
3. **14:12–17.** When you hear of the downfall of a powerful political or media personage, what sympathy do you have for that person? What do you think happens to such a one after the downfall and humiliation have occurred? What (if anything) does it teach you about your own conduct?
4. **16:3–5.** Refugees flee from danger, often to neighboring countries that are not happy to receive them. How should refugees be received? How should they be cared for? How long should they be allowed to stay in your country?

Chapters 17–20

For understanding
1. **17:1–11.** What is the historical backdrop of this oracle against Damascus (Syria) and Ephraim (Israel)? What does Isaiah contend regarding Judah? On the positive side, what will the catastrophe prompt survivors in Israel to do?
2. **18:1—20:6.** What is probably the historical setting behind these oracles against Ethiopia and Egypt? How was the conspiracy destined to end? Though Isaiah foresees the coming catastrophe, how does he look beyond it?
3. **19:1.** How does the image of the Lord thundering toward Egypt in his battle chariot draw from the imagery of Canaanite mythology? However, how is the Lord approaching? According to St. Jerome, how does the Lord "riding on a swift cloud" refer either to the body of the Virgin Mary or to that of Christ? According to Eusebius of Caesarea, what does the saying prophesy? What is the attitude of the idols of Egypt?
4. **19:16–24.** What is scheduled to begin on "that day"? How does this particular oracle stand out from its surroundings? What does it show?
5. **19:19.** Where did Jewish colonies in Egypt construct temples in OT times? However, since the laws of Deuteronomy prohibit sacrificial offerings outside the central sanctuary, what is Isaiah looking beyond these cultic restrictions to see? To what does the "pillar to the LORD" refer?

For application
1. **17:10–11.** How did you feel if you have ever experienced an apparent bonanza turn to loss, a nearly complete project collapse, or a garden that promised fruit fail to bear it? How much personal investment went into such ventures, and how did their failure affect your faith in God?
2. **19:19–24.** During the Communist era, how did Christianity fare in the Soviet Union? At Fatima, what did the Blessed Virgin predict about Russia? How have the fortunes of Christians in Russia changed since the collapse of the Soviet Union? How might the conversion of Russia become a blessing for the rest of the world?
3. **20:6.** When the economy goes into recession and your bank fails, where do you turn for support? Ultimately, where does your security (financial or otherwise) lie?

Chapters 21–23

For understanding

1. **21:9.** What does this verse announce? In Isaiah's day, what does the vision serve to discourage Judah from doing? In the sixth century, however, how was this happy news for Judah? How often do these words appear in the Book of Revelation, and for what purpose?
2. **22:1.** When is the likely historical occasion for this oracle? What happened when Assyrian forces eventually invaded Judah? Where perhaps is the "valley of vision"? As another possibility, why might Isaiah be speaking sarcastically?
3. **22:15–25.** In these verses, who is stripped of his office, and who replaces him? When would Eliakim have become the royal steward, or prime minister? What does the account show about the corruption of faith and life?
4. **22:22.** What body part symbolically bears the weight of government? To what does the text perhaps allude? What symbolizes the royal authority entrusted to the chief steward? Being the king's representative, what is he authorized to do? In the NT, how does Jesus, as the messianic King from David's line, elevate Peter to chief steward?
5. **23:18.** In what way does Tyre's conversion appear to be in view? What do similar prophecies in later chapters portray about Gentile nations? Since Deut 23:18 forbids dedicating a prostitute's income to the Lord's sanctuary, what will become of Tyre's riches?

For application

1. **21:3.** The simile of a pregnant woman going into labor appears frequently in Scripture. What is the image supposed to convey? Have you ever faced a situation for which this simile would be appropriate?
2. **21:6.** Read the note for this verse. Who are the watchmen for the Church? On what watchtower do they stand? For what are they on the watch?
3. **22:9–13.** Read the note for these verses. What preparations is your country making for its defense? What attention has the country given to spiritual defenses, such as acts of repentance?
4. **22:12–13.** These verses contain a well-known proverb. Does the proverb intend to communicate a sense of joy and gladness or a sense of despair? What does the prophet mean to say by quoting it?
5. **22:22.** What does it mean for the prime minister of a country to have the final authority to "open and shut"? The note for this verse alludes to Mt 16:19, the giving of the "keys of the kingdom" to Peter. In terms of papal authority, does it mean that the pope can do whatever he wants? If not, what are the limitations on his authority?

Chapters 24–26

For understanding

1. **24:1—27:13.** What is the Isaiah Apocalypse? Expanding beyond the horizons of chapters that stress the Lord's sovereignty over individual nations, in what four ways—literarily, historically, eschatologically, and theologically—do chapters 24–27 affirm the Lord's sovereignty over the world?
2. **24:22.** Where will rebel spirits and kings be detained to await their final sentencing? To what later Jewish tradition did this vision seemingly give rise? Which are some passages of the NT that have links with Isaiah's vision?
3. **25:6–8.** What kind of banquet do these verses describe? What will be served to the guests at this banquet? What does the future banquet on Zion teach about Jerusalem, and to what promises is it also related? What linkage did the vision inspire later Jewish writings to make? How does Jesus likewise depict the kingdom of God as a pilgrimage and a wedding banquet? How does the Book of Revelation evoke Isaiah's prophecy? According to St. Cyril of Alexandria, on what is the feast of wine and joy founded?
4. **26:19.** As one of the clearest affirmations of bodily resurrection in the OT, how do some interpret the language of resurrection in this text? What is more likely the point? How is the singular Hebrew expression ("my body") apparently intended? How does the Greek LXX read? What is the significance of dew in this context?

For application

1. **24:5.** To what does our culture attribute the pollution of the earth? To what did Isaiah attribute it? Which is right? Whichever side you take, what is the solution to the problem?
2. **25:6–8.** How do these verses affect your vision of what heaven is like? Why in the NT is heaven compared to a banquet rather than, say, to the vision of God? What sorrows would you like to have wiped away?
3. **26:9a.** What time of day is your best time for prayer? Why do you think the prophet prefers the night? What yearning for the Lord do you experience? When are you most likely to feel a longing for the presence of God?

Chapter 27

For understanding

1. **27:1.** Which oracle does this verse conclude? What is Leviathan, and what does he represent? How does the Bible depict him? Although a terrifying menace to mortals, who has the power to subdue him? In the NT, who is he unmasked to be? Although some scholars hold that Leviathan is a symbol of Babylon, the city that the Lord will punish with a sword for its monstrous wickedness, what will be the ultimate fulfillment of this promise?
2. **27:2–6.** What does this new Song of the Vineyard look beyond? How does this song differ from the first song?
3. **27:8.** Why is the chastisement of Israel carefully administered? What does Scripture teach about the discipline of the Lord? According to the next verse, what is the suffering and scattering of Israel among foreign nations meant to induce? What does the east wind symbolize here?
4. **27:13.** What does the "great trumpet" signal? What does Jesus foretell at the sound of a trumpet, and of what does Paul speak? Of what is the holy mountain Zion the focal point?

For application

1. **27:1.** The note for this verse says that Leviathan the sea monster "represents primordial chaos in ancient Semitic mythology", something only God can conquer. How do you imagine total chaos? Of all reptiles, which do you most fear? What evil does that reptile represent to you?

2. **27:2–4.** Aside from anything produced by it, why do people enjoy gardening? What might make the challenge of combating weeds enjoyable? What spiritual benefit might a dedicated gardener enjoy?

3. **27:13.** Why does the military use trumpets or bugles for various signals? Why is an angelic trumpet regarded as the signal for the end of time?

Chapter 28

For understanding

1. **28:1—39:8.** What shift occurs in the central section of Isaiah? What dilemma do Judah and Jerusalem face concerning the rising threat of Assyria? How does Hezekiah of Judah stand out in this section?

2. **Word Study: Woe (28:1).** Appearing roughly 50 times in the OT, how is the word *hôy* (Heb.) variously translated? How did it originate? When a prophet utters a "woe" on himself, of what does he seem to despair? Ordinarily, why do prophets pronounce "woes"? As what do they function, and what is the underlying idea behind them? At times, how are the "woes" of the prophets strung together? In Isaiah, how does one encounter them?

3. **28:10.** What is the Hebrew that is translated here as "precept upon precept, line upon line"? As what were sounds such as these apparently uttered? How, then, will God's punishment fit the crime? Rejecting divine instruction, what will the drunkards of Ephraim be forced to suffer?

4. **28:11.** Who are the "men of strange lips"? What point does Paul make when he cites this passage in 1 Cor 14:21? Although a gift of the Spirit, what limits the charismatic gift of speaking in tongues? As in Isaiah's prophecy, of what can tongues that no one understands be a sign?

5. **28:16.** What is the Lord laying in Zion? What new work will the Lord accomplish there? On what kind of foundation will it rest? What does the "cornerstone" seem to represent? In the Aramaic *Targum of Isaiah*, as what is the stone identified? About whom is Isaiah 28:16 a messianic prophecy? According to St. Ambrose, what does Jesus, as the foundation of the Church, enable us to do?

For application

1. **28:1.** Given the explanation of the word *hôy* (Heb.) in the word study for this verse, what do these various interjections mean to speakers of modern English? Have you ever pronounced or heard pronounced a "woe" on anyone, and, if so, what did the speaker intend? When you hear the Yiddish expression *Oy veh!* in casual conversation, what do you think it means? How is the scriptural use of the expression so much more serious?

2. **28:10.** According to the note for this verse, to what are these expressions, as phrases of dismissive mockery, equivalent in everyday speech? Have you ever been dismissed in a similar way? How personally do you take such a dismissal? How personally might God take it?

3. **28:11–13.** Despite modern translations that strive for readability, the Bible seems to speak to many people in a language that they claim not to understand. What do you think is the real problem with understanding biblical language? What do you think of Isaiah's opinion at the end of v. 12?

4. **28:24–29.** How would you rephrase these verses in your own words? For example, what are you supposed to do once you have made preparations for a project? What does that say about how you are to progress in the spiritual life?

Chapter 29

For understanding

1. **29:1.** As a poetic name for Jerusalem, how can the name Ariel be translated? For what is Jerusalem coming to judgment?

2. **29:10.** What is the "spirit of deep sleep" that the Lord brings upon Judah? Why are the purposes of God incomprehensible to Judah? How does Paul apply this verse in Rom 11:8? Though some of his kin accepted the gospel, what prevented many of them from accepting it? Who are normally expected to understand God's actions and purposes in history?

3. **29:13.** What does it mean that Judah's leaders are charged with hypocrisy? Instead, what do they do? When Jesus cites this passage in his criticism of the Pharisees, for what is he faulting them, and what does that say about their leadership?

4. **29:16.** In what way is the thinking of the rulers of Judah upside-down? On what does Paul insist when he alludes to this passage in Rom 9:20–21?

For application

1. **29:9–10.** What seems to be the area of Catholic theology that is most susceptible to controversy? How does the secular world want Catholic teaching to change? How are theologians responding? How *should* they respond?

2. **29:13.** How would you apply this verse to your own relationship to God? How is your heart far from him? How routine is your practice of the faith? What would it take to change the direction of your heart?

3. **29:16.** What right do you have to tell God how he should treat you? Have you ever taken that right to yourself? What benefit have you derived from it? In reality, what rights does God have over you, given that he has granted you free will?

Chapters 30–33

For understanding

1. **30:18–26.** In his impassioned appeal to Jerusalem, about what is Isaiah adamant? To receive God's mercies, what is all that they have to do?

2. **32:1-20.** What does Isaiah foresee regarding the house of David? As a time of spiritual renewal, what will it follow? What must Judah's leaders first come to see? With what will these blessings coincide?
3. **32:15.** What will be the future "blessing" that God will pour out on his people in the time of messianic fulfillment? How does this, as one among several OT passages, envision the Spirit? When is it ultimately fulfilled?
4. **33:1.** Against whom is this cry of lamentation directed? In whom is Assyria represented? What suggests that Isaiah has a typological view of history? How will Sennacherib deal treacherously with Jerusalem?

For application
1. **30:1-2.** When personal circumstances (financial, marital, medical, etc.) get difficult, where do you turn first for help? How many resources do you have available to you? In such circumstances, how quickly (or slowly) do you turn to prayer?
2. **30:10-11.** What do you think of leaders who only listen to people who tell them what they want to hear? How often do you seek out such people yourself? From what kind of counselors do you want to hear?
3. **30:20-21.** How do you discern the will of God for your life? How willing are you to trust that the Lord will guide you in a way that is fulfilling for you?
4. **33:14-16.** According to these verses, how do you know you are right with the Lord? What would you add to this list of behaviors to work toward spiritual perfection?

Chapters 34-35

For understanding
1. **34:1—35:10.** What is the theme of these oracles? How certain is the historical background of these sayings? How do they show parallels with earlier as well as later parts of the book?
2. **34:4.** What beings comprise the "host of heaven"? How does Isaiah's vision reappear in the Book of Revelation?
3. **35:3.** What kind of message is Isaiah giving the covenant people in exile? What is the good news? When does the Book of Hebrews allude to the LXX version of this passage?
4. **35:8.** How is the way of returning to God pictured, and where does it lead? Why is the way called holy? How did the earliest Christians understand adherence to the gospel? When might Jesus himself have had this theme from Isaiah in mind?

For application
1. **34:9-17.** How would you describe what a once-populated region would look like following nuclear irradiation? What, if anything, would live there? How long would that kind of devastation last? How would that image compare with Isaiah's vision here of God's judgment?
2. **35:3-4.** Those "of a fearful heart" need to be encouraged, that is, have their hearts strengthened. Where do you find courage? What Scripture passages renew your hope or strengthen your trust?
3. **35:5.** What do physical healings have to do with the proclamation of the gospel? Why does proclamation of the Word often result in healing?

Chapters 36-37

For understanding
1. **36:1—39:8.** What do these chapters cover? What is the historical setting? Why are the stories presented out of chronological order? Theologically, how does the Lord feature in these stories? Canonically, what accounts do these stories parallel in Scripture?
2. **36:1.** Who is Hezekiah, and for what is he admired in Scripture? With whom was he apparently co-regent, and for how long? Why did Sennacherib, king of Assyria, invade Judah in 701 B.C.? What do the surviving *Annals of Sennacherib* describe?
3. **37:2.** Who were Hezekiah's delegates to Isaiah? What are some hallmarks of Isaiah's distinctive language and style that appear in this chapter? What does sending delegates to Isaiah say about Hezekiah?
4. **37:26.** What do the Assyrians wrongly suppose about their status as a mighty empire? On the contrary, what does the God of Israel—who is likewise the God of all nations—predetermine regarding these events? What does Isaiah stress about the Lord?

For application
1. **36:2.** Read the note for this verse. What implicit point is being made by observing that the upper pool is the same place where Isaiah had challenged Ahaz years before?
2. **36:7.** What is the Rabshakeh implying by charging that Hezekiah has removed the Lord's high places and altars throughout Judah in preference to the Temple? If someone asked you, as a Catholic Christian, why it's so important to worship the right God in the right way, how would you answer?
3. **37:23.** What makes the mockery of anyone in authority a dangerous act? What especially makes blasphemy against the Holy One of Israel so grievously sinful?
4. **37:26-29.** What is Isaiah telling Sennacherib in vv. 26-27? What apparently has caused God to change his mind regarding Sennacherib's purpose in God's plan (vv. 28-29)? Does that mean that God's mind is changeable?

Chapters 38-39

For understanding
1. **38:8.** What kind of miracle is performed here? On what instrument does it take place? What does Hezekiah witness?
2. **38:9-20.** As Hezekiah's psalm of thanksgiving, what does it recount? As what illustration does the psalm serve? In view of the larger context, what parallel between the personal fate of Hezekiah and the collective fate of Jerusalem can one see?

3. **39:1.** Who is Merodach-baladan II? What do many believe about the motives of his envoys in coming to Jerusalem? What is he probably seeking? Why does Hezekiah lead the Babylonian dignitaries on a tour of his royal treasures?
4. **39:5-7.** What does Isaiah foretell about Jerusalem more than a century before its occurrence? What does he warn about a partnership with Babylon? What did Isaiah often advise about faith?

For application
1. **38:2-3.** Hezekiah, told to prepare for death, reminds the Lord of how virtuous he has been. For what was he implicitly asking? Have you ever similarly reminded the Lord of your good behavior? For what were you likewise asking?
2. **38:9-20.** When you are ill, how easy is it for you to pray? Under those conditions, how do you pray for yourself? Why is it appropriate to give thanks to God even before you know the outcome of your prayer?
3. **39:1.** According to the note for this verse, why did Hezekiah most probably show the Babylonian envoys Israel's treasures? What would our government be likely to show foreign diplomats whom they wished to impress? How does such an attitude filter down to your relations with your neighbors and business associates?
4. **39:8.** What do you think of Hezekiah's reply to Isaiah? How concerned is he for the future stability of Israel? If you were told that the economic security you enjoy today would not be around for your great-grandchildren, what would be your response?

Chapter 40

For understanding
1. **40:1—55:13.** What message do chaps. 40-55 proclaim to the Judean exiles in Babylon? For this community, how current is Isaiah's prophecy of the conquest of Jerusalem? What historical vantage point does the book now take? On what does the prophet's message center, and what must the covenant people do in the meantime? What do these chapters stress about the kind of deity that the God of Israel is?
2. **40:3-5.** When the Lord rescues his people from Babylon, where will he lead them? Although deliverance from Babylon replicates the former exodus from Egypt, what greater salvation does it anticipate? How will the glory of the Lord be most fully revealed? According to St. Augustine, if the Baptism by Jesus is not by water only, by what is it accomplished?
3. **40:6-8.** How certain and lasting is Isaiah's message of good news? What does it say about the prophetic word of God? What relation does Peter make of this passage to the message of the gospel? According to St. Basil of Caesarea, what should you think about when you look at something grassy or a flower?
4. **40:22.** Where is the Lord enthroned? How was this belief represented in the sanctuaries of Israel? To what could the "circle of the earth" refer? To what is the work of creation, with the sky suspended over the earth, compared, and what belief does it reflect?

For application
1. **40:1-2.** Have you ever been severely punished for something that happened or was allowed to happen, even if you were not directly responsible? How did you feel about the punishment? Where would you turn for comfort in such a circumstance?
2. **40:6-8.** In the context of the message of hope in vv. 1-5, why does the prophet remind Israel here of the passing of generations? What point is he making in v. 8? What point is St. Peter making by quoting these verses in 1 Pet 1:23-25?
3. **40:9.** How often have you been told of your responsibility as a Christian to announce the gospel of the Lord? What have you done in response? What do you think your role is in evangelizing others? How afraid are you to use words?
4. **40:18.** Despite knowing that God is not like anything in creation, how do you imagine God? Why is it impossible for humans to avoid imaging what God "looks like"? How do the comparisons we make of Divinity to things we know limit our understanding of God? How can we know him without comparing him to created things?
5. **40:29-31.** In what sorts of situations are you most likely to feel in control? When are you least likely to feel confident of yourself? What did Jesus mean when he told St. Paul that "my power is made perfect in weakness" (2 Cor 12:9)? How do you rely on such strength?

Chapter 41

For understanding
1. **41:2.** Who is the "one from the east" named in 44:28 and 45:1? How did he establish the Persian Empire? When Babylon itself surrendered to Persian forces in 539 B.C., what happened to its foreign captives? What does Isaiah emphasize about Cyrus' remarkable rise to power?
2. **41:14.** To what does the term *go'el* in Hebrew refer? How might this refer to the Lord? At what does the language of redemption hint?
3. **41:17-20.** What is made available in Isaiah's vision of the desert highway from Babylon to Zion? What do these images symbolize? Of what do these provisions evoke memories?
4. **41:21-29.** About what issue are the gods of the nations summoned to testify before the Lord? What are they challenged to do? Why do none of the gods respond?

For application
1. **41:4.** What do the Greek letters alpha (A) and omega (Ω) symbolize to Christians? Who in the NT claims that they are pointing to his identity? As suggested by the note for this verse, what do these symbols say about him?
2. **41:10.** Numerous times in both the Old and New Testaments, the Lord assures warriors, kings, prophets, and his disciples that he is with them. What does that assurance enable his servants to do? How does the Lord's presence reassure you, and for what purpose?

3. **41:14.** The note for this verse defines the Hebrew term *go'el*. According to the note, what is the relationship of the *go'el* to the one he redeems? How might that understanding change your view of Jesus as your personal *go'el*? How can you participate in his redemptive work?
4. **41:24.** What, or who, are some of the pagan gods worshiped today? Why do people reject Christian revelation in order to choose them? How do you think Isaiah would describe the spiritual state of those who do?

Chapter 42

For understanding
1. **42:1–9.** This is the first of how many "Servant Songs" in Isaiah? At one level, who does the Servant appears to be? However, what considerations make this identification improbable? In view of this, what kind of figure does the Servant appear to be? Which passages in the NT reference this first Servant Song in connection with Jesus as "the servant of the Lord"?
2. **42:1.** In what does the Lord's Spirit instruct the Servant, and what does it empower him to do, as it did with David? With what does the statement here stand in contrast? What does the Hebrew word *mishpaṭ* denote? According to St. Cyril of Alexandria, if Jesus, being divine, was not sanctified by the Spirit (since he is the one who sanctifies), how is he sanctified and anointed, and for what purpose?
3. **42:6.** What is a covenant a formal means of creating? In a way not explained, how will the Servant accomplish this in himself? How will the Servant's work compare with other prophetic expectations? What is the light referred to here? In essence, what national vocation of Israel does the Servant fulfill? According to Thomas Aquinas, why does the Lord God foretell the sending and exaltation of his Son?
4. **42:18.** To what is the spiritual condition of Israel owing? Despite being the Lord's messenger, what does Israel still need?

For application
1. **42:5–7.** Although these verses are addressed to the Servant of the Lord, how do they apply to you? As part of God's covenant people, how are you a "covenant to the people" and a "light to the nations"? Specifically, what does that involve for you personally?
2. **42:10.** What does music add to the act of worship? How does singing enhance prayer? From where should the words for sacred hymns be derived?
3. **42:19–20.** What is the difference between seeing and observing or between hearing and listening? Have you ever come to realize that you have been spiritually blind or deaf in your spiritual life? Where do you think the Church in your country should be more spiritually attentive?
4. **42:23–25.** Pay attention to the pronouns in these verses. Who is the speaker? To whom is he speaking? Who is included in the "we" and the "they" of v. 24? When preachers use such pronouns in their homilies and exhortations, do you include yourself among those being addressed?

Chapter 43

For understanding
1. **43:1.** How is Israel's calling viewed? What does the Hebrew verb *yaṣar*, which also describes Adam's creation in Gen 2:7, suggest? What points to an intimate personal relationship between the Lord and Israel? What does it reaffirm?
2. **43:5–7.** What do these verses promise? How did the Israelites become sons and daughters of the Lord? When does Jesus probably allude to this passage?
3. **43:10.** To what can Israel, entrusted with divine revelation, testify? Unlike other nations, what were the covenant people in a unique position to know and believe? When does Jesus draw from this passage? What does the expression "I am He" mean?
4. **Essay: The New Exodus in Isaiah.** Of what is the epic story of the Exodus viewed as a pattern in Isaiah? At the same time, what do the People of God need more than a land to call their own? What are seven ways in which Isaiah's use of Exodus imagery speaks to both of these issues? According to the New Testament, how does the new exodus find its completion in the redeeming work of the Messiah?

For application
1. **43:1.** Although this verse is addressed to a group, how could you apply it to yourself? What does it mean to you that the Lord knows your name and regards you as his?
2. **43:2.** How precious are you to the Lord? How honored? How loved? How do you assure yourself of the truth of these words despite the suffering you endure? As you apply them to yourself, how do they change your image of yourself?
3. **43:11.** How convinced are you that there is no salvation except in Jesus Christ alone? Why is it necessary to work for the conversion of believers in other religions? How do you answer a critic who contends that Christian missionaries should not insinuate their religion into other cultures?
4. **43:25.** When you go to confession, how confident are you that your sins are truly forgiven? If God says that he will not remember your sins, why do you still feel guilty about them?

Chapters 44–45

For understanding
1. **44:6–8.** What is monotheism? What does the Bible acknowledge about the worship of pagan nations, and about what does it warn Israel? What theological conviction, attributed to Moses, stood alongside this practical reality? With what does Scripture identify false gods, represented by idols, and what does that make of their worship?

2. **44:28.** How will Cyrus II, founder of the Persian Empire and victor over Babylon in 539 B.C., be the Lord's instrument of deliverance? Because it is unusual for prophets to identify persons to come in the future by name, what controversy was sparked by the appearance of Cyrus' name in this verse and in 45:1? What two solutions are proposed? How will Cyrus, like Moses, who was called from the pasture to rescue captive Israel, fulfill the role of "my shepherd"?
3. **45:1.** What is the Hebrew word for "anointed"? Of whom is it used in Scripture? How often is the title given to a Gentile in the OT? What does the title "anointed" signal about Cyrus? What responsibility of the Davidic king is Cyrus given?
4. **45:17.** What constitutes the chief benefit of God's "everlasting love" for Israel? How does Paul reaffirm this statement?
5. **45:23.** Why does the Lord swear a divine oath? How effective are words spoken by God? On what two occasions does Paul draw from this vision in his letters? Since Paul identifies Jesus with the divine Lord of Isaiah's prophecy, what does he imply?

For application
1. **44:3.** Read the note for this verse. In terms of the imagery used, what would be the difference in meaning if the verse were phrased "I will sprinkle my Spirit", rather than "I will pour my Spirit"? How generously does the Father intend to be with giving the Spirit? How generous is your response?
2. **44:12–20.** Many Christian commentators say that our era is reverting to paganism. If so, how are our gods fashioned? Since most modern idols are not cast or carved statues, how does the prophet's satire on idol manufacture apply to them?
3. **45:8.** This verse is prayed by the Church during the Advent season. What righteousness is the Church praying the heavens to rain down? How is righteousness like a seedling?
4. **45:9–13.** The context is about God's selection of Cyrus, a pagan emperor, as a tool. Why would an Israelite object that Cyrus is a pot with no handles or an illegitimate child? When the Lord allows misfortune in your life, do you view his methods as providence or as punishment?

Chapters 46–48

For understanding
1. **46:1.** For what god is Bel another name? Who is Nebo, and where is reference made to him? How were idol images of these gods handled during the city's annual New Year's festival? What is the contrast between the lifeless gods of Babylon and Israel's living God?
2. **47:1–15.** For what is judgment about to fall on Babylon? When will it happen, despite the army of wise men and astrologers who claim to predict the future? At another level, what may Babylon be said to represent?
3. **47:9.** When judgment comes, with what will Babylon be left? What are some superstitious practices of Babylon?
4. **48:1–22.** Why is the end of the Babylonian Exile not something the covenant people deserve? Instead, why will it come about? What is the Jewish community in Babylon urged to do?

For application
1. **46:10.** If you could describe God's plan of salvation in a few sentences, how would you summarize it? Would seers within pagan religions have been able to identify any plan for history from their gods? If so, how would they go about it? When the Christian God says he has a plan for your life, how will you be able to know it?
2. **47:8–11.** According to the note for v. 8, what is Babylon claiming for itself? In our culture, who seem to make similar claims? What thoughts cross your mind when you witness the downfall of once powerful and respected people? What if such disgrace happened to you or those near you?
3. **48:3–5.** As suggested by these verses, what attitudes caused Israel to mistake both the coming of the Messiah and his identity? If you had been alive in Galilee in Jesus' day and heard what he said about himself, what would you honestly have thought of his claims?

Chapter 49

For understanding
1. **49:1–7.** In this second "Servant Song" in Isaiah, where the Lord's Servant is closely identified with the people of Israel (49:3), how is he at the same time distinguished from them? What does the Servant thus appear to be? Whereas Cyrus is granted the political power to bring exiles back to Jerusalem, with what is the Servant armed? From earliest Christian times, with whom is the Servant of the Lord identified and to whom does his salvation apply?
2. **49:5.** How does the Lord form the Servant? When does God become intimately involved in the life of each person? What spiritual mission does the Servant have?
3. **49:6.** To what does the "tribes of Jacob" refer? In what respect does the Servant embody all that Israel was called to be? How does Paul read this passage?
4. **49:16.** What is marking the hands a way of saying and of what is it a sign? To what does "your walls" refer? When would they be rebuilt?

For application
1. **49:2.** For good or ill, how is your mouth like a sword? What can it do either to help or to harm? When Jesus is represented as a warrior with a sword coming from his mouth (Rev 19:15), what is this sword?
2. **49:4.** Do you ever feel as if the spiritual life is a never-ending struggle, with little progress in holiness to show for it? If so, how do you deal with such feelings? What considerations bolster your trust in God?
3. **49:14–15.** How do these verses speak to you at times of spiritual desolation? How do they reassure you of the Lord's love for you?
4. **49:16.** Why do people write notes on their hands? Why might it be important that the word in this passage is not merely "written" but rather "graven"?

Chapter 50

For understanding

1. **50:1.** Who is the mother of exiles? Why is a bill of divorce necessary? What is significant about the fact that the necessary documentation is lacking in this instance? What is the legal background from Deuteronomy? In biblical times, how could the head of a household pay off personal debts? According to St. Ambrose, why was Christ sold, even though he was not forced to pay the price of sin?
2. **50:4-11.** In this third "Servant Song" in Isaiah, as what does the Servant appear? While he represents the people of Israel, how is he still distinct from them? Where does Christian tradition see a fulfillment of these verses? According to St. Athanasius of Alexandria, how does Jesus give us an image of all that is virtuous and an example for conducting ourselves?
3. **50:8.** Who vindicates the Servant, and when? How does Paul show that he has this passage in mind? What is implicit in his comments?

For application

1. **50:4.** What kind of spiritual formation have you received? Which persons or institutions have been the most formative influences in your spiritual life? How did they teach you? If you have had no such formation, where do you think you might go to get it?
2. **50:5.** The Scriptures and related Church teachings contain many "hard sayings", moral teachings that many find especially challenging. Are there any that you find irksome to the point of rebellion? If so, what decisions have you made about applying them to yourself and your life?
3. **50:6.** Notice the words "gave" and "hid" in this verse. What do they say about the Servant? What can you learn from the Servant of the Lord about facing opposition in your practice of the faith?
4. **50:10.** How prepared are you to be accused of bigotry and hatred because of your Christian beliefs or to resist laws that endanger your ability to earn an income? How ready are you to abandon trust in the economy and social acceptance and rely on the Lord for your welfare?

Chapter 51

For understanding

1. **51:2.** In what ways are Abraham and Sarah the ancestors of Israel? Of what are they held up as models here? What does that model say to the Jewish community in Babylon?
2. **51:5.** To what does the term "islands" refer? Of what is the Lord's arm an image? How should we understand descriptions of God as if he had a body?
3. **51:9.** What does the prophet implore the Lord to do? What is Rahab, and what does he represent? When did the Lord demonstrate his mastery over the sea? Whose evil power does Rahab sometimes represent?
4. **51:17.** Of what is the "cup of wrath" an image? To what are its effects likened? When did Judah and Jerusalem drink of this cup? What is it now Babylon's turn to taste?

For application

1. **51:1-2.** Who is your Confirmation patron saint? What prompted you to select that person? What do the saints have to teach you about how to grow in holiness? What writings by or about them have you read?
2. **51:6.** How often do you look at old photographs and wonder what happened to the people in them? How well or badly have friends and relatives aged compared to what they looked like when young? How have you aged? What do you have that is not transitory? Where can you go for what is permanent?
3. **51:9-10.** By recalling the miracle of the Exodus, what is the prophet asking of God? As you look around you, do you see the miracles of Pentecost still happening, or are such things ancient history? How should the Lord strengthen his arm in our day?

Chapter 52

For understanding

1. **52:7.** To which mountains does this verse refer? What does Isaiah envision a herald racing to Jerusalem to announce? What is Paul saying by citing this passage? What is the essence of the good news proclaimed to Zion? How does the rabbinic *Targum on Isaiah* render this statement?
2. **52:11.** What does the phrase "from there" (Heb., *mishsham*) imply about the prophet who wrote these words? With what views is this consistent, and for what hypotheses are they problematic? Why should the returning exiles "touch no unclean thing"? To what "vessels of the Lord" is the prophet referring?
3. **52:13—53:12.** In this fourth "Servant Song" in Isaiah, how does the Servant appear? How does he show himself to be faithful? In the end, how does tragedy turn to triumph? Theologically, what is the central mystery of the song? Rhetorically, which voices speak in the song about the Servant and what he achieved? How does the NT read the fourth Servant Song?
4. **52:15.** What does the alternative translation "sprinkle" suggest the Servant will do? Why will people shut their mouths, and what will they see and understand? Why does Paul quote the Greek LXX of this verse? According to St. Thomas Aquinas, what is the prophet Isaiah foretelling here?

For application

1. **52:1.** The prophet imagines Zion "putting on" strength as if it were a suit of clothes. When you have worn the same clothing for too long, how does donning fresh clothes make you feel? What does St. Paul mean by suggesting that we "put on" Jesus Christ (Rom 13:14)?
2. **52:11.** What are some of the liturgical vessels used in connection with the Eucharist? Who is permitted to handle them? What are the restrictions on cleansing them after use? What message do such restrictions communicate?

3. **52:12.** When an army is on the move, what is the function of the advance guard? Of the rear guard? At the Exodus, how did the Lord perform both functions? What is the difference between the urgency with which the Israelites left Egypt and their pace in leaving Babylon?
4. **52:13.** What do you think Isaiah's prophecy means by promising that the Lord's servant shall be "lifted up"? What did Jesus mean by it (Jn 3:14)?

Chapter 53

For understanding
1. **53:4.** How are sin and suffering conceived in this verse? According to the Gospel of Matthew, how is this verse fulfilled in Jesus? What did people initially think of the Servant, and what did they realize later? What does Paul claim about Jesus?
2. **53:7.** What does the sign of obedient submission indicate about the Servant? How is this response fulfilled in Jesus? What does the comparison of the Servant to a lamb mean, and how does it apply to Jesus?
3. **53:10.** How does the prophet view the suffering and death of the Servant? What is an "offering for sin" known as in Levitical law, and how would a person who profaned something holy offer one? How does the Greek LXX translate this? How is the expression "shall prolong his days" a mysterious statement, and at what does it hint from a Christian standpoint?

For application
1. **53:1–2.** Who is the speaker here? What is the speaker's attitude toward the Servant? How does that attitude resemble your own toward someone you grew up with and thought of no account?
2. **53:3.** What is your instinctive reaction when you see someone with a disfigured face? What is your impression of the person behind the face? How do you deal with any revulsion you may feel?
3. **53:5.** Where is the justice in having someone else be punished for an offense you committed? In the case of your sins against God, why will punishing you not suffice to make amends to him? How does the innocent suffering of the Servant bring about a different outcome?

Chapter 54

For understanding
1. **54:1–17.** What are these verses about? In what four ways is the city of Jerusalem described, and how do they express what the city will experience from God? How do Paul and the Book of Revelation draw from this passage to describe the heavenly city?
2. **54:5.** When did the Lord wed himself to Israel? Thereafter, what provoked him to jealousy? What attitude does Isaiah underscore?
3. **54:10.** What does the phrase "my mercy" express about the Lord? What is the "covenant of peace", and what will it bring about?
4. **54:17.** What heritage is referred to here? Who are the servants of the Lord, and how do they resemble the messianic Servant? Who will this community of servants include?

For application
1. **54:2.** If a sudden influx of Christian refugees were to join your parish, how would you make room for them? How would you determine what their needs were? How would you handle cultural differences and still maintain a united parish?
2. **54:7–8.** St. Ignatius Loyola says that an active spiritual life tends to alternate between relatively short periods of desolation and consolation—spiritual "ups" and "downs". Have you ever experienced periods of desolation? What should you do when desolation comes? How do you recognize the consolation that comes after it?
3. **54:10.** Do alternations of desolation and consolation mean that God's love for you is vacillating? How can such variation indicate that his love really does not alternate but is constant? What do these alternating periods indicate about your spiritual life?
4. **54:15.** What is the objective of the discipline that God's servants receive from him? How can apparently random misfortunes help us to grow in self-discipline?

Chapter 55

For understanding
1. **55:3–5.** What promise will the new covenant fulfill? How should these verses be interpreted: as a *transfer* of God's commitments or as an *extension* of the Davidic covenant? How does Paul relate this passage to the Resurrection of Jesus in Acts 13:34? According to St. Jerome, why will this covenant not be brief and confined to a single period of time but will abide forever?
2. **55:4.** What does this verse recall, and how was David "head of the nations"? How is that pattern of international rule expected to play out?
3. **55:6–8.** What do these verses appeal to Israel to do? Now that deliverance is near at hand, what is this is a prime opportunity for Israel to do?
4. **55:8.** From whose "ways" are the Lord's ways drastically different? How abundant are the mercies of the all-holy God?

For application
1. **55:1–2.** If it is not possible to earn entry into the Heavenly Banquet, why does it seem that the Christian life is so hard? If your good actions do not merit the kingdom of God, what does?

2. **55:6.** What does it mean to seek the Lord? Does the text of this verse mean that there are times in life when the Lord might *not* be found or that he might not be near?
3. **55:8-9.** If the divine mind is so different from the thought patterns of the human mind, how does one learn what the Lord is thinking? Why is it never safe to assume that the Lord thinks the way people do? How does one acquire the "mind of Christ" (1 Cor 2:16)?
4. **55:10-11.** The Lord promises through his word in Scripture and in numerous other ways that he loves you. How do you reconcile that promise with the misfortunes that come your way? If he promises victory for you, what does that promise imply about how you attain it?

Chapter 56

For understanding
1. **56:1—66:24.** What are these prophecies about? Why is Isaiah 56–66 designated Third Isaiah? Why was this a time of high expectation and low morale? Into what groups was the community clearly divided?
2. **56:2.** Why is the sabbath important? Of what is the observance of this weekly day of rest an acknowledgment? Why was keeping the sabbath an especially serious concern in the postexilic period?
3. **56:3-8.** By what is the salvation to come marked, and whom will it include? On what is acceptance based? In essence, beyond what restrictions does Isaiah look? How is the fulfillment of this prophecy signaled in the Book of Acts? When may Jesus have had this passage in mind?
4. **56:7.** What "holy mountain" is envisioned here? Who will be allowed to bring their sacrifices there? What had Solomon envisioned, and how does Isaiah expand this vision? When does Jesus quote this passage?

For application
1. **56:2.** What is the law of the Church regarding observance of the Lord's day (see CCC 2042)? Why do you (or do you not) obey it? Why is more than mere observance of the law necessary? How is observing the Lord's day a blessing for you and your family?
2. **56:4-5.** Who are the eunuchs to whom this prophecy is addressed? Aside from professed celibates (e.g., priests, consecrated religious), who else might be included in that number? What monument and name might they be given?
3. **56:7.** What does the adjective "catholic" mean? How truly "catholic" is your parish? Who are the foreigners who come to your church door?

Chapters 57-59

For understanding
1. **57:19.** For whom is the blessing of peace available? To whom is it proclaimed? When does Paul allude to this verse?
2. **58:3.** Why can fasting be done? What makes it a form of supplication here? If Isaiah's polemic is not against fasting per se, at what is it aimed? What does Jesus affirm about fasting?
3. **59:3.** What does specifying different parts of the body related to the mouth and hands illustrate? Why are people's hands defiled with blood? What suggests that deceptive and untruthful speech was a pervasive problem in the postexilic community?
4. **59:20-21.** What benefit does making a new covenant with God's people offer them? In reference to whom does Paul cite this prophecy? Whom does the new covenant embrace?

For application
1. **57:1.** What attention do you give to the situation of Christians being persecuted in other countries? What help, material or spiritual, do you give them? How does their situation affect yours?
2. **57:8.** Where is pornography most available to you? How does looking at it harm you and those you love? If the saying "You become what you look at" is true, what does that say about you if you are viewing pornography?
3. **58:3-7.** What is the purpose of fasting? What kind of fasting do you do, and when? What kind of fasting is the Lord advocating in these verses? How does that kind accord with your practice?
4. **58:13-14.** To whom does Sunday belong, to you or to God? If the latter, what do you do to give him his time? How should you be spending Sundays (cf. CCC 2184-88)? How much of them do you claim for yourself?
5. **59:4.** We live in a litigious society. If you have ever sued anyone, what was the reason for the suit? Among fellow Christians, how legitimate is it to sue one another? Why was Paul so upset that Christians were taking each other to court (1 Cor 6:1-7)?

Chapter 60

For understanding
1. **60:1-22.** How does the vision describe the future Zion? How does the Book of Revelation draw from this vision? Of what kind of city do both passages speak?
2. **60:4.** Who are the sons and daughters mentioned in the verse? How does Isaiah envision Gentiles participating in Israel's restoration? How does St. Methodius apply this passage to the Church?
3. **60:6.** Who are Midian and Ephah? What was Sheba, and for what was it known? What does the mention of caravans of camels bearing gold and frankincense call to mind?
4. **60:19.** What is the "everlasting light" mentioned in this verse? Where in Scripture does the image of divine glory outshining the brightness of the sun and moon reappear, and for what is it used?

Study Questions

For application
1. **60:1.** When someone you have long known suddenly seems more cheerful and at peace, to what might you attribute the change? How would the person's face signal the change? Has your face ever seemed to radiate an inner light?
2. **60:5.** Read the note for this verse. For what is the wealth of the nations to be used? When the Lord increases your wealth, how should you use it?
3. **60:11.** What are the modern equivalents of city gates? Since walls and gates are no longer useful, how do modern cities ensure their own security? How can you make your home a place of praise?
4. **60:18.** In an age of violence and terrorism, what would it take to realize this vision in the modern world? What needs to change for salvation and praise to become realities in our communities?

Chapter 61

For understanding
1. **61:1–3.** For what ministry is the one who speaks anointed by the Spirit? Though he is not otherwise identified, what do parallels with earlier verses in Isaiah show about him? Contextually, for what purpose does he appear as God's anointed agent? What does Jesus, after reading this passage in the synagogue at Nazareth, claim?
2. **61:2.** To what does "the year of the LORD's favor" refer? How did this year begin? What is the "day of vengeance"? When does the Book of Sirach echo this and the following verse?
3. **61:6.** What renewal does this verse envision? For much of biblical history, to whom was the priesthood restricted? What dramatic expansion does Isaiah foresee? To what does "the wealth of the nations" refer?
4. **61:7.** What is the "double portion" referred to here? How else is this inheritance also fitting?

For application
1. **61:1.** What are some ways that persons not in a physical prison can still be bound as if imprisoned? How can you participate in the mission of the Messiah to unbind them?
2. **61:2.** Jesus proclaims blessed all who mourn (Mt 5:4). What are some differences between the kind of mourning that Isaiah has in mind here and that which Jesus has in mind? Since Isaiah is talking about Israel's exiles, might there be any similarity?
3. **61:3.** What is a faint spirit? How will a "mantle of praise" fortify a faint spirit?
4. **61:6.** According to the *Catechism*, Baptism and Confirmation enable you to participate in the priesthood of Christ (CCC 784, 1546–47). How do you exercise your ministry as one who belongs to the "common priesthood of the faithful"? If you are ordained to the ministerial priesthood, how does that common ministry expand?

Chapter 62

For understanding
1. **62:1–12.** In another announcement of Zion's salvation, what will happen to the glorified city? What key idea is introduced at the outset?
2. **62:2.** What new name is revealed in 62:4? According to St. Cyril of Jerusalem, what new name will all believers in Christ bear? According to St. Cyril of Alexandria, what kinds of things are made new in Christ?
3. **62:5.** What odd notion does this verse introduce about sons and their mothers? What alternative translation from the Hebrew do others prefer? What support for this alternative can be found in Scripture? On this reading, to what is Zion compared?
4. **62:8–9.** What oath does the Lord swear? In particular, from what does he pledge to preserve Zion?

For application
1. **62:2.** Quoting St. Cyril of Jerusalem, the note for this verse says that "Christ grants all believers to bear his name." Why is that important? What does the name "Christian" mean to most people? What does it mean to you? What should it mean?
2. **62:4.** This verse contrasts Zion's old name (Forsaken, Desolate) with its new name (My Delight Is in Her, Married). Despite the experiences of some married couples, what are the ideals of a marital relationship (for example, how intimate is it and how long should it last)? If you have ever felt forsaken by God, how does the reality of being "married" to him change that?
3. **62:5.** Why is prior virginity considered important to a marital relationship? Why has modern society rejected the ideal of virginity at marriage? Even though successful marriages occur when one or both partners have lost their virginity before the wedding, what is lost even then? If virginity is a virtue, how can it be regained if lost?
4. **62:8.** Read the note for this verse. Why would an ancient society such as Israel use the right hand as the proper hand for swearing an oath? For what was the right hand commonly used? Why not the left hand?

Chapter 63

For understanding
1. **63:3.** What is a wine press? For what does the crushing of the fruit and the likeness of red juice to blood make the wine press a potent image? What help does God need to accomplish the work of salvation and judgment?
2. **63:7.** What Hebrew term does "steadfast love" translate in this verse, and to what does it refer? To what might use of the plural of the Hebrew word *ḥesed* be a reference?
3. **63:10.** How had Israel rebelled against God? To what does the Lord's Spirit refer in this context a reference? How does Paul adopt the language of this passage in Eph 4:30? What does Christian tradition infer from this expression? Why must the Spirit be a personal force? According to the verse, how did God fight against the rebels?
4. **63:16.** What is the unusual way of addressing God in the OT? Where else in the OT is he addressed this way? On what is the language of divine paternity in the OT based? How is a new dimension of God's fatherhood opened up in the NT? Who are the founding fathers of Israel?

For application
1. **63:7.** How often do you recount to yourself how the Lord has shown his steadfast love for you over the years? How does reviewing these experiences with gratitude strengthen your trust in him?
2. **63:10.** Read the note for this verse. How is it possible to "grieve" the Holy Spirit? Why does Paul urge Christians not to grieve the Holy Spirit (Eph 4:30)? How does being "sealed" in the Holy Spirit become a motive for not grieving him?
3. **63:16.** The note for this verse states that "if invoking God as Father is rare in the OT, it becomes routine in the NT." How habitual is it for you? How does experience with your earthly father influence your view of God as Father? Which Person of the Trinity do you invoke most often, and why?
4. **63:17.** The note for this verse talks about hardening of the heart as coming from God; but Ps 95:8 suggests that it also comes from ourselves. Is hardening of the heart something that happens instantaneously, or is it a gradual process? Is hardening of the heart mere stubbornness, or is it something more insidious?

Chapters 64–65

For understanding
1. **64:1.** How are the heavens imagined in this verse? What is the prayer to the Lord being made here? How might this verse lie behind Mark's account of the Baptism of Jesus?
2. **65:1–2.** Despite a divine plea for repentance that goes unheeded, what does the Lord say he is ready to do? What response does he receive from the people he has chosen to be "a light to the nations"? By quoting the LXX of these lines in Rom 10:20–21, how does Paul apply them to the Gentiles and to Israel? According to St. Thomas Aquinas, when has God spread forth his hands in giving many benefits to Israel?
3. **65:17–25.** On what does this vision of God's new creation mainly focus? What sharp contrasts does the highly poetic language draw? What kind of a place will the holy mountain be? How will the righteous who dwell there live?
4. **65:17.** How long will the new heavens and earth remain? What other "new things" will be awaited by God's people? How is Isaiah's prophecy of a new creation here and in 66:22 utilized in NT descriptions of the world to come? According to St. Jerome, what does newness mean?

For application
1. **64:1.** How does Isaiah's desire for God to tear the heavens open and come down reflect your own wishes? If he did, what would you want him to do? How has God actually answered that prayer?
2. **64:6.** Read the note for this verse. Some Christians take the verse to mean that all human actions are unclean and polluted in God's sight. What is your opinion? When you do an act of devotion, how pure are your motives? If your motives are mixed, what will it take to purify them?
3. **65:5.** Can a person fulfill all religious duties faithfully and yet keep the Lord at a distance? How can someone be active in Church ministry and yet have no personal relationship with God? Why do some people feel that letting the Lord into their lives is not safe?

Chapter 66

For understanding
1. **66:1–24.** To whom are these verses addressed? Although there is a remnant of devout "servants" (66:14) who "tremble" at God's word, what is the state of the masses? What does the Lord thus promise to do?
2. **66:1.** As God's sanctuary, how is the mystery of creation artistically represented? What is the house that the returnees are building? Instead of a building, where is God's presence more reliably located? To what does the expression "the place of my rest" traditionally refer?
3. **66:7–12.** To whom does Mother Zion miraculously give birth, and how? On that day, what will she do for her little ones? According to St. John of Damascus, what was characteristic of the way Mary gave birth to Jesus?
4. **66:18–21.** When the Lord plans to gather all nations to Mount Zion and reveal his glory to them, how is this grand event expected to take place? How does Paul show that he has this prophecy in mind that finds a partial fulfillment in his own life? What does he state as his mission?
5. **66:23.** What day of the month is the new moon? What day of the week is the sabbath? What literary device does the conjunction of "new moon" and "sabbath" form?

For application
1. **66:1–2.** Rather than looking to the Temple as a place of his rest, God looks to the human heart. What does it mean for him to find rest there? Why are humility and contrition so important? What does it mean to "tremble" at God's word?
2. **66:5.** How would you define joy? Why do many (including fellow Christians) evaluate the life of a Christian according to one's experience of joy? If joy is supposed to be visible, what are the signs that one has it?
3. **66:10–14.** How does joy characterize your life? How is the Church like a mother caring for an infant? How do you take nourishment from what the Church provides?
4. **66:21.** One of the goals of Catholic missionary efforts is to establish a native clergy in lands being evangelized by missionaries. In your diocese, how serious is the shortage of priests? How many men are preparing for ordination, and how many are likely to be ordained in the near future? Does your diocese send out missionaries, or does it receive clergy from other countries? What does that say about whether your diocese is a mission territory or an established church?

BOOKS OF THE BIBLE

THE OLD TESTAMENT (OT)

Gen	Genesis
Ex	Exodus
Lev	Leviticus
Num	Numbers
Deut	Deuteronomy
Josh	Joshua
Judg	Judges
Ruth	Ruth
1 Sam	1 Samuel
2 Sam	2 Samuel
1 Kings	1 Kings
2 Kings	2 Kings
1 Chron	1 Chronicles
2 Chron	2 Chronicles
Ezra	Ezra
Neh	Nehemiah
Tob	Tobit
Jud	Judith
Esther	Esther
Job	Job
Ps	Psalms
Prov	Proverbs
Eccles	Ecclesiastes
Song	Song of Solomon
Wis	Wisdom
Sir	Sirach (Ecclesiasticus)
Is	Isaiah
Jer	Jeremiah
Lam	Lamentations
Bar	Baruch
Ezek	Ezekiel
Dan	Daniel
Hos	Hosea
Joel	Joel
Amos	Amos
Obad	Obadiah
Jon	Jonah
Mic	Micah
Nahum	Nahum
Hab	Habakkuk
Zeph	Zephaniah
Hag	Haggai
Zech	Zechariah
Mal	Malachi
1 Mac	1 Maccabees
2 Mac	2 Maccabees

THE NEW TESTAMENT (NT)

Mt	Matthew
Mk	Mark
Lk	Luke
Jn	John
Acts	Acts of the Apostles
Rom	Romans
1 Cor	1 Corinthians
2 Cor	2 Corinthians
Gal	Galatians
Eph	Ephesians
Phil	Philippians
Col	Colossians
1 Thess	1 Thessalonians
2 Thess	2 Thessalonians
1 Tim	1 Timothy
2 Tim	2 Timothy
Tit	Titus
Philem	Philemon
Heb	Hebrews
Jas	James
1 Pet	1 Peter
2 Pet	2 Peter
1 Jn	1 John
2 Jn	2 John
3 Jn	3 John
Jude	Jude
Rev	Revelation (Apocalypse)